British COLUMBIA

The Romantic History of Dawson Creek
in Four Complete Novels

Janelle Burnham Schneider

BARBOUR
PUBLISHING, INC.
Uhrichsville, Ohio

ISBN 1-57748-795-8

All Scripture has been taken from the King James Version of the Bible.

Published by Barbour Publishing, Inc., P.O. Box 719, Uhrichsville, Ohio 44683 http://www.barbourbooks.com

Member of the
Evangelical Christian
Publishers Association

Printed in the United States of America.

JANELLE BURNHAM SCHNEIDER

Janelle published her first five books with **Heartsong Presents** under her maiden name of Janelle Burnham. She put her writing aside during her own true-to-life romance, wedding, and the birth and infancy of her daughter Elisabeth. They have added a son to the family, but writing is a desire she cannot ignore. As a military wife, she has lived various places across Canada, including British Columbia, New Brunswick, and Alberta, collecting new story ideas and learning much about real romance.

River of Peace

To B.J. Hoff, whose stories challenge me, whose writing inspires me, and whose friendship encourages me.

Chapter 1

1930

All off at Hythe! End of the line!"

Ida smiled at the conductor's air of importance as she stood, collecting her lunch basket and handbag. His strutting authority almost hid his inexperience, but his booming announcement to a mere handful of passengers betrayed him. Her mother would have had fun imagining how he had acquired this job and what his family was like. The thought generated a giggle, along with tears. Mom's life had been sucked away by consumption just a few months ago. Now Ida was alone at the end of the Northern Alberta Railway. A school awaited her in a town forty-five miles farther northwest, but she hadn't been told how she would get from here to there. "Looking back only keeps you from seeing opportunities," Mom had often said, along with, "Ships with folded sails can't catch the wind." Despite her weariness after a full day on the train, Ida straightened her shoulders as she'd often seen Mom do when faced with uncertainty. She smoothed the folds of her heavy cape and forced herself to walk confidently toward the door.

To her surprise, a sign with her name on it swayed above the small crowd around the station. "Ida Thomas, new schoolteacher for Dawson Creek." The sign was being held by a large, brown hand, but she couldn't see the person to whom it belonged. She directed her steps toward the sign. It came down abruptly and a short, stocky person detached himself from the crowd. "Miss Thomas?"

"Yes." She extended her hand and felt it engulfed briefly in a crushing grip.

"Lars Harper. Your trunks?" His friendly manner softened the impact of his abrupt speech.

"I have just one."

"This way." He shouldered his way through the people milling around the freight area. "Kelly." His gruff voice caught the agent's attention. "Miss Thomas's trunk and all Dawson Creek freight."

Mr. Kelly touched his hat in greeting to Ida, then gestured to the piles

7

of boxes. "Load these into Mr. Harper's truck, Peterson."

The young assistant's gaze traveled from Ida's deep green hat down to her shoes, lingering a few moments longer than appropriate. She felt grateful for the concealing bulkiness of her cape. Having grown up in Edmonton, a new city close to the edge of the frontier, she had had to endure bold gazes such as his since her early teen years. Mom's frequent warnings about her attractive face and luxuriously thick blond hair drawing unwanted attention from uninhibited men seemed especially appropriate now. The untamed wilderness to which she'd come often attracted the same kind of men. She moved from beside Mr. Harper to slightly behind him.

"I'll take the lady's luggage," Mr. Harper addressed the agent.

"Right here." Mr. Kelly lifted the long wooden box from among the several sacks of flour. "I figured you'd be taking her with you, so I made sure Peterson put this with your freight."

"Obliged." Mr. Harper hefted the trunk without visible effort and strode purposefully toward an ancient-looking red truck. Still holding her trunk on his shoulder, he opened the passenger door and silently gestured Ida inside.

She studied her surroundings while he finished loading. From her perspective beside the frame building, the town appeared to start with the station and extend to the east. Bright sunlight shone warmly into the truck, despite the late afternoon hour. Trees on the other side of the tracks swayed in a light wind. Blue sky and green poplar leaves provided the only colour alternative to brown dirt and buildings. A dust devil swirled toward the truck, pelting the metal with grit. The sound reminded Ida how filthy she felt. She hoped her new home wouldn't be too many hours away.

As if reading her thoughts, Mr. Harper settled himself behind the steering wheel with an abrupt announcement. " 'Bout two hours to home. Horse'n wagon's a nicer trip, but truck's faster." The vehicle rumbled as he started the engine.

Having already observed that her companion wasn't a talker, Ida let her mind drift. The school committee had written to her that she would "have lodging with one of Dawson Creek's most distinguished citizens, Mrs. Barry." Using her mother's favorite way of passing time, Ida tried to picture her hostess. Probably a tall, sparse woman. "Distinguished citizen" conjured an image of more dignity than humor. She hoped she could find someone to laugh with. That's what she'd missed most since Mom died.

Mr. Harper raised his voice over the noise of the engine. "I'll answer questions if you've got 'em."

She spoke her first thought. "Do you have children in the school?"

He nodded. "Three."

"How old are they?"

"Teddy's seven, never been to school before. Nettie's ten, goin' on twenty. Thinks she knows everythin' since she can read. Jed's fifteen. Helps on the farm, so he schools part-time. Doesn't like that, but his mother's dead set on his getting an eddication."

"Is your farm near Dawson Creek?"

"Close to where the town is, but farther from where it will be." A faint smile twitched his lips.

"Pardon me?" Ida couldn't figure out how to interpret his statement.

"Thought I might stump ya." Humor in his voice removed any possible sting from his words. "Railroad guys want to build their track 'bout two miles away from where the town is. Say it's too hard to build closer, so we're movin' the town. Train won't come to us so we're goin' to it."

Silence settled once again. Ida felt uncomfortable shouting her questions, and Mr. Harper had apparently volunteered as much information as he wanted. She wouldn't have minded taking a nap, but the jolting ride made that impossible. Her driver expertly avoided the worst potholes, but the truck still bounced in and out of numerous ruts. She tried to imagine what her school would be like. The letter from the committee had said thirteen children, sometimes seventeen, so apparently three other students attended part-time like Jed Harper. She'd never taught before, as Mom had become ill shortly after Ida's graduation from Teaching School. Her trunk held many excellent textbooks and her heart an abundance of love for children, but would that be enough? She firmly reminded herself this wasn't the time to drop anchor, as Mom would have said.

Almost two hours later, the truck labored up a steep hill. Suddenly a town sprawled before her gaze. "Is this Dawson Creek?" She tried to speak loudly enough to be heard, but without shouting.

Mr. Harper shook his head. "Pouce Coupe." The name sounded like "poos coop-ee." "Almost home, though."

Ida tried to settle the fluttering in her stomach while she took in the landscape around her. Mountains appeared distantly on the horizon. Square fields had been carved from among trees covering nearby hillsides. At least twenty shades of green blended into one another, along with the gold of wheat and ever-present dust brown. The road curved sharply ahead of them, leading to a cluster of buildings that seemed hardly more than a hamlet.

"That's it." Mr. Harper waved his hand at the sight.

Ida hardly knew what to say. Her apprehension abated slightly as a couple of passers-by waved. The place seemed friendly enough.

"I'll take you to Mrs. Barry's right off."

Unease gripped her again. She wished irrationally that the committee had found her a hostess less distinguished. The truck stopped in front of a two-story frame house flanked by an addition on either side. Though the building appeared large in comparison to nearby houses, it would have been overshadowed by almost any residence in Edmonton. It looked too small to house more than a small family. Mr. Harper came around to open her door, then lifted her trunk from the truck bed.

They'd taken less than a dozen steps when a short, white-haired woman hurried down the front steps. "You must be Ida Thomas, and after riding all the way from Hythe with Lars, I'm sure you're ready for a good chat. I don't suppose he thought to tell you anything!" Irrepressible twinkles in her blue eyes brought a smile to Ida's face. "I'm Lucetta Barry and delighted to have a lady with me for a change. Running a boardinghouse is great fun, though rather boring with only men around."

Talking continually, Mrs. Barry led Ida into a bright kitchen almost filled by an average-size table. Doors stood invitingly on either side. A third doorway across from the entrance led into a hall. Mrs. Barry gestured to the left. "Put her trunk in the yellow room, please, Lars, while I rustle up a bite to eat. You're welcome to stay, though we might be too chatty for you."

Mr. Harper's face reddened, though a grin twitched his mustache again. "Thanks, Mrs. Barry. Store's waitin'." He set the trunk by the door indicated and left with a wave for both ladies.

"I told the school committee they ought to send someone else to meet you, but Lars goes to the train every week for freight and mail so the men couldn't see why anyone else should go. Did you find out anything about us?"

Ida found herself divested of basket, handbag, and cape and gently pushed onto a chair. A steaming cup of tea flanked by a sugar bowl and a creamer appeared almost magically, followed by a dish heaped with warm rolls. "He told me his name; said he has three children—seven, ten, and fifteen; the town we passed through was Pouce Coupe; and Dawson Creek is planning to move to meet the railway."

"Obviously, you've won his approval. Many people don't hear that much from him in a year. Thankfully, his Kate's more outgoing or their children may never have learned to talk."

Ida laughed delightedly. "My mother would have loved to know you.

She used to make the same kinds of observations about our neighbors."

"Does she live in Edmonton?" Lively interest without a hint of nosiness sparkled in the elderly lady's eyes.

"She died this past spring from consumption." Saying the words aloud brought unexpected tears.

Mrs. Barry's face sobered compassionately, and she laid a gentle hand over Ida's fingers. "I'm sorry, dear. It's hard. I take it your father's gone, too?"

"In 1916 during the Great War." Ida smiled to let her hostess know she didn't mind the questions.

"I lost my Kelvin at the beginning and found my William near the end, only to lose him six years later. Death always brings difficult adjustment, though the Lord's love has made it bearable for me. I hope you'll feel you can confide in me when you need a friend or even a mother."

Ida felt a bubble of joy. "I think we're already sisters in the faith."

"You look like someone who's found peace." Mrs. Barry beamed. "We can't help but be friends. Now, would you like to clean up first or unpack?"

Ida again became conscious of travel grime clinging to her. "Could I take a sponge bath?"

"I'll give you something better. I've got hot water and a big tub we can set up in your room. My son put a big stove on my back porch so I can cook and heat water in the summer without heating the entire house, the way this big cookstove does."

In less time than seemed possible, Mrs. Barry had the tub filled. "I'll put your trunk here beside your bed so you can reach clean clothes. Take as long as you like, dear." She looked closely at Ida's face. "You look exhausted and it's already past seven. Why not just tuck yourself into bed after your bath? There's a chamberpot under your bed if you need it. We can deal with unpacking tomorrow."

The suggestion sounded too good to be refused. With Lucy's help, Ida tugged her trunk inside her room. As soon as the door closed behind her hostess, she let down her hair and brushed the travel dirt from it. Short haircuts were becoming more fashionable for young ladies, but Ida had never been tempted. Her dad had loved to brush the tangles from her waist-length blond hair while she sat on his lap. Cutting her hair would feel like severing her last tie with him. With the skill of much practice, she quickly braided her smoothed hair and pinned it into a bun on the back of her head. She then lowered herself into the steaming water. What luxury! She soaked as long as she dared without falling asleep, then got out while pulling on her long-sleeved nightgown. She hadn't been in Dawson Creek a full day yet, but Mrs. Barry had already made it seem like home. Snuggling between fresh-smelling sheets, she wondered if the other residents, especially the parents of her students, would be as welcoming.

Chapter 2

Ida slept deeply and peacefully. She dreamed of her mother and awoke prepared to tell her about Mrs. Barry. She opened her eyes, gazing around the pretty, well-furnished room. A nearby wall clock declared the time to be shortly after six. Already bright sunlight streamed past ruffled curtains at the windows. Mother would love the house as much as the lady who owned it. Then increasing alertness brought clear recollection. Mom was gone. That's why Ida had come here. She planned to teach, to support herself because there was no one left to do it for her.

But Mom would scold her soundly if she gave in to self-pity. "Time to set your sails," Ida reminded herself with a grin. Becoming part of this community as well as a good teacher would take hard work and determination. "But then life without challenges would be no fun," Mom had often said.

As she dressed, Ida wondered why she remembered so many of Mom's little sayings without the feelings of irritation they had brought while she was growing up. The creases had come out of her periwinkle dress nicely. Looking at the ivory lace around the stand-up collar and the French cuffs, she remembered Mom painstakingly stitching it in place. For the last several months of her life, sewing was all Mom could do without inducing the terrible coughing, so she had sewn a beautiful collection of undergarments as well as skirts, blouses, and three nice dresses. When Ida had asked where she'd found the fabric, Mom had only smiled. "I won't be leaving you much money, but being well-dressed will help you make a good impression in getting a job. Besides, every time you wear these, you'll remember you're loved." Ida remembered, with tears, smiles, or sometimes both. This morning the tears came easiest. She wiped them away with the edge of the pillowcase as she made her bed.

A desk sat under her bedroom window. She seated herself for a few moments of Scripture reading. A picture-perfect view stretched before her. Sunlight brought out variations of the many shades of green she'd noticed yesterday afternoon. Dew still shimmered on the ground. Suddenly she could hardly wait for evening to see how the picture before her would change. She opened her Bible to Lamentations 3 to find the two verses that had come to mean so much to her since Mom's death. "It is of the LORD'S mercies that we

13

are not consumed, because his compassions fail not. They are new every morning: great is thy faithfulness." She looked out at the dew on the ground, fresh every morning like God's mercy.

Noises from the kitchen indicated Mrs. Barry had also awakened. Ida hurried out to see if she could help. Swathed in an apron covering all but the sleeves of her dress, which reached halfway between her knees and ankles, Mrs. Barry already had bacon sizzling, coffee perking, and a batch of pancake batter waiting.

"Did you leave anything for me to help with?" Ida asked in greeting.

"Good morning, dear. For this morning, no. Until you get settled in, I'd like to spoil you. But if you'd like to chat while I work, you're welcome to sit there at the table. I'll bring you a cup of tea in a jiffy, unless you'd prefer coffee." Mrs. Barry's hands didn't slow while her words tumbled out. "Chat" seemed to be one of the lady's favorite words, as well as activities.

"It's been awhile since I've had anyone to talk with this early in the morning," Ida admitted. "I hadn't realized until now how much I missed it."

"Your mother?"

Ida nodded.

"What did you chat about?" Mrs. Barry set a cup of fragrant liquid in front of Ida.

"Usually what we'd read from Scripture that morning. It always seemed to get the day started right. Is this peppermint tea?"

"Made from leaves grown just outside my back door." Mrs. Barry beamed with pride. "Would you mind continuing that morning ritual with me? It's been awhile since I've been able to talk first off about God's early morning mercies."

"Actually, that's what I read this morning. The dew sparkling in the sunlight reminded me of the verses in Lamentations that talk about God's mercy being new every morning. Those thoughts have somehow kept me going almost every morning since Mom's funeral." Ida sipped the tea, hoping the hot liquid would dissolve the lump in her throat. She wanted to face her new beginning courageously, yet she still missed Mom terribly. Would she be able to become the kind of teacher Mom had wanted her to be?

Mrs. Barry let the silence linger for a few moments before replying in a gentle tone. "I know what you mean. Some verses from Isaiah did the same for me when my husbands passed away. One of these days I'll tell you about it. But for this morning, I've been thinking about Psalm 37:23 and 24. 'The steps of a good woman are ordered by the LORD: and she delighteth in his way. Though she fall, she shall not be utterly cast down: for the LORD upholdeth her with his hand.' One egg or two?"

"Just one, please." Ida laughed. "Obviously you take Scripture personally, Mrs. Barry."

She looked straight at Ida. "Is there any other way to read it?" The twinkles took over her eyes again. "You almost had me thinking you were one of those people who think the Bible is only for inspiration. And would you please call me Lucy? That's what my friends call me."

"You're so much like my mother, it won't be easy." Ida grinned. "But I'll try."

The door at the far end of the kitchen opened. "Woulda slept with them chickens if I knowed you was organizin' a Sunday mornin' gabfest," a short, wiry man growled, stumbling to the end of the table closest to him. His hair stood on end in wild disarray and his beard looked little better.

Mrs. Barry chuckled indulgently. "Miss Thomas, meet Mr. Carey, our resident grouch. Mr. Carey, meet Miss Thomas, Dawson Creek's new schoolteacher." She set a mug of coffee near his hand. "Mr. Carey works at the feed store, and he believes the day shouldn't start until after lunch. Three eggs or four, Mr. Carey?"

"Bein's how it's Sunday, lunch'll be pretty scarce. Better stoke up with four." He lifted his head slightly, and Ida glimpsed mischief in his eyes.

"If you'd come to church with us, you'd have plenty to eat," Mrs. Barry informed him briskly.

"Gotta write my sister a letter." Ignoring the spoon nearby, he tilted the sugar bowl so a cascade of sweetener flowed into his cup.

Lucy set a plate loaded with two pieces of toast, four pieces of bacon, and an egg in front of Ida, then looked squarely at Mr. Carey. "Is that the sister who died three years ago or the one who won't speak to you because you insulted her husband?"

Mr. Carey slurped his coffee loudly before answering. "Smart-aleck, interferin' woman! Make ya' a deal. Don't mention church for a month and I'll go with ya' once. Just once. Just to get ya' offen my back."

Mrs. Barry smiled smugly. "Deal. Now let's see if we can get you to comb your hair before you come into polite company."

Mr. Carey glared at her, then looked at Ida. "Some wimen ain't content less'n they're reformin' helpless men. How long am I gonna hafta wait for them eggs, Miz Barry?"

Lucy waved her wooden spoon at him. "S'pose I say 'until you learn to be polite.' We have a young lady with us now. Perhaps you'll brush up on your manners a bit."

"Mebbe so. Mebbe not." He muttered, taking another long slurp from his cup and reaching for the plate she extended. In an amazingly short amount of time, he inhaled four eggs, four pieces of toast, a stack of pancakes, and countless strips of bacon. "Good eats, ma'am, and welcome to Dawson Creek, Miss Thomas." The door to his room banged shut behind him.

"And so you've met your fellow boarder." Lucy sat across from Ida with a plate of pancakes and an egg. "Most of my business comes from people passing through or farm folks stranded in town by weather. I don't charge local folks anything, but they always pay me somehow, usually with food or firewood. Do you feel up to coming to church with me?"

Ida nodded. "I'm looking forward to it."

"We don't have a pastor yet, so our men take turns reading Scripture to us. Mostly we just sing and talk about God's goodness during the week. Since we don't have our own building, my son has volunteered the use of an empty one-room cabin on his farm. We hope to buy a lot at the new town site next summer and start building then. We're still a small group, so the cabin works well for now. After our meeting, we have potluck lunch. There's not much visiting time around here, so Sunday afternoons are always special."

At the little cabin, one of the men led some familiar hymns accompanied by a guitar. Another read a Scripture passage and commented on it. Prayer requests were heard and prayed over and a blessing asked over the food. Children outnumbered adults at the church service, but even the smallest sat quietly until the final "Amen" had been uttered. Ida noticed a skinny, red-haired girl leave immediately after prayer.

A woman even shorter than Ida with sparkling green eyes introduced herself right away. "I'm Nina Spencer, Lucy's daughter-in-law. My husband, Lionel, is the tallest of the men over there." Her gesture indicated a sparsely built man with a kind face and light brown hair. "I won't try to tell you which of the children in this bedlam belong to me. Maybe Mom can bring you out tomorrow for a proper visit. Come, let's fill our plates before the youngsters get all the food."

Ida ate and listened to the friendly chatter, trying to discern how these people related to each other. Four overall-clad men congregated at one end of the table and seemed to be discussing farm-related subjects. She recognized her escort from yesterday among them, though he didn't appear to be talking more than he had then.

"You must be the new schoolteacher." A well-rounded woman with blond braids wrapped around her head set a full plate on the other side of the table from Ida and continued speaking without giving Ida a chance to reply. "I'm Kate Harper. My husband met you at the train yesterday, though I don't guess he told you anything about us. We're some happy to have a proper school for our young'uns. Why'd you move all the way here from Edmonton? I know you came from Edmonton because my husband's on the school board. You don't have any family? Somehow I kind of thought you must be an orphan. You have that look about you. Well, it'll make you that much better of a teacher, I say. It's easier to relate to children when your own childhood hasn't been that happy. I hope you'll stay with us for a good long time and that we can become friends, as long as you don't mind being friends with the parents of your students. I should actually say the mothers of your students, since it wouldn't be proper for you to be friends with their fathers. My Lars says I never give anyone else a chance to say anything, but then most people don't seem to want to talk when I'm around. If they did, they'd interrupt. Take Nina Spencer, for instance. When she wants to say something, she just starts in. That always tells me in the nicest possible way to hush up. My pa used to say I could talk the twitch right out of a cow's tail. My Lars, on the other hand, doesn't talk even when the room's silent." She laughed, an infectious, friendly sound. Before she could continue her monologue, a girl who looked almost identical to her interrupted with a heated tale of wrongdoing. Both Nina and Kate left the table temporarily to restore peace.

Ida's attention drifted to a quiet, elegantly dressed lady seated beside her. Her hair had been swept up into an attractive style contrasting sharply with the simple buns the other ladies wore, yet her shy smile betrayed no arrogance or superiority. She noticed Ida's glance and introduced herself. "I'm Cynthia Pierce. My husband's the dark-haired, handsome man sitting beside Lionel Harper."

Ida asked the logical question. "Do you have children?"

"Two with us and three with the Lord." Moisture hovered on the edges of her thickly lashed blue eyes. "My Sara is six and can hardly wait to learn to read. Theodore is sixteen and a good student, too. He wants to be a doctor."

"Have you talked to him about that?" Kate had returned to her lunch. "I may be wrong, but I've never thought much—"

"Shush, Kate," Nina interrupted firmly. "We all know learning to be a doctor is hard work, and I think it's admirable young Theo has decided to do it."

The topic of conversation changed, once again leaving Ida free to study her companions. She felt she could easily become friends with Cynthia and

Nina. Kate might be more of a challenge. Her comments about Ida's past still stung, though she'd obviously had no cruel intentions. As soon as Ida learned her way around, she'd make an effort to get to know all three ladies better.

She expressed her intentions later to Lucy on the way home. "If I tried to go visiting now, I'd probably cause a town crisis by getting lost."

"You'll catch on, dear. Nina offered today to have Lionel bring her horse into town if you'd like to borrow it. She's in the family way again and won't be needing the animal over the winter."

"That would be lovely." Ida quickly recalled many visits to a horse ranch owned by a friend's father. Despite her mother's mild disapproval, Ida hadn't been able to resist the sense of freedom she felt while astride a galloping horse. "How many children do Lionel and Nina have?"

"This will be their fifth, and my seventh grandchild. My son Kelvin and his wife have two girls."

Ida thought again of the sad, young face she'd noticed during the service. "Lucy, did you notice a young girl sitting by herself near the door this morning? I didn't see her at lunch. Who is she?"

"That's young Ruth McEvan." Sadness shadowed Lucy's eyes.

"I didn't see anyone with her. What of her family?"

Lucy traced the edge of her ever-present teacup for a few moments before answering. "They came from the prairies by wagon five years ago. Last year, the mother and three children drowned in a river accident. Timothy McEvan's been a man destroyed ever since. We've offered in as many ways as we can think of to help him with the three children who are left, but he's determined to do it alone. I've never seen such a heartbroken family." She sat silently for a couple more minutes, then bustled to her feet. "Let me give you a quick tour of the house and outside before I start peeling potatoes for supper."

As Ida suspected, the door to the right near the end of the short hall led into a simple but nicely furnished parlor. "I'd like you to feel that this is your home," Lucy emphasized. "If you want to have a private conversation with any guest, feel free to bring them in here. Of course, the kitchen table is where I do most of my visiting and you're welcome to do the same." To the left, stairs led to an upper level. "This is my room." Lucy gestured toward an airy room to the left. A doorway in the center and one to the right led to two smaller bedrooms. "These rooms are perfect for overnight guests or for storing coats and sleeping children when the family comes over." They descended the stairs, and Lucy led Ida out the door at the end of the hall.

To the right stood a small barn where Lucy's horse and now Ida's would be sheltered, and discreetly beyond that stood a tidy-looking outhouse. Lucy waved toward the buildings. "Lionel and his boys make sure the barn is kept clean and the horse curried. They'll take care of yours, as well. All we have to do is feed them in the morning."

"I'd like to do that," Ida offered eagerly. "Since Nina's horse will be here for my use, I'd like to help out."

"Do you have a couple of riding skirts?" Lucy glanced at the straight skirt Ida had chosen for her first Sunday.

"My mom made me a nice split skirt since she couldn't keep me from riding. She didn't think it was ladylike." Ida's cheeks warmed. She hadn't intended to sound critical of Mom.

Lucy didn't seem to notice. "Good idea. But it's probably made of heavy cotton, right?" Pausing for Ida's nod, she continued. "It will work well for now, but it won't be warm enough for winter. I have some extra wool fabric in a trunk upstairs. Would you mind if I sewed you another split skirt? You'll be spending a fair bit of time riding in the winter. We can't lose our first real teacher to frostbite." She chuckled and gave Ida a quick, one-armed hug around the shoulders.

Ida wandered to her room to finish unpacking. She already felt more loved and welcomed than she'd dared hope. Her thoughts turned back to a young face aged by grief lines and stayed with the memory until sleep took over.

Chapter 3

The week passed quickly as Ida settled into her new home and acquainted herself with the town. Dawson Creek was a friendly place, with a population under fifty. As Lucy explained while drawing a map for Ida, the real centers of business in the area were Rolla, several miles to the north, and Pouce Coupe to the south, which also contained the only hospital in the area. However, each of the villages served farming families scattered throughout the Peace River region.

"When homesteaders first came west," she continued, "they built their homes as close to each other as possible. The result has been small communities of farms. You'll hear people talk about Sunset Prairie, Progress, Fellers Heights, and a host of other names. They're just clusters of farm families who've created their own community. They help each other build, plant, and harvest, as well as create schools for their children. Your school is an example."

"So the school I'll be teaching in isn't in town?"

Lucy shook her head, pushing the piece of paper across the table. "I've drawn a circle to represent Dawson Creek. These two larger circles are Rolla and Pouce Coupe. Lionel's farm is a mile due north of Dawson Creek. Lars and Kate Harper's place is also a mile north of town, but about half a mile west from Lionel's. Their land borders the farm owned by Lars's brother, James, just to the north. About a mile west of Lars Harper's is Timothy McEvan's farm, and the school is on a piece of his land closest to the road. About a mile and a half west of the school is Doug and Cynthia Pierce's place. If you ride past their farm another five miles or so and a bit to the south, you'll encounter Arras."

"That means Lionel and Nina's children are a mile and a half from school." Ida studied the map disbelievingly. "It seems like quite a distance."

"Distance is relative around here." Lucy continued her patient explanation. "We're a day's travel by horseback from the railway, so an hour's walk to school seems reasonable."

"But what about winter? I've heard it can get pretty cold in the Peace Country."

"It can," Lucy said calmly. "Unless there's a good wind blowing, the children just bundle up warmly in blankets with heated rocks beside them and ride to school in the wagon. Young Lionel is good with a horse and wagon, and the other families have older sons. Except for the McEvans," she added as an afterthought. "But they're closest to the school, so walking isn't a problem. Since Nina has invited us out for a visit, how about if I take you the long way so you can get a feel for things?"

Lucy detailed her family's story while they rode. She had been born and raised in England, where she met and married her first husband, Kelvin Spencer. After his death in the early days of the war, she joined the military and met a Canadian, William Barry. After his medical discharge, they married and he brought her to the Peace area. Kelvin, Jr. chose to remain in England with his sweetheart. Lucy's younger son, Lionel, had come with his mother and stepfather. "In those days," Lucy recalled, "a man could claim land just by living on it for a year and building a cabin. Lionel got his start that way, with help from the inheritance he'd received from Kelvin, Sr. Since his claim bordered William's land, when William passed away, Lionel bought our farm. That money helped me set up the boardinghouse."

The trail branched ahead of them. Lucy slowed the horse and gestured to the left. "You can't see it from here, but the school's down that way. You'll see Lars Harper's place on the left just before we get to Lionel's."

Ida silently marveled at the rough beauty around her. She still couldn't believe young children trekked over a mile in the winter just for school. The closeness she'd observed among the families yesterday had led her to believe they lived much closer together. Instead, it appeared at least an hour's walk separated each family from another.

Lionel met them as they entered the farmyard. "Welcome, Miss Thomas. I'll take care of the horses if you ladies would like to go on inside." He helped them down from the buggy. "Nina's been hardly able to wait for you to get here."

Nina greeted each lady with a hug, then set a plate of warm cookies and cups of steaming tea on the table in front of them. "How do you like the Peace Country, Miss Thomas?"

"It's a lot different from the city, but I like what I've seen so far."

"Good. We'll do what we can to keep you here. What has Mom told you about us so far?"

"Just a basic sketch," Lucy put in. "Mostly about William and I and how Lionel got started."

Nina laughed. "The only time I've been jealous over Lionel was right

21

after he filed the claim. There's never been anyone else for either of us since we met the first Sunday he and his mom were in Canada, but he wouldn't marry me until he had the farm going. I was only fourteen at the time. That year and a half seemed like forever." A soft smile lingered on her face as she stared out her kitchen window into the farmyard where Lionel worked with a colt in the corral. "Then one marvelous autumn day, he came calling. When I greeted him at the door, he said real solemn-like, 'Nina, I've come to speak with your father.' Dad took him out on the porch where they could be alone, but I listened at the door. 'Mr. Watson,' he said, 'I've just come from town where I deposited ten dollars from this year's crop in the bank. My farm's running well, I have all the stock and equipment I need, and I've already paid for next year's seed. I'm ready to support a wife, and I'd like to marry your daughter, with your permission, sir.' Dad didn't answer for the longest time. He and I had discussed Lionel so often, I thought I knew what he was going to say, but that pause almost had me fooled. Then he said, 'Reckon you'll have to settle that with Nina, son. But if she'll have you, my blessings on you both.' Ten years and almost six children later, here we are with twice as much land as he started with. He's a wonderful provider."

Ida met the three boys and two girls later around the lunch table. Only six-year-old Tommy had anything to say to the new schoolteacher. "I have to learn to read so I can be as smart as Young Lionel." His description of his nine-year-old brother brought smiles to all the adults' faces.

Ida commented on the children's helpfulness while she and Lucy traveled home in the buggy with Nina's horse, Misty, plodding behind. "I've never seen youngsters so cooperative," she marveled.

"Their parents have done a great job raising them so far," Lucy agreed. "They all know nothing makes their dad more upset than for Nina to have to do something the children should have done. Even as a small boy, he used to insist on lifting pails and hauling firewood for me. He and Young Lionel come into town every evening to clean out my horses' stalls and make sure there's plenty of hay, feed, water, and firewood. In the early days of his marriage, I worried that he might be tied too tightly to my apron strings to be a good husband. Nina quickly set me straight, though. She told me one day, 'My mother always said a man will treat his wife as well or as poorly as he treats his mother. He's never neglected me to take care of you, and I'm glad to see he cares so much about your well-being.' When those two married, I definitely gained a daughter rather than losing a son."

Briefly, Ida wondered if she'd ever have a mother-in-law like Lucy or find a husband like Lionel. But then, as Mom had often said, God brought

Eve to Adam, so in the right time He'd bring the right man for Ida. "You don't have to go beating the bushes for a mate," she'd say firmly.

Ida's next discovery was the schoolhouse, built on a fenced triangle of land about six miles from town. Lucy took her there the next day, the buggy full of cleaning supplies. "It's been almost a year since the last teacher left us," she explained. "I'm sure the place is a mess."

She hadn't exaggerated. Sunlight struggled through dirt-encrusted windows. Spider webs hung from corners and desks that were covered with layers of dust. "Where are the books?" Ida asked, devoutly hoping no one had been careless enough to leave them here.

"I think the Pierces have been storing them, though we don't have a lot." Mrs. Barry opened the door of the woodstove. "Good, not many ashes. Bring me the kindling and the matches, would you, please?" In short order she had a fire blazing and a large pot of water heating.

Ida attacked the floor with a long-handled straw broom. "How many teachers have been here before?"

"Just one. He stayed for just a couple of months before the trustees caught him coming out of the Rolla saloon. They've been searching for a replacement ever since, but no one seems to want to come this far west and north."

"Where have the children been going?"

"Most have been learning what they can at home."

"Isn't there a school in town?"

Mrs. Barry scrubbed at the bench seats with an old rag. "There is, but they've had to split it into three different locations in order to make room for all the students. A new building is planned once the town moves."

"So how did this school happen?"

"Lars, Lionel, and Timothy McEvan decided it was time they had their own school. They talked to Lars's brother James as well as Doug Pierce, and the five of them built this building on this corner of Timothy McEvan's land. That proved to be the easy part. You're the answer to our prayers about the hard part."

"Timothy McEvan. He's the man you told me about on Sunday?"

"Yes. If the school hadn't been beneficial to his children, I doubt he'd have taken any interest in the project. The way he helped us, though, showed me what a fine man hides under all that guilt and grief."

"Yoohoo. Anybody need help here?" Kate Harper peered into the room.

"You'd be welcome," Lucy responded. "I think the water's heated just perfectly, so let's start scrubbing windows. Cleaning the rest won't do any good until we can see what we're doing."

"I brought a couple of buckets and some rags." Kate bustled back to her wagon, a stream of unintelligible chatter drifting behind her. As she returned, the words began making sense. ". . .you girls out here cleaning all by yourselves. Ruby, that's my sister-in-law," Kate offered the explanation with a glance at Ida, "is in the middle of making cheese, so she couldn't come. Nina said she'd be here later, though I'm not sure it will be good for her, and I think Cynthia's coming, too. She said something about bringing books." Kate trudged back to the wagon for more rags, so Ida took advantage of the pause.

"Will Kate's sister-in-law's family be coming to school?"

Kate overheard the question. "They will if I have to take a switch to them. James and Ruby didn't get much past the reading stage in their own schooling, so they're not too dedicated to it for their kids. That farm's all they think about. But I keep telling Ruby, it's not big enough for the whole brood. If they don't get some learning, how will they find anything else? Young Jim will try to skip as much school as he can, and his dad will let him because it means the boy can help on the farm more." She continued a commentary on each of her six nieces and nephews. ". . .and young Julie is three. Can that child ever have a fit! I'll never know how such placid parents as James and Ruby produced a temper like that one has. I love them all, but why anyone would want seven children is beyond me! Speaking of big broods, here comes Nina. Now, girls, we can't let her do anything heavy. As early in her time as she is, too much could do her harm." Kate raised her voice as Nina reached into the back of her wagon. "No, Nina, I'll carry that in for you."

Not long after Nina, Cynthia arrived with several crates of books. She rolled up the sleeves of her fashionable print dress and started scrubbing book shelves. By the middle of the afternoon, the schoolhouse gleamed. Sunlight streamed through clean windows onto well-dusted desks. Just inside the door, a clean washbasin sat on a wooden table.

"What are those pegs for?" Ida asked, looking at the double row just above the washstand.

"Towels," Kate informed her. "Each child will bring his or her own towel and cup. The men will keep the water bucket filled before winter. Once the snow starts, you can melt it for washing and drinking water. You won't believe how dirty the children can get just during a brief recess. Mark my words, you'll be glad for those towels before the first day is out."

Despite her interaction with her students' mothers, Ida still felt unprepared. She had no doubts about her academic abilities. But could she meet the needs of seventeen students? Thirteen to seventeen distinct personalities? She wished Mom were here, too, with some helpful advice.

She walked to school the first day to get a feeling for the trek her students would make every day. Teddy and Nettie Harper arrived only a few minutes after she'd settled at her desk. Nettie not only resembled her mother in appearance, but also in behavior. Her "Good morning, Miss Thomas," was quickly followed by, "Teddy's shy, but I'm not. My cousin Patricia taught me to read after her mother taught her. I've read every book Mrs. Spencer's loaned me, plus Mama's Bible twice. I can help you teach the little kids if you want."

Ida welcomed them both with a smile, recognizing thirst for learning behind Nettie's self-importance. She greeted other new arrivals, grateful for a reason not to answer Nettie's offer. After a brief Scripture reading and a quick prayer, she began sorting the children into groups. Five youngsters were eager to learn to read—Tommy Spencer and Teddy Harper, as well as red-haired, freckle-faced Phillip McEvan, whose brown eyes invited mischief, shy Karin Harper, and dainty Sara Pierce. Ida assigned Teddy a seat as far from Nettie as she could manage, sensing the boy needed a break from his overbearing older sister. On the other hand, their cousin Karin looked like she might burst into tears any time she lost sight of Patricia, one of Ida's oldest students. Karin had to be on the front row with the rest of the new readers, so Ida asked Patricia to sit right behind her. Little Sara Pierce kept looking around for her older brother, but seemed content as long as she could see Theodore.

The rest of the students sorted themselves out as Ida asked questions about their knowledge and abilities. Patricia's assigned seat to the left of the classroom caused the older students to gather there, as well. The part-time students had come for the first day, so they staked out their seats at the back. Justin Harper's eyes sparkled as Ida asked him arithmetic questions of increasing difficulty. When he finally paused over an algebra problem, she guessed he'd probably be ready for graduation by the end of the year, along with Theodore Pierce. Jed Harper was somewhat behind Justin and Theodore in academic ability and not quite as eager to learn. His cousin Jim obviously didn't want to be in school, though he treated Ida with courtesy. During harvest, Patricia Spencer and Ruth McEvan would be Ida's only students in the older group.

Ruth McEvan remained a mystery. She rarely spoke, even when spoken to. Ida handed her one of the newest readers available. The girl's eyes sparkled briefly, then resumed their sad, almost hardened gaze. She answered Ida's questions so quietly the teacher had to strain to hear her. Ida also noticed that

Theodore waited until Ruth had chosen a seat, then picked one beside her for himself.

Aside from Ruth, Ida felt her biggest challenges would be among the middle group. David Spencer seemed quiet for an eight year old, reluctant to interact with others. His older brother, Young Lionel, seemed a typical nine-year-old boy, despite his air of responsibility. Ida could tell he'd been told to watch out for the younger ones. Michael Harper was obviously a typical ten year old, full of energetic ideas for getting reactions out of others, particularly Nettie, whom he teased to distraction. His younger sister, June, obviously would have preferred to be outside climbing trees. With the others' distinct and attention-grabbing personalities, Clara Spencer's quiet studiousness could be easy to overlook.

After getting her students seated and organized, Ida assigned all but the youngest a short exercise in which they were to write one page about themselves. She gave the five youngest students a bucket of colored blocks, which she asked them to organize according to color and size. Though both assignments would help her understand her students better, they also gave Ida a few moments to collect her thoughts and watch the students as a whole.

It wouldn't be difficult to distinguish among the family groups, she decided. All of James and Ruby Harper's children looked typically Scandinavian—stocky build, white-blond hair, and blue eyes. Both McEvan children had red hair and freckled noses. Theodore and Sara Pierce were black-haired, though Sara's eyes were blue while Theo's were dark brown. Jed Harper was the image of his dad, and his sister and brother looked too much like their mother to be mistaken for their cousins. The four Spencers varied most in appearance, but Ida felt better acquainted with them than the rest of her students. She hoped that feeling wouldn't last long.

By two o'clock, Ida felt grateful she had arranged for classes to let out early. Many of the children were overly excited, making discipline difficult to maintain. The younger ones had become fidgety, and the older ones were obviously ready to escape their studies. An hour later, after they had departed, she closed the door with a sigh.

"Surely teaching school isn't that bad already," a male voice interrupted her thoughts.

She turned her head with a start in the direction of the voice to find a well-dressed young man lounging against a tree. He looked vaguely familiar and his smile seemed pleasant enough, so she smiled back. "The first day is always tough."

"Then it's good I'm here to carry your books home for you. I'm Ken Danielson. I didn't get an opportunity to introduce myself at church a week ago." He reached out a hand for the textbooks from which she planned to create special assignments for Justin and Theo.

She let him take the books, while declining to place her hand on the arm he offered. "I'm afraid I've met so many people these last two weeks, I don't remember seeing you. But thanks for the escort, just the same."

"I'll bring the buggy tomorrow."

His assumption that his presence would be welcome annoyed her. "That won't be necessary. I'll be on horseback. Besides, I enjoy the time by myself after the children go home."

"We can tie your horse behind. I want to get well acquainted with you." He winked flirtatiously.

Ida decided not to press the point for the time being. They discussed general topics—weather, town news, and harvest, though he didn't seem to know much about the latter. At the end of the boardwalk leading to her new home, she stopped and reached for her books. "Thanks for escorting me home, Mr. Danielson. I'll see you Sunday?"

A glimmer of something uncertain showed in his eyes before it was quickly replaced with a smooth smile. "Or perhaps before, Miss Thomas." He lifted his hat in salute and left her wondering who on earth he really was.

Chapter 4

The next month passed more quickly than Ida would have believed possible. Though her classroom had appeared to organize itself into three groups on the first day, by the end of the first week, she felt as if she were teaching thirteen different classes. Even her new readers were at different levels. Sara Pierce already knew her letters, while Teddy Harper still struggled distinguishing colors. Tommy Spencer learned his letters quickly, as long as Young Lionel was at school. The days his older brother stayed home, Tommy's mind seemed everywhere but on his studies. Karin Harper soaked up schooling like a thirsty sponge and would catch up to Sara in no time. Hopefully the two girls would help each other once they learned to read. Then there was Phillip McEvan—mischievous, energetic, affectionate Phillip. He liked nothing better than to sit on his teacher's lap and would have spent every recess there if Ida would have let him. He greeted her each morning with a hug, began and ended each recess with a hug, and wouldn't leave in the afternoon without a hug.

"The child seems starved for affection," Ida explained to Lucy one evening during the second week. "I don't want to appear to play favorites, but denying him a hug or a cuddle seems as bad as slapping one of the other children."

"How does Ruth treat him?" Lucy's hands stilled in their work for once as she gave complete attention to Ida's answer.

Ida couldn't help the sigh that felt like it came from her toes. "She's another challenge. I've tried several times to get her to talk with me, but all I get are one-word answers. She seems as close to happy as she ever gets when left completely alone. Her sadness is like a shield against life in general, including her little brother."

"Does he try to hug her?"

"Usually he just tries to hold her hand. She'll tolerate him for a few minutes, then makes him let go."

"Does she have any friends?"

Ida grinned. "Theodore Pierce. She tries to ignore him like she does the rest of us, but he never gives up. He brings treats for her lunch and often walks her to and from school."

Lucy resumed stirring her cake batter. "Sort of like another young man I often see at the end of my boardwalk."

"If I felt he were as much my friend as Theo is Ruth's, I wouldn't work so hard at avoiding him." She felt surprised at how easy it was to talk to Lucy, almost like old times with Mom.

"Why do you say that, dear?" Lucy poured the batter into two round pans, which she placed in the oven. She dipped steaming water out of the boiler on the back of the stove into the dishpan. Ida would have liked to help her, but Lucy preferred to let the dishes air dry. She used rinse water so hot the dishes were ready to put away by the time she finished wiping the counters.

"He talks mostly about himself and his own world. He's nice enough, but he doesn't seem interested in me as a person. He tries too hard to impress me."

Lucy poured a cup of tea for each of them and settled at the end of the table where Ida had been grading arithmetic quizzes. "Oh?"

"Oh, yes. I know all about how his dad was one of the town's earliest businessmen and now owns the only hardware store. As a result, his family is so well off, Ken doesn't have to work, which is why he can meet me after school almost every day. Then you should hear him talk about his concern for Dawson Creek's spiritual well-being. Apparently the entire community is comprised of unrepentant reprobates." Ida couldn't stop her giggle.

Lucy grinned in response. "Has he mentioned the Presbyterian group who meet at James and Ruby's place twice a month or the Catholic priest who comes through on a regular basis? There's also an Anglican church being planned for building in Rolla next summer."

"Like I say, if he didn't try so hard, I might be more impressed."

"And how's Nettie doing?" Lucy's eyes twinkled, remembering the girl's eagerness to be in charge.

"Periodically I have to remind her who the teacher is and who is really responsible for keeping discipline in the classroom. Mostly, I just try to keep her so busy she doesn't have time for meddling."

"Is that difficult?"

"Yes and no. She has learned quite a bit on her own, but only what she wanted to learn. She can whip right through the eighth level readers, but anything more than simple arithmetic is difficult. It's easy to find plenty she needs to work on. Motivating her to do it is the hard part."

"You're showing a lot of wisdom in working with those youngsters, Ida. Your mother would be proud of you." Lucy patted Ida's arm. "God sent you here for a special reason. I'm more convinced of that by the day. And also grateful He put you with me."

Unexpected tears filled Ida's eyes. Lucy had an uncanny knack for finding her sore spots and saying just the right thing to ease them. "Thanks, Lucy. Some days I wonder if I really am fulfilling a purpose or just muddling through."

Lucy's voice softened. "I can imagine. But isn't that what the New Testament calls walking by faith? It seems to us we're just muddling through. But our Father sees the whole picture and orders our steps accordingly."

"I know He ordered my steps to put me here," Ida replied, putting her hand over Lucy's. "I don't know how I would have managed these first few months without Mom if I hadn't been with you. Still, though, I would want her to be proud of what I'm doing if she were here. But if she weren't gone, I wouldn't be here." She laughed self-consciously. "Don't I sound mixed up?"

Lucy blinked away tears of her own. "It is hard getting used to being without those we love. I hope you won't be reluctant to let me know when you need some mothering."

"A hug right now would be nice." *Would that assuage the torrent of insecurity a difficult school day seemed to bring?*

Without hesitation, Lucy enfolded Ida in a loving hug. She said nothing else, just simply held the younger woman tightly until Ida relaxed her own embrace to reach for her handkerchief.

"Thanks. I'd hoped I'd miss her less with being busy, but it seems I miss her more."

"That's the way it is, honey, at least for the first little while. As long as you don't try to avoid the pain, it will get easier in time."

Ida stacked her papers. "I'm going to go to bed early. By the way, I won't be here for supper tomorrow evening. The Pierces have invited me out to their farm. I'll walk to school in the morning, and Mr. Pierce will drive me in after supper."

"That's lovely." Lucy's face beamed. "I knew it wouldn't take folks long to want to get acquainted. Are you having any trouble with the schoolhouse stove? It can be difficult at times."

Ida wrinkled her forehead in puzzlement. "I haven't had to do much with it. Since it's started getting cold overnight, I've found a fire already built when I arrive each morning. The boys keep it stoked during the day, and all I have to do is close the dampers before I leave in the afternoon."

"You have no idea who's doing it?"

"No. The schoolhouse is nice and warm when I get there, so whoever it is comes fairly early."

"That's quite a trek for anyone. Probably if you're supposed to know who it is, you'll find out eventually." Lucy shrugged and grinned.

Except for her mysterious morning visitor, "getting acquainted" hadn't been a problem for Ida. Not only did she see most of her students and their families on Sundays, but one parent or another usually stopped by the schoolhouse every day. Nina had invited Ida and Lucy for a meal at least once a week since school started. Friendship grew quickly between the two younger women. Kate Harper visited regularly, almost always on Saturdays, and she'd already had Ida out to their farm for a supper. With Nina's assistance, Ida was learning to understand Kate and even appreciate the caring she concealed behind unending talk. Timothy McEvan remained the only parent whom Ida hadn't met.

Having seen the Spencers' log farmhouse and Lars Harper's log cabin, Ida was awed by the gracious frame home in which the Pierces lived. Surrounded by a whitewashed picket fence, the house looked like it had been transplanted from one of the city's nicest neighborhoods. "What a lovely house!" she couldn't resist exclaiming as she, Theodore, and Sara walked up the drive.

"Father always says this is Mother's reward for being willing to live out at the edge of nowhere so he can have the farm he wants." Theo's ready smile lit his eyes.

"I'll show you my room," Sara offered, eager to have some of Teacher's attention, too.

Actually, Ida received a grand tour of the entire home, conducted by both her students. Theo's explanations gave her a sense of the life from which his mother must have come, while Sara's comments told her what a loving atmosphere Cynthia had created for her family. When they finished, Cynthia had tea and dainty cookies waiting in the sitting room.

"Doug won't be in from the field until dark, around seven," she explained, "so I thought a little refreshment would keep us going until supper time. Have you washed?" She examined Sara's hands gently. "Go wash your hands and face and comb your hair. We won't eat everything before you get back." She hugged the small girl and gave her a kindly push toward the small room beside the porch. Ida had never before seen a room set aside exclusively for washing and bathing.

Theo had obviously anticipated his mother's expectations. His hair looked damp from where he'd used water to help tidy it. Though the teacup and saucer looked too dainty for his hands, which were beginning to look like a man's, he handled them expertly. He responded to his mother with surprising gentleness and deference, though without appearing like an over-mothered sissy. After about thirty minutes, he excused himself for chores.

"So how do you like teaching school?" Cynthia inquired. Though her voice carried unmistakable traces of her cultured background, it communicated genuine interest.

"It's a challenge." Ida smiled reassuringly at Sara. "I have five new readers, each of whom is at a different level. It's sort of that way throughout the entire classroom."

"I've spent some time working with Sara here at home. Would there be anything I could do to help?" Cynthia's eyes lit eagerly. "I've already asked Doug, and he wants me to do whatever I can."

"From what I've seen of Sara's learning, I think you could help me quite a lot. Most of my work with her age group is just repetition. How about if you come in whenever you're able, and I promise I'll be able to put you to work."

"I would really enjoy that. I've always loved children and wanted a houseful of my own. Somehow, though, I've only been able to keep two." She scooped Sara close to her with a fierce hug. "And I love them both dearly."

She declined Ida's offer of help with the tea tray or with supper. "You've had a long day. I'd be pleased if you could just relax while I finish in the kitchen. If you'd like, help yourself to one of our books, or if you prefer to nap, Sara can show you to the guest room."

Ida smiled her thanks. "A book sounds wonderful. I've had little time to read just for enjoyment since school started."

Theo's attitude toward his mother explained itself as soon as Doug Pierce entered the house. Ida noticed he stopped first at the washroom to clean off the dirt of the field. He then vanished upstairs to return quickly, clad in clean pants and a fresh shirt. His light brown hair had been dampened and combed into place. Only then did he venture toward the kitchen, where Ida could hear him greet his wife. When Cynthia called everyone to the table a short time later, Doug helped her carry serving dishes from the kitchen, then held her chair for her as she sat down. He and his son then seated themselves. After asking the blessing, he made sure his wife was served first.

The adults' conversation soon expanded to include Theo and Sara. Ida was impressed with the way both parents gave importance to their children's opinions and thoughts.

"When is the town going to move?" Theo asked his dad, following Ida's account of her trip from Hythe with Lars Harper.

Doug stacked dishes while his wife brought out bowls of fluffy vanilla pudding topped with fresh raspberries and whipped cream. "Last I heard, it's scheduled for mid-November."

"How do you move a town?" Sara wanted to know.

"Mr. Harper told me they'll use huge chains to hook a building to a big machine or maybe to horses that will tow it," Theo explained patiently.

The tiny girl looked puzzled. "What's tow?"

Her dad laughed. "That means to pull. The buildings will roll on logs that will be on top of planks."

Sara's brow remained wrinkled. "I still don't understand."

"That's okay," her mother reassured. "It's hard to explain. We'll have to take you to watch."

"But what if I'm in school?"

Doug tweaked her braid. "We'll work out something, sweetheart."

Ida already knew what would be worked out. Listening to the family talk, she'd decided to cancel classes so families could watch the event together. The process sounded mysterious even to her. It promised to be an exciting event that would draw spectators from miles around.

Theo offered to drive her home. Ida was delighted his father agreed. Theo probably had some insight she needed, but she didn't think he'd want to discuss it with a group, even if that group were simply his parents. Besides, darkness made it easier to share confidences.

She hugged Sara good-bye, thanked Cynthia for the delightful meal, and shook Doug's hand. Theo helped her into the buggy. She waited until they were out of the yard before she asked, "May I ask you some personal questions, Theo?"

His voice in the dark sounded perplexed. "Sure, Miss Thomas."

"I've noticed your efforts to befriend Ruth McEvan. How well do you know her?"

He didn't answer right away. "Probably as well as anyone, though you've probably noticed she doesn't give much more attention to me than to others. Why?"

"I'm worried about her."

"Me, too." His voice sounded heavy with the weight of his concern.

"Has she told you what's troubling her?"

"Do you know what happened to her mother and brothers?"

"Yes."

"We've talked about it some after church or on the way home from school. She thinks it's her fault and that she has to make it up to her dad and other two brothers."

"There's another brother?"

"Greg. He's only three, a lot like Phillip, but quieter."

"Does anyone help them, like cooking, cleaning, sewing, that kind of thing?"

"Mr. McEvan and Ruth won't let them. They both insist they can do everything themselves."

Ida couldn't imagine the fourteen-year-old girl being mother and housekeeper as well as going to school. No wonder she kept to herself. She didn't have time for normal childhood friendships—except for this friend who wouldn't let her be alone. "How does she find time for her studies?"

"She's real smart, Miss Thomas. Most of her work she can do in school. If she does have to study at night, her dad makes supper and takes care of the boys." His tone told how proud he felt of her accomplishment.

"Do you mind if I ask why you work so hard to be her friend? It seems to me if it weren't for you, she'd let herself be alone."

He paused again. "That's why I do it. She doesn't know yet how much a friend can help. So I stick close for when she realizes she needs someone."

"That shows a lot of caring and maturity on your part, Theodore. More than most fellows your age." She wasn't sure how he'd respond to the praise, but she had to tell him how she felt.

"My dad's the same way—always helping the folks that don't think they need it. He says that's what Jesus did for us, dying for us before we realized we were sinners. He says a true friend is the kind that doesn't expect anything in return. People respect my dad. Some of the ones he helped are the ones who were there for us when Mother got so sick. He also says true friends are there when no one else wants to be. Ruth tries to make people not want to be around her, so I just stick that much closer. She'll be all right one of these days."

Ida felt like she'd lost her breath. With heart and understanding such as his, this boy—no, young man—would make a fantastic doctor. "What if Ruth never changes, Theo?"

"She will. God told me so."

His quiet confidence shook Ida afresh. "Would you mind telling me how you know for sure?"

"I was praying for her one morning while reading my Bible, and I saw a verse I'd never seen before. It says, 'Weeping may endure for a night, but joy cometh in the morning.' I know God never lies."

They had reached the edge of town, so Ida spoke quickly. "Sorry for all the questions, Theo, but I have one more. You've told me some pretty personal things tonight. Why did you trust me so easily?"

He didn't answer until he stopped the horses in front of Ida's boardwalk. "Partly because I know you really care about all of us, that you're our friend."

Ida didn't want to pry, but she sensed the unspoken part of his answer was the most important. "Can you tell me the other part?"

"You won't tell anyone else?"

"No. Everything you've said tonight stays with me."

"The first Sunday I saw you, I felt like God told me you are the person He'll use to help Ruth."

Chapter 5

When Ida looked out her window Wednesday morning, she gasped with surprise. A thick white layer of snow coated everything. She dressed quickly and hurried out to the kitchen. "Lucy, did you notice what happened last night?"

"That there's snow," Mr. Carey responded from where he sat at the kitchen table still slurping coffee. "It's part of the scenery most of the year hereabouts."

"She knows that, you old grouch," Lucy fussed, filling a plate for Ida. "It is pretty, isn't it?"

"Misty won't have any trouble in it, will she?"

"It might take her a few minutes to adjust, but she'll do fine." Lucy patted Ida's shoulder reassuringly. "At least the school will be warm when you get there." Her eyes twinkled over the mystery.

"I suspect Theo comes over early, since they live nearby." Ida returned to her room for warmer clothing. She tugged on the beautiful woolen riding skirt Lucy had made, then folded another skirt into her bag. A shelter for the horse had mysteriously appeared near the school about a week after school started. With its door closed, she had a private place to change into more appropriate clothing for the day.

"Theo's sure a fine young man, isn't he?" Lucy called through the closed door.

Ida fastened her heavy black woolen cape around her neck. This was the first time she'd worn this garment since Mother had finished it the week before her death. She swallowed back the inevitable tears before answering. "He is." She came back into the kitchen, tying a pink knitted scarf around her head. "He hasn't missed a day of school yet. Even when the other boys are helping with harvest and butchering, he's at school. I wonder how Doug manages without him."

"I wouldn't know, but from what Doug and Cynthia were saying during lunch on Sunday, they're just as eager for him to become a doctor as he is. Maybe Doug's making a few sacrifices of his own to make sure his boy gets a good education."

"I'm glad and a little scared if they consider my teaching good education." Ida laughed, trying not to remember Mother's pale face as she'd sewn the big pink buttons down the front of this cape and the pink trim around the edges.

"From watching the pains you take here at home and the way you worry over those children, I haven't a doubt they're getting the best education possible." Lucy gave Ida a floury hug. "Oops, didn't mean to get bread-making all over your lovely cape." Her voice softened. "Is that another of your mother's projects?"

She nodded.

"Wear it like a hug, girl. Let it remind you of her love, not just her absence."

Ida squeezed her friend's sticky hands. "Thanks, Lucy. Now I've got to get out of here. The children will never let me live it down if I arrive after they do."

"My prayers are with you!" Lucy called out the back door.

Ida saddled Misty almost without thinking about it. Riding had grown from an enjoyable recreation to an instinctive part of her life in the past weeks. She breathed deeply of the crisp, clean air, wondering briefly if this kind of life would have restored Mother's health. Then the rhythmic clop of Misty's hooves and the stillness of winter's first morning replaced her sadness with peace. Lucy had been right. Time made grief easier to carry—not less, just easier.

What would it take to help Ruth and her dad discover that secret? Ida had tried everything she knew to find a crack in Ruth's self-imposed barrier. She'd even borrowed Lucy's buggy for one day so she could offer Ruth and Phillip a ride home.

"Thanks, Miss Thomas, but we wouldn't want to trouble you. It's not that far, anyway." Ruth had grasped her brother's hand and they had set out before Ida could think of a reply.

Ida remembered Theo's gentle defense. "She doesn't mean to be rude, ma'am. I think she actually likes you."

Ida had turned to her young friend in amazement. "Where did you get that idea?"

He'd smiled. "I've seen her watching you. She adds bows and lace bits to her blouses like you do and even tries to walk like you."

Now, as she rode Misty through the new snow, she wondered again if his conviction about her helping Ruth wasn't the product of his caring imagination. Yet Lucy's comment about Ida's special purpose in Dawson Creek added validity to Theodore's idea. *Or was it God's idea?*

To Ida's surprise, a new face appeared at the dinner table that evening. Lucy introduced the light-haired man as Pete Miller. "He's a carpenter from Grande Prairie come to help with the move. He'll be here a month or so."

"Where is Grande Prairie?" Ida wondered.

Their guest didn't seem bothered by her ignorance. "It's a ways south of Hythe."

"How will you be helping?"

"Some of the old buildings need reinforcement, and there's a heap of new ones being built at the new site. You'll find yourselves overrun with carpenters in the next few days. Seems to be plenty to keep us all busy. Sure is good food, ma'am," he complimented Lucy.

Maybe Pete could explain something Ida had noticed yesterday. "Can you explain the shallow holes being dug behind some of the buildings?"

"I'd be glad to. They're to make room for skids."

"What are skids?"

He took a couple swigs of coffee before answering. "It's what they call the lumber they put under the building to make it easier to move. If the building wasn't on the skids, it would be pulled apart when they drag it to the new site."

A few days later, Ida saw a different approach to the same task. It took her a few moments to realize what looked different about the boarding-house. Gradually she realized boards around its base had been removed, revealing the stone pilings on which it sat. According to Pete, there was just enough distance for skids between the base of the house and the ground. One by one, homes and businesses began disappearing from the old town site. Some were slowly dragged by the large crawler tractors that had been used to construct the railroad grade. Others were pulled by farm tractors, and horses moved the rest.

Lucy and Ida visited the new town site Saturday afternoon. Several houses and stores had already been settled on new foundations, while brand-new buildings stood in various stages of construction nearby. Pete had been right about the number of carpenters who had come to participate in the building boom. Most of them chose to stay at the three-story Dawson Hotel, which took the better part of two weeks to relocate. As it crawled along towed by horses, guests wandered in and out just like it was stationary.

The boardinghouse moved on Tuesday. Ida and Lucy packed all their breakables into crates padded with linens and removed wall hangings. Lucy used the crates to brace cupboard doors closed.

"Think you can find your way back this afternoon? Home will be two and a half miles farther away." Lucy giggled at her own joke.

The old town site looked strange when Ida rode by after school. Now that the boardinghouse was gone, she also noticed how many other buildings had been moved. Another home was being prepared while she watched.

The school trustees had given Ida permission to cancel school the next day so everyone could watch the co-op store being moved. She and Lucy spent the early part of the day putting their belongings back in order. Mr. Carey came in for lunch, mumbling the entire time.

"Who's lousy idea was this anyway? Buildings weren't made to be moved like someone's satchel. It's easier to lay railroad track than it is an entire town. And people are acting like it's some big party, all lined up out there waiting for the co-op like it's the queen or something."

Lucy had prepared ham and beans, and she set a steaming plate in front of him. "I'm sure a warm, healthy lunch will help you feel better."

"And what if I don't want to feel better! That's the trouble with this world. Wimen always tryin' to fix things!" He wolfed his lunch in six bites and stomped back out the door.

"Poor man. It's so hard to stay grouchy when this world is full of excitement." Lucy giggled, dipping herself another small helping of beans. "More for you, dear?"

"No thanks. I've had plenty. It was delicious as usual."

Lucy grinned again. "When you've had as much practice as I've had, you'd better know how to make a meal tasty."

By the time they finished dishes, the co-op was within sight. They grabbed thick coats, shoved their feet into warm boots, and rushed outside to join the crowd across from the store's new location. The store's skids rested on logs that rolled across planks laid along the ground. Ropes connected the building to the bottom of a large metal post, which had been secured in a hole some distance away. A horse had been hitched to each of four poles extending at right angles from the post. As they circled the post repeatedly, the ropes wound around the post, towing the building so slowly it barely seemed to move. A crew of men formed a continuous chain of activity, picking up planks and logs from behind the building and repositioning them in front. Meanwhile, a stream of people wandered in and out of the store.

"They said they wouldn't close for a moment during the move. I think most people are just going in to see what it's like in a moving building." Kate Harper's familiar voice nearby caught Ida's attention.

She looked over at her friend. "And have you been shopping today?"

Kate's face turned faintly pink, and she nodded. "Of course. We were almost out of flour."

"Miss Thomas!"

Ida felt a small body hurl itself at her knees as her legs were caught in a viselike grip. She looked down at disheveled red hair. "Phillip! I'm glad to see you." She pried his arms away from her legs so she could bend down and return his hug. "What are you doing today?"

"Ruth and Papa wanted to see the store, and I wanted to see you. Will you come with me? I want to show you my little brother." Phillip hopped from one leg to another in his excitement.

She let the small boy grab her hand and drag her down the block. "Papa! Papa! I found Miss Thomas." Ruth stood beside a tall, red-haired man who looked like he hadn't eaten a decent meal in months. His clothes hung on him as though he had once been stockier. *He would have been a huge man*, Ida thought, imagining him big enough to fit his coat properly.

A smile stretched the man's mouth, but didn't touch his grief-filled blue eyes. "Was she lost?"

"No. But she's my teacher and I wanted Greggy to see her." Phillip tugged at the foot of a small red-haired boy his father held. Mr. McEvan placed the boy on the boardwalk so the youngsters could talk. Ida knelt down to be at the boys' eye level. "Greggy, this is Miss Thomas. She's the pretty lady I told you about. She's teaching me to read so I can teach you. She likes hugs, too." Phillip demonstrated his point by giving his teacher another neck-crushing embrace. Before she could return it, Greg had joined the hug.

Ida squeezed them both, then kept her arms around them while she chatted. "How old are you, Greg?"

"Free." He struggled to show her on the fingers of one hand while putting his other thumb in his mouth.

"Do you help your papa at home while Phillip goes to school?"

The boy nodded solemnly.

"I'm teaching him his letters like you teach me," Phillip informed her. "He wants to come to school when he's as big as me."

"I'm sure he'll be as good a student as you are." Ida hugged them both again before standing up. She lifted her gaze to find their dad watching her. "I'm pleased to have met you, Mr. McEvan."

"Likewise," he replied gruffly with a stiff nod. "You've been good to my children."

She didn't know how to reply. The pain in his eyes grabbed her heart.

She had a crazy impulse to embrace him as she had his sons, as if by doing so she could absorb some of his agony. She met Ruth's gaze, surprised to see a hint of friendliness there. "I'm glad to see you, too, Ruth." Without thinking, she hugged the girl. To her amazement, she felt the hug returned.

Greg and Phillip were now busy drawing designs in the mud made by melting snow, chatting happily to each other. Ida didn't know what to say in parting. Neither Ruth nor her father offered any comment.

"Miss Thomas!" Ken's friendly greeting interrupted the almost-awkward silence. He strode quickly toward them. "The cafe windows face this way. Please share a soda with me while we watch."

His almost childish enthusiasm grated on her nerves. But maybe his carefree approach was what she needed to break the spell McEvan's sadness had put over her. She patted Ruth's shoulder as she smiled at Ken. "Sure. See you tomorrow, Ruth."

Ken extended his elbow, but Ida declined the offer. "How did your parents' store survive the move?"

"No problems at all. We thought about leaving the house at the old site and building new here, but Father didn't think we could be finished before winter."

She noted his inference that weather, not money, had been the deciding factor. At least she needn't feel guilty about him spending money on her, she mused while waiting for him to return to the table with their treat. Spending money seemed to be his favorite form of entertainment.

The massive soda glass he carried almost overflowed as he set it down. "Doesn't that look tasty. Here, I brought an extra spoon."

She couldn't remember having ever tasted anything so rich. "Mmmm. It's almost addicting." She smiled her thanks before taking another bite.

"I've been thinking about this new house of my parents'," he commented several mouthfuls later. "Spring might be a good time for me to build a house of my own so they wouldn't have to build with me in mind. What do you think?"

Ida almost choked on her ice cream. What did it matter what she thought? "It could be a practical idea, if that's what you really want to do. Do you know for sure you're going to settle in Dawson Creek?"

"If I decide to move, I can just sell the house. But I probably won't be leaving for awhile."

Ida wondered if he'd finally found employment that interested her, but was afraid to ask. Ken's continuing monologue relieved her of the need to reply.

"I've always wanted to travel a bit, but I'm not wild about doing it alone. I just realized I could get the house started in the spring, leave on a honeymoon right after school's out, and the house would be finished by the time we got back."

She choked back laughter. "How long would this honeymoon be?"

"Six months at least. Oh look, they've just about got the store in place! Isn't it just amazing the way we've been able to relocate this entire town?" His tone made it sound as though he'd played a vital role in the move.

"Mrs. Barry's probably looking for me. Thanks for the soda."

Ken stood with her. "I'll escort you back. No telling what could attack you in this wild town."

Ida looked at him with a smile, expecting to see an answering twinkle over the joke. Instead, she could tell he took himself quite seriously. The notion strengthened her impulse to giggle. She held the laughter back, not wanting to hurt his feelings.

Both she and Lucy did laugh out loud later when she related the story. "That boy has no more sense of reality than Nina's new baby, Tabitha." Lucy shook her head.

"Besides, if I were in any danger, I'd want a man with working muscles, not a storekeeper!" Ida giggled again. Then a stray thought doused her mirth. Timothy McEvan had obviously been quite solidly built at one time. Could misplaced guilt over being unable to protect his family be what troubled him? As though a cloud had passed over the sun, she no longer felt like laughing. Somehow the McEvans' grief had made its way into her heart.

Chapter 6

School demanded all Ida's patience Thursday. A day off had left the children as fidgety and excitable as they usually were on Mondays, except she didn't have Cynthia's help as she did at the beginning of the week. Anticipating some of the excitement, she had planned some discussion for the beginning of the day. Each child had an opportunity to tell what he or she had seen or heard. They would have dragged the conversation out all day if Ida would have let them. She set the youngest students to drawing pictures of the move and asked Ruth, Patricia, and Theodore to write essays about it. The three older boys were missing this week to help with the butchering.

"Time for arithmetic drills," she announced to the middle group. "I've written addition problems on the board. As soon as I say 'Go,' you write down answers as quickly as you can. Ready, set, go!"

Usually the informal competition motivated each of the children to work as hard as they could. Today, Nettie deliberately set her pencil down in the middle of the paper and stared out the window. It seemed like an attention-getting scheme, so Ida ignored her. A squabble broke out among the younger students. While she tried to settle the disagreement, she heard an irritated exclamation from David.

"Nettie! I'm trying to work."

"You're as boring as Teacher," Nettie whispered back.

Ida stood as quickly as she could without tripping on her skirt. "Nettie Harper, sit down."

Nettie deliberately walked away from her desk. The altercation had gripped everyone's attention by this time. Even the older students had ceased writing. Ida knew she had to handle Nettie carefully or lose any discipline she'd carefully cultivated so far.

"Nettie, if you take another step, you can keep walking until you get home." She kept her voice calm.

"Makes me no never mind." Nettie tossed her head. "You don't like me anyway."

Ida fervently wished Nettie would have chosen a more private moment for her declaration. As it was, the challenge had to be answered before the entire school. She wondered if Jed's absence had anything to do with Nettie's timing. "How about if you come sit down, and we'll all talk about it?"

"You can't make me."

You need a good spanking, Ida thought, even while acknowledging that solution would only embarrass and alienate Nettie. Somehow, though, she had to overcome the child's will. "Nettie, you can either discuss this with all of us now, or I personally will take you home and explain to your dad what has happened." If she had to, she'd leave Theo in charge.

After an interminable pause, Nettie's defiant gaze dropped, and she slowly shuffled back to her seat.

Ida moved close enough to rub her hand across her student's hair. "Can you tell us why you feel I don't like you?"

"You never let me do fun stuff."

"Like what?" The older students had resumed writing, and the younger ones were drawing peaceably.

"I told you I could help you teach the little kids. All you ever let me do is stupid math pages."

Ida knelt so she could look into Nettie's eyes. "I appreciate your wanting to help me, Nettie. But you need to learn more before you can really help me."

"I already know how to read. I can read Jed's books." Tears trembled at the edges of Nettie's eyes.

"I know you can, and that's important. But you also need to know how to write neatly and how to add and subtract, multiply and divide."

"But I hate math!"

Ida hugged her close. "I can understand that. I hated math, too. But my mother always used to tell me that if I only did the things I wanted to do, I'd grow up lazy and good for nothing. You don't want to be lazy, do you?"

Nettie shrugged, which Ida took for as much agreement as she would get out of the strong-willed girl.

"How about if we start the math time test over again? Whoever does all the sums correctly can have fifteen extra minutes of recess."

By the end of the day, Ida felt completely worn out. Friday contained no major confrontations, but she still felt frazzled. That evening, Ken came for a visit and presented her with a box of fresh carnations.

"Where did you get such gorgeous flowers?"

He grinned, obviously pleased with himself. "Father had to go to the city this week and I asked him to bring them back."

"They're marvelous. Lucy, come smell." The reds and pinks along with their sweet fragrance lifted her spirits.

Lucy sniffed appreciatively. "They are lovely, Mr. Danielson. How about if I put them in a bowl of water for you, Ida, and I can bring you each a cup of hot cocoa in the sitting room?"

"Thanks, Lucy." Ida impulsively hugged the older woman, then led Ken to the little used room down the hall from the kitchen. Several chairs covered in fancy material sat against the walls, with a small, low table in the center of the room. Ken held a chair for Ida, then chose one beside her for himself.

"I've been doing more thinking for the house and wanted to get your opinion. I'd like to make it three stories, with the master suite taking up the entire second floor and the children's rooms on the third floor. There should probably also be a room up there for a nanny. What do you think?"

Again Ida felt seized by a fairy-tale world. "It sounds like a house any woman would love. Where would you put the kitchen?"

"I thought of putting it in a wing off the ground floor so it wouldn't heat up the main part of the house during the summer. The wing would also have a couple of rooms in it for the cook/housekeeper."

"It sounds unbelievably luxurious." She permitted herself only a small smile lest she burst out laughing.

"Only the best for my wife, I say. What do you think of a summer honeymoon?" Apparently this scheme was no fairy tale to him.

She wondered how to detach herself gracefully. "Wouldn't you want to be engaged before you started planning your honeymoon? Your wife-to-be might have her own ideas."

Fortunately, Lucy arrived at that moment with the hot cocoa. The expression on Ken's face told Ida he hadn't even considered the possibility of his future wife not agreeing wholeheartedly with his plans. She sent an appealing message to Lucy, who interpreted it correctly.

"I'll just trot back to the kitchen for the popcorn and join you two in a moment."

Ken's expression turned mildly sulky until Lucy returned and inquired, "Did I hear you say something about building your own house, Mr. Danielson?"

The opportunity to talk about his pet project cheered him up immediately. "Yes, ma'am. I won't do the actual building, but I'm planning to design it myself."

Lucy listened attentively as he described various features, including rooms for the live-in help. To Ida's amazement, she also made suggestions.

"I'd think you'd want at least four bedrooms for the children, wouldn't you?"

Ken pondered for a moment. "That seems about right. Two boys and two girls would make a nice family."

"Since you'd have all that space on the second floor, would you build separate dressing rooms? I'd think it incredible luxury to have his and her dressing rooms, one on each side of the bedroom. You know, nice big rooms, each with a couple of chairs, maybe even a single bed in case one of you is ill."

Ida could see Ken visualizing the layout. "I hadn't thought about that."

"If you'll pardon an old lady's opinion, nothing wins a woman's heart like having her own space within a large master bedroom. If you plan it right, you could even have both dressing rooms open onto a common sitting room. Wouldn't that be lovely, Ida? A private sitting room off the master bedroom?"

Ken looked expectantly at Ida, who shrugged, feeling as though the conversation were running away from her. "I wouldn't know. I shared a room with Mother all my life. I've never even imagined the kind of luxury you're talking about." She listened to the two of them continue the discussion. Lucy's kind heart would never make fun of Ken. Why, then, did she embellish his notions?

Ken carefully stood to leave fifty-five minutes after he arrived. "Thank you for a lovely evening, Miss Thomas and Mrs. Barry. I've enjoyed your company."

"Thank you for the flowers," Ida replied, relieved she didn't have to offer any more opinions.

Lucy closed the front door behind him and turned to Ida with twinkling eyes. "I don't believe him! He left right on time, too."

"What do you mean?"

"In fancy places where life is more formal than it is here, a man who spends any more than an hour in a young lady's home is considered to be taking unfair advantage. You have to admit, his manners are flattering."

Sniffing her flowers again, Ida nodded. "I never dreamed I'd get flowers like this from anyone, especially here on the edge of nowhere."

"Wealth has its advantages, dear." Lucy's eyes sparkled again.

"But why did you encourage him in there? You know I'm not interested!" Ida heard an unfamiliar edge of hysteria creep into her voice.

Lucy wrapped a comforting arm around her. "I'm sure my encouragement, as you call it, isn't going to make him think you're serious. He wanted to talk about his house, so that's what we talked about. I didn't think it would hurt you to hear how his wife will be taken care of."

"Like some bird in a fancy cage with nothing to do. Did you hear him? A housekeeper to do all the cooking and cleaning and a nanny to take care of the children. What's the use of having a family if you don't care for them yourself?"

Lucy turned Ida so they could look into each other's eyes. "I'm glad to hear you say it. I wouldn't worry about Ken if I were you. He'll have a new project planned by Christmas, and this one will be forgotten."

Ida sighed. "I just hope he doesn't get seriously interested in me. About an hour at a time is all I can take of him."

"How about getting a good night's sleep? I'm sure this won't look nearly so serious in the morning." Lucy hugged her and gently pushed her toward her bedroom.

But as Ida tossed on her bed that night, it wasn't Ken, his flowers, or his house that kept her awake. No matter what else she tried to think of, she couldn't free herself from Timothy and Ruth's sadness. This made the third consecutive night their grief-filled eyes had interrupted her sleep. She awoke Saturday morning, listless and weary. After lunch dishes had been washed and put away, Lucy poured the inevitable cups of tea and seated herself across the table from where Ida sat staring into space.

"You haven't been yourself for a couple of days. Is it Mr. Danielson?"

Ida sipped her tea, made from raspberry leaves, one of her favorites. "It's Ruth and her father."

"What about them?"

"I met Mr. McEvan on Wednesday. Phillip introduced me to him and Greg. Lucy, I've never seen so much sadness in a person. It's more than just grief. It's like he's given up hope of ever being happy again. And Ruth's the same way. It makes me wish Mother were here. She'd know what to do."

Lucy reached across the table to place her hands on Ida's arms. "You can't fix everyone's problems, dear girl. I know you want to help Ruth, but sometimes we have to let time do what we can't."

"But it's like they're locked behind a wall. How does a person get through?"

"Maybe if I tell you a bit of my story, you'll understand. Do you mind?"

The tone of her voice made Ida feel as though she were about to discover something well aged and precious. "Not at all."

"Kelvin Spencer and I were married in England when I was just sixteen. He was personable, good looking, and reasonably wealthy. We adored each other in the way only very young newlyweds can. Two years later Kelvin Jr. was born and Lionel a year after that. Kelvin Sr. did his best to protect me from anything unpleasant, other than childbirth, which he couldn't do much about. Nothing prepared me for losing him in 1914 at the beginning of the Great War. We would have been married fifteen years the day after I received the news. I simply went to pieces inside. We had sent the boys to live with their grandmother in the country before Kelvin left, so I didn't even have them to think about.

"Of course, nobody around me knew how bad I was. Kelvin and I had attended a wonderful little church ever since we were youngsters, and I worked hard to keep up the front I felt they expected. Many people told me how much they admired my strength. Little did they know how angry I was at God. Eleven months later, I volunteered as a WAC and got sent to France. Everybody thought I was so brave and patriotic. I actually hoped to be sent to the front so I'd be killed, too. I just got worse. Seeing all those truly brave young men getting killed or maimed increased my bitterness. Where was the good God I'd been taught about?

"Then one night in early 1916, two truckloads of us were on our way to the coast to be shipped back to Britain for reassignment. The other truck got blown to bits. I was hit on the head and woke up in a British hospital unable to remember who or where I was. Gradually, it all came back to me and with it my anger at God. By now the list of reasons for my anger had grown to an incredible length. One day, as I reviewed the list, I began to have thoughts like I'd never had before. I can still remember them like they came yesterday. The first one was, if God wasn't the loving God I'd thought He was, who lied? That troubled me for days. Since I was too weak to get out of bed, I had no way of running from the question. God says about Himself that He cannot lie. That meant my understanding of Him must have been warped. Eventually I asked the nurses for a Bible and began reading at random, searching for clues as to Who God really is. No matter where I read, I found myself confronted with God's compassion. At the same time, I saw innumerable instances of His allowing situations that seemed to be inexplicable in light of His love. It was the book of Job that pulled the two concepts together for me. God doesn't make sense to me because He is God. His love and His sovereignty at times seem totally unrelated. But if I could understand Him completely, He wouldn't be God. He'd be a construction of my own imagination.

"That's when I began learning about faith, the ability to trust Him even when He isn't making sense. It means refusing to give up on what He says about Himself, knowing that He cannot lie. About the time I'd made peace with Him, I was declared well enough to be sent out again. I had plenty of days where it would have been easier to retreat into anger, but God Himself had planted the seed of faith in me. I knew if I didn't choose to trust Him, I'd lose my sanity. Six months before the war ended, I met a Canadian soldier named William Barry, and Lionel and I followed him to the Peace Country.

"Five years later, influenza took him, too. This time faith carried me through the grief. It made all the difference."

The crackling of the fire in the cookstove made the only sound in the kitchen for several minutes. Ida finally found her voice. "Mother used to say, 'God's bigger than I am, so I just have to assume He knows what He's doing.'"

Lucy nodded with understanding. "A lot of people think faith means admitting God caused my husbands to die, or your parents, or Timothy McEvan's family. I don't believe He arranges for these things to happen. I do believe, though, they happen within His control, and only He can explain the whys. I can't base my love for Him on knowing why."

"But how does that help me with Ruth?"

"Faith allows you to let God do the healing, even when it looks like He's doing nothing."

"I just wish I could do something. I can't even sleep at night from thinking about them."

"God could be trying to give you an assignment. Maybe all they need is someone who loves them enough to keep praying for them."

Ida thought immediately of Theo's disclosures the week before. She had her own grief to cope with. Perhaps that would help her reach Ruth. But why would God ask her to care about Timothy McEvan's sorrow as well?

Chapter 7

Carnations were only the first in Ken's series of unbelievable gifts. The next week, a massive box of chocolates arrived in the mail with a tag bearing the words "Regards, Ken Danielson" on the inside. Then a complete set of Jane Austen's writings.

Even Mr. Carey noticed during Sunday morning breakfast. "A body would think you wimen wuz settin' up your own store, the way things are piling up around here. At least there ain't any more of them smelly flowers."

Lucy just smiled sweetly at him. "Some men know how to give women something other than complaints. By the way, Mr. Carey, I haven't mentioned church to you for two whole months now. Care to go with us this morning?"

For once he didn't have an immediate answer. Lucy's eyes had begun to gleam with triumph when he coughed slightly. "I dunno. Working out in the chilly wind seems to be givin' me a bit of a head cold. Think I'd best stay inside today."

Ida choked on her pancakes. The ongoing debate between the two always amused her, but this morning both were in rare form.

"Chilly wind, my eye!" Lucy sputtered. "We've had the warmest autumn this year we've had in a long time. Tomorrow's the first of December, and it's just barely cold enough to keep the snow from melting. You're just looking for an excuse not to come."

"Could be right," Mr. Carey allowed, pushing himself back from the table. The click of his bedroom door ended the conversation.

Lucy stood in the middle of the kitchen, hands on hips, watching him go. "That man! Some days I think he says things just to get me riled."

"Could be right," Ida echoed, trying not to chuckle.

Lucy whirled to face her. "Whose side are you on, anyway?" Ida smirked, then both women laughed aloud.

"I guess it's God's job to get hold of him, not mine," Lucy muttered, clearing the table. "I just wish He'd let me help."

"I know what you mean." Ida put the salt and pepper shakers in the cupboard.

"How's Ruth doing?" A stack of clean dishes grew rapidly beside Lucy's dishpan.

"She talks to me a little more, as in greets me in the morning and says good-bye in the afternoon. She still looks incredibly sad, though."

"God seems to delight in doing things the slow way. I guess that teaches us more about trust. Remember, it took Him thirty years to give Abraham a son."

Ida meditated on the events of Abraham's life as they drove to the farm for church. Could she be as patient while waiting for God to bring relief to this student for whom she'd come to care so deeply?

Doug Pierce gave the sermon that morning, using Hebrews 10:36 as his text. "For ye have need of patience, that, after ye have done the will of God, ye might receive the promise." Ida sat straight up in her chair as soon as she heard the verse. It was as if Doug had been listening to her thoughts this morning. "Sometimes God gives us concerns we don't understand," he said. "It may be a neighbor who doesn't know Him yet or a dream for our own lives. He lets us know what he wants to accomplish, then seems to go completely silent. Sometimes everything in the world goes contrary to the dream we feel we received from Him. That's when faith becomes crucial. If we can believe He meant what He said, regardless of what circumstances look like, we bring joy to Him. Look with me at Luke chapter 22, verse 32. Jesus tells Peter, 'But I have prayed for thee, that thy faith fail not: and when thou art converted, strengthen thy brethren.' As an illustration, I'd like to tell you a bit of our family's story." The group was seated in an informal circle. Doug had remained seated while he talked, and he reached for Cynthia's hand as he closed his Bible.

"Most of you know we lost three babies after Theodore was born. You probably don't know that each of those babies seemed like an answer to prayer. When we were first married, a doctor had told us Cynthia wouldn't be able to have children. Theo was our first miracle, and we'd asked God for one more so he wouldn't have to grow up an only child. For the first year after he was born, it seemed like every time we opened our Bibles, we found a reference to God giving children. We wrote each passage down and kept praying. After a year or so, we stopped getting such dramatic reassurance. We reviewed the early promises and kept praying. Four years passed before another little one appeared. She lived less than an hour. I was ready to give up on God at that point, but my wife wouldn't let me. 'God doesn't lie,' she'd say. 'We just have to wait some more.' Two years later, another baby died. Then another three years later. When I'd get discouraged, Cynthia would remind me of the promises. When the grief would get too much for her, I'd feel confident God would come through.

"Theodore grew up with our hope and disappointments. In the year before Sara was born, it seemed he had more faith than both his parents. We were almost afraid to hope when we learned another baby was on the way. Somehow Theo was positive this would be our 'promise baby' as he called it. Sure enough, little Sara was born healthy, and she's been a joy to us ever since. When you're wondering if God's really there, take a look at my family. We've seen Him do the impossible, and we want to strengthen your faith."

Through her tears, Ida noticed Ruth in a corner wiping her eyes. She quietly moved to put her arm around the girl. "Are you okay?"

Ruth tried unsuccessfully to stop crying, then turned and buried her face in Ida's shoulder, sobs shaking her. Ida held her close. Gradually Ruth was able to speak. "Why did God do that for them, but He killed my mother and brothers?"

Her grief caused Ida's eyes to overflow. "I don't know why He let it happen, honey, but He wasn't the one who killed them. The river did that."

Ruth sobbed some more. "If I hadn't been there, it wouldn't have happened."

"What do you mean?" Ida rubbed her back gently. The rest of the group had moved to the table for lunch, except for Theo, who stood watching them from a distance.

"If I hadn't been there, the raft wouldn't have been too heavy."

"Ruthie," the endearment came naturally. "We don't know that. I know little about what happened, but I don't think we'll ever be sure why it happened. Just like I don't know why God let my daddy be killed in the war or my mother get sick and die last spring."

Ruth pulled back to look at Ida. "Your mother died, too?" Little hiccups still shook her. "And your dad?"

Ida nodded. "That's why I came here. I had to find a job because I was all alone."

"Do you miss them all the time?"

"Yes." She had to wipe away more tears.

Tears still ran down Ruth's cheeks, too. "Daniel was my twin brother, my best friend. We told each other everything. I saw the log hit him and he disappeared. I was too far away to do anything. Mama tried to hold Sam and Benjamin up, but the river just carried all of them away. I was holding Greg, so I couldn't swim to help her, either."

"But you did save Greggy." Ida used her handkerchief to wipe Ruth's face.

"I know, and I wish I could feel grateful, but I don't. Most times, I'd rather have Mama and Daniel here than Greg. And then I feel so guilty for that, too." She sobbed into Ida's shoulder some more.

"Honey, feeling guilty won't bring your mama or your brother back. I'm sure you did all you could."

"But why didn't God let it be enough? Why Daniel instead of Greg?"

Ida wished she had an easy answer. "I don't know, Ruthie. It's one of those hard questions only God knows the answer to."

"Sometimes I hate Him, too." The words were whispered into Ida's collar.

"That's all right. He can handle it. One day, you'll be ready to love Him again, and He'll be waiting for you."

"Why would He care about me? I've said such awful things to Him when nobody else can hear." Ruth looked into Ida's eyes questioningly.

Ida hoped the conviction of her soul came through in her voice. "He loves you just because you're you."

"It's just so hard. I feel like there's nobody in the world who understands. You were a grown lady when your mama died."

"Maybe it seems that way to you. Sometimes I still feel like a little girl. Some nights I miss her so badly, I can't help crying into my pillow."

Ruth studied Ida's face for a long moment, then wiped her eyes again.

"Ruth, you have another friend, someone else who understands a little bit."

Her eyebrows puckered. "Who?"

"Theodore. Remember what his dad said?"

"Yeah." She plucked at the frayed edges of her sleeves. "I guess so. But you heard what his dad said. He'd think I was awful for hating God."

"I doubt that. You should talk to him some time."

"Maybe." Ruth considered it. "But you won't tell anyone what I said. Please?"

"Of course not. I hope you'll come to me if you need to talk again. I can't say I understand, but I'd like to listen. Holding it all in just makes you feel worse."

She nodded. "I know. I already feel better than I have since the river. I just wish I didn't miss them so badly."

Ida pulled her into a hug. "I know. Believe me, I know. But Mrs. Barry says it gets easier after awhile. How about if we go see how much lunch is left?"

"I hope I don't look too awful."

Ida smiled and took her hand. "I'm sure no one will mind."

They filled their plates, finding seats a little away from the rest of the group, who gave Ida reassuring glances, but didn't ask any questions. Theo quietly sat beside Ruth.

Ken waited until they'd finished eating before approaching Ida. "Would you go for a sleigh ride with me this afternoon? I brought my dad's sleigh in case you said yes."

She felt too emotionally drained to cope with him. Then a look at Ruth's face gave her an idea. Maybe an hour or so looking at the countryside would help them both collect themselves after the storm. She felt badly for using Ken, but it would be for a good cause. "That sounds like a lovely idea. Would you mind if Ruth comes, too?"

His eyes told her he minded very much, but good manners asserted themselves. "Of course not. I'd be flattered to have two lovely ladies with me."

Theo rolled his eyes, bringing a faint smile to Ruth's lips. "Thanks, Miss Thomas," he whispered, as he took Ida's plate, then Ruth's.

"Let's go then. Your dad won't mind?" She felt compelled to ask.

Ruth shook her head. "He always cooks lunch for him and the boys on Sunday afternoons, and they take long naps."

Ida quickly told Lucy where they were going. "I'll try to be back in about an hour."

"Is Ruth all right?"

The smile threatened to split her face. "I think she's on her way."

Lucy closed her eyes. "Thank the Lord."

"You said it." Ida hurried out to the sleigh where Ruth was already seated. Ken stood waiting to help her in. She noticed he'd maneuvered things to have her beside him. Three would be a tight fit. She'd have preferred Ruth between them, but oh well. Just an hour wouldn't hurt her. And it might help Ruth a lot.

Snow blanketed everything in sight, including hay stooks. The hills in the distance displayed varying shades of gray and white, laced with the black of bare tree branches.

"Looks like winter's here for good," Ken commented companionably.

"What's it like here?" Ida asked, mostly to make conversation.

Ruth answered emphatically. "Cold."

"It probably seems colder out on the farm." Ken's voice conveyed just a touch of superiority. "In town, we have sleighing parties, music nights, and plenty of activities to keep us from noticing the cold."

Ida wondered if this had been such a good idea. Ken apparently didn't mind Ruth's presence as long as she kept quiet. She looked over at Ruth, who seemed unaware of Ken's attitude. Well, the girl needed Ida's company this afternoon, and Ken would just have to put up with it. "What does your family do in the wintertime, Ruth?"

"Just the usual stuff. Dad usually works out in the barn when I'm home to watch the boys. Once I've done everything that needs doing, it's time for bed." Ruth sighed, a tired woman kind of sigh.

Lord, why was it necessary to turn a child into an old woman? This girl should be excited about sledding, and popcorn by the fire, and Christmas. On the edges of the thought came Mother's voice. "Without challenges, you'd be lazy and good for nothing." *Isn't this challenge a little much for a teenage girl? I'm sorry, Lord. I choose to trust you, since I can't understand.*

Ruth grabbed Ida's arm. "Oh, look! There's a moose over there."

Ida's gaze followed the line of Ruth's arm and pointing finger. "Ken, would you stop the sleigh for a moment?"

He gave her a long-suffering look, but halted the horses.

In a patch of willows stood the strangest looking animal Ida had ever seen. His snout was as broad as his forehead, though the center of his face was tapered like an hourglass. Long ears flopped on either side of his head. Large flat antlers made him look top-heavy in spite of the long, deep-chested body behind and below them. Long, skinny legs with bulbous knees held the animal up. "Those legs look too awkward to be real," Ida whispered.

"Can we leave now before he decides to charge at us?" Ken asked impatiently, clucking to the horses without waiting for a reply.

"They don't charge unless you get between a mother and her calf. The males only charge at each other during mating season," Ruth informed Ida quietly. Her whisper held a wealth of disdain for this city man who was frightened of wild animals.

"Ruth, would you like to come home with me for supper?" Ida asked the question specifically so Ken wouldn't feel invited.

"How would I let my dad know?"

Relieved Ruth didn't immediately decline, she quickly improvised. "We'll have to pass your farm on the way back. I'm sure Mr. Danielson wouldn't mind stopping for a moment. I'll even go in and ask for you." She felt Ken stiffen beside her, but didn't care. His childishness had become tiresome.

Ruth looked directly at her for the first time since they'd left the Spencers. "If he doesn't mind, I'd like that."

Mr. McEvan had just closed the barn door when they pulled into the farmyard. Ida noticed how clean and tidy everything looked. "Ken, I'd like to get out, please."

He clambered off the sleigh and helped her to her feet.

"Mr. McEvan?"

"Yeah?" Though he didn't smile, he didn't sound disgruntled by their presence.

Since he hadn't seemed to recognize her, she decided an introduction would be the best first move. "I'm Ida Thomas, Ruth and Phillip's teacher."

"Phillip introduced us awhile back." Again, those deeply pained blue eyes arrested her attention.

"I wasn't sure if you remembered." She tried to smile. "Ruth accompanied Mr. Danielson and me on a ride after church today, and I was wondering if you'd mind if I took her home with me for dinner. Mrs. Barry and I will bring her back before it gets too late."

He looked at his daughter, who nodded. "Sounds okay. I guess I don't have to tell you she has school tomorrow." From another man, the comment would have sounded like a good joke.

"Thank you, sir. I'll take good care of her."

He touched his hat brim and proceeded toward the house without a look back.

Ken stayed silent the rest of the way into town and helped them out of the sleigh without a word. He looked like one of Ida's first-graders in a pout as he drove off.

"I guess I kinda ruined your drive," Ruth commented.

"Not mine," Ida assured her. "I invited you, remember?"

"Yeah, but your beau wasn't too happy."

"He's not my beau. Lucy, I brought a guest."

Never happier than when fussing over company, Lucy welcomed Ruth warmly. "I'm glad to see you, child. I hope you'll pardon Mr. Carey's manners. He's had a bad cold today, so he's too wobbly in the knees to stand. Mr. Carey, this young lady is Ruth McEvan, one of Ida's students."

He nodded at Ruth before taking another loud slurp of his coffee. "Done tole you, Miz Barry, you're too late to try reformin' me."

"I wouldn't think of reforming you, Mr. Carey," Lucy shot back. "God's the one who can do that."

"Now don't start preachin' at me, woman. If I'd huv wanted a sermon, I'd huv gone to church." He winked at Ruth, whose eyes had gone round at their bickering.

"And it wouldn't have harmed you a bit. Ida, would you mind showing Ruth around? I have this pie crust almost ready to roll."

Ida gave her the tour, ending at her own room. Ruth went straight to the window, that showed a similar panorama as it had at the old location. "What a beautiful view!"

"I know. I fell in love with it first thing, even though it always makes me think of my mother."

Ruth turned to face her. "Why?"

"The last few years, we lived in an apartment that had only tiny windows that faced another building. Mother always wished we could have had a prettier view."

"I wish I could have met your mother." She trailed her fingers across the edge of Ida's desk.

"And I wish I could have met yours."

Ruth blinked a couple of times, but didn't break down. "I do, too, and Daniel." After a long pause she continued. "I also wish my dad would cry."

"Why is that?" Ida felt like someone had punched her in the stomach. She could picture the shattered blue gaze without trying.

"Because it helps. I always thought it would make me feel worse if I cried, so I kept it all tight inside me. Then when Mr. Pierce was talking, I looked at you crying and I couldn't help myself. I tried to stop. I felt really embarrassed, then you hugged me and I had to cry harder. I'm glad you were there."

Ida pulled her down so they could sit side by side on the bed. "Ruthie, you've had more sadness in your life than a lot of people ever have. My mother always used to say God gave us tears to keep us cleaned out inside. If you keep the tears in, it just makes you hurt worse."

"I know that now, and I wish my dad did." Ruth laid her head against Ida's shoulder.

"May I tell you something else?"

"Yes, ma'am."

She put her arm around Ruth's skinny shoulders. "You're going to feel like crying more before you're better. Will you promise me you won't try to keep it back? Even if you're at school and need to go for a walk so you can cry, please tell me."

Ruth sniffed. "I just feel like I'm going to cry for the rest of my life."

"You won't. I promise. Some days I feel like that, too, but Mrs. Barry says it gets better."

Ruth raised her head with a smile. "She's a nice lady, isn't she?"

"She's wonderful. I'll bet if we go out there now, she'll offer us both some tea. Shall we do it?"

"But first," Ruth hesitated, "would you mind praying that my dad'll cry, too? He's been so sad and mad, like me, only he doesn't have anybody to talk to."

Ida placed her hands over Ruth's. "I'll do that, if you'll promise you'll let yourself cry when you feel like it." Only she knew she couldn't have stopped praying for Timothy McEvan if she'd wanted to.

They'd barely opened the bedroom door when Lucy held a chair out from the table. "Sit here, Ruth. Would you like a cup of tea?"

Ruth's eyes twinkled at Ida briefly. "Yes, please."

Ruth and Ida managed few words during supper. Ida suspected Lucy kept goading Mr. Carey just to entertain their guest. "I suppose that cold of yours has your appetite down to normal size, so I'll just give you a single slice of roast."

He seemed to warm to an audience as well. "Whatcha tryin' to do, starve me? I'll let you know if I'm not hungry."

"That'll be the day. I'd probably think you were dying."

"Then you wouldn't have anybody to pick on. Mind if I eat now?"

A grin flitted across Ruth's face just before Lucy turned to her. "Are you getting enough? Mr. Carey tends to clean the dishes out before visitors get a fair chance."

"I have plenty, thank you." Obviously Ruth's mother had trained her well in their few years together. Once the meal was over, she quietly helped clear the table.

To Ida's surprise, Lucy handed the girl a dishtowel. "If you don't mind helping me, dear, we'll get this place cleaned up in a trice." She carefully drew the girl out as they worked, asking questions about recipes she used and her brothers' food preferences. After dishes were done, she made tea, which she served in fine china cups Ida hadn't seen before.

Before they took Ruth home, Lucy took one of her hands and one of Ida's, then bowed her head. Ruth and Ida made the circle complete as they listened to a prayer that brought an almost tangible feeling of comfort into the room. Though Ruth couldn't have known, Ida knew the older woman was praying from her own experiences of bereavement. Doug Pierce had been right. Faith that had been severely tested became a source of strength for others in need.

Chapter 8

School brought more challenges on Tuesday. Another thick layer of snow had fallen during the night. Its undisturbed whiteness lay just beyond the windows, inviting Ida's students to come out and play in it. She gave them extra long breaks at recess and lunch, hoping to burn off some of their energy. Thankfully, the Young Lionel and Jed had come today. Their presence always seemed to stabilize the younger ones. Jim, who missed more school than any of them, was absent today as well. Ida had a hunch education didn't carry the same priority with him or his parents as the farm. So be it. Many of the farmers in the area knew little more than how to read, write, and add. They still took care of their families well and contributed to the well-being of the community.

By afternoon recess, Ida realized further studies were a lost cause. Maybe this was the right time to introduce an idea she'd been toying with since moving day. She insisted everyone be seated, then waited for Michael and David to finish their whispered conversation.

"What does snow make you think of?" She smiled at their ruby-cheeked faces, eyes sparkling with the joy of a new season.

Without putting her hand up, Nettie suggested, "Snow angels." The schoolyard gave mute evidence of this being on more than one child's mind.

"Good. How about if we take turns making suggestions? Put your hand up if you have an idea, and I'll make sure everyone gets a chance. Next?"

Clara shyly suggested hot chocolate. Michael thought of snowball fights. Tommy mentioned toboggan rides and Young Lionel hockey games. This made Patricia think of skating on the river. Just when Ida thought they'd never make the suggestion she wanted, Karin whispered, "Christmas." Popcorn, candy, presents, Christmas trees, carols—the barrage of resulting ideas was deafening.

Ida laughed and held up her hands for silence. "Wait just a minute. I can't hear if everyone talks at once." She wrote the ideas down on the chalkboard until interest started dwindling. Then she asked, "Have you ever put on a Christmas concert?"

Total silence reigned for a minute, then bedlam erupted. It seemed everyone had a question. Ida answered them as quickly as she could. Yes, a play would be fun. Yes, everyone would get a part in the concert. Even the youngest ones, too, Phillip. The parents would probably help with the costumes and props, although if Jed and Young Lionel wanted to help there, too, that would be fine. When asked what kind of play they'd do, Ida threw the question back at them. "What kind do you want to do?" To her surprise, most of them wanted to do a Nativity play. In a way, it was a relief. The story was familiar, so the lines wouldn't be hard to learn. But what would she do to make this concert different from the average? Maybe Lucy would have some ideas.

They spent the rest of the afternoon discussing their project. To her amazement, everyone agreed Patricia would make the best Mary. "She's so pretty and quiet," Nettie explained. The six-year-olds all wanted to be shepherds, and Nettie wanted to be Herod. Ida would have to figure out a way to redirect that ambition.

When school let out, she had to resist the urge to collapse at her desk for a quick nap before heading home. She leaned her head back as far as she could, stretching out the tight neck muscles. When she straightened up again, Ruth was standing just inside the door. Ida smiled at her reassuringly. Since their talk on Sunday, Ruth had seemed to retreat into herself, though Ida had noticed her talking to Theo during recesses. Her eyes had seemed a bit brighter, as well, but she'd made no more gestures of friendship to Ida.

The teenager approached Ida's desk hesitantly. "Are you busy?"

"No, I'm actually too tired to get anything done right now. Sit here, if you'd like." She patted the edge of her desk.

Ruth smiled shyly. "The kids were ornery today, weren't they?"

Ida nodded, pleased she'd noticed anything beyond herself.

"I think your idea of a Christmas concert is wonderful." Ruth studied her hands, then continued in a rush. "But what I really wanted to tell you is thanks for Sunday. I didn't say anything before because I didn't want the other kids to think I'm trying to be teacher's pet or anything. But I'm feeling lots better than I have in a long time. And when I miss my mother or Daniel so much I think I'm going to scream, I remember what you said about it not always being like this." Tears trembled on her lashes when she looked back up at Ida.

Ida felt a lump in her own throat. This girl's pain was so similar and yet so much more devastating than her own. At least she seemed willing to talk. "May I show you something, Ruth?" She lifted her cape off the hook near the blackboard and tucked it around the girl's shoulders. "This is the last garment my mother ever made for me."

"Did your mother make all your clothes?" Ruth whispered, running her hands over the soft wool.

Ida nodded. "She wanted to make sure I had pretty things to help me find a job after she was gone."

"My mother didn't have time to do anything for me before. . ." She couldn't continue.

"I know, Ruth." Ida dared to enfold her in a hug. "That's why I thought it might help if I shared some of the special things my mother did for me. I have a feeling your mother would have done the same if she'd known what was going to happen."

"If we'd known, we wouldn't have let it happen." With a quick gesture, Ruth angrily flung Ida's cape to the floor.

Ida didn't stoop to pick it up lest she break eye contact. "I know."

"No, you don't." Like a summer thunderstorm, the girl's anger seemed to rumble out of nowhere. "You say you do, but you don't. My mother left me nothing. Nothing, do you hear? Nothing except nightmares of watching her drown. It wasn't your twin brother that drowned with her, it was mine. Mine." A sob cut off her words, but she wasn't finished. "All I have left are two little brothers who can't remember anything and a dad who never even looks at me anymore. You can't know." She ran out, slamming the door behind her.

Ida stooped to retrieve the cape. How had she destroyed the budding friendship so quickly? She made sure the fire in the small stove was down to embers, bundled herself up, and started home. Thankfully, Misty seemed to know the way, so Ida could let her thoughts tumble at will. Once the animal was stabled and rubbed down and the saddle hung in its place, she wandered absently into the house. Somehow, Ruth's outburst had returned her healing heart to its previous painfully wounded condition. The hurt went too deep for tears.

"Ida, honey. Whatever is the trouble?" Lucy took one look at the teacher's troubled face and began fussing around her, unbuttoning her cape, pushing her into a chair, placing a steaming cup of tea before her. "You look done in."

As unemotionally as she could, Ida related the events of her day. "I just don't know what I did wrong, Lucy. I thought she was doing so well."

Lucy didn't demean Ida's pain with an immediate answer. Only the scrunch of her knife against the potatoes she peeled and the crackling wood in the stove broke the long silence. Eventually, she faced Ida and asked almost in a whisper, "How often did you get angry before your mother died?"

Remembering her outbursts still brought guilt. Ida recalled her unrelenting rage, particularly in the early days of her mother's illness. "More often than I'd like to remember."

"Of course you did, child. It's part of grief. You felt it beforehand because you knew what was coming. Young Ruth feels it now because she didn't."

"But it was like she blamed me." Even as she said the words, she remembered accusing her own mother. She'd known at the time her mother wasn't to blame, but she couldn't seem to help herself.

Lucy's kindly gaze seemed to perceive Ida's thoughts. She only suggested, "Why don't you take a bit of a rest before supper?"

By the time Ken arrived later in the evening for his inevitable visit, Ida felt more like herself. Maybe Ruth had simply reacted as Ida herself had done not so long ago. Ken's offering of another bunch of carnations helped also. She found herself excitedly discussing the Christmas concert with him and Lucy. "I'm not sure how we're going to make a Nativity play into something that won't bore the parents, but at least my students are enthusiastic about it."

"Could I lend some help building backdrops?"

Ken's offer almost stunned Ida into speechlessness. "I'll be grateful for any help I can get. How about if I let you know when we've decided what we need?"

"Sounds good." Ken beamed at her.

Ida looked at Lucy, wondering at his unusual demeanor. Lucy gave a slight shrug while saying, "Are you interested in an old lady's suggestion for your concert?"

"Sure!"

"Why not use the Nativity play as a background for each of the students to do some kind of performance? You could have the little ones sing a song. Maybe the older ones would like to do a Christmas-type recitation. You could make these special bits something that relates to the difference Jesus can make in lives now."

Anticipation made Ida tingle all over. "And the ones who don't want to do something special can have parts in the play. You're a genius, Lucy!"

Ken shifted a bit in his chair while they planned, but he didn't try to change the subject. He laughed when Ida mentioned Nettie's comments. "Would she settle for being one of the three wise men? If you give her a poem to recite as well, that might keep her busy enough to forget about Herod."

"He might have an idea, there," Lucy offered as she left to answer a knock at the front door.

Ida could hear Lionel and Nina's familiar voices explaining they'd been out for a drive and just stopped in for a few moments. She noticed Ken studying her with an uncertain expression on his face. "What is it, Mr. Danielson?"

He grimaced. "I really wish you'd call me Ken, and I'd like to call you Ida. What I mean is. . .uh. . .well, actually. . ." He cleared his throat, took a deep breath, and tried again. "Would you mind if I came courting?"

Ida had always hoped such a moment would fill her with a bubbly sort of delight. Right now, she only felt as though she were about to board a train for an unknown destination. She didn't want to hurt his feelings, but neither did she want to agree too quickly. "I don't know what to say, Ken." The use of his first name brought a sparkle of pleasure to his eyes. "I'm flattered, but I'd like time to think it over if you don't mind."

His suave polish gradually reasserted itself. "Of course. I'll be counting the minutes."

What for? she wanted to ask, but that would sound churlish. "Thanks for understanding."

He nodded and stood. "I need to leave now, but I'll see you on Sunday." He reached for her hand, which she tucked behind her back.

She let him out the front door, then joined the others at the kitchen table. Lucy took a clean cup and saucer out of the cupboard. "I've just been telling Lionel and Nina about your Christmas concert."

"It sounds marvelous to me," Nina declared, laying a hand on her rounded stomach. "Since I'm not too active these days, I'd be happy to help sew costumes, and I'm sure Kate would help, as well. She's a better seamstress than you'd think."

Lionel covered Nina's hand with his own. "I'll make sure my wife doesn't overdo."

"Oh, Lionel." Nina looked at her husband with affectionate exasperation. "A bit of sewing won't hurt me, especially since you insist on the kids doing most of the housework. Having babies has never given me any trouble."

"That's because I make sure you're taken care of." His firm comment closed that part of the discussion. "But Miss Thomas, do you think it would be possible to invite more than just parents to the concert?"

"Of course," Lucy interrupted. "Grandparents will be welcome, too, or I'll know the reason why."

Lionel protested through the laughter, "That's not what I meant, Mother. I'd like to see some of the townfolk come out, too."

"Would there be enough room in the school?" Ida couldn't envision the necessary space.

"I think there's an empty storeroom in the co-op building. Lars might be able to get us permission to use it, if you'd like. A couple of us men could hammer together a sturdy stage, and I'm sure we could round up enough chairs."

The project had suddenly blossomed far past Ida's imaginings. "Do you think the children could handle performing in front of strangers?"

"Why not leave the decision with them?" Nina suggested. "Much as we'd like to show them off, if they're too shy, we'll respect that."

But when Ida mentioned the idea the next day, the class gave their resounding approval. Even Jim, who'd heard about the excitement and decided to check it out, thought it would be fun. "If we know the townfolk'll be there, too, it'll make us work harder to do it right," he commented.

Nettie didn't like that. "We'll do it right anyway, Jim! We're not a bunch of babies, you know."

Recognizing family rivalry for what it was, Ida deftly changed the subject. "I have one other idea. I'd like to hear some of you sing Christmas songs, or recite Christmas poems, or something like that, if you want to."

"Can we pick our own?" Patricia wondered.

"I'd like to check them out first, but yes, I'd like you to pick what you want to do."

From there, the last hour of every school day was devoted to preparing for the concert. The excitement even spilled over to the church gathering on Sunday. It took Lionel several tries to get everyone seated so the short service could begin. Just before he bowed his head for opening prayer, Ruth McEvan slipped in, followed by her father and brothers.

Ida watched them out of the corner of her eye. The boys behaved well, though they kept trying to wave to her. Ruth often glanced her way, as well. But Timothy's face captured Ida's most frequent notice. He seemed familiar with a churchlike setting, but uncomfortable at the same time. As Lionel read from Psalm 91, Ida thought for sure Timothy would leave. But he stayed and even joined the line for lunch after Doug assured him there was plenty for everyone. "The ladies each bring enough for their families, plus a few more, and we always have leftovers. We'd love to have you." He clapped Timothy on the shoulder and ruffled Greg's hair. "I'll bet there's even a piece of chocolate cake over there your size, young man."

"Me, too?" Phillip wanted to know.

"If your dad says yes." Doug carefully handed the question over to Timothy, who nodded with a small smile and herded his troupe to the table.

"Miss Thomas." Ken startled her out of her preoccupation. When she looked at him, he lowered his voice conspiratorially. "I'd like to take you to my parents' place for lunch today, if you don't mind. My mother said you'd be welcome."

Ida had met his parents during one of her first weeks in town and saw them often when she and Lucy did their weekly shopping. It wasn't like she'd be eating with strangers, but for some reason she couldn't define, she didn't want to miss out on today's "family lunch" as they called it. "I appreciate the invitation, Ken, but I don't often get to visit with my students' parents in a group like this. I'd prefer to stay here."

His knitted eyebrows indicated his preferences weren't often crossed. But he quickly put on a smile. "I'll just go on myself, then. See you later this week."

Nothing dramatic happened or was discussed during the meal. Both Phillip and Tommy spilled their milk, Nettie tried to help herself to three pieces of cake, and Tabitha spent more time crawling under the table than eating. Ida noticed neither Timothy nor Ruth ate much, but at least they were there. Somehow it made her glad she'd stayed.

Chapter 9

Just a single day later, Ida glanced up from her work-covered desk. Though the other students played in the snow outside, Ruth hovered by the door with Theodore beside her. "Hello, you two."

Ruth's face turned pink, while Theodore nudged her arm. Ida could barely make out his whispered comment. "It's okay."

Ruth cleared her throat, a small, strangling sound. "Miss Thomas. . ." Her voice trailed off.

Ida kept her voice as gentle as possible. "How about coming next to my desk. It's hard to say anything across a room. Now what is it?"

"I'm just sorry." Once she found the courage to talk, Ruth kept her gaze locked on Ida's. "I didn't mean all those awful things I said. I know you miss your mother, too."

Ida stretched out her arms, letting Ruth choose whether or not to receive the hug. "I know you didn't mean it." She cradled the thin shoulders. "I said lots of terrible things to my mother when I found out how sick she was. It's hard to get used to being without them, isn't it?"

Ruth pulled back. "I didn't think you knew how to be not nice."

Ida chuckled. "I think everyone's born knowing how, Ruth. We just learn how to choose to be different."

"I was so scared to come talk to you."

"Why?"

"You'd been so nice to me ever since you came and then I ruined it." She looked into Ida's face anxiously. "I wasn't really mad at you."

"Well, since we've talked it over, let's just pretend it never happened. Okay?"

The first real smile Ida had ever seen on Ruth's face touched the girl's eyes before turning up the edges of her mouth.

"Told you she'd be good about it," Theodore reminded his friend triumphantly. "Now you can stop worrying."

Ida handed Ruth the bell. "Would you call the others in, please?" As Theo held the door open for Ruth, Ida felt like the sun had come from behind a long-lasting cloud. Even Nettie's temper tantrum later in the afternoon couldn't mar her happiness.

On Friday, Theo came to school bearing fancy envelopes that he handed out at the end of the day to the oldest child of each family represented, with one left over for Ida. "We're having a toboggan party at our farm tomorrow afternoon, and everyone's invited. The paper in the envelopes will tell your parents everything." He looked at Ida. "Mother said to make sure Mrs. Barry knows she's welcome, too."

Ida had more fun than she dreamed possible. Bundled up in woolen socks and flannel petticoats beneath her heavy skirt, two heavy sweaters beneath her cape, a knitted hat, a similarly knitted scarf tied around her head and neck, and woolly mittens, she could hardly move. But as Lucy had said while digging the warm clothes out of a closet, "You can't have fun at a sledding party if you're cold."

Ida had wondered if people might think her too undignified if she participated in the sledding, but Lucy pooh-poohed that idea. "Nina'd be out there if it wouldn't give Lionel fits. You just have fun enough to include those of us who have to stay in by the fire."

Each of the children, including the older boys, insisted on giving Teacher a ride. Before Ida had her fill of sledding, the older Lionel started a snowball fight with Doug Pierce that escalated into war. Those who had been surprised to see the entire McEvan family show up were further amazed when Timothy crammed snow down the back of Lionel's jacket. Doug had built a large bonfire at which the participants warmed themselves periodically. Before the younger children could get too tired, Cynthia called everyone inside for supper—steaming bowls of chili, hot buns fresh from the oven, and mugs of hot cocoa. Dirty dishes seemed to vanish, and someone started humming a familiar tune. Others filled in the words. Ida didn't notice when the songs changed to hymns, which the children appeared to know as well as the adults.

She did notice Timothy McEvan. He sat quietly while everyone chattered during supper. He didn't participate in the singing, though he seemed in no hurry to leave. During one of the hymns, she noticed the glint of moisture just above his beard.

A strange noise outside brought the singing to a halt. Doug hurried to the door. "Would you look at that?" he intoned.

When Ida could finally catch a glimpse through the bodies crowding around, she wondered if she was seeing right. Having lived in the city, she recognized a car when she saw it. It was the identity of the driver that amazed her, though she realized later it shouldn't have. Ken Danielson. "Is

Miss Thomas in there?" he inquired, barely concealing his pride at the stir he caused.

The crush miraculously thinned, allowing her to get through. "Wherever did you get an automobile, Mr. Danielson?"

"We went to the city for it this week. Do you like it?"

What else could a person say at such a moment? If she could have been honest, she would have admitted that it seemed ill-mannered to flash such a purchase before farmers such as her friends who worked hard to keep food on the table and homes in good repair. But Ken would never understand that, and her friends would be embarrassed if she tried to explain it. She merely said, "It looks nice."

"Well, grab your coat and I'll take you home."

Ida felt intensely uncomfortable as she searched for her cape, sweaters, socks, hat, and scarf in the pile of winter clothing. Lucy quietly joined her. "All you'll need is your cape, which is right here. I'll bring the rest when I come."

"I feel like I'm breaking up the party." Ida searched Lucy's gaze for comfort.

It came in the form of a hug. "Nonsense. It's time to get the children home for bed, anyway. I'm sure not a soul here blames you."

Ida made sure she thanked Cynthia for the marvelous afternoon, then waded through a progression of hugs from her students. Ken stood just outside the door. *Strange that Doug hadn't invited him in. But then, where would one more person have fit?*

"At last. I thought I'd lost you forever in that crowd." He opened the passenger's side door with a flourish. She couldn't see the vehicle clearly in the dark, but she could feel the smooth seat coverings. A smell of newness surrounded her when he shut her door. After seating himself, he carefully maneuvered the car out of the driveway and turned onto the road heading away from town, the car's headlamps dimly illuminating the snow-covered trail ahead.

"I thought you were taking me home!" Ida protested.

"The long way," he explained, with a trace of smugness in his tone. "So what do you really think of my car?"

Ida tried to laugh. "It seems, oh, I guess a little extravagant. Although it's very nice," she hastened to reassure him.

"But that's what the Danielsons are all about. Luxuries farmers can only dream about." His arrogance jarred her nerves.

"Farmers are the kind of people I work with every day, Ken."

"I know, and I admire you for it. I admire you for a lot of reasons."

What had taken over him? It seemed as though his manners had been just a veneer that now peeled off. She tried to pass it over with a joke. "Now, Ken, if you're going to embarrass me, I'll have to ask you to take me home."

His voice grew soft. "I'd never want to embarrass you, Ida. I've never met a woman like you. You're perfect."

Perfect for what? She chose another question. "How did you know where I was?"

He chuckled. "That old bird who lives at the boardinghouse told me. He didn't seem too happy Mrs. Barry hadn't stayed around to cook his supper."

"Mr. Carey's always fussing about something." She said it affectionately, feeling a strange resentment at Ken's reference. *Was it possible he didn't see value in anyone other than those with whom he chose to associate?* She tried to make the question sound casual, a getting-acquainted kind of inquiry. "Who are your friends in this area?"

"In Dawson Creek?" He seemed to find the idea highly amusing. "I have just one, a beautiful, kindhearted lady with gentle green eyes and soft-looking blond hair."

She hadn't expected that kind of response. "Do you have many friends, then?"

"Lots in the city. They're always coming up with something different to do. You wouldn't believe some of it."

Ida felt sure she wouldn't. How could fine, ordinary folk like Mr. and Mrs. Danielson have produced a son such as the young man with whom she now rode? Actually, the automobile explained a lot of the problem. Over-indulgence. It had ruined many children. "Shouldn't we be turning around? I don't want to be out too late."

Silently, he backed and turned the car until they were facing back toward town. "I'm not going to quit trying, Ida."

She could think of no reply. They passed the Pierces' driveway. Just before reaching the turnoff for the school, she noticed something strange by the side of the road. "What is that?" She thought she recognized the figure standing beside a wagon. "Ken, please stop." She barely waited for the car to cease moving before she yanked her door open. "Mr. McEvan, are you all right?"

"Miss Thomas? I thought you went home a long time ago."

She chose not to explain. "What happened? Are the children with you?"

"My horse seems to have gone lame. The children are in the wagon. I told them to stay under the hay and blankets. If I can get word to Doug, he'll be able to help." For once, he didn't seem reluctant to talk.

The idea came to her from nowhere. "I'm sure Mr. Danielson wouldn't mind if I took the children home with me. That way you can do what needs to be done for your horse without worrying about them alone at the farm or here getting chilled."

"I really hate to put you out."

"It's not putting me out in the slightest. I'm glad for an excuse to have your children with me. Come on, Phillip. How would you, Greg, and Ruth like to spend the night at my house?"

Timothy reached over the side of the wagon and helped his daughter down first, then his sons. Ida thought he looked at her strangely, but in the dark she couldn't be sure. Greg had already started shivering, so she tucked him inside her cape. "Ken, we need to hurry and get these children warm."

Phillip and Ruth clambered into the rumble seat. Ida kept Greg cuddled in front with her. Ken's silence told her loudly how much he resented her changing his plans. Couldn't he see the children needed help? To give him credit, however, he didn't dawdle getting them back to the boardinghouse.

Thankfully, Lucy had already arrived home. As soon as she saw the children, she bustled upstairs, returning with an armload of clothing that she laid out on chairs pulled near the stove. "I'm glad I've kept some of the grandchildren's clothes here. Ida, how about a warm bath for Phillip and Greg while I make up some beds? Ruth, I'll tuck you here next to the stove with a hot cup of tea so you can get warm while we tend your brothers."

By the time Ida had finished bathing the boys, their pajamas had warmed through. She folded a blanket around each. "Mrs. Barry has two lovely beds upstairs. Would you rather sleep there or in my room?"

"With you," Phillip murmured sleepily.

Ruth caught Ida's attention and beckoned. "They can't sleep in the same bed," she whispered. "Phillip thrashes so much he keeps Greggy awake. I can take Greggy upstairs with me."

"In this house, you're a lady of leisure." Ida shook her head, feeling a tingly sense of delight at being able to remove a little of the burden from this girl's shoulders, even for a night. "Greggy can sleep with me." Phillip fell asleep almost before his head reached the pillow as Ida folded the blankets around him on his floor pallet beside her bed. Greg had drifted off while sitting in the kitchen. She gently moved him to her bed, making sure the covers were pulled snugly around his shoulders.

Ruth could barely keep her eyes open, but she wanted to talk. "Miss Thomas, have you noticed my dad is different?"

"I don't know your dad that well." She had suspected change, but how could she admit to watching him?

"Well, he is. He noticed I wasn't so mad all the time and asked me why. I told him about what you said and what happened after that." She blushed, still embarrassed over her outburst. "That's when he said he'd start coming with me on Sundays. Mr. Pierce has been asking him for a long time, but he wouldn't do it until now."

Ida's curiosity had been piqued. "Does Mr. Pierce visit your dad a lot?"

"Not visit, exactly. He's just there whenever my dad needs help. He says he comes because he likes my cooking, but I think he just says that so Dad won't feel beholden. Sometimes Theo comes, too." Ruth yawned widely. "What I wanted to say is, I think God's answering our prayers for Dad."

Lucy entered the kitchen in time to catch Ruth's yawn. "If you'd like a bath, there's still lots of hot water. Unless you'd rather just go straight to bed."

"I am sleepy, but a real bath sounds heavenly. I usually just take sponge baths at home. Can I just sit in it for awhile?"

Ida swallowed the instinctive urge to correct Ruth's grammar. "Sit as long as you like."

Once Ruth's bathtub had been hauled to her room and filled, Ida and Lucy returned to the kitchen for chamomile tea and private conversation. "What brought this on?" Lucy wanted to know.

Ida explained about seeing the family by the side of the road, then remembered something. "I never did notice Ken leaving. He's probably feeling extremely put out with me."

Lucy watched her closely. "Would you have done anything differently to make him happier?"

"And leave those children out in the cold? Of course not." She felt miffed that Lucy could even ask.

Lucy grinned mysteriously. "Just checking. It's not every guy in town who can bring you flowers, candy, and a car, not to mention offering you a custom-built house with servants."

Ida swirled the tea in the bottom of her cup, thinking about her conversation with Ken as they drove. "I discovered something tonight. His gifts matter more to Ken than people do. The way he talked tonight, I felt almost like I'd been bribed." She chuckled. "He told me tonight I'm the perfect woman."

Lucy snickered. "Perfect for what?"

"I didn't ask. Somehow I didn't feel complimented."

"He wants to offer you anything money can buy, Ida."

"I know. But there's still something missing. I don't know what it is. If I did, I'd feel less like a shrew for not appreciating him."

Lucy put her hands over Ida's in the familiar gesture. "Honey, the book of Psalms tells us that if we delight in Him, God will give us the desires of our hearts. I think He's referring to the want itself as well as the satisfaction of the want. If He hasn't given you a desire for Ken's friendship, then cooperate with Him. He knows your heart and his. He has something planned for each of you that's better than either of you can imagine. Ken may be so self-centered he misses it. But I don't think you will."

"Thanks for the confidence." Footsteps upstairs indicated Ruth had finished her bath. "I'll help you dump the tub, and then I'm going to bed. This day has been almost too much."

Despite the unfamiliarity of another body in her bed, Ida slept dreamlessly. She awoke Sunday morning to find Greg had snuggled himself against her with his arms wrapped around one of hers. Cuddling with him felt so right, so. . .maternal.

Both boys seemed to wake simultaneously, Greg slowly stretching, Phillip talking immediately. "I forgot I was sleeping at your house, Miss Thomas. Do we have to go home today?"

She thought his choice of words amusing. "It depends on when your daddy comes for you. Maybe you'll get to go to church with Mrs. Barry and me."

Breakfast was a noisy affair. Greg had awakened to full voice by that time, and Phillip hadn't slowed a bit. Ida expected Mr. Carey to make some grouchy comments. Instead, he listened to the chatter with a half-smile on his face and even helped Greg cut his pancakes. The women pretended not to notice. Lucy found some more clothes of her grandchildren's that sort of fit the boys. With a bit of tucking and basting, Ida's green and yellow plaid skirt fit Ruth, topped by a green sweater Lucy'd also found. All five of them bundled into the buggy to head for the "meeting house" at the Spencers' farm. Mr. Carey once again declined Lucy's offer to accompany them, though she'd assured him the boys would love to have him along.

"I can tell I'm getting to him," she told Ida gleefully, expertly guiding the horse out of town. "He turned me down politely. It won't be long now before he lets God take over."

Despite Phillip's earlier eagerness to remain with Ida, he launched himself from the buggy as soon as he saw his dad, who'd just arrived with the Pierces. Ida couldn't hear what he was saying, but he obviously had plenty to tell Timothy. Surprisingly, Greg didn't seem to want to let her go.

He insisted on sitting on her lap during the service, while Ruth sat on one side and Phillip snuggled closely on the other. Timothy settled a little awkwardly beside Phillip. Afterwards, Greg wanted Ida to fix his plate for him, which she managed to do while listening to Phillip describe his dream to her. When she caught Timothy watching, she smiled quickly before Greg directed her attention elsewhere.

Not until dishes had been cleaned up did Timothy finally speak to her. "Doug has loaned me one of his horses until Blackie's foot is better, so I can take the children home this afternoon."

"Would you like me to bring their clothes on Monday to save you the trip into town?" Greg was clamoring for another hug, so she picked him up.

Refusal had shown in his eyes until Greg hugged her. "I would appreciate that, ma'am."

Greg leaned over for a hug from his dad, so Timothy took him. Ida smiled at them, then turned to accompany Lucy out the door.

"Miss Thomas?"

She looked back at Timothy's uncertain expression.

"Thanks for. . .well, just thanks for everything."

Chapter 10

With the Christmas concert only ten days away, Ida used most afternoons for rehearsals. Patricia would play the part of Mary, and Young Lionel would be Joseph. Nettie, Michael, and June were the Three Wise Ones. They couldn't be Wise Men " 'cause Nettie and June are *girls*," Phillip had pointed out with all the disdain small boys have for females not mature enough to be called women. David and four of the six year olds made credible shepherds. Tommy was the Star in the East, and Clara and Ruth formed a lopsided pair of angels. Clara wanted to do the talking, though she couldn't seem to remember her first line, "Glory to God in the highest." Ruth showed amazing patience, reviewing the words over and over with the small actress. The older boys preferred to work on scenery and props, though Ida had persuaded Justin, Jed, and Theodore to do a short choral reading. She wanted to include Jim, as well, but he missed most practices.

"Had you thought about having some singing?" Cynthia asked, the Monday after the tobogganing party.

Ida had wished many times she could. "I'd love to, but I haven't figured out how to teach them without a piano. I don't sing well."

"Why don't you bring them over to our place? We have a piano, and I'd enjoy playing for them. I'm sure Doug wouldn't mind us using the team and wagon to get them back and forth."

Ida couldn't help contrasting the Pierces' generous sharing of their financial security with Ken's selfish squandering, then rebuked herself. *Don't be too hard on him. Maybe he hasn't been taught any differently.* But the feeling wouldn't go away.

The students reveled in the music practice sessions. Even the older boys, from whom she'd expected opposition, joined in the singing. Most of the children happily, though not always accurately, carried the melody. Justin was developing a marvelous bass voice, and Theodore had obviously already learned how to use his tenor. Ruth picked up alto harmony almost instinctively, and Patricia followed along well. Nettie's strong voice didn't surprise Ida, but its sweetness did. Her little choir would do her proud the week before Christmas.

Friday afternoon, Nina and Kate delivered the costumes. Ida couldn't imagine where they'd found the ideas. Creativity had transformed hand-me-downs into garments fit for stage, complete with sparkling jewelry for the Wise Ones and perfectly sized staves for the shepherds. Teddy and Phillip started a jousting match with theirs, so Ida declared the staves off limits until the dress rehearsal. She had a hunch Teddy would steal the show with his star costume, a huge six-pointed piece of cardboard with something sparkling stretched over it. His arms fit through straps on the back, and his cherubic face peeked through a hole near the center.

"You ladies are marvelous!" she exclaimed when the last piece had been revealed. "How did you think of so many great ideas?"

"Raising children develops a woman's creativity." Nina laughed, reaching for little Tabitha, who balanced precariously on top of a desk.

"In that case, you should be close to a genius," Kate remarked drily. "I've been thinking you must be trying to beat Ruby's record. I still can't figure out why anyone would want that many children. Of course, if all kids were as well behaved as yours, it would make a difference. My two youngest can drive me insane without half trying." She seemed oblivious to both standing well within earshot.

Michael chose that moment to pull Nettie's hair, launching a scuffle that demanded Ida's immediate attention, and the two mothers left.

By Friday, Ida felt frazzled. Christmas excitement had invaded her classroom. While Justin, Theodore, and Ruth managed to maintain their studies, the rest of the students were far too wound up to concentrate. She tried to start the day with the customary arithmetic drill. Only David made any pretense of working, and over half his answers were incorrect. Next, she tried a spelling bee, but the six year olds couldn't participate and distracted everyone. All at once she remembered a box of colored paper Cynthia had given her. "Who wants to make Christmas cards?" She distributed the colored paper, glue, and scissors, thereby exchanging pandemonium for organized confusion. The project only required her mediation skills for settling debates as to who got to use which piece of paper and whose card looked prettiest. By the time the cards were finished and the classroom restored to tidiness, she could justify calling lunch. She allowed twenty minutes for eating, then shooed everyone outside. Hopefully, fifteen to thirty minutes of solitude would restore her supply of patience. The older children would have to settle any schoolyard debates. She was going to pretend she couldn't hear a thing. Folding her arms on her desk, she let her head fall forward.

"Miss Thomas?"

The whisper roused her from the brink of sleep to see Ruth standing beside her. Her smile came easily. "What can I do for you?"

Ruth extended a piece of paper. "I was wondering if I could read this poem at the concert."

Ida read. "It's beautiful, Ruth. Where did you find it?"

She studied Ida's desktop self-consciously. "It was just in my head."

"You mean you wrote it? I didn't know you were a poet."

"I'm not, really." The girl beamed, albeit shyly. "I just wanted to read it because it tells what I feel about Christmas this year. You won't tell anyone I wrote it, will you?"

"Of course I won't, if that's what you want. But why not?"

"I don't want them to laugh at me." She shrugged and wrinkled her nose.

Ida could understand. Reading the verses as part of a planned program was one thing. Admitting to having written them would be opening her soul for observation, not all of it gentle or kind. "I won't tell."

Afternoon practice didn't go much better than morning classes. No one remembered their lines correctly, the shepherds refused to stand still, and even the choral readers couldn't seem to get their timing correct. At two o'clock, she gave up and sent everyone home. "Theodore, will you please tell your mother we won't be coming?" She thought she saw understanding in his smile as he nodded, but he didn't say anything.

As soon as the last child had bundled up and disappeared down the road, Ida saddled Misty. If she stayed around to clean up, this would be one of the days Ken would show up to accompany her home. This way, he'd only find an empty schoolhouse.

"The day must have been brutal," Lucy observed when she arrived home. "It's early, and you look like you were pulled through a knothole backwards."

Ida chuckled, feeling some of the day's tension drain away. "I'm almost ready to outlaw Christmas. Even Patricia, who rarely says an unkind word to anyone, told Matthew he was a stupid donkey for stepping on the edge of her costume. Karin burst into tears because David made a face at her, and Nettie spent the day telling me how I should do things differently. Justin, Theo, and Ruth were the only ones who achieved anything remotely resembling studying."

"Just one day like that won't hurt any of them," Lucy soothed, pouring her a cup of peppermint tea. "You did right sending them home early. Let their parents cope with that excess energy. Why don't you take a rest and I'll wake you in plenty of time to freshen up for supper."

Ida could feel her eyelids drooping at the mere suggestion. "You're sure you don't need help with supper?"

"I'll call when you're needed." Lucy smiled mysteriously.

Dusk had already darkened her window when Lucy's gentle tap brought her awake. Her disorientation lasted only until she heard, "You've just enough time to freshen up, dear."

Time? Ida checked the wall clock, remembering Lucy's strange expression earlier. Just past five. What was her friend up to? She'd just barely finished pinning her hair up again when she detected a ruckus in the front entry.

"I'm here, Miss Thomas. Are you s'prised?" As soon as Ida came out of her room, Phillip launched himself into her welcoming arms. "Mrs. Barry asked us to come for supper and not to tell you 'cause it was s'posed to be a s'prise. I didn't say anything at school today or yesterday or the day before, did I? Are you s'prised?"

"Slow down, Son," Timothy advised, putting a large hand on Phillip's head as he passed.

"Yes, I'm surprised," Ida assured the excited boy, helping Greg climb into her lap, too. "And how are you, Mr. Greg?"

"I'm just Greg," he informed her solemnly. "Know what I did today?"

"No. What?" Ida looked up briefly to give Ruth a welcoming smile.

"We built a fire at school."

Ida was sure she hadn't heard correctly. "You what?" The blush creeping out from the edges of Timothy's beard indicated maybe the story wasn't so farfetched.

"Daddy goes to school every morning before it gets light outside, 'cause he says he has to make it warm." Phillip started the story, but Greg took over quickly, his head bobbing emphatically. "I woked up before he left, and Ruthie was busy, so Dad tooked me with him. I helpted him, didn't I, Dad?" He looked at his red-faced father for confirmation.

"You did, Son."

Somehow this piece of knowledge created a funny feeling in Ida's middle. She tried to ignore her reaction and ease Timothy's embarrassment. "You must have done a good job, Greg, because the school was just toasty when I got there. I've really appreciated that fire every single morning, but I had no idea you and your dad made it." Her gaze met Timothy's over the boys' heads. For the first time, his contained something other than heart-rending grief, something almost personal. A warm tingle spread along her spine. Where did she get the feeling his early morning trips to the schoolhouse were a personal gesture? Impossible. He still mourned his wife intensely. She shifted her eyes guiltily as she realized the direction of her thoughts, only to find Lucy watching.

Lucy's gaze dropped to the children. "Boys, how about giving Miss Thomas some room to breathe? If you'll go upstairs to the room with the door open, you'll find some toys. Ruth, would you set the table for me?"

Ida turned abruptly to show Ruth where to find plates and eating utensils. The boys returned, each with a wooden truck that they rushed to show their dad. Timothy gave each son several moments of individual attention, then addressed them both. "Just make sure you don't get in the ladies' way, boys, and be ready to come as soon as Mrs. Barry calls us."

"Yes, sir," they chorused. Loud simulations of truck noises soon emerged from the hallway.

Ida kept herself busy mashing potatoes and putting fresh rolls into a towel-lined bowl. It didn't help. Timothy's presence created a tingle of awareness she couldn't escape. She found herself smiling at his gentle conversation with his sons, impressed with the way he gave each individual attention. *Doug Pierce and Lionel Spencer treated their children similarly. Why should Timothy seem so remarkable?* She took care to avoid eye contact with him during supper, not an easy feat since Lucy had placed them across the table from each other. A knock at the door during dessert offered her escape. "I'll get it, Lucy."

Ken Danielson stood on the step, holding a carefully wrapped package. "Hi! May I come in?"

Ida stepped aside wordlessly. The familiar light scent of his aftershave almost caused her to cringe. His gift held no appeal, either. His hands caught her attention—white, carefully groomed, no dirt ground into the pores, no rough callouses.

"Is this a bad time?" he asked softly, as if trying to keep the conversation private from those seated at the table behind Ida.

She lifted her gaze to the cultured lines of his face, forcing a smile on her own. "No. Lucy just has guests for supper, but you'd be welcome to share pie with us."

"I'd rather just be with you. Would you mind going for a walk?"

For some reason she couldn't identify, she minded very much. "I've had a difficult day at school. I'd rather stay inside. I hope that's okay."

He caught at her hand, a frown creasing his forehead. "I was hoping we could really talk tonight."

"About what?" She pulled back, wishing he'd quit trying to be so personal. Whispers and footsteps behind her indicated Lucy had shepherded everyone into the sitting room.

"I asked you awhile ago if I could come courting. You've never said yes or no." Rather than uncertainty, his eyes revealed only displeasure.

A mental picture suddenly intruded into her dilemma—a tall, skinny man kneeling in front of the schoolhouse stove, hurrying to get wood burning so he could leave without being seen, then his blush when his son revealed his activities; a brokenhearted gaze warming ever so slightly. The scarred soul she'd glimpsed held far more appeal than the polished creature who now waited for her answer. She would probably never see more of the inner Timothy McEvan. What she had seen convinced her she couldn't be satisfied with Ken's luxuries. She craved character more than culture, depth more than polish.

"Ida?"

"I'm sorry." She directed a half-hearted smile at him. "I've just been thinking."

"And your answer?" He squeezed her hand so hard it hurt.

"It wouldn't work."

He let go abruptly. Disbelief twisted his expression. "But. . .but. . .but why? You would make a beautiful wife. You'd never have to teach again and would never have to do without anything."

She touched his arm to stop the flow of words. "I'm sorry, Mr. Danielson. I've enjoyed your company, but I don't feel toward you as a woman should toward any man she permits to court her."

"That doesn't matter." His voice grew louder with fervency. "I care enough for both of us."

His selfishness eliminated her fear of hurting him. "The answer is simply and finally no. I think you should just go now." She was hardly aware she was whispering fiercely in reaction to his loud protest while she thrust the unopened package into his hands. "Good night, Mr. Danielson."

He said nothing more as he left, his expression sullen. Ida stood in the open doorway, momentarily oblivious to the biting cold that swirled around her. She'd just refused what probably represented her only opportunity for marriage in this tiny community. But she couldn't feel regret. Despite his age and size, Ken remained little more than a boy. Somewhere, somehow, she hoped to meet a man. Someone who had matured inside as well as outside. Someone with whom she could share her soul with all its scars and bruises and who would share his in return.

"Are you all right, Ida?"

Lucy's voice from behind returned her to reality. She nodded reassuringly as she shut the door. "Sorry about the draft. It was Mr. Danielson."

"He didn't stay long."

"He saw we had company." She mentally reached for a smile that would mask the turmoil into which her emotions had been stirred.

The rest of the evening passed pleasantly enough. Mr. Carey and Timothy discussed crops, weather, and animals—those subjects of perennial interest to farmers. Ruth and Lucy visited cheerily over dishpans. Greg and Phillip took turns telling Ida long-winded stories.

After a final cup of coffee, Timothy bundled his family up for the ride home. "Thanks for the dinner, Mrs. Barry."

Lucy beamed at him. "You'll have to come more often."

Ida accepted a round of hugs from the children, wondering at the gleam in her friend's eyes. And why did the room seem so empty when the McEvans departed?

Chapter 11

The five school days prior to the Christmas concert left Ida little time to feel Ken's absence. She insisted on diligent study in the mornings that required as much effort from her as from the students. Friday right after lunch, Doug Pierce arrived with a wagon filled with hay to take the excited group into town for "dress rehearsal" in the makeshift performance hall. Ida gasped with delighted surprise at the changes Lionel and Lars had created in what had been a dingy storage room.

A sturdy square wooden platform stood at one end. Temporary curtains basted from Nina's linen supply hid all but the center area from spectator view, providing "backstage" changing and waiting areas. The men had scrounged enough benches from somewhere to provide seating for a sizable crowd. She wondered if more than the first few rows would be filled.

The different environment increased the students' already fever-pitch excitement. Clara forgot her opening line again and burst into tears. Nettie suddenly announced she was "tired of this stupid play." Ruth moved to comfort Clara while Ida tried to find the reason for Nettie's temper. Meanwhile, the shepherds got into another squabble, which resulted in a broken staff. More tears.

Just when Ida felt she'd burst into tears herself, Doug stepped in. "Students, let's give Miss Thomas a break for a moment. Come sit down here." He waved toward the benches.

Hearing his quiet authority, even Nettie cooperated. No one fidgeted as he continued to speak in gentle tones. "You students have done a wonderful job preparing for this concert. You'll be a real credit to Miss Thomas, and your parents will be proud of you. But can anyone tell me why you're doing this?"

" 'Cause it's fun?" Michael piped up.

"I suppose that's part of it," Doug affirmed, glancing apologetically at Ida, who presently felt like the project was anything but fun. "There's more to it than that, though. Why are you singing the kinds of songs you are and doing the play you're doing? Why not some other story?"

They thought for several moments, then Justin raised his hand. "It is

81

Christmastime, sir, so that's our theme."

"And what's so special about Christmas?"

"That's when Jesus was borned," Sara answered promptly.

"So you're really doing this program because of Jesus, right?" Doug raised his eyebrows in question. When several nodded enthusiastically, he inquired, "Do you think maybe Jesus wants to help us all remember our lines, listen to Miss Thomas, and get along with each other?"

Ida noticed Nettie's softened expression. Somehow she hadn't credited the girl with enough heart to care about spiritual matters. Mentally asking divine forgiveness for overlooking the positive in one of her most troublesome students, she heard Doug ask the children to bow their heads.

"Let's pray right now and ask Jesus to help us all tell His story the best we can. Lord Jesus, we're all here today because we want to celebrate Your birth by telling others how You came. We've never tried anything like this before, and we're all a little jittery about it. Would You please help each one of us to remember what we're supposed to do and say and give us willing spirits to get along with one another? Please bless Miss Thomas for working with us so patiently. We want others to find out how wonderful You are through what we do here tonight. Thank you. In Jesus' name, Amen."

Everyone calmed down miraculously after that. Even the youngest children seemed to have taken Doug's words to heart. By the time the wagon full of students left shortly after three, Ida felt relatively confident the evening would be a success.

The house was still when she entered. *Lucy must be resting*, Ida thought as she eased her bedroom door open so it wouldn't squeak, then stopped abruptly. A gorgeous dress hung from a hook on the wall. Made from a deliciously rich shade of red satiny fabric, it had long puffy sleeves fastened with tiny pearl buttons on each long lace-edged cuff. A high collar rimmed with lace topped a form-fitting bodice. Yards of the shiny material hung in long, graceful folds from an impossibly small waistline. She felt Lucy's presence behind her even before she spoke.

"Well, what do you think?"

Ida turned to her friend. "It's lovely. Where did it come from?"

Lucy's excitement gentled into compassion. "I thought you might be missing your mother's fine needlework for Christmas and decided to try to fill the gap."

Tears stung. Ida hadn't been aware until now how hard she'd been trying not to think about past holidays. Lucy's embrace softened the loneliness. Her beautiful gift made Ida realize how much she'd gained since last

Christmas even though she'd also lost much. "Thank you, Lucy." She pulled back and wiped her eyes. "It looks too small, though."

"Only because you're used to wearing clothes almost too big for you," Lucy replied briskly. "Try it on. I'll bet it fits perfectly."

It did, too. Despite the unaccustomed snug fit, Ida felt gorgeous rather than indecent. "How did you figure out my size?"

Lucy laughed. "I just borrowed a couple of dresses while you were at school, then adjusted the measurements for the different pattern. I've had a hunch a lovely figure hid behind your baggy clothes."

Ida felt a twinge of discomfort, which she didn't know how to explain without hurting Lucy's generous heart.

But Lucy guessed what she was thinking, and her voice softened. "It's not a sin to be pretty, you know."

"Mom always said beauty was dangerous, that it could get me into trouble."

"If you flaunt it, yes. Any of God's gifts can be dangerous if used contrary to His purposes." Lucy reached for both of Ida's hands. "But, my dear girl, your gentle, pure spirit shines out through those lovely green eyes so brightly, no one could ever accuse you of misusing His gift of beauty."

Ida raised her gaze to Lucy's eyes. "A gift? I've always thought of it as a temptation, pride for me, and wrong thoughts for men."

"It's the way God made you, isn't it?"

Ida nodded.

"Then it's His gift to you." She paused. "And to the man He'll bring as your husband."

Ida could feel warmth spreading up her neck, but she had to pursue the subject. "What do you mean?"

"God has made men to be attracted by physical beauty. That's why flaunted prettiness does tempt men to impure thoughts. You've learned to keep your appearance disciplined by discretion, and I think God will use it as a special joy for someone who needs an extra daily reminder of how good He is. Now, why don't you let me set up a nice, hot bath for you down here. Soak as long as you want, and I'll bring supper in when you're finished so you can eat in your dressing gown. That way you can rest and spend as much time as you need prettying up."

Ida pondered Lucy's words while she reveled in the warm, scented water. The tub was just large enough so she could sit with her legs bent comfortably. She chuckled to herself. If she were any taller, she would have been cramped. As a teenager, she'd often wished she were at least three inches taller and quite a bit plainer. Mom's warnings about her appearance had made her feel like an invitation to trouble. *Had Mom been overzealous?* It felt horribly disloyal to be questioning her views when she couldn't explain herself. Another of Mom's quotes came to mind. "Think for yourself, girl. That's why God gave you a mind that works." Of course, that statement had always been used to answer Ida's questions about views she heard in her classes that were different from the way she'd always thought. Ida looked again at the crimson gown. Mom would have thought the color too attention-getting, as well. But Lucy loved God as much as Mom had. She wouldn't have given Ida the dress if she felt it were sinful, either in color or style. Maybe Mom's perspective on Ida's appearance was simply personal preference, rather than divine guidance. Ida decided to wear it to the concert and watch people's reactions. If it elicited any kind of attention that she felt was improper, she'd simply explain the problem to Lucy and not wear it again.

But once Ida arrived at the scene of the night's entertainment, all thoughts of personal appearance fled. One of the curtains needed a quick fix. Students began arriving, dressed in their best, some already exhibiting signs of stage fright. Theo, in black trousers and a white shirt, handed over the repaired shepherd's staff, while Ruth looked at her with wide green eyes. "Miss Thomas, are you sure my poem's good enough to read out loud?"

Ida took time to hug her. "Do you think I'd let you do something that would embarrass you?"

Ruth pulled back and looked into Ida's face for several moments, then down at the floor. "I guess not."

Ida gently pulled on the girl's chin until her head lifted again. "I love you, Ruth, and your poem is just right. What you've written may be exactly what someone needs to hear tonight."

Ruth pulled in a deep gulp of air. "I'm just scared they'd laugh if they knew I wrote it."

"No one will laugh, I promise." Ida smiled reassuringly. "You look lovely."

Ruth pulled self-consciously at her deep green skirt with its ruffled flounce. A lace-trimmed cream blouse brought out the deep highlights in her wavy red hair, which she'd tied into a simple low ponytail with a bow matching her skirt. "Mrs. Pierce made it for me for the concert. You look really nice, too, Miss Thomas."

"Thank you, Ruth." She silently lifted a prayer of thanksgiving. She'd noticed how drab Ruth's few dresses had become. *Bless Cynthia for doing something about it for this evening.* Maybe Nina would make a couple more if Ida bought the fabric. She glanced quickly around the rapidly filling room, but to her relief, Ken hadn't come. For just a moment, her gaze intercepted Timothy's. Something she saw made her conscious once again of her appearance. She turned quickly back to her students.

The play went off without a hitch. Clara remembered her lines, the shepherds behaved themselves, and no one tripped over anyone else's clothing. Both the choral reading and the group singing with two-part harmony brought enthusiastic applause. Ruth's poem was the last item of the evening. The packed room fell silent as the girl knelt beside the makeshift manger and began to speak in a quiet, yet resonant voice.

> *"They say he's just a baby,*
> *And in part they're right.*
> *He cries, drinks only milk,*
> *And awakens through the night.*
> *It seems almost unreal*
> *This mewling infant could be more*
> *Yet Scripture had foretold*
> *His coming here so long before.*
> *His Father called Him Mighty God,*
> *Wonderful, Prince of Peace.*
> *He offers life eternal*
> *Amazing love that will not cease.*
> *Many years have passed.*
> *Happily we celebrate His birth.*
> *But what He does for me each day*
> *Is of much more worth.*
> *My life had turned bleak shades of gray*
> *Then windy storms turned clouds black.*
> *But then I saw Him standing there.*
> *His smile rolled storm clouds back.*
> *No matter where I am,*
> *I know He's on my side.*
> *Within His healing love,*
> *I'm learning to abide.*
> *He is my Prince of Peace."*

Ida knew the audience's knowledge of Ruth's family added meaning to the simple words. Sure enough, she could hear light sniffs and quiet blowing of noses as Ruth disappeared behind the curtain. Under Ida's direction, the audience sang "Silent Night" in closing. Before the carol ended, Lionel Spencer had joined Ida at the front of the room and indicated he wanted to speak.

He cleared his throat when the last musical notes faded. "Well, folks, I'm not much of a public speaker, but someone had to say these words. We thought the superintendent of our school board ought to do it, but Lars declined." Everyone chuckled at the idea of the silent Lars Harper addressing a crowd. "First, we want to thank you townfolk who graciously came to see our children's program tonight. We'd like to give credit to the special lady who made it possible. Miss Ida Thomas came to us from Edmonton in September to teach in our country school. As you witnessed tonight, she's done a wonderful job. Miss Thomas, in thanks from all the parents of your students, please accept this gift."

Ida couldn't blink fast enough to keep the tears back as the entire audience stood and clapped enthusiastically. She could feel the love these usually reticent people were trying to express in their applause. Lionel motioned for her to open the brightly wrapped package. She untied the red yarn bow, then folded back green paper. Inside lay a pair of navy blue woolen mittens trimmed in pink nestled on top of a pink scarf with navy tassels and a navy-trimmed pink hat. "I don't know what to say." Her voice wouldn't come out loud enough. "Thanks for the gift, and thanks for the privilege of working with your children."

Another round of applause broke out, then the crowd began filing to the tables at the side of the room where the ladies had placed a mouth-watering array of baked goodies. Ida turned toward the platform, where her students waited as a group.

"We did it, Miss Thomas." Young Lionel beamed.

Clara's eyes sparkled. "And I didn't forget my words."

"You all did very well." Ida gave each student a touch on the shoulder, hand, or head to let them know how proud she felt. "I want you all to have a wonderful two weeks off and be prepared to study hard when you come back."

There were a few groans at the suggestion, but everyone was smiling. The younger children started the round of hugs, which ended up including every student, except the three older boys, who confined themselves to manly handshakes.

When the last one vanished in the direction of the goodies, Ida turned to find Nina waiting to speak with her. "I just wanted to tell you how beautiful you look tonight, Ida. That color suits you wonderfully. Is that dress another of your mother's creations?"

Again Ida had to choke back tears. "No. Lucy made it for me."

Nina gathered her into a hug. "This time of year can't be easy being in a totally new place with people you hadn't met until four months ago. I hope it helps to know how much we've come to love you."

"Thanks." Ida wiped her wet cheeks.

Nina smiled understandingly, then moved through the crowd toward her husband.

Ida watched, feeling an unfamiliar twist of envy. Everyone here had someone. Her gaze found Doug and Cynthia talking to a couple from town, Doug's arm draped around Cynthia's shoulders. She made her way to the door. Maybe some time outside looking at the stars and breathing the sharp, cold air would restore her perspective. Her cape lay near the bottom of the pile of wraps beside the door. She found it and wrapped it around herself, feeling more desolate than ever. If only Mom were here to share this evening with her. If only she could feel Mom's arms around her, rather than this lifeless reminder of her absence. Moving into the shadows beside the door, she leaned against the building, willing herself not to break down completely. She began to whisper into the cold night air. "Mom, I don't know if you can hear me, but I need to talk to you. You don't know any of these people, so I can't even imagine that you're rejoicing at what we accomplished tonight. Even the dress I'm wearing isn't something you would have made for me, probably isn't even a dress you'd like. I'm changing, Mom, and I feel like I'm losing you in the process."

Changes. Ida pondered all that had happened since she'd come to Dawson Creek. She felt like she was becoming part of this remote community. Not so remote anymore, she reminded herself. The first train ever was due to arrive sometime in the new year and would provide weekly service. Maybe Ken would be able to find a bride in the city and bring her back on the train. The thought of him marrying someone else brought relief. At least she'd know she hadn't hurt him irreparably. But would she ever find her kind of mate?

A sound beyond the edge of the building caught her attention. She listened for a moment longer. There it was again. A heart-wrenching sob broke from the shadows. Cautiously, she stepped away from her hiding place and moved toward the sound. Gradually, she could make out a form against the neighboring feed store. She couldn't be sure, but she thought she recognized the long, skinny outline.

"Mr. McEvan?" she called softly. When no response came, she paused. She really had no right to intrude, but his and his children's agony had almost become her own. Yet another change on her inner landscape since— Another sob interrupted her thoughts. A compulsion moved her close enough to confirm her conclusion. "Timothy, it's me, Ida." The shadow against the wall seemed to change posture slightly. *Had he heard her?* "I only heard you because I've been out here grieving, too. Somehow Christmas makes death so much harder to bear." She paused to see if he would respond. She had almost decided to leave him alone when muffled words stopped her.

"It's just not fair."

How well she knew that feeling! Somehow she had to keep him talking. "What do you mean?"

Through the darkness, she could barely see him turn to face her. "Janet should have been here to hear Ruthie tonight. Daniel would have been so proud of his sister, and of Phillip. And Sam and Benjamin. They all would have been here if I hadn't failed them."

Ida felt like his anger had grabbed her around the middle. She forced her voice not to tremble. "How is it your fault, Timothy?"

"I should have taken the rafts over myself one at a time. I should have waited until winter so we could have crossed on ice. I don't really know what I should have done. If I'd just done something different, I wouldn't have lost them." Another sob broke from him.

She prayed for the right ideas, the right words. Was there any way she could pull this man back from the precipice of guilt and heartbreak? "I never knew your wife, Timothy, but Ruth has told me a bit about her and a bit more about Daniel. I don't think either one of them would want you to beat yourself up over what happened. I know you miss them. I still miss my dad and he's been gone thirteen years."

He replied brokenly, "But my wife. My boys. I'm supposed to protect them. I failed."

She moved close enough to lay her hands on his arms. "You're not God. You couldn't have saved your family from the river any more than I could have saved my mother from tuberculosis. It's hard to go on without them, but we have to. Both of us do."

"How?" The single syllable was cut off by another sob.

"I don't know exactly. I just take one day at a time. When the hurt starts to overwhelm me, I remind myself that God understands what I can't. I don't have to explain what He allows, only trust Him to help me bear it."

He shook her hands off his arms and moved a couple of steps away. "I used to love God. How can I now? That hurts as much as anything. Now when I need Him so much, I can't feel anything toward Him except anger for what He's taken away." His voice dropped to a ragged whisper. "Sometimes I even hate Him."

Another plea for divine help launched itself from Ida's heart. She stepped close enough to touch him again. "He knows. Scripture tells us He's felt everything we feel and that He captures each of our tears and keeps them in a bottle. If He cares enough to collect our tears, I think He understands our anger."

"But will it ever end?" He bowed his head onto her shoulder. Her cape absorbed his tears.

Awkwardly, she wrapped her arms around his heaving shoulders. Some might think her actions improper, but God knew her heart. Maybe for the moment, He saw them only as two human beings clinging to each other in their search for Him. She had no idea where the thought came from, but it gave her courage to speak as she tightened her embrace. "I think the pain and anger only end when we stop trying to fight them. As long as we resist grieving, we only make the wounds worse. When we let ourselves hurt, we allow His healing to touch us."

Gradually, his weeping stilled. He straightened, then reached for her hand. "This is the first year my children have asked about Christmas since the river. I know it would help them, but I just can't do it."

The words came without conscious thought. "Why don't the four of you join Lucy and me at the boardinghouse on Christmas Day? You don't have to do anything except come."

He squeezed her hand, then let it go. "I'd better hitch up the team and get my family home."

Ida stayed outside awhile longer to give her emotions time to settle. For some reason, Timothy had bared his broken heart to her. In the uncharacteristic act of embracing him, she absorbed some of his hurt into her own bruised soul. Shared pain had formed a fragile bond between them.

Chapter 12

At Lucy's insistence, Ida did nothing but rest the first four days of Christmas break. She slept until she felt like waking up, lounged around the house during the day, and went to bed early. By Wednesday morning, she felt more refreshed than she believed possible. "What can I do to help you get ready for company tomorrow?" she asked as she accepted a plate of pancakes for breakfast.

"Company," Mr. Carey snorted. "Good thing I'm leavin' for Hythe this afternoon, else I'd be trapped in this house with Merry Christmases and Scripture readings all day!"

Lucy's eyes twinkled. "You don't have to run off, Mr. Carey. We're having roast turkey and dressing, with mashed potatoes and the gravy you like so well, along with sweetened yams, boiled carrots, cranberry sauce that I made myself this summer, and three kinds of pie for dessert. I'm sure there will be plenty for you. We'll even warn you before we say 'Merry Christmas' so you can get out of earshot."

"Harrumph," was all he said as he left the table.

"Poor man," Lucy commented.

The phrase reminded Ida of Timothy huddled against the side of the feed store after the concert. *Would he and the children come tomorrow?* She'd heard no confirmation, but then he hadn't said they wouldn't come.

When she'd told Lucy about it, the older woman had smiled with a knowing twinkle in her eyes. "I'm glad you're feeling enough at home to invite people over. Let's plan on them being here. If they don't come, we'll just have extra food we can send home with Lionel and Nina."

Ida couldn't decide whether or not she wanted the McEvans to show up. Would she and Timothy even be comfortable in the same room after their intensely personal discussion? Yet if they didn't come, the rejection would feel equally personal. Just in case, she managed to find small gifts for each of the children: a red wooden truck for Greg, a blue one for Phillip, and a clothbound blank book Ruth could use for a diary or in which to write more poetry. Nina and Lucy had also managed to create two skirts and three blouses from fabrics the ladies had picked out together. Nina and Lucy had insisted on contributing to the cost. The parcel would be presented to Ruth from the three of them. She hadn't decided whether or not to find a gift for Timothy.

The family hadn't even attended the Sunday service at the Spencers' farm. She had a feeling Timothy was still struggling with his feelings about God. For his sake, she hoped he could find peace. After that. . . She refused to let herself indulge in daydreams. At present, she felt strongly attracted to a widower who still felt married. Until he made peace with himself and his God, she'd best not let herself get carried away. But that didn't stop her from mentioning his name frequently in prayer.

She and Lucy scrubbed, swept, and baked all morning. By midafternoon, the house glowed with cleanliness and shimmered with delicious smells. After a light lunch, they lingered at the table over cups of tea.

"I think I'll take a bit of a rest," Lucy commented. "Lionel said he'd drop by around five with our tree. Thanks to you, everything else is ready. I'll make the dressing and stuff the turkey just before bedtime so it can bake overnight. Is there anything you'd like to do, any way I can help make Christmas more like your mother used to?"

Ida smiled gratefully. Lucy's offer brought both pain and comfort. "This Christmas has already been more lavish than anything I can remember after Dad went off to war. We never had enough money to do anything but read the Christmas story and give each other a single, simple gift." She paused. "Our life together was often difficult, but I'd go back in a minute if it meant I'd still have Mom."

Lucy nodded. "I don't doubt you would, dear. Speaking of wealth and poverty, I haven't noticed Mr. Danielson around much."

"When he stopped by the other night while the McEvans were here, I told him I wasn't interested in being courted."

"What brought you to that conclusion? Or do you not want to talk about it?"

Ida looked into Lucy's compassion-filled eyes. If Mom had been here, she would have spilled out the whole story days ago. Maybe it was time to start letting go of Mom and accept Lucy's mothering. "He's too much of a little boy who's used to getting his own way. He offered me every luxury he could think of, but he wouldn't take the time to discover the person I am inside."

"And?" Lucy seemed to be expecting a different kind of answer.

Ida studied her teacup. "He's not the kind of man I could spend the rest of my life with."

"How did you discover that?"

Lucy's gentle inquiry compelled Ida to be honest. "Timothy McEvan."

A familiar glint shone in Lucy's eyes. "I suspected as much."

"There's a lot of strength and goodness buried in him. He's just hurting too badly to let it show."

"It seems to me a certain schoolteacher is luring it into the open."

Startled, Ida looked straight at Lucy. "What makes you say that? As near as I can tell, he still thinks of himself as married to Janet."

"Timothy used to keep himself strictly apart from his neighbors. I'm not sure what would have happened to him if Doug Pierce hadn't refused to be rejected. The only thing that surprised me more than seeing him at Sunday meeting was when he accepted my invitation to dinner. He studies you pretty carefully, you know."

"What do you mean?"

"Take the night of the concert, for instance. He watched you the entire evening, or at least until Ruth recited her poem."

"What happened then?"

"He just sort of seemed to crumble inside. As soon as Ruth joined him, he handed Greg to her and left. I didn't see him again."

"I did," Ida admitted softly.

"I noticed you going outside, but I thought you were just looking for a few moments to yourself."

"I was." Tears filled her eyes, remembering. "Everything around here is so different from what Mom and I lived. I feel like I've settled so securely into life here that I'm losing touch with Mom."

"That's what healing's all about, honey." Lucy placed her hands over Ida's. "And I'm sure your mom's glad to see it."

"I don't know." Ida shook her head. "I just had to get outside where I could talk to her without people thinking I'm going crazy. Somehow it helped."

"Sure it did. I still talk to both Kelvin and William from time to time, especially when my children or grandchildren make me proud. Those we've loved will always be part of our lives even though we have to live without them. That's why Timothy's going to need an exceptionally understanding wife if he decides to marry again." She refilled their teacups.

"He's a long way from that yet." Ida related what had happened by the feed store. She laughed self-consciously. "I'm glad no one could have seen us. They'd have been scandalized to see their proper schoolmarm embracing one of the parents who'd hired her." She searched for understanding in Lucy's gaze. "Maybe I am going a bit crazy, but I had the feeling God didn't see us so much as man and woman at that moment, but as two individuals seeking and giving comfort."

"It's not crazy at all, Ida. Scripture teaches that in Christ there is no Jew or Gentile, bond or free, male or female. Granted, here on earth, there's certainly a difference. But every once in awhile, He gives us an opportunity to share His love in a way that goes past traditional barriers. Heart attitude is what makes the difference between that kind of ministry and simply disregarding His principles. You have a wonderfully generous heart. Don't be surprised if God is using it in unusual ways."

"Then I guess that's my excuse for inviting them all over here for Christmas."

"No need to apologize. In fact, I'm glad to see it. I have a hunch God has a very special place for you in Timothy McEvan's life. Had you thought about gifts for them?"

"I have something for each of the children, but I can't decide what, if anything, I should do for him."

Lucy thought for a moment. "I have an idea. I'll be right back."

Ida heard footsteps upstairs, then Lucy returned with something in her hand. "My William used to like to carve. He made a set of these for me less than a year before he died. I'd be pleased if you'd give this one to Timothy from you and me."

There certainly could be nothing improper about a gift from both of them. Ida studied the carving Lucy had placed on the table. It depicted an eagle with wings outstretched, each feather etched with meticulous detail, the wood polished to a glowing luster. "It's beautiful."

"William loved eagles. He used to read everything he could find about them. Did you know they seem to be able to sense when a storm is coming and will fly directly into the wind until they're on top of the disturbance? He used to say that's the way he wanted to be as a Christian. But he also found out there are times when an eagle will wait out a storm. Rather than flying above it, he'll sit huddled on the ground or in a tree or up against a rock face. That was my favorite fact. Scripture says God will give us wings like eagles, but there are some times we just aren't able to fly above our heartaches. There's nothing wrong with waiting them out, as long as we don't stay huddled in our tree after the sun's come out."

Ida chuckled at Lucy's analogy. "That is a wonderful thought. I'll give this to him from both of us, and maybe some day I'll be able to tell him what you've told me."

Christmas morning dawned bright and cold. Sunlight glinted off the snow in dazzling sparkles, yet the chill took her breath away when she went out to the stable to feed the horses. *Surely Timothy wouldn't bring his children out in this cold just for dinner.* She tried to push away disappointment.

Less than an hour later, the Spencers arrived, heralded by bells Lionel had attached to his team's harness. Tabitha went immediately to the parlor, where the tree stood splashed with colorful fabric decorations. She squealed when she saw gifts piled around it.

"Not yet, Tabby," her mother admonished, adding two more packages to the collection. "We have to wait until Grandma tells us we can open them."

Tommy had to show Miss Thomas his new picture book "with words in it since I can read now," he declared proudly.

"And what do you have?" Ida asked Clara.

The shy little girl just tugged on the red scarf that hung around her neck even though her coat had been taken to the upstairs bedroom. David and Young Lionel joined the discussion, describing the puppies they'd received but had been unable to bring to Grandma's. In the middle of Young Lionel's description of his puppy, her concentration vanished. Had she heard arrivals at the front door?

A moment later, Phillip's familiar call confirmed her hopes. "Miss Thomas! I'm here."

She couldn't help the grin that plastered itself across her face. "I have to go greet our other guests," she informed the group around her. Even when she saw Timothy behind his children, she had trouble believing he had actually come. A quick glance at his eyes revealed the ghost of a smile.

Ruth reached out for a hug. "I can't believe we're here, Miss Thomas," she whispered. "Dad told me you'd invited us, but he didn't make up his mind until this morning. I thought he was going to decide it was too cold."

"Me, too," Ida whispered back. She untied the boys' scarves, lifted woolen hats, tucked mittens into coat sleeves, and carried the pile of wraps to the designated bedroom upstairs. When she returned, Phillip and Greg were playing trucks with Tommy, Ruth was helping Lucy and Nina in the kitchen, and Lionel had engaged Timothy in discussion while standing guard on the Christmas tree. While she added her assistance to meal preparation, she kept an ear tuned to the men's conversation. Though she couldn't distinguish words, she felt relieved to hear Timothy's rumbling tones regularly. She'd feel terrible if he didn't enjoy himself.

"Time to gather around the tree," Lucy announced after checking the turkey. "By the time we're finished, this bird should be ready to eat."

Lionel pulled an extra chair from the kitchen that he placed beside the armchair in which his wife sat. Lucy settled into the armchair closest to the tree, leaving only the small sofa for Timothy and Ida. Greg and Phillip eliminated any possible uneasiness over the seating arrangement by both trying to squeeze into the small space between their dad and Phillip's teacher. Ida pulled Greg into a hug at the same moment Timothy lifted Phillip onto his lap.

"We settled that pretty quickly, didn't we?" Timothy's eyes twinkled slightly with the humor Ida had known he possessed but had never seen. She simply nodded.

Lucy was speaking. "I'm thankful each of you were able to make it today. There's nothing quite like being able to share Christmas with those you love. Both Ida and the McEvan family have lost loved ones recently. Though there's no way a holiday can be the same as it was, we hope you'll find comfort and joy in the love of our family. Lionel." She turned to her son, who had a Bible spread on his lap.

He began reading the Christmas story. For the first time, Ida became aware that Mary and Joseph were separated from their loved ones on that "first Christmas." More importantly, that which made Christmas possible was Jesus' willingness to be separated from His Father, first in leaving Heaven, then in the abandonment He suffered on the cross. Her eyes stung. Thankful for Greg's little body shielding her from open view, she ducked her head and let the tears flow. Startled, she glanced sideways when Timothy pushed a large handkerchief into her hand. Compassion hovered there in his suspiciously bright eyes.

She had recovered by the time Lucy handed out the first package. The room quickly filled with excited chatter and abandoned wrapping string. Greg and Phillip were ecstatic over their trucks. "Thanks for choosing two different colors," Timothy murmured. "Squabbles will be much easier to settle this way."

Ida nodded with a grin. "I spend my days figuring out how to mediate childhood disputes."

Ruth's eyes lit up when she saw her gifts. "It's wonderful, Miss Thomas! Now I won't lose my writing. Maybe I can even keep a diary." She stood to hold the skirts against herself. "And I love the pretty new clothes."

Lucy reached toward Timothy with a small, awkward-looking package. "This is from Miss Thomas and myself."

Timothy cradled the bundle in his hands. "I don't know what to say."

"Just open it," Lucy urged.

Delight spread across his features as brown paper fell away. "I've always wanted to be able to do something like this. Where did you find it?" he asked, his voice gruff as he looked at Ida.

"Mr. Barry used to make them."

"And one of these days you'll have to get Ida to tell you the story behind this one," Lucy announced.

"I have it on good authority she's a marvelous story-teller." Timothy gave Phillip a quick hug.

"We've heard much the same rumor," Lionel commented, ruffling Tommy's hair.

She felt embarrassed to be singled out, yet somehow also warmly accepted. Almost like part of the family. Lucy handed her two bundles from the rapidly shrinking pile. "It's your turn." One contained a long navy wool skirt from Lucy and the other a blouse that Nina had made from a matching print. Then Lionel handed her another package. It appeared perfectly normal. Brown paper had been wrapped around a cardboard box and careful printing on the paper read, "To Miss Thomas from the McEvan family." However, when she held it, she could feel something moving inside. She heard scratching and soft mewling. Pulling the paper away, she saw a tiny gray kitten.

"Do you like her, Miss Thomas?" Greg asked eagerly.

"Dad said we had to ask Mrs. Barry if a kitten would be allowed here, and she said yes," Phillip informed her.

Ida lifted the kitten out gently. The creature fit well in her cupped hands. "She's so tiny. How old is she?"

"Not quite six weeks," Ruth explained. "Dad said she probably wasn't quite old enough, but he figured you'd love her enough to make up the difference."

Timothy's face turned redder than it had when Greg had revealed his early morning trips to the schoolhouse. Ida looked back at the kitten to give him time to recover, his comment settling into her heart with a warm glow. "Of course I'll love her. Isn't she pretty, Lucy?"

All of the children gathered closely, each wanting a chance to touch the soft fur. "What should I name her?" Ida asked them.

Several suggestions were offered. Tommy suggested "Rover," which David informed him was a dog's name. Nina quickly intervened with "Joybelle" before a fight could erupt.

"I like that!" Ida exclaimed. "She's a Christmas gift, so she ought to have a Christmassy sounding name. Would you mind if I called her Belle for short?"

"Not at all," Nina assured her. "Young Lionel, would you bring our gift from Grandma's bedroom?"

The boy returned quickly, carrying a woven basket. "We didn't know how to wrap it, so Grandma said we could keep it upstairs until you opened your other presents." He offered the basket to her. "It's from us, the Spencers, I mean."

Cradling Belle in her lap, which Greg had vacated in the excitement, Ida examined the basket. A soft pad lined the bottom, making it a perfect bed for her pet. "How did you know?"

"When Ruth told me what they were doing, I dropped a hint to Lionel and Nina. Quite simple, actually." Lucy giggled.

Ida resisted the tears pushing at her eyelids. She'd thought this Christmas would be lonely and painful. Instead, some of the finest people she'd ever met had taken her to their hearts and lavished both love and material gifts on her. When Lucy reached over the basket to give her a hug, she lost the battle. Lucy held her for several long moments, allowing Ida's tears to soak her shoulder. When the wave of emotion had passed, Ida pulled back. "I'm sorry."

"For what?" Lucy's eyes glistened, too.

"Christmas isn't supposed to be tearful."

Nina knelt awkwardly beside Ida to give a hug of her own. "Nonsense. Christmas is about love, and sometimes love brings tears."

Phillip pushed into the circle for a hug, then Greg, then Tommy, then Tabby. Their enthusiastic embraces pulled a chuckle from Ida. "I have to be the most blessed teacher in the world to have students like you." She glanced at Nina and added, "And families like you, too."

"We're blessed to have you."

The gruff remark startled Ida, who'd forgotten Timothy seated beside her. She met his gaze directly for the first time that day, touched by the gentleness she saw there. "I just hope I'm worth your confidence."

"You already have been." He smiled at Ruth, who now sat against the wall with a dreamy look, running her fingers over the cloth covering her new diary.

Ida laughed softly. "It looks like genius is stirring." The veil of restraint she'd felt with him so far gradually lifted.

Dinner lasted well over an hour, as everyone lingered over the delicious food. At Lucy's insistence, Nina lumbered upstairs with Tabby for a dual nap. The men took the rest of the children into the sitting room so Lucy and Ida could clean the kitchen in peace.

With the last pot dried and put away, Ida joined the men and children. "Where's Mom?" Lionel inquired.

"She wanted a bit of a nap." Ida returned Phillip's ever-present hug.

Timothy grimaced at his two sons. "I wish a couple of people I know would make the same choice."

"Surely not with all the excitement in the air. We might miss something." Ida couldn't resist teasing him gently. He looked more peaceful than she'd ever seen him. His eyes even contained a hint of a twinkle.

"Read me a story," Greg demanded with a tug on her skirt.

"Please?" his father prompted.

"Please," the boy echoed dutifully.

"What story would you like?"

"This one." Tommy held up his Christmas gift.

Ida had no sooner seated herself on the sofa than small bodies crowded around her. Greg immediately claimed her lap, while Phillip and Tommy snuggled close on either side. Clara and David sat by her feet, leaning against the sofa. Young Lionel sat on the other side of Phillip, not wanting to be left out. Timothy smiled indulgently at the pile of little people. Ruth had found a pencil and was huddled in her familiar position against the wall, already intently writing in her new book. Lionel dozed in a chair in the opposite corner.

Ida packed as much expression into her reading as she could, her audience's affection pulling the drama out of her. Less than halfway into the story, she felt Greg go limp against her, his even breathing indicating he'd finally succumbed to weariness. As she turned a page, she glanced up at Timothy, who extended his arms in a silent offer to take Greg. She shook her head, not wanting to disturb the boy or change the quiet atmosphere surrounding her. Phillip and Tommy also dozed off before the story's end. Timothy and Lionel took the little ones upstairs, and the rest of the afternoon passed quickly in numerous games of pick-up sticks and tic-tac-toe with the older children. Lucy awoke in time to serve coffee and more pie before the men decided to take their families home. "The cows still expect to be milked, even on Christmas Day," Lionel explained. With hugs all around, the Spencer family departed.

Lucy went upstairs to fetch a second load of winter wraps. Ruth helped Phillip gather the family's gifts from the parlor, and Ida found herself alone with Timothy in the kitchen. He looked down at the sleeping child he'd just brought from the upstairs bedroom. "You've been really good for my children," he commented softly.

"It must be because I love them." She didn't know what else to say.

Some of the softness disappeared from his gaze. "Any child would be blessed to have you as a mother. From what I've heard, it won't be long before you and Mr. Danielson will be creating a family of your own."

Ida looked directly into his blue eyes, wishing she could remove the splinters of pain she still saw there. Her reply came without forethought. "Mr. Danielson knows my heart isn't available. I seem to have fallen in love with someone who already has a family." The words had hardly left her mouth when she realized what she'd said. Mortification overwhelmed her and she fled to her room without waiting for a response.

Chapter 13

For days afterward, Ida wished she could have retracted those words. What an unseemly thing to have said! She stroked Belle's downy fur and the kitten mewed as if in sympathy. *Why did Timothy McEvan's presence elicit emotional responses from her so contrary to good sense? If Mom had been here, she wouldn't have gotten so carried away*, she thought irrationally. Finally, Lucy cornered her. "Ida, you need to talk."

To her dismay, tears threatened to destroy her composure. She hadn't opened the subject before for fear she'd cry rather than talk. She shook her head.

Lucy grasped her hands. "You're just going to make yourself sick if you don't get this out where you can deal with it. Now what is it?"

The unusual sternness in her voice startled Ida into cooperation. She related the entire humiliating conversation, ending with, "I'm embarrassed, Lucy. How could I have been so forward?"

Silently Lucy gathered the weeping young woman into an embrace until the sobs ceased. "Ida, do you truly believe every detail of your life is under God's control?"

The answer came without thinking. "Yes."

"Including your mistakes?"

That question made Ida think. "I guess so."

Lucy nodded with a comforting smile. "Do you really believe that, or is it just the right answer for this quiz?"

"If He couldn't control my mistakes, He wouldn't really be omnipotent." Ida smiled shakily.

"It sounds to me like you're convinced. May I tell you what I think about what happened?" Lucy poured out cups of steaming tea.

Ida nodded and wrapped her hands around the cup's warmth.

"I don't pretend to know what God has planned for you or Timothy. But I have noticed how well you compliment each other when you're not trying to pretend there's no attraction between you. You look to me like a perfect fit." Lucy's words created a warm gush of joy within Ida. "Maybe your admission was just what Timothy needs to encourage him to leave

100

his grief and guilt behind."

Ida wanted to believe her friend, but one thought wouldn't go away. "My mother would have been horrified."

"You don't know that."

"She told me more times than I can count how important discretion is, how men don't respect women who let too much of their feelings show."

"Maybe Timothy isn't the only one who needs to leave a bit of the past behind."

The quiet comment stopped Ida's whirling thoughts midsyllable. "What do you mean?"

Lucy again grasped Ida's hands. "From what you've said, I know your mother was a fine lady. But Ida, dear, she's now at home with the Lord she loved. You can't live the rest of your life wondering how she'd handle what you're facing. She taught you as well as she knew how. You now answer only to your Heavenly Father for the choices you make. You'll never go wrong asking yourself how to respond as He would."

It made sense to Ida. Yet, as she pondered the conversation over the next few days, she still resisted her loss. Acting contrary to what she remembered of her mother felt like betrayal. Through the mental clamor, she recalled Timothy's grief-filled eyes. Was she as reluctant as he to let go?

As had become habit, she discussed her thoughts with Lucy. "I'd never realized before how much Mom's opinions mattered to me."

"Of course they do." Lucy thumped her bread dough one last time, plopped it into a bowl, and set it near the stove to rise. "She was both your mother and your friend. The danger is when pleasing her becomes your sole reason for what you do."

"I've been reading Proverbs lately," Ida mused. "It talks as much about a person's heart as it does about actions."

The counter now clean, Lucy sat at the table across from Ida. "You're right. Jesus talked often about heart. He even went so far as to say that doing the right thing, such as keeping the law, with a wrong motivation makes the action wrong, too."

"I haven't been able to forget what you said about asking myself what Jesus would do. By always thinking about what Mom would do, I've made her more important than God."

"And in so doing, lost track of the beautiful uniqueness of yourself," Lucy replied gently.

Startled, Ida looked up from her tea questioningly.

Lucy smiled. "When God made you, He gave you certain characteristics for a purpose. Trying to be exactly like your mom, Ida, says the way He made you isn't good enough."

Ida pondered for several moments. "I never thought of it that way. I've just been thinking in terms of making Mom proud of me if she were here."

Lucy patted Ida's hands in the familiar gesture. "From what you've said of your mom, I'm sure she's proud of you. Nothing makes a mother happier than to see her children becoming the people God meant them to be."

Despite her other personal discoveries, Ida still wondered about Timothy. She had seen him a couple of times in town, but his greeting was nothing more or less than that of a respectful acquaintance. She couldn't help wondering if their comfortable camaraderie of Christmas Day had vanished forever.

∽

The second Sunday of the year brought the coldest temperatures Ida had yet experienced. Lucy warned her to bundle up well for their trip to the Spencer farm. "As long as the wind isn't blowing, we'll be fine."

Ida donned three thick sweaters. The top one had been one of her first knitting projects and had turned out too large to be worn alone. At Mom's insistence, she'd kept the garment. With gratitude, she realized its size made a perfect fit over the rest of her clothing. By the time she met Lucy at the back door, they both wore so many layers they could hardly waddle. Ida giggled. "No one could accuse us of flaunting our figures."

Lionel met them at the barn almost before the buggy had stopped. "Ma, I was afraid you'd do this."

Lucy favored her son with a tolerant glance. "It's like I told Ida. If we let a little cold keep us at home, we won't budge until March."

"But what if something had happened? You'd freeze to death."

"Not as long as we're walking." She allowed him to help her down, then patted his arm. "Thanks for your concern, Son, but I've lived in this country long enough to know when it's dangerous. If we'd had any wind, I would have kept us at home."

"Just hurry inside, please, and I'll take care of the horse."

From Lionel's reaction, Ida wondered if anyone else would brave the weather. However, it appeared most people shared Lucy's perspective. The pile of blankets, sweaters, coats, and other winter wear in the corner grew to mammoth proportions as each family arrived. She greeted Cynthia Pierce enthusiastically. "I'm so glad to see you. Theo told me you'd not been feeling well since Christmas."

Cynthia returned her hug. "It always happens when I let myself get overtired. Hopefully, I'll be able to make it to school this next week."

"Much as I appreciate your help, please don't push yourself unnecessarily."

"She won't," Doug assured her, putting an arm around his wife's shoulders.

Lionel started singing, accompanied by his guitar. Conversation stilled to a minimum as everyone found seats. Ida chose a place beside Lucy. When a blast of frigid air behind them indicated more arrivals, she knew without looking who had come. Her suspicions were confirmed when a well-clothed small person clambered into her lap uninvited. "Hi, Teacher. We comed even though Daddy said it was almost too cold," Phillip informed her in a stage whisper.

She put a finger on his lips to shush him while she removed his coat and other winter gear. "Go put these on the pile, and then you can come back and sit with me if your dad says it's okay." Since the youngster rejoined her quickly, she assumed he obtained permission. She refused to let herself look for Timothy to confirm. However, she found herself unable to concentrate on the songs they sang.

Lionel eventually stood and put his guitar to one side. "Your presence here today is encouraging to my wife and me. Though we would have condemned no one for staying home, your being here in spite of the weather lets us know these afternoons of worship together are just as important to you as they are to us. I didn't prepare anything to talk about today, so I'm wondering if anyone else has something."

After a brief pause, Ida heard a rustle behind her. "Yes, Lionel, I think I do." To her amazement, Timothy strode to the front of the room. "I'm not much good at talking in front of people, but you people have been so good to me and my children, I feel like you're family." He cleared his throat, then sat on the chair Lionel had vacated. "I'd like to start with a Scripture reading. Lamentations chapter three, verses 22 through 26." Ida noticed his fingers trembling as he found the passage in his Bible. " 'It is of the LORD'S mercies that we are not consumed, because his compassions fail not. They are new every morning: great is thy faithfulness. The LORD is my portion, saith my soul; therefore will I hope in him. The LORD is good unto them that wait for him, to the soul that seeketh him. It is good that a man should both hope and quietly wait for the salvation of the LORD.' "

He cleared his throat a couple more times before continuing. Ida felt like she sat on the edge of an important discovery and silently prayed he'd have the composure to say all he wanted to say. "Eighteen months ago, my wife and three of my children drowned. I've blamed both God and myself. In my anger, I almost committed myself to never being whole again. As a result, I haven't been a very good neighbor or father. But you people refused to let me bury myself in bitterness." He looked at Doug Pierce, and for a moment Ida thought he would break down completely. He swallowed hard. "Through you I've realized remaining angry at God was cutting me off from my only true Source of comfort and healing." Now his gaze met Ida's. Rather than looking away in embarrassment, she found she wanted to be able to see all the way into his soul, to realize the depth of what he was trying to say. "You've also provided the love and guidance my children needed while I found my way back to my Heavenly Father. I've seen the faith and courage with which you face your heartaches, and it has challenged me to do the same. Just before Christmas, I opened Janet's Bible for the first time since the river." He had to pause for a couple of moments. "This passage I've read to you was underlined. It seemed to be a message to me, both from Janet and from my Heavenly Father. I will probably never be able to explain why God allowed half our family to be swept away. But I've come to know that His love for us is no different than it was before. He's been waiting for me to let Him show me how to cope and heal. We as a family will always miss Janet, Daniel, Sam, and Benjamin. But because of the healing I've decided to accept, we're now ready to let them go, knowing they're waiting for us in a better place. It's up to us who are left to make the most of the future God has put before us." His gaze traveled around the room, making eye contact with each person there, then returned to Ida. "We'll continue to need your love and prayers, even as we thank you for what you've already done." He sat down.

Silence gripped the room. Then Doug thumped over to Timothy to enfold him in a great bear hug. Lionel followed. Their wives sat smiling and crying at the same time. Even Kate Harper seemed touched. Ida became aware of the tears trickling down her own cheeks. She'd felt Timothy's pain; now she'd experienced his first steps toward healing. It wouldn't be an easy path to travel, but at least he'd found the One who would make it possible.

Chapter 14

When Ida awoke Monday morning, her first conscious thought was of Timothy. A prayer of thanksgiving bubbled from her heart. "Thank you, Father, that he's found You again." *How Mom would have rejoiced! But then, Mom had never met Timothy.* The familiar twist of pain shadowed Ida's joy. Remembering the solace he had found in Lamentations, Ida quickly readied herself for the new day so she could spend a few moments studying the passage again. "His compassions fail not. They are new every morning. . ." She read the verses a second and a third time.

The clattering of stove lids in the kitchen told her Lucy was up, too. She grabbed her Bible and raced out to share her discovery. "Lucy, listen to this!"

"Good morning to you, too." Lucy's eyes twinkled. "Let me guess. You've been reading Lamentations."

Ida smiled self-consciously. "Yes. And I found something I've never seen before." She read the verses aloud. "It seems like every morning when I get up, I have to face all over again the fact that Mom's not here." Lucy nodded understandingly, but didn't interrupt. "It's like the grief is fresh each day. But these verses say God's compassion is also new every morning. It's almost like He matches His compassion to my hurt."

Lucy's eyes moistened. "That's beautiful, Ida. I don't know how many times I've read those verses, but I hadn't understood them that way before."

Grumbling from the opposite doorway brought their conversation to a halt. "How's a working man supposed to get his rest with you two wimen blabbering all the time?"

"Good morning, Mr. Carey," Lucy responded. "You're just in time for fresh coffee."

"Might as well have something to get me going since you made sure I can't sleep." He winked subtly at Ida.

She almost gasped. While she'd grown accustomed to his complaining, she'd always thought he was serious. At least this morning, it seemed he was simply acting to see what reaction he'd get out of Lucy.

"But morning's the best time of the day." Lucy set a steaming mug in front of him. "Maybe if you spent more time enjoying it, you wouldn't be so grouchy the rest of the day."

"What have I told you about tryin' to run my life?" he growled.

"Just a helpful suggestion," she replied innocently, grinning at Ida when he wasn't looking.

But even the playful bickering couldn't take away Ida's wonder at her discovery. She and Mom had read through the Bible together many times. Somehow, there always seemed to be a new personal message in it from her Heavenly Father.

∞

The next few days at school were hectic. The students hadn't yet settled back into routine. In addition, Dawson Creek's first train was due to arrive Thursday evening. The excitement that gripped the entire town also invaded her classroom. She dismissed her students early Thursday afternoon so everyone could get chores done and supper eaten before the locomotive's arrival.

To her astonishment, Mr. Carey met her and Misty as they entered the barn. He appeared to be feeding Lucy's horse and cleaning out stalls. "I'll rub her down for you, ma'am."

"Thank you, Mr. Carey."

"I wasn't doin' nuthin' anyway," he excused himself gruffly. "Just don't expect me to do it all the time."

She thought she caught a glimpse of his roguish twinkle, but couldn't be sure. On her way through the kitchen, she paused to whisper to Lucy, "You'll never guess who's out in the barn."

"He came home from work about an hour ago, madder than a wet cat they'd closed the store early. He devoured pie and coffee, then disappeared out the back door."

"He did warn me not to expect this of him all the time."

Lucy grinned. "I don't think he has anything to worry about."

"How long before supper?"

"The train's due at six, so I thought we'd eat in about thirty minutes. I'd like to leave for the station early."

"I'll be out to help in a few minutes," Ida promised as she closed her bedroom door. She quickly shook the chalk dust out of her black wool skirt, then removed her riding clothes. For the evening's activity, she wanted something festive-looking. Her Christmas gift from Lucy seemed just right. Her outfit would be covered by her shawl, she reminded herself. It didn't matter. She felt like dressing up, so she would.

A crowd had already gathered by the time Lucy and Ida arrived.

Thankfully the temperature had warmed enough to make waiting outside possible. Several people moved aside so the two ladies could get closer to the front.

"Hello, Mrs. Barry and Miss Thomas," Mrs. Danielson smiled at them as they found a place to stand. "Isn't this a wonderful evening?"

Lucy returned the greeting. Surprise took away Ida's power of speech. She hadn't expected pleasantness from the Danielsons after what had happened between her and Ken. She scanned the crowd, but didn't see him. A tackle around her knees almost sent her tumbling, while a firm grip on her elbow steadied her. She grinned down at Phillip. "I'm glad to see you, too." Timothy's hand lingered a moment longer than necessary, which she found strangely pleasant. "Thank you, Mr. McEvan."

He chuckled. "It's the least I can do until my son learns how to say hello less exuberantly."

Greg leaned from his dad's arm to give Ida a hug, bringing her into even closer contact with Timothy. She directed her attention toward Ruth, accompanied as usual by Theo. "What do you think of us getting our own train?"

"Dad says now that we have regular shipments from the city, we might even get a lending library. Do you think so, Miss Thomas?" The girl's eyes sparkled.

"It's possible. What do you think, Theo?"

"It would be wonderful. The train will also make it easier for me to come home for visits after I start medical school."

"I'm sure your mother likes that idea." Ida smiled at Cynthia, standing just behind her son.

A distant whistle interrupted conversation, causing a rumble of excitement through the crowd as everyone strained forward to see down the tracks. More quickly than seemed possible, the black smoking engine roared up to the tiny station building, pulling several freight cars and a passenger car behind it. Several railroad dignitaries disembarked. The new stationmaster shook hands importantly.

"What's she doing here?"

Ida barely heard Timothy's muttered exclamation, though she felt his tension behind her. She looked back toward the passenger car, where a well-dressed woman hesitated at the top of the steps, loathe to contaminate herself with what she saw around her. Her gaze swept through the crowded yard almost unseeingly until she found Timothy. At once, her face hardened. She moved toward them purposefully.

"Mother Carrington! How kind of you to visit us." Timothy strode forward, greeting her with more warmth than Ida felt the lady's expression deserved. "Ruth, Phillip, and Greg, this is your grandmother Carrington, your mother's mother."

Phillip clutched Ida's leg more tightly, while Greg ducked his head into his father's shoulder. Only Ruth appeared willing to become acquainted. "Hello, Grandmother. I'm glad you're here."

"Well, I'm not." Mrs. Carrington lifted her nose as if smelling something disagreeable. "I've come to take you children back to Toronto where you can be cared for properly. I would have come much sooner, but I didn't fancy riding in an open wagon or an outdated truck from that hamlet they call Hythe."

Ida watched the man she loved age abruptly. The grief lines that had been fading around his mouth and eyes deepened. He looked at her, helpless agony in his expression. She held out her hand to the uninvited guest. "Mrs. Carrington, I'm Ida Thomas, the children's schoolteacher. You would be more than welcome to spend the night at the boardinghouse where I live. Tomorrow we'll take you out to the farm so you and your family can discuss your plans in private." She didn't know where the words came from, but they brought a light of gratitude to Timothy's stricken eyes.

Mrs. Carrington didn't thaw a bit. "I suppose that's my only option, since no train departs this Godforsaken place tonight. Timothy, be sure your children's bags are packed when I arrive tomorrow. From their appearance now, I'll be ashamed to have them seen in Toronto, but they will need something to wear until they get there." She looked imperiously at Ida. "If you'll direct your driver and carriage over here, I'll get that stationmaster to bring my bags out."

Ida mustered her most courteous smile. "I'm afraid we don't have a driver or a carriage. If you'd like to walk with Mrs. Barry and me back to the boardinghouse, I'm sure Mr. McEvan will be happy to bring your bags in the wagon."

Mingled fear and fury showed in the lady's face. "I should have known Timothy would bring my precious daughter and grandchildren to some place so primitive. In Toronto, no true lady is seen walking anywhere."

Lucy's reappearance saved Ida from an unwise answer. "Mrs. Carrington, this is Mrs. Barry, the lady who owns the boardinghouse. Lucy, this is Mrs. Carrington, Mr. McEvan's mother-in-law."

Lucy extended her hand in greeting. "We're glad to have you with us."

Mrs. Carrington ignored the hand. "I'm certainly not glad to be here."

She expanded on the theme throughout the short walk downtown. The buildings were ugly, the weather sharp enough to ruin a lady's complexion, the paths shoveled through the snow far too narrow, and the piles of horse droppings offensive in the extreme. "Why you people don't invest in something clean and sensible like automobiles, I'll never know." Her mood didn't improve when they reached the boardinghouse. No carpeting, no powder room, no indoor "privacy room," and so the list continued.

Ida had never admired her friend and landlady so much as during that interminable evening. Though nothing provided for their guest was good enough, Lucy remained gracious and attentive.

The following morning brought no relief. Mrs. Carrington wanted to set out immediately after breakfast, in spite of Lucy's insistence that they wait for daylight. Ida saddled Misty and rode out of the yard with a feeling of guilty relief. At least she could escape to school.

She recognized Pierce's team in the shelter as she approached, then Cynthia came running out of the schoolhouse. "Ida, would you let me take classes for you this morning so you can go over to the McEvans'?"

Surprise stole Ida's reply. Finally, she found a coherent thought. "Why? Has someone been hurt?"

Cynthia shook her head. "Doug and I were talking about it last night after watching what happened at the train station. Both of us think you could help Timothy just by being there."

Ida had felt the same way since awaking, but it seemed horribly presumptuous. "Won't he think I'm interfering?"

"I think he'll be grateful for the support. We'll be praying for you."

Ida held Misty still for several more moments. Mom would be horrified that she'd even contemplated arriving uninvited at a single man's residence. But that thought was quickly replaced by another. What would God's compassion have her do? She smiled at Cynthia. "Thanks for the offer. I just hope we're doing the right thing."

She guided Misty automatically down the winding trail to the McEvans' farm. Two bundled figures ahead in the predawn shadows caught her attention. She reigned the horse to a stop and dismounted to talk to them. "How are you two this morning?"

The usually voluble Phillip had nothing to say. Ruth explained. "He's afraid Grandmother is going to convince Dad we have to go with her."

"That's understandable," Ida replied, kneeling in the snow and holding out her arms to the silent boy. "Would a hug help?"

Phillip ran into her with such force she almost toppled over. He buried his head into her scarf as sobs started to shake his small body. "She can't make us leave, can she, Teacher? I don't want to go away from you or my dad or the horses and cows and chickens. How does Daddy know she's really our grandmother? Maybe she's just a horrid old lady who steals children."

She hugged him tightly through their layers of winter clothing until he calmed enough to listen. "Do you really think your daddy would let you go anywhere that wasn't good for you?"

"But she didn't ask him." He hiccuped. "She told him, and he didn't say no."

"But he didn't say yes, either, did he?"

"No." Phillip sniffed loudly. "I think I need a hanky."

Ruth pulled one from the cloth bag that carried her books and their lunch. "What do you think, Miss Thomas? Is he really going to let her take us away?"

Ida stood to put her arms around the girl. "I don't know, Ruth. The only thing I do know is that God isn't going to stop taking care of you now. Would it help if I prayed with you?"

Both nodded, their eyes filled with a trust so sincere it brought tears to her own. She bowed her head, while hugging them both close. "Lord Jesus, Ruth and Phillip are worried this morning because they don't know what their dad is going to decide. We know you know their grandmother wants to take them back to Toronto, and they don't want to leave. Will you please give them peace today so they can learn well, and give their dad wisdom as he makes his decision? In Jesus' name, Amen."

The two hugged her again, then suddenly seemed to realize which direction she'd been riding. "Aren't you going to school this morning?" Ruth asked.

Even for these two, Ida felt embarrassed to explain. "Mrs. Pierce offered to take classes for me this morning. She and Mr. Pierce think I can help your dad. Do you think so?" She appealed to Ruth for confirmation.

The teenager didn't even hesitate. "Yes. He doesn't know it yet, but he needs you."

Ida didn't dare explore further. "Then I'd better see what I can do. You'll be good for Mrs. Pierce, won't you, Phillip?"

"Yes, ma'am." He flashed his usual fun-filled grin at her, then trudged off through the snow behind his sister.

He needs you. . . The thought wouldn't complete itself nor would it leave. *What had led Ruth to such a conclusion?* Timothy had made great strides in dealing with his grief, but was he really ready to admit another woman to his life? The sight of him entering the barn ahead made her put her contemplations aside.

"Daddy, look who's here!"

She heard Greg's happy announcement as he followed his dad. Abruptly, Timothy came back out. Relief gentled his expression when he saw her. "What brings the schoolteacher here?" He reached up to help her dismount.

How could she explain without seeming forward? "The Pierces and I thought you could use some moral support this morning."

"Cynthia's at school?" The gentleness in his eyes didn't change.

Ida nodded. "I met Ruth and Phillip on the way."

"He's pretty upset, isn't he?"

"Probably no more than you are."

He didn't answer until he'd put Misty into a stall with fresh hay. "She can offer them so much more than I can."

Ida knew if she pursued his thoughts further, she could be accused of meddling. Yet she felt compelled. "Like what?"

He scooped Greg onto his shoulders. "Nice clothes, higher education, all the advantages of city living."

"Mr. McEvan." Though she thought of him as Timothy, she carefully didn't let it slip. "Would you mind telling me why you and your wife came out west?"

He looked at her intently for several long moments, then shifted his gaze off into the distance. "We wanted our children to learn—" His voice trailed off as if he couldn't find the words to explain himself.

"Independence?" She made the guess from what she knew of his character.

"In part." He nodded slowly. After a few moments' contemplation, he continued. "Janet often said city living encourages people to forget God's simplicity."

She sensed the process of putting his thoughts into words would help him make a decision. "I think I understand, but can you explain a little more?"

"Like this." He waved toward the gradually lighting horizon. "City folk are often too busy to watch the sun come up. They never pay attention to the seasons except to complain about the hardship of rain or snow. They don't think about where their food comes from. We wanted our children to enjoy what they eat because they helped plant and harvest it. Am I making sense?" He finally looked at her again.

She nodded, amazed at the sheer quantity of words he'd used. *Had she said enough? Too much?* Lucy's favorite verse came to mind. "The steps of a good woman are ordered by the Lord. . ." Leaning against one of the stalls, she watched him ponder and remember. *"Father, he needs to feel your presence like he never has before,"* she prayed silently.

The jangle of harness coming toward them punctured the quietly intent mood. "Here she comes." He touched her arm. "I'm glad you're here. Would you hold onto Greg while I unhitch the horse? And please keep praying."

She held out her arms and the toddler tumbled into them. How had Timothy known she was praying? His perception gave her an odd feeling of intimacy with him. He helped his mother-in-law out of the buggy.

"That lady's mad at Daddy."

Greg's whispered confidence startled Ida. She glanced at Mrs. Carrington, whose disapproving countenance hadn't altered since breakfast.

If Lucy was surprised to see Ida at the farm, she didn't let on. She beckoned, strain showing in fine lines around her eyes. "Maybe Greg and I could play out here in the barn."

Greg bounced excitedly in Ida's arms. Ida smiled at him, then at Lucy. "That's a great idea."

Lucy accepted Timothy's assistance in getting out of the buggy, then held out her arms for the small boy. "If you don't mind, Mr. McEvan, Greg and I will stay out here and talk with the horses. With the door closed, we'll keep nice and warm."

Timothy looked up from the harnesses he had unhitched. "Much obliged, Mrs. Barry."

Mrs. Carrington barely gave him time to turn the horse into the corral before demanding, "Well, are you going to leave me out here to freeze?"

"No, Mother. Come inside and I'll brew us all a pot of hot tea." Timothy motioned the two ladies ahead of him into the small log cabin.

For once, Mrs. Carrington remained silent, though she inspected her surroundings carefully. "I wouldn't have expected you to do this well without Janet, Timothy." Her tone made sure Timothy didn't think he'd been given a compliment.

"Ruth has been a fine little housekeeper," Timothy responded as if he had been commended.

"That's my point exactly," Mrs. Carrington exclaimed. "All that girl should be thinking about is party dresses and hairstyles, not trying to turn this hovel into a home."

"When you saw her last night did she appear unhappy, Mother?"

"Don't call me Mother." The woman sat up straighter, if that were possible. "You lost all relationship to me when you killed my daughter. I'm only here to rescue my three remaining grandchildren from your foolishness."

Pain knifed through Timothy's face at the accusation, but peace quickly replaced it. "It doesn't matter what you think of me, Mrs. Carrington. I'll always love you because you raised the woman I loved. For awhile, I blamed myself for her death, but I don't anymore. In time, you won't either."

"Sentiment isn't going to change my mind, Mr. McEvan. The fact remains that my grandchildren no longer have a mother. It's my duty to make sure they're well cared for."

"I don't agree." Timothy's voice remained calm.

Obviously, few people dared disagree with Mrs. Carrington. She seemed shocked into silence, if only briefly. "And what can you provide for them that I can't? You've already deprived them and me of my daughter."

"No one has mourned my wife's death more than I." Timothy set his cup down on the table and stood as if to shake off invisible bonds. "Nevertheless, I'm as much the children's father as she was their mother. We're still a family even though four of us are no longer present. Our family love hasn't changed."

"Noble thoughts, Mr. McEvan, but they won't give my grandchildren the finer things of life that they deserve."

"Fancy clothes can't replace love, Mother."

"Your so-called love didn't keep my daughter alive."

"And you want to punish me by taking our children away." Timothy turned to face his mother-in-law directly.

Mrs. Carrington didn't deny the charge.

"I know you loved Janet. Breaking her children's hearts isn't going to bring her back."

"The children will adapt. When they realize what I can offer them, they won't even look back."

"Yes, they will, Mother. Janet and I brought our family out here because we wanted more for them than we felt city life could offer. They've become part of this farm. You won't be able to transplant them back."

"You can't raise them without a mother."

"I don't intend to try."

Mrs. Carrington seemed to become aware of Ida's presence for the first time. Ida willed herself not to blush under the woman's squint-eyed scrutiny. Timothy's words had fanned a flame of hope within her, but she couldn't afford to let her countenance reveal it. Mrs. Carrington looked back at Timothy. "What woman in her right mind would move into this place and take on three children just to marry you?"

"The right one," Timothy answered calmly.

Mrs. Carrington made a sound that in a less cultured person would have been a snort. "You always were a dreamer. I'll make a compromise with you. I'll take Ruth and you can keep the two boys. I wouldn't know what to do with them anyway."

Ida bit back her protest at the lady's callous disposal of Phillip and Greg. Timothy's quick glance reminded her that any input from her would strengthen Mrs. Carrington's determination.

"Mother Carrington, you are not taking even one of my children. God gave them to Janet and me. Since Janet's gone, it's now my responsibility, and mine alone, to care for them."

"They're all I have left of my daughter. Can't you understand that? I tried to get here as soon as I received your letter, but as you well know, there was no civilized means of travel to your town until yesterday." Her tone implied that Timothy could have done something about it had he wished. "With Ruth to remind me of her, maybe I'll be able to forgive you for what you've done."

Timothy's lips whitened. His eyes turned steely gray. "My children are not for sale for any price. I've forgiven myself for the river accident. Whether you ever do or not is your choice. In any case, you're not taking Janet's daughter away from me."

A spot of bright color appeared above each of Mrs. Carrington's sharp cheekbones. "Are you denying me contact with my own grandchildren?"

"You know I would never do that." Timothy refilled the teacups. "You may write to them as often as you like, and I'll encourage them to reply to your letters. If you want to invite them to come live with you when they finish school, I'll let them make their own decisions. Until then, they remain with me on the farm Janet wanted for them."

Mrs. Carrington didn't say anything for a while. Finally she stood and fastened the coat she'd refused to remove. "May God forgive you for breaking my heart. I know I can't. If you should change your mind before the train leaves this afternoon, you know where to find me."

Chapter 15

Mrs. Carrington slammed the door behind her as she sailed out. Timothy turned to Ida, his sagging shoulders beginning to straighten. "Who is going to tell her the train doesn't leave until next week?"

"I guess Lucy will have to." Ida noticed his mischievous smile closely resembled Phillip's. He finally looked released from an overwhelming weight.

His expression sobered. "I can't tell you how much I appreciate your being here, Miss Thomas."

"I didn't do much."

"You prayed." His tone told her how much he'd relied on it. "From the first time I met you, I noticed the way peace hovers around you. It rescued me today."

If she hadn't watched the battle of emotions on his face during the past hour, his description would have seemed melodramatic. She knew he'd just fought for a life beyond grief and guilt. "One of my favorite Scripture passages says God wants to give us peace like a river. Maybe He wanted to show you today that His river can give as much as another river took away."

"He gives more, Miss Thomas, much, much more." With that enigmatic statement, he held her cape for her. "Mrs. Barry could probably use my help hitching up the buggy."

"And I should return to my classroom."

"Thank Mrs. Pierce for me, will you please? I don't know if I could have handled Mother without you." His hands rested on her shoulders after he settled her cape into place, leaving a tingling warmth after he reached for the door. They walked in silence to the barn, where Lucy led the horse from the corral. Mrs. Carrington's usual stream of complaints had dried up for the moment.

Ida and Timothy waved the two ladies off down the lane, then Timothy saddled Misty. "Your horse certainly is beautiful, Miss Thomas." He patted Misty's nose.

"She's actually just on loan to me from Nina Spencer. It's been wonderful to be able to ride to school, especially after the town moved." She

115

accepted his help up into the saddle, while Greg watched from a nearby pile of clean hay. "Have a great day helping your dad, Greg."

Greg grinned at being acknowledged. He pulled his thumb from his mouth long enough to wave. "Bye, Miss Thomas."

Phillip and Ruth detached themselves from the group milling in the yard for recess. Ida realized she should have asked Timothy what to tell them. "What happened?" Ruth inquired, while Phillip wondered, "Is that lady taking us with her?"

"Let me get Misty put away, then we'll talk." Ida laughed, hoping to reassure them. When the horse had been taken care of, she knelt in the snow outside the shelter so she would be on Phillip's eye level. "Phillip, who is supposed to decide whether or not you leave?"

He didn't hesitate. "Daddy."

"That's right. So would it be fair of me to tell before he's had a chance to talk with you?"

Phillip ducked his head. "I guess not."

Ida glanced up at Ruth, then tipped Phillip's head up so she could look into his face. "I know you're both worried. I would be, too, if I were you. Just remember, we talked to Jesus about it this morning, and the Bible tells us He makes everything work out the way that is best for us."

The shadow of fear lifted from Ruth's eyes first, then a sunny smile broke out on her brother's face. "I'd better go play before Mrs. Pierce rings the bell."

By day's end, Ida felt grateful Cynthia had stayed beyond the morning. For some reason Ida didn't want to investigate, she seemed unable to concentrate. Usually she had no trouble listening to the first graders read while keeping an eye on the middle grades in case someone got fidgety and watching for signs of difficulty among the older students. Today it was all she could do to keep her mind focused on the lesson being recited. "I don't know what I would have done without you," she told Cynthia after the last student left. "I wouldn't have been much use alone."

Cynthia smiled gently. "I expected that. Was it too awful this morning?"

Ida checked to make sure no young ears hovered too closely and lowered her voice to a whisper. "I think it actually brought out the best in Mr. McEvan. I've never seen him more confident. She accused him of killing her daughter, and he refused to accept the blame."

"He's come a long way this winter," Cynthia observed. "You've done more for him in five months than Doug has been able to do in almost two years."

"Me?" Ida stared at her friend in amazement. "What have I had to do with it?"

"I don't know for sure, but you've certainly made a difference."

Ida just shook her head.

Cynthia tied her parka hood. "I don't think God is finished with you in Timothy McEvan's life. See you Sunday, if not before."

Ida stared at the closed door for a long time. Cynthia's comment made the second mention today of the deepening relationship between her and their neighbor. Ida knew her feelings for the widower hadn't made sense from the beginning. According to Ruth's earlier observation, the attraction was mutual. Timothy himself had as much as told his mother-in-law he was considering remarriage. Could it be possible?

She didn't pay much attention to Misty's progress on their way home. Her mind tumbled with possibilities. Nearing town, Ida realized trying to figure out what might happen would simply make her miserable. She prayed silently. "Father God, I don't know what Your plan is for Timothy and me. I've prayed for him as You directed, and I've done for him what I felt You wanted me to do when he turned to me for help. You know how much I care about him and his children. I trust You to accomplish your best in all of our lives. Please help me not to worry about it anymore." Peace gradually settled over her thoughts.

Ruth and Phillip met her early the next morning at the warm schoolhouse, where a fire blazed as usual in the barrel stove. Their faces beamed. "Dad told us we don't have to go," Phillip stated unnecessarily and threw his arms around Ida's neck in a stranglehold. "I'm so glad I don't have to go away from you."

"How do you feel, Ruth?" Ida looked over Phillip's head at his older sister.

"Relieved and glad to see Dad looking so happy. He's acting really different, and he even whistles like he used to before. . ." Her voice trailed off.

"Isn't it strange how some things can be like they used to, while other things will never be the same?" Ida asked softly.

Ruth's eyes softened. "I guess you kind of know what it's like."

That was Ida's only bright spot in the next four grueling days. Mrs. Carrington resented every moment standing between her and the next train out of the Peace River Country. Though it hardly seemed possible, she became more critical and demanding each day. Belle found herself confined to the bedroom after Mrs. Carrington's shriek of horror at discovering the kitten roamed the house at will. The second evening, Mr.

Carey didn't even stay at the table long enough to eat dessert. He excused himself with a nod toward Lucy and Ida that clearly excluded Mrs. Carrington. "Pardon me, ladies. I'm sure your pie would be right tasty, Mrs. Barry, but my innards aren't workin' right tonight. Not that your cooking is a'tall responsible," he added before shutting his door with an emphatic thud.

Ida and Lucy had all they could do to keep their expressions appropriately sober. Mrs. Carrington quickly filled the brief silence. "What a rude man! I'm surprised you have any business at all, Mrs. Barry, if you allow creatures like that to eat at your table."

Tuesday afternoon, a strange silence shrouded the boardinghouse when Ida came home from school. She tiptoed into the kitchen, where she found Lucy at the table with a cup of tea and her Bible. "It's so quiet," she whispered.

Lucy smiled. "I know. I've been enjoying it ever since the train left at noon." Her eyes turned wistful. "I just wish Mrs. Carrington could discover how good God wants to be to her, if she'll let Him."

"Sometimes I forget that myself," Ida admitted, cuddling Belle, who was purring delightedly at being released from confinement. "I know how I want things to turn out and I forget to trust Him." She reflected on the number of times in the past few days she'd felt frustrated over Timothy. They had chatted briefly on Sunday, but Ida saw no clues to confirm Ruth's and Cynthia's comments. Disappointment clutched at her each time she remembered. Each time it became easier to turn her thoughts into prayers for the man she'd come to love.

Lucy nodded understandingly. "You're not alone in that, dear. How would you like to join me here with your Bible? I've missed our morning discussions."

Quiet confidence seeped into Ida's soul during that hour. It stayed with her during the rest of the week at school, even when Ruth handed her a note on Thursday afternoon. "Dad asked me to give this to you this morning, and I forgot until now. I'm sorry."

"That's all right." She gave the girl a quick hug. "I'm sure it's nothing serious. Are you studying with Theo this afternoon?"

Ruth shook her head. "Dad asked me to come straight home. He needs me to keep the boys inside while he takes care of something. He didn't say what."

"He'll let you know if it's important," Ida reassured her. She waited until the last student had disappeared down the road before opening the paper that seemed to burn in her hand.

Dear Miss Thomas,

Please do me the honor of waiting at the schoolhouse after the children leave. I need to ask you something.

Timothy McEvan

She studied the masculine scrawl. *Why here? Why not at church on Sunday or the boardinghouse this evening? All I can do is wait,* she reminded herself. Knowing she wouldn't be able to concentrate on grading the older students' essays, she dipped some warm water from the pot on the back of the stove and began scrubbing desktops. The students probably wouldn't notice the difference, but it would keep her busy.

Half a dozen clean desks later, she heard a knock at the door. Timothy entered uncertainly. He looked reassured to see her there. "Thanks for waiting."

"I'm glad to help when I can." The words sounded stiff and formal, but what else could she say?

He cleared his throat several times before he could speak. "Miss Thomas, I feel like a fool for coming to you this way, but the more I pray about it, the more it seems like the right thing to do. Not that I don't want to; it just feels awkward since we haven't done hardly any courting." He stopped and studied the floor.

Ida slowly realized what he seemed to be trying to say. She waited, afraid he'd change his mind before he finished.

"The more I try to lead up to it easy-like, the more of a muddle I make." He looked straight into her eyes for the first time. "Miss Thomas, would you marry me?"

She felt like someone had just pulled the floor out from under her. While she'd hoped and prayed, she hadn't expected results this suddenly. Before she gave the answer she'd had waiting since Christmas, she wanted to hear something else. "Why?"

His expression didn't change, but she saw hurt in his eyes. "I'm sorry. I shouldn't have been—"

She grabbed his arm as he started to turn away. "I haven't answered you yet, Timothy." Her use of his name brought hope back into his face. "I have to know something first, though. Why do you want to marry me?"

"I need you," he stated simply.

Once again, she thought she knew what he meant, but she wanted to hear him say it before she committed herself. "Because you told your mother-in-law you'd find a mother for your children?"

It took a moment for her meaning to reach him. When it did, the tenderness she'd been watching for dawned in his eyes. He grasped both her hands with his farm-roughened fingers and looked directly into her eyes. "I need you more than they do." He stopped as though searching for just the right words. "Your faith gave me courage to find God again. Your gentle spirit has helped me find peace." Uncertainty clouded his face. "I'm still not saying it right."

"Why, Timothy, that was almost eloquent!" she teased gently, knowing he needed reassurance before his confidence totally crumbled. Yet she still felt compelled to search for more. "Are you sure friendship isn't enough?"

He dropped her hands with a helpless sigh. "I'm sure." He looked into her eyes again. "I need you with me for always, or at least as long as God leaves us both on earth."

His last words reminded Ida of the difficult path he'd come and the hurdles still facing him. "How can you be certain? It hasn't been that long since you lost Janet." She didn't want to hurt him by seeming reluctant, but she had to know his heart.

He claimed her hands once more. "In June, it will have been two long years. I'm finally ready to let myself care again. Christmas Day, you said you'd fallen in love with someone who has a family, and I've dared to hope I'm the one. Have you changed your mind?"

She felt the heat creeping up her neck and cheeks while she shook her head. "You don't know how often I've wished I hadn't said that."

"If you hadn't, I probably wouldn't be standing here now."

She looked into his eyes, waiting for the explanation. "Why?"

"I don't have much to offer a bride. My farm isn't much yet. I have three children who can be difficult. We're always going to remember and talk about Janet, Daniel, Sam, and Benjamin. In other words, I'm just a poor widower with three children and a lot of memories. You gave me hope we could be a whole family again."

Ida pulled her hands free so she could wrap her arms around him. "I'm just an orphaned schoolteacher with a lot of memories. I guess that's why I loved you so quickly."

He slowly returned her embrace. "Say that again," he whispered into her hair.

"I love you, Timothy McEvan."

"Does that mean you'll marry me?" He smiled gently, his eyes twinkling like Phillip's.

She teased him back. "Only if you love me, too."

A solid glow replaced the twinkles. "Always."

Chapter 16

I da peeked out from behind the curtain that had been strung across one corner of the "meeting cabin" at the Spencers' farm. Just as quickly, Lucy pulled her back. "Stop that! He'll see you," she whispered fiercely.

"How can he? He isn't here," Ida whispered back.

Lucy pulled Ida around to face her. "Ida Thomas, it's still ten minutes before the ceremony is to start, and you know how muddy these roads are with spring runoff. Timothy isn't going to change his mind now."

Ida forced a smile. "I know. I just want to see him."

Lucy adjusted the long, filmy veil. "After today, you'll be able to do just that every day for the rest of your lives. Shush now and calm yourself."

For the first time in three days, Ida allowed herself to sit idle. Nina and Cynthia had decided school should be canceled Friday to allow her time to finish preparations for her wedding, as well as to get her belongings moved to the McEvan farm. She and Lucy had finished her rose-toned wedding dress on Friday. Ida had felt the colored fabric would be more serviceable later than white. Lucy found some handmade cream lace in one of her storage trunks along with the cream-colored veil she had worn at her own first wedding.

Saturday, Ruth and Ida had moved furniture in the McEvans' tiny two-room cabin. Timothy had shared a room with the two boys, while Ruth occupied the other room. A curtain now divided Ruth's old room into two cubicles. An addition to the cabin was planned for later in the summer, but for now Ruth would share her already minimal space with her brothers. When Ida apologized for the third time for making Ruth give up her room, the teenager stopped tucking in the sheets around Phillip's bed to look straight at her. "I've prayed for a long time that God would let you be our next mother. Why should I complain since He's answered my prayer?" Tears welled in Ida's eyes remembering Ruth's sincerity. How she wished her own mother could share this day with them! Busyness had kept thoughts of Mom in the foggy background of her mind. Now emotion threatened to overwhelm. What would she have thought of Timothy?

A handkerchief dabbing at her cheeks brought her back to reality. "I didn't tell you to start crying and turn your eyes all red!" Lucy's scolding brought a shaky smile to Ida's face. "That's better. What is your bridegroom going to think of you crying on your wedding day?"

Ida recalled his gentle smile on previous occasions when her emotions had overflowed. "He'd just give me his handkerchief. He's used to tears by now." In the three months since he'd proposed, they'd spent every possible moment together, talking while they cleaned the barn, repaired the corral, cooked supper, or just sat in Lucy's parlor. Her love for him grew as he continued to struggle to share his heart. While they worked to make sure the children didn't feel left out, Lucy, Nina, and Cynthia worked equally hard to give them plenty of time for private discussions, as well. Despite their short and strange courtship, Ida felt friendship and love had grown together. They had become as much best friends as sweethearts.

The door rattled. Before Ida could get up for another peek, Lucy pushed her firmly back into the chair. "I'll check this time." She moved the curtain slightly, then looked over her shoulder with a broad smile. "He's here now. You can relax."

Ida heard the beloved, familiar tread approaching their cubicle moments before Cynthia's stern, "Don't you dare, Timothy McEvan. She'll be out when it's time."

It seemed to take forever for everyone to get settled, then Lionel started playing on his guitar "All the Way My Saviour Leads Me." Cynthia had offered to have Doug move the piano to the Spencers' cabin so she could play a traditional wedding march. Though touched by her offer, Ida and Timothy had agreed the hymn would be most meaningful for their wedding. When their friends started singing, Lucy finally allowed Ida to step out of hiding. Only a half dozen steps separated her from her groom and the visiting preacher who would unite them. Timothy's beaming smile made the effort to surprise him worth it. She couldn't have stopped her own answering grin if she'd wanted to.

The preacher spoke briefly of the love between man and wife being an earthly symbol of the love between Christ and His church. Timothy and Ida gazed at each other throughout the short sermon, silently giving and accepting commitment. She revelled in the gentle affection in his eyes. For once, no hint of pain hovered there. Each of them had come a long way to find the other. Together they stood as testimony to God's ability to turn heartache into peace.

"Do you, Ida Thomas, take this man to be your wedded husband, to love and comfort him, for richer or for poorer, in sickness and in health, until death do you part?" The preacher's formal question brought an answer straight from her heart.

"I do."

Author's Note

On November 11, 1930, the town of Dawson Creek completed moving its buildings to a new location two and one-half miles northeast to be nearer the approaching railway line. Details of the move are similar to descriptions in this book. Passenger service ended at the town of Hythe until January 15, 1931, when Dawson Creek's first passenger train arrived. All other events and characters in this book are fictitious.

Beckoning Streams

To Colleen L. Reece
Thanks for your encouragement, suggestions, and friendship.

Chapter 1

Flanked by two men she had known since childhood, Ruth McEvan choked back the urge to flee the schoolroom crowded with strangers. Nervously, she checked the waistband of her dark green knee-length skirt to make sure it hadn't folded over and that her green print blouse remained well tucked in. She hoped her red shoulder-length hair hadn't been too badly mussed by the ride into town in Mr. Pierce's buggy. Her knotted stomach told her this meeting couldn't possibly bring good news. To her best recollection, there had never been a gathering of all the teachers and trustees in the district before. Each school had been managed by its own trustees and taught by teachers selected by those trustees, a system that had worked well for Peace River area farm families since a handful of parents had opened the first school twenty years ago. The provincial Department of Education had provided few guidelines and even less financial help over the years, leaving each school relatively autonomous. A meeting such as this could only signal changes.

She accepted the chair indicated by her own school's superintendent, Lars Harper, and tried to ignore the tension threatening to turn her stomach inside out. During the past seven years, her little school had become her life. She'd been just fourteen when it had opened on a bit of land donated by her dad, built by five nearby families, and taught by a petite, gentle lady from the city, Ida Thomas. Ruth knew she hadn't been an easy student in the beginning. A river accident had claimed her mother and three of her brothers less than two years previously, leaving her confused, angry, and responsible for helping her devastated father care for a toddler and a first-grader. Miss Thomas's compassion had worked its way past Ruth's bitterness and helped her begin to accept the tragic changes life had thrust upon her. Friendship had gradually developed between the two.

Ruth's dad, Timothy McEvan, had also been drawn to the schoolteacher. Ruth had rejoiced to see twinkles return to his eyes as he had spent increasing amounts of time with Ida Thomas. At the end of Ida's first year of teaching, they had married. It seemed natural for Ruth and her brothers to call their dad's new wife "Mom." Her caring heart provided the tender mothering they needed. The boys had been young enough that they didn't feel any conflicting loyalties. Ruth envied them their lack of memories. Her own memories of their mother and her twin brother, Daniel, sometimes brought feelings that she was betraying them by loving her new mother. She still couldn't understand why God hadn't prevented the accident. As she'd done often in recent months, she pulled her thoughts away from the unsettling question.

A year after Timothy and Ida's marriage, Ruth had graduated from the country school. Ida had encouraged her to continue her education in the recently established high school classes in town. Two years later, Ida had left teaching to have her baby, and Ruth had been asked to take her place. The trustees' request had come as a shock since Ruth had had no formal teacher training. But they'd insisted they had confidence in her abilities, so she'd taken the job.

Her lack of education weighed heavily in her thoughts as a well-dressed, balding man at the front of the room called the meeting to order. "As near as I can tell, we have a representative from each of the schools in the area. Seems like schools have sprouted around here like quack grass." Several chuckled at the intended joke. Ruth wasn't sure she liked the comparison. "The situation is this, ladies and gentlemen. There are thirty-nine schools around the area, not counting Dawson Creek's high school. Some of our schools are well funded while others are just getting by. A few of us have been talking amongst ourselves and consulting with the Department of Education and we've come up with a solution that we hope will put all schools on an even footing without overtaxing certain districts. The plan is to consolidate all our schools, which should make them easier to administrate, as well. Gustav Olafson will explain how this proposal will work."

A tall, sparse man moved to the blackboard. In a deep voice that carried well, he explained as he drew a map of the area south of the Peace River. "This," he explained, making an X near the center of the board, "represents Dawson Creek. Rolla is here." He placed a mark northwest of the first and another to the southwest. "And this is Pouce Coupe. Basically, the South Peace River block will be divided into three sections. All the students in a given area will attend a single school until they're old enough for high school." Three lines illustrated his point. "As you can see, a town is located in each area, giving us a logical location for the schools. Since Dawson Creek already has the high school, that town will have two facilities."

"What about the teachers?" one man toward the back wanted to know.

The bald man took over. "With so many students in each area, we'll certainly need more than one teacher for each school. Those with certification who have taught the longest will have first chance at those jobs."

Ruth tried to ignore the feeling of loss that hit her like a blizzard. Her school gave her worth and purpose. Without it, she'd be nothing more than a spinster stranded in her parents' home. Nevertheless, she couldn't crumble. Not here in public.

The other trustee from her school, Doug Pierce, lifted his hand for recognition. "Is this plan mandatory for everyone?"

She could have hugged him for asking, even though she knew the answer wouldn't change anything. It felt good to have someone else fighting for what had suddenly become so precious.

The bald man smiled benignly. "Of course not. However, the proposed four schools will be funded by district taxes. Independent schools will not be eligible for this funding, so parents would end up paying twice for their children's education if they tried to maintain an independent facility."

"When will the new plan go into effect?" Mr. Pierce pushed for more information.

"We hope to have facilities ready for the first week in September. We'll use existing buildings in Rolla, Pouce Coupe, and Dawson Creek, but they'll need additions and improvements. Several carpenters will be kept busy throughout the summer." His tone implied pride in providing employment.

"What about transportation?" someone else inquired. "Many of the youngsters in our area will have a four- or five-mile drive to get to one of the new schools."

Ruth didn't bother trying to follow the answer. While some country schools might get a reprieve due to distance, hers was one of the closest to town. She had less than three more months of the job she cherished. Then, as a result of a single bureaucratic decision, she'd be tossed aside like vegetable peelings.

Doug Pierce didn't waste any time leaving the meeting. With a firm hand on her elbow, he guided her through the crowd out to his buggy. He didn't bother trying to make small talk as they drove home. His sympathetic silence reminded her of his son, Theodore.

She let her thoughts linger on the young man she hadn't seen since Christmas. In the months immediately following the McEvans' tragedy, Theo Pierce had proven himself the truest kind of friend. Though Ruth had tried to push him out of her life along with everyone else, he'd refused to leave. He didn't force his way into her confidence; he'd merely waited until she felt ready to talk. Doug Pierce had spent hours helping Timothy McEvan around the farm, and Theo often accompanied his dad. He'd sit at the table with his textbooks while Ruth cleaned, cooked, and mended for her father and brothers. If she started talking, he'd close his books and give her his undivided attention. If she didn't feel like talking, he studied silently. When he had left the Dawson Creek area for medical school in Edmonton five years ago, she felt like part of her went with him. He'd kept his promise to write to her regularly and always made time for a visit on his infrequent trips home. If only he were around tonight! She visualized his dark, gentle eyes that seemed able to read her heart before she'd found words to describe her feelings, his straight black hair, and tall skinniness. She gave herself a mental shake. Theo wasn't here and wouldn't be for quite some time. She had to cope alone.

Mr. Pierce reined the horse to a stop in front of the McEvan farmhouse. Climbing out of the buggy, he reached up to assist her. Retaining his grasp on her arm, he seemed to struggle for words. "Miss McEvan, Ruth." Thick dusk obscured his face, but Ruth heard the compassion in his voice. "I'm really sorry for what happened tonight. If there were a way to avoid closing your school, we would have found it."

"I know." She tried to put a smile into her tone.

"You're not only an excellent teacher but a very special person. Cynthia and I think of you more as a daughter than a neighbor. If we can help you in any way, even just by listening, please let us know." He hugged her tightly. "You need to talk with your dad, so I won't linger. Just don't forget we love you."

Lamplight flickering in a window indicated Dad and Mom had waited up for her. She opened the front door uncertainly, not sure how to explain the evening's events. Her parents sat in their favorite places at the end of the table nearest the stove, holding hands. Mom's waist-length hair hung down her back the way Dad liked it, firelight from the stove giving the blond strands a ruddy glow similar to Dad's rumpled curls. Dad let Ruth hang her coat on the hook and remove her boots before asking, "How was the meeting?"

Ruth met his blue-eyed gaze directly. "My school is being closed." She fought to say the words without choking up.

Mom instantly jumped to her feet and reached toward Ruth. "My poor girl." Though several inches shorter, she pulled Ruth's head down onto her shoulder in a purely maternal gesture of comfort.

Her caring proved to be Ruth's undoing. The tears she had choked back for hours now poured out in a hot torrent. A strong arm wrapped around her back as she felt both herself and Mom enfolded in Dad's embrace. In their comfort the intensity of her feelings ebbed. Mom led her to the table. "Do you feel like talking about it?"

She didn't really, but they deserved an explanation. She outlined the proposed changes much as the bald man had done.

Dad's expression looked thunderous. "You mean we're being forbidden to keep our own school?"

His defense of her school felt so good, a shaky smile stretched her lips. "No. They say the goal of the plan is to keep taxes low and schools well funded. If parents are willing to support an independent school in addition to paying taxes, no one will object."

His temper abated as quickly as it flashed. "I have to admit it makes sense." He shrugged. "Pierce and Lars Harper have been trying to get more funding from the Department of Education, and I'm sure other schools have been doing the same."

Mom patted Ruth's arm. "It still hurts, though, doesn't it?"

Ruth nodded, tears scalding her eyes again. "I feel so useless."

"Why is that, Ruthie?" Dad's work-roughened fingers stroked her hair.

"What am I going to do once school is over?"

He grinned mischievously. "Rest, plant a garden, read, make pies."

She couldn't see the humor. "In other words, sit around like an idiot. Where am I going to find another job?"

"Why do you need one?"

She looked for understanding in their eyes, but saw only compassion. "I can't be dependent on you forever!"

"Why not?" Dad looked almost pleased.

"Because I'm a grown woman, that's why." Ruth struggled to keep her voice low enough to avoid waking the children. "You have the younger ones to take care of. I should be helping, not adding to the burden."

"You're never a burden, sweetie. In fact, I'm honored to be able to take care of you. That's my role as your dad. If the school hadn't needed you, I wouldn't have wanted you to work in the first place."

Ruth shook her head, desperation making her voice shrill. "You don't understand."

Mom placed a hand on Dad's arm to stop his reply. "Perhaps not. But because you're hurting, we hurt, too. We only want to help if we can. Can you trust us for that much?"

With effort, Ruth reined in her emotions and nodded. She shouldn't expect anyone to understand what she couldn't explain. No words she could think of would adequately describe the ache filling her chest. She'd lost more than a school or a job. She'd lost her identity.

Chapter 2

Ruth left for school the next morning before her brothers finished the chores. She needed to be alone and counted on the extra hour before class to subdue her still roiling emotions. If only the meeting had been scheduled for a Friday or Saturday evening, rather than a Thursday. Now she had to face her students before she'd had a chance to adjust to the news. The proposed changes that monopolized her thoughts probably wouldn't be common knowledge for another couple of days. Even then, she had no intention of discussing them in her classroom. It would be up to parents to inform and reassure their offspring. Besides, she doubted any of them would be nearly as distraught as she felt.

She paused for a moment on the step in front of the schoolhouse door to look around. Bright sunshine promised change in the snow-blanketed landscape. Spring had always been her favorite time of year as snow gave way to dark earth, sprouting vegetation, and new leaves. But today, sunshine didn't bring the familiar tingle inside. It only reminded her that the last day of school hovered only ten weeks away.

Opening the door, Ruth stepped into the familiar room. Desks sat in tidy rows facing a blackboard on the far wall. Her own desk occupied the center front of the room between the blackboard and her students' desks. Off to the left, a small stove radiated warmth from the fire Dad had built earlier in the morning, as he had every chilly day for seven years. She hung her coat and scarf on the highest peg beside the door. In forty-five minutes, the short wall from the door to the corner would be filled with winter wraps. She'd never been able to figure out how her fourteen students could fill two rows of ten pegs each and still squabble over who had stolen whose peg.

She hoped today would be a peaceful one; she didn't think she'd be able to cope with any petty disputes or recalcitrant youngsters. "Please, just cooperate," she whispered pleadingly to the empty desks.

The routine tasks of preparing for her day brought a feeling of order. She organized papers to be graded, found a passage of Scripture for everyone to read together, wiped the blackboard with a damp cloth, and wrote the daily arithmetic quiz in place. At least for today, she was still a teacher.

Doug and Cynthia Pierce's thirteen-year-old daughter, Sara, arrived first. "I wanted to get here early so I could give you this," she explained with a shy smile. As much as her brother, Theo, resembled their dad, she looked like her mother. She had the same silky-looking straight black hair and gentle blue eyes. Though Cynthia stood about the same average height as her husband, Sara looked far more petite. She held a wrapped package toward her teacher.

Ruth accepted the bundle. "What is it?"

"Just some cookies." Pink tinged the girl's cheeks. "Dad told us what happened at the meeting last night, and I wanted to let you know we still love you."

Her gentle affection brought tears to Ruth's eyes, though she blinked them away quickly. "You don't know how much you've helped me," she managed to say and let a hug communicate the rest of her feelings.

Sara seemed to understand. Her eyes lit with merry twinkles. "There's also a letter from Theo in there."

Ruth felt like sunshine had finally broken out from behind a cloud. "Just for that, you'll get top marks on your next essay."

Sara just grinned and scampered outside to join the Harper and Spencer girls, who were giggling together. Ruth wanted to rip the package open immediately. However, she'd enjoy Theo's letter more if she could read it privately and uninterrupted. She slid the box under the edge of her desk. Just knowing what was in it would add cheer to her entire day.

Despite her hopes for a tranquil day, spring sunshine had given everyone the fidgets. Papers rustled, pencils broke, and books dropped. Just an hour before lunch, indignant shrieks shattered the tense semi-silence. "Phillip McEvan, I hate you!" Little blond Julie Harper glared at the innocent-looking redhead behind her.

Ruth looked up from guiding Audrey Spencer through a word list in time to see Julie slap Phillip with all the force of her ten-year-old indignation. "Miss Harper?" Ida had always said treating students like adults often brought out their best behavior.

"He pulled my braid, Miss McEvan, just when I had my penmanship page almost finished. Now it's totally ruined and I hate him." The girl dissolved into tears.

"Mr. McEvan?" Ruth looked to her young brother for an explanation.

"I was just teasing!" Phillip's blue eyes, so much like their father's, filled with reproach. Rather than having a typically redheaded temper, thirteen-year-old Phillip approached life as though it were an adventure, everyone a friend. His casual approach to responsibility and good behavior gave his parents and his older sister many moments of despair. Ruth knew from experience the futility of trying to discuss the matter with him. His logic perceived the problem to be Julie's for overreacting. Similar situations in the past had taught her to give his seemingly boundless energy the outlet it required.

"I think you need to go outside and chop some kindling for the stove, Mr. McEvan. Julie, let's look at your page and see what can be done to fix it." A few rubs with an eraser eliminated the errant marks. As usual, the problem hadn't been nearly as severe as Julie's outburst had indicated. Her Norwegian family's emphasis on neatness gave the child more reasons than most for emotional displays. Anything that threatened the tidiness of her little world brought on tears or temper.

She'll learn soon enough how untidy life can be, Ruth commented to herself with a twist of bitterness, which she quickly squelched. Best to concentrate on the matter at hand, improving the six year old's reading skills.

An exhausting four-and-a-half hours later, she waved the last of her students off toward home, then snatched the box from beneath her desk. Lying on top of delicious-smelling oatmeal cookies was an envelope marked in familiar handwriting. *Please give this to Ruth McEvan*, it said. With the cookies in one hand and the letter in the other, she settled herself in the sunbeam streaming through the open doorway.

> *My dear friend,*
>
> *I take a few moments during this endless night on duty to let you know I've been thinking of you. I confess to envy as I consider spring coming to the Peace River Country. Every year I've been away, I've intensely missed our tramps in the bush hunting pussy willows and other signs of spring. If you get a moment, would you take some pussy willows to my mom for me? Is the creek high enough to cover the beaver dam? Remember the year it got so high you couldn't even tell the dam was there? That's kind of the way I feel around here. There's so much to be done, I sometimes wonder if it's really me taking temperatures, bandaging wounds, and listening to heartbeats. But I'm not unhappy or complaining. This is excellent training for whatever God wants me to do next. As Mrs. Barry's favorite Scripture verse says, 'The steps of a good man are ordered by the Lord.'*
>
> *Your last letter was wonderful. I love hearing what all your students are doing. I know you're teaching them well. While I enjoy reading about the happy things in your life, I hope you'll never hesitate to*

*let me know if things aren't going so well. Though I can't be there in
person for you, please remember I'm no less your friend now than I've
been in the past.*

*Oops. I hear one of the nurses calling, so I'll have to close for now.
I'm praying for you.*

Your pal,
Theo

Ruth let the pages drop into her lap. The words brought comfort even
while they made her miss him even more. He'd understand her feelings,
maybe even help her make sense of them. Right now she wouldn't even be
able to find the words to write to Theo. If God were so determined to let
this happen to her, why hadn't He made sure her best friend were around to
help her cope? The sour thought startled her. When had it become so easy
to blame God for everything?

She stuffed the letter into her satchel, made sure the dampers in the stove
were closed, shut the schoolhouse door firmly, and took a thin trail through
the bush toward home. Having worn this trail as a student in an effort to avoid
her brothers on their daily treks to and from school, she usually enjoyed its
solitude in her transition from teacher to sister and daughter. Today the pleasure had vanished. In its place she felt anger, betrayal, abandonment, even
confusion. Her trail joined the lane to their house just before the farmyard.
Dad was working with a spirited young horse in the corrals beside the barn to
her left. He waved and smiled in greeting, the fabric of his shirt stretching
tightly across his muscled chest. It felt good to see him so happy. In the two
years immediately following her mother's death, he had lost so much weight
his clothes had hung on him like a stick scarecrow's garb. Grief had stooped
him to almost normal height. Several months of Ida's love and cooking had
finally straightened him to the broad, smiling giant of her childhood.

"How was school?" he called, letting the horse roam the corral while he
bent over to lean his elbows on the rails. His rusty hair, which he'd passed
on to Ruth and her brothers, lay in rumpled disarray from his efforts to control the skittish horse.

She quickened her steps to join him. They didn't often get time to visit,
just the two of them. "Tiring."

"I didn't expect the day to be easy. I hope Phillip didn't make things
more difficult."

His perception took her by surprise. "Actually, they were all on the edge
of wild today. Spring sunshine does that."

"Phillip?" he insisted.

"He pulled Julie's braid this morning, though according to him the resulting war was her fault for slapping him."

Timothy chuckled. "That sounds like Phillip. What then?"

"I sent him outside to chop kindling. He came back with dirt streaks all over his pants. I didn't bother to ask what he'd been doing. After that, a muddy leaf just 'accidentally' landed on Julie's desk. He knows she's fanatically neat, so he delights in seeing how many ways he can find to make her mad."

"From what you and your mother have told me, it doesn't take much." His blue eyes twinkled.

She scowled at him. "Now you look like Phillip. Maybe I ought to get Mom to take the switch after you when he misbehaves."

He shrugged, now looking innocent. "Why me? I'm just his dad." Pushing back from the log rails, he straightened and reached for the reins he'd been using. "I'd better get back to work. I want to have Star ready to help me with planting. If the snow keeps melting like it has so far, I could be out in the fields by the end of next week."

Ruth continued leaning on the corral, watching Star. As far back as she could remember, she had loved horses. They had a grace she didn't see in any other animal, and all she'd met so far seemed genuinely affectionate. Star lunged at the end of the reins, not yet ready to accept Dad's direction. He hung on patiently until the animal settled.

Wearily, she turned toward the house. Once a simple two-bedroom cabin, it now boasted additions front and back. The front one had been built the summer after Dad and Mom's wedding and contained a porch and two bedrooms, one for Ruth and one for the boys. The back one had followed the birth of Beth, who was now close to two. It contained another two small bedrooms used by Beth and three-year-old Timmy. Ruth had offered to share her room when Beth grew old enough to be moved out of what was now called "the baby room," a cubicle near Mom and Dad's room that Ruth and the boys had shared until their rooms had been built.

"Thanks for the offer," Mom had said, "but you're an adult now and need your own space. The pigs sold well last fall, so we can afford it."

This afternoon, Ruth blessed Mom's wisdom. It felt heavenly to shut the rest of the world out for a little while. A stack of arithmetic tests and English compositions overflowed accusingly from her satchel, but she ignored them. She lay back on her bed, staring at the ceiling, finally letting feelings come to the surface. What if she ended up an old maid, living with her parents even after her hair had turned gray? That seemed to be all the future held for her. Guilt added to her gloom. Sure, Dad had said he'd consider it an honor to continue to support her, but had he considered the length of time he'd probably have to do it? She felt as if she stood at the edge of an endless progression of bleak years without purpose, fulfillment, or even identity.

Another alternative came to mind. She fished under her bed for the box in which she stored letters she wanted to keep. Most of them bore Theo's handwriting. Near the bottom lay one with perfectly scripted words, still holding a delicate scent. Ruth's earliest memory of Grandmother Carrington was seeing the stately, well-dressed lady descending the steps of Dawson Creek's first passenger train, her expression looking like she'd just stepped into a nightmare. Without even greeting her son-in-law or grandchildren, she'd announced she'd come to "take poor Janet's only remaining children back to civilization where they can be raised properly." Ruth had been sure her dad would give in until she saw the look on Ida's face. Though no formal courtship had yet developed between Ida and Timothy, the schoolteacher had looked ready to give her blood to keep the McEvan children in Dawson Creek. She'd even ridden out to the McEvan farm alone in an uncharacteristic breach of etiquette. Ruth remembered her kneeling in the snow to reassure Phillip as they'd passed her on their way to school. They'd never found out what she'd said to their dad, but Grandmother had returned to Toronto alone. Nevertheless, she'd written to Ruth at least twice a year, offering every enticement she could present to persuade her granddaughter to come east. Her most recent letter had arrived last week.

My dear granddaughter,

I trust this letter will reach you in time for your twenty-second birthday. However, since your father insists that you live far beyond the reach of civilization, I won't be surprised if it is late. Please know I wish you the happiest of days.

Since I have received no notice of your impending marriage, I have to assume your father has been as remiss in this area as in all others relating to your growth into a young lady. Should you decide to accept my long-standing offer to come live with me, I can assure you there will be no lack of young men seeking your hand. I'm sure I could arrange a marriage for you with one of our city's wealthiest families.

If you prefer to further your education for a couple of years first, I could arrange entrance for you into one of our best schools, despite your age.

I love you, dear, and truly wish to see you as happy as you can be. Your loving grandmother.

Ruth stared at the fine paper, for the first time seeing beyond Grandmother's continuing disapproval of Dad. Maybe she should go east. At least she could further her education. She couldn't imagine living in the city forever, but maybe she could tolerate a year or two. Yet the thought twisted her heart. She'd miss seeing young Timmy and Beth grow up, being part of life on the farm she loved, watching her brothers become young men. Which would be worse, alienation from everything she knew and loved or remaining helplessly useless in a familiar environment?

The impossible choice brought a wordless exclamation of frustration to her lips. Why did everything have to be so complicated? She flung the box back under her bed, then yanked a work dress over her head in place of her teaching clothes. Thinking wasn't getting her anywhere. She might as well make herself useful in the kitchen.

Mom sat at the table peeling apples. "Other than dealing with your brother, how did your day go?" Her understanding smile mellowed Ruth's mood.

"Not too bad. How did you hear about Phillip already?"

"I asked him about his day when he got home. He told me you'd sent him outside twice today."

"Spring has them all wound up," Ruth observed, hoping her tone wouldn't betray her tension. "Would you like me to make biscuits?"

"That would be perfect with the stew I have in the oven." Mom wiped the back of her hand across her forehead. A few blond locks straggled wearily around her face, having come loose from the graceful twist at the back of her head. "I'd planned to get this pie done earlier in the day, but I haven't had much energy. It's been all I could do to keep up with the little ones." Her usually vivid green eyes appeared faded.

Concern stabbed at Ruth. "Are you feeling all right?"

"Pretty good, all things considering." Whatever she had been planning to say was interrupted by a small, howling red-haired boy. "What is it, Timmy? Stop crying so Mommy can understand what you're saying."

Between sobs, the three year old managed to talk. "I just wanted to play with Gweggy's twuck, but he hitted me!"

"Let's ask Greggy about this, okay?" Mom scooped Timmy into her arms and headed purposefully toward the bedroom.

Ruth heard scraps of the conversation, but didn't pay much attention.

Altercations like this were common. Timmy tried valiantly to keep up with his older brothers, but they didn't want to be bothered with a toddler. Greg had been the baby of the family until Timmy had been born and then Beth just a year later. Though proud of the babies, neither of the older boys had much patience with the curious little ones who managed to investigate everything in the house. She formed one last biscuit from the leftover dough and set the full pan over the warming oven, ready to be baked as soon as the stew pot came out. In only a few more minutes, she had the pastry mixed, rolled out, and folded into two pie plates. After peeling and chopping the apples Mom had started to prepare, she mixed them with cinnamon and a touch of sugar and filled both pies, which she covered with another layer of pastry. The stew could simmer on the back of the stove while the biscuits and pies baked.

Mom returned just as Ruth shut the oven door. "Thanks, Ruth. I didn't intend for you to have to cook supper after a full day at school." She sank wearily into the rocking chair in the corner, Timmy snuggled against her shoulder.

"I used to have to do this all the time," Ruth reminded her, "and I didn't have stew waiting, either."

"I've often wondered how you kept up with your studies so well with all you had to handle here at home."

"I guess a person just does what has to be done." Ruth shrugged.

"Scripture does say God never gives us more than we can bear," Mom replied. His feelings soothed, Timmy wiggled off her lap, though Beth quickly took his place. Almost from birth, she'd been a cuddly baby and still never lost a chance for a hug or a snuggle.

Ruth silently set bowls around the table. There it was again—the reminder that the all-powerful God she'd been taught to love had betrayed her. Sure, she'd survived, but His lack of action that day at the river still felt like a burden heavier than she could carry. He didn't seem prepared to bestir Himself to save her school, either. When she needed Him most, He became remote, hidden behind lofty-sounding Scripture verses. The anger felt so intense, she glanced over to see if Mom had noticed, but the two in the rocking chair were almost asleep.

Dad came inside just as she lifted the biscuits from the oven. "Smells heavenly in here." He breathed in deeply, then leaned over to kiss his wife.

She stirred, her eyes fluttering open. They brightened to their normal color as she saw the big, red-haired man leaning over her. "Hi, honey."

Dad studied her intently. "How're you feeling?"

"Pretty good after a short snooze." Mom pulled his head down for a long kiss.

A silly grin played around his lips. "Hmmm. That's quite a welcome." Concern replaced the grin. "I don't like to see you so tired, though."

Her eyes glowed with the special light meant only for him. "You don't need to start worrying just yet."

"Can't help it," Dad muttered, turning toward the wash basin.

The undercurrent more than words or actions seemed familiar to Ruth. Dad's fretting. Mom's weariness. No explanation presented itself. She glanced at Mom stroking Beth's blond curls with a look of supreme happiness. How would it feel to be so cherished by a husband, so fulfilled as a mother?

Dad's arrival brought the three boys barrelling from the bedroom, chattering excitedly. Dad tossed Timmy into the air, rumpled Greg's hair, and thumped Phillip's shoulder. "And how are my two scholars? Did you make Ruth's day a good one?" He winked at his daughter.

All three boys tried to talk at once while Dad herded them toward the basin to wash their hands for supper. Ruth's doldrums lifted as the family settled around the table. Phillip and Greg bantered back and forth as usual, keeping the adults laughing. Dad praised the biscuits. Mom complimented the pie filling. Before Timmy left the kitchen, he held his arms up to Ruth for a quick hug and Beth copied him. Their simple affection left Ruth with a smile as she washed dishes. Nothing in her life had been predictable since that day at the river. Things were changing again, but she still had a family who needed her. Their love would have to be enough for now.

Chapter 3

"A re you ready, Ruth?" Mom called from just outside the closed bedroom door.

Ruth made no effort to move off the bed where she had lain for the last couple of hours. Though exhausted from two nights with little sleep, her mind hadn't slowed down enough to let her rest. Whatever she'd been scheduled to do, she didn't feel up to it.

"Ruth?" Mom pushed the door open gently. "What's the matter? We're supposed to be at the Harpers' bonfire party in thirty minutes."

"I think I'll just stay home." Ruth kept her gaze focused on the ceiling.

"It might be good for you to go." Mom lowered herself gently onto the edge of the bed. "I know you feel like being alone, but you'll just lay here and think. An evening out in the fresh air could be just what you need to help you sleep tonight."

Ruth doubted Mom's logic, but knew better than to argue. She pushed herself into a sitting position. "Maybe so. It will just take me a minute to change." A denim skirt that reached several inches past her knees and a navy-and-white striped blouse made a comfortable outfit. The long, green wool shawl Mom had given her for Christmas several years ago would keep off the evening's chill. Since spring thaw conditions required rubber boots, she pulled on a pair of thick navy socks. A brush brought some semblance of order to her wavy hair.

The rest of the family had already piled into the wagon when Mom and Ruth came out of the house. Dad helped Ruth onto the plank, benchlike seat near the back of the wagon and Mom onto the front seat with him. Phillip and Greg sat with Ruth while Timmy and Beth played in some straw between the two planks. A cloudless sky indicated perfect weather for an evening outdoor party. Dusk wouldn't intrude until around nine o'clock. Only dirty patches of unmelted snow and a chilly breeze provided reminders that spring had only just begun.

Ruth ignored Phillip and Greg's conversation about a tree fort they wanted to build. A feeling of isolation settled around her like a heavy wool blanket. *This is what the rest of your life will be like*, she told herself. *You might as well get used to it.*

A mere thirty-minute ride brought them to James and Ruby Harper's well-ordered farmyard. A two-story farmhouse stood off to the left of the driveway that continued toward a massive barn. Just a couple hundred yards behind the farmhouse, a small cabin peeked out from behind some trees. It had been James and Ruby's original home and was now occupied by their oldest son, Jim, and his wife, Norma. Across the driveway from the house, a large area had been cleared where a number of people already milled around a crackling blaze.

Jim came running from the barn to greet the newcomers. "Good evening, Mr. and Mrs. McEvan. If you'd like to join the others at the fire, I'll take care of your horses." He lifted his hat toward Mom and then Ruth.

"Thanks," Dad replied, handing Jim the reins. Jumping down from the wagon, he lifted Mom down, then handed her the basket of cookies she'd brought. Phillip leaped over the side to go join a muddy soccer game near the barn. Greg waited until Dad had helped Ruth to the ground, then handed Beth and Timmy down. Despite her mood, his thoughtfulness made Ruth smile. At ten, he already resembled what she remembered of Daniel.

Mom's basket of cookies joined the array of baked goodies on a long table made of rough planks laid over sawhorses. Ruth followed her family to the logs arranged like benches around the fire. With all the people who had come, she found it easy to remain unnoticed, which was just how she wanted it. She didn't feel like socializing, though watching everyone else gave her something neutral to think about.

Her school superintendent stood talking with his brother near the fire. Lars Harper's slender frame appeared short and emaciated beside James's stocky, broad-shouldered height. Lars had straight blond hair, but James had only a fringe around his ears. James appeared to do most of the talking while Lars listened.

Both Harper farms had become large, successful enterprises. Lars and his grown son, Jed, raised some of the best horses in the country, while James and his son, Jim, were developing a dairy herd and increasing their pasture and cultivated acreage annually. The fuel for tonight's bonfire had come from their continual clearing efforts. Both Jed and Jim had been among Ruth's first classmates when the school had opened. They had only stayed a year, however, choosing the next fall to become full partners in their parents' farms.

Jim's younger brother, Justin, had graduated from the country school in its second year, though he hadn't followed Mrs. McEvan's encouragement to go on to high school. Instead, he'd found a job in Dawson Creek's telegraph office and moved into town soon after. To Ruth's surprise, he'd come to the party tonight. His matching pants and vest with a white shirt seemed rather dressy for the evening's activity, but that was Justin. Fancy clothes suited his long-legged, slender frame well. He kept his blond hair carefully slicked back at all times. In the five years he'd been working in town, he'd gradually assumed sophisticated mannerisms. Some people said he thought himself too good for farm folks. His work brought him into contact with exciting events in the world beyond Dawson Creek, and he loved to talk about them. He seemed to fancy himself a dispenser of superior knowledge, yet Ruth found his revelations fascinating. Sometimes he showed up at the McEvan farm to try to persuade her to accompany him to a town function. She usually declined. The thought of being alone with him made her inexplicably uncomfortable.

As usual, tonight he'd found an audience. His sister, Patricia, and her husband, Bruce, looked only slightly bored as he imparted his knowledge. Only a few months younger than Ruth, Patricia had married Bruce Henderson soon after finishing school. In four years, they'd developed a small farm three miles northwest of her parents' and increased their family with three children. Envy stabbed at Ruth. Why couldn't her own life have turned out as comfortably?

Her attention shifted to a matched pair of sorrel horses pulling yet another wagon into the driveway. The breeze ruffled their light-colored manes against their golden coats. She wished she could pet the beautiful animals without drawing attention to herself. If she ever had enough money to buy her own horse, she'd find either a sorrel or a bay. The solid color with contrasting mane seemed to her the best accent for a horse's grace and strength.

As the wagon came to a stop, she finally noticed its occupants, the Spencer clan. Mom hurried over to greet Mrs. Spencer, one of her closest friends, with a hug while Mr. Spencer relinquished his reins to Jim. Meanwhile, five of their six children dashed off toward the soccer game. Only the eldest, young Lionel, stood still, as if looking for someone. Ruth glanced at Sara Pierce in time to see her eyes light up and a flush spread across her cheeks. Young Lionel tried to appear casual as he made his way over to where Sara and her mother sat.

With her attention on the two youngsters, Ruth didn't notice the approach of a plump woman until it was too late to move. Lars Harper's wife, Kate, was the last person she wanted to visit with. "So, I hear you're out of a job come June," the lady announced as she approached. "That's too bad, but then maybe it will give you a chance to get married and settle down." She perched on the edge of the log beside Ruth. "It won't be long before you're past the marrying age. You know, I always thought you and Theodore Pierce would make a match of it. He must have decided he wanted to be a doctor more. Funny what men think sometimes, isn't it? I'm sure he'll be looking for a nurse, now. I'll have to remember to ask Cynthia if she's heard anything."

Ruth wished Mom or Mrs. Spencer were there to stop Mrs. Harper's flow of words. They were the only two she knew who could do so. Besides, she needed desperately to hear Mom's oft-repeated explanation. "Mrs. Harper doesn't mean any harm. She's just so interested in people, she doesn't think before she speaks." Tonight of all nights Ruth didn't feel up to being understanding.

The monologue continued. "Did you see my Nettie here with her husband? He's just as besotted with her as the day they were married. Now that she's in the family way, he treats her like fine china. You should come over and meet him. I haven't heard him mention having an unattached older brother, but we could ask."

Ruth suppressed a cringe, wondering how to decline gracefully. With a feeling of intense relief, she saw Mrs. Spencer beckoning. "Is Mrs. Spencer looking at you or at me?"

"Probably me." Mrs. Harper chuckled infectiously. "It's been nice visiting with you."

Ruth searched through the crowd for Nettie Harper, or Williams, as her name had become. She remembered the rambunctious know-it-all from her days as a student. Nettie had mellowed a bit by the time Ruth took over as teacher, but there had been a few tense days just the same.

"Would you like a cup of juice?" a quiet male voice inquired from behind.

Ruth turned to see Jed Harper extending a full mug. From under one arm his hat protruded, its imprint still showing on his curly light brown hair. Lines around his gray eyes already testified to hours spent in the outdoors squinting against the sun. In overalls and a faded flannel shirt, he looked every inch a typical Peace River farmer. Almost as soft-spoken as his dad, he'd never said more than "hello" to her. Curiosity about his motive kept her from irritation at being disturbed again. She tried for a friendly but neutral tone as she stood to take the cup. "Thank you for thinking of me."

"No trouble. I just noticed you weren't watching the soccer game and thought you might like some refreshment."

"I get to watch soccer every day at recess. Do you not like soccer?" She smiled to see if he would respond in kind.

His lips twitched slightly in what appeared to be his version of a smile. "After a full day following two horses and a plow, it's a treat to sit still."

"I imagine your mares will be foaling soon."

A sparkle of interest replaced shy hesitation in his eyes. "Hopefully we'll get a full dozen this year."

"Are they all thoroughbreds?"

"No." He set his wide-brimmed hat on the log and stuffed the hand that had been holding his hat into his pocket. Tapping one foot nervously beside his hat, he continued. "Thoroughbreds make nice riding horses, but they're no good for heavy farm work. We only breed a couple each year. The rest are either draft horses or mixed breeds." He stopped as though suddenly realizing he'd said more than a dozen words. Red tinged his ears.

She tried to think of a reassuring reply. "I like horses."

He nodded. "So do I." His well of conversation seemed to have dried up completely. They stood in uneasy silence for a few moments before he reached for his hat. "I'll be going now."

Ruth settled back onto the log. If he were a polished charmer like his cousin, Justin, she would have thought he brought the juice as an excuse to talk with her. Talking obviously made him uncomfortable, so why had he come?

"You look thoughtful. I hope they're pleasant thoughts." A short, comfortably rounded woman with white hair sat down beside Ruth as if she'd been invited.

"Grandma Lucy!" Ruth impulsively gave her a hug. "I didn't know you were here."

"I came with Lionel and Nina. They refuse to let me miss out on anything around here." A wide smile made her plump cheeks even fuller.

"I must have been so busy watching your grandson I didn't notice you." Ruth felt her gloom vanishing. Grandma Lucy actually had no biological relationship with the McEvans. She'd offered a room in her boardinghouse for Ida Thomas when the teacher had been hired seven years ago. She and Ida became close friends as the younger woman adjusted to a new place and to living without her mother who'd died just six months before Ida came to Peace River. Lucy Barry had seen the attraction between Ida and Timothy even before they recognized their own feelings. On Ida and Timothy's wedding day, Lucy had insisted on taking Ruth, Phillip, and Greg for a week so the newlyweds could have time to themselves. That was the week Ruth and her brothers had started calling Mrs. Barry "Grandma Lucy." All of the children's natural grandparents still lived in Ontario, where the McEvan family had lived before coming to homestead in the Peace River area, so they cherished their adopted grandmother.

Grandma Lucy's eyes sparkled with interest. "You mean the one who has eyes only for young Sara Pierce?"

Ruth giggled. "Yes, that's the one. He tried to be so subtle, but their faces gave it away."

"He reminds me of his father at that age. My Lionel looked just the same the first time he laid eyes on Nina. Eighteen years later, they're still sweethearts. Have you heard from Sara's older brother lately? He's almost finished with medical school, isn't he?" Grandma Lucy had a way of asking personal questions in a way that conveyed loving interest rather than just curiosity.

"Actually, he finished school a year ago, but he has to do an internship at a city hospital before they'll let him work on his own."

"Any idea when he's coming home? I know Doug and Cynthia miss him terribly."

"He hasn't said yet. I'm sure if he'd made any plans, Sara would have announced it the next day at school."

"Do you think he'll stay in the city?" Grandma asked with an oddly intent look.

Ruth shrugged. "He hasn't mentioned anything like that. I know his mother keeps hoping he'll come back here to set up his practice."

"And what do you hope?"

"I haven't thought much about it," Ruth answered truthfully. "He's still my best friend, so it would be nice to have him home."

Grandma patted Ruth's hand. "Have you written to him yet about your school closing?"

She shook her head. "I don't know what to say."

"It hurts pretty badly, doesn't it?"

Tears stung her eyes, but she blinked them back. "I haven't thought of much else since the meeting Thursday night."

"I've been praying for you." The simple words conveyed infinite empathy and concern. "I hope you won't hesitate to come for a visit if you need to talk."

"Thanks." Ruth dredged up a genuine smile.

Grandma Lucy didn't say any more. Ruth couldn't help but feel the contrast between this silence and that which had fallen between her and Jed. The other had been isolating. This was the comfort of being both understood and loved.

Chapter 4

*L*ife is strange, Ruth mused, watching the children at recess. Only a month ago, she'd been content in her role as schoolteacher, with rarely a thought for the lack of romance in her life. Now it seemed she saw couples wherever she looked.

At the edge of the schoolyard, two figures wandered apart from the rest. Sara Pierce and young Lionel. *At least they never try to sneak out of sight*, she thought with relief. Both responsible youngsters alone, they had earned even greater trust from their parents in their conduct together. Though they often pulled apart from a group for private discussions, they always stayed in full view of adults. Ruth had yet to see them try to so much as hold hands. If she had to have lovebirds in her classroom, she thanked the Lord they were these two.

The rest of the children were playing a screeching game of "Kick the Can." She reflected on how much her students had grown during her three years as their teacher. She'd started with most of them at the middle level. Young Lionel Spencer would start high school next year and his brother, David, would follow him a year later. Their sister, Clara, had another two years before deciding whether or not to go beyond grade eight. It had been difficult to persuade June Harper to stay in school this year, so she probably wouldn't be back after the summer. Mom's first class of readers, all five now in their teen years, were now in grade seven. Her middle students, Julie Harper, Greg McEvan, and Tabby Spencer, would be in the new school for several years to come, as would Ruth's lone new reader, Audrey Spencer.

Ruth sighed. No matter which way she looked at the possible future, this school would be no more. It probably would have closed soon, anyway, since there wouldn't have been any new readers next year. "Consolidation," as it had been called, was obviously the best idea. But its effect on her life remained too painful to contemplate just now. Time to call her students in. She rang the bell. As usual, her three thirteen-year-old boys, Tommy Spencer, Teddy Harper, and Phillip, were the last to make it inside. She opened her mouth to reprimand them when Sara tugged on her sleeve. "Miss McEvan, look at what Lionel and I found."

A tiny nest snuggled in Sara's hand. A couple of spotted eggs lay inside.

Ruth gasped at the delicate beauty of the woven twigs. "Where did you find this?"

"Over by that stump." Sara pointed. "There were feathers scattered all around, so Lionel said it looked like a fox or something had killed the mother."

Ruth grinned at the young man hovering nearby. "If you say that's what happened, I'll take your word for it." Young Lionel had already gained a reputation for being an exceptional tracker and reader of the bush country surrounding them. "I'll get everyone settled and you can tell us about your discovery." She turned toward her desk, then stopped. Her three "troublemakers" stood in front of it, holding a crudely lettered sign that read, "Happy Birthday, Miss McEvan!" From where she stood, she could read where each of her thirteen students had signed the banner and written a personal message. "I don't know what to say. This is a wonderful surprise." She blinked back tears that seemed to flow too easily these days.

"That's not all." Clara and Tabby scurried out the door and returned carrying a saddle blanket woven in tones of blue. "Greg and Phillip said you like blue, so we pooled our money to buy this for you."

Ruth looked at her students in amazement. Few of them ever had spending money, so parents must have contributed heavily. Regardless, her students had gone to incredible effort to provide her with a memorable birthday gift. She took the blanket from the girls to feel its roughness against her cheek. If only she had a horse to put it on. *Someday*. "I thank each of you. I can guess how you found out it was my birthday," she pretended to glare at her brothers, "and it means a lot to me that you'd work so hard to make it special."

"Can we go home early then?" irrepressible Phillip asked.

"No. We still have arithmetic quizzes to take." But by midafternoon, she relented. Early dismissal for one day wouldn't hurt any of them. Her brothers were the first out the door, but she called them back. "Would you take this home for me, please, and let Mom know I'll be there in awhile?"

"Sure," Phillip answered amiably, reaching for the blanket, but Ruth pulled it back.

"Can you keep it out of puddles, off the ground, and away from blanket-eating trees?"

"Of course." The familiar reproach showed in Phillip's eyes.

"I'll take care of it," Greg offered. "We won't do anything else until we've put it in the house."

Ruth smiled her thanks. She knew Greg would keep his word. Phillip didn't mean to be irresponsible; he just got distracted easily. Leaving the schoolhouse door open, she sat on the step to grade quizzes. The warm sunshine felt soothing. Two of Julie's precisely written answers were incorrect. Tomorrow Ruth would have to explain yet again that incorrect answers didn't mean failure. On the other hand, Phillip wouldn't be at all disturbed by the fact his paper contained more wrong answers than right ones. Would their teacher next year make allowances for their different personalities? *Of course,* she reassured herself. The person wouldn't have been hired unless he or she was a good teacher. But Ruth's concern lingered. She'd miss seeing Tommy's eyes light up when he figured out how to do six-digit multiplication or Sara's dreamy expression while she worked on an English composition. All at once, she knew how to write to Theo so he would understand.

She retrieved a couple of sheets of clean writing paper from her drawer. Using a textbook as a lap desk, she began.

> *Dear Theo,*
>
> *Thanks again for taking time to write to me. The reminders of your steadfast friendship were exactly what I needed.*
>
> *Your letter arrived at the right time. Just the day before, I had attended a meeting of all the school trustees in this area. To put it succinctly, all of the one-room schools in the south Peace River district are being consolidated into four centrally located schools. While some teachers will be reassigned, others of us won't be.*
>
> *My life has been so centered around this school, I feel like its closing is almost the end of me. As I graded papers this afternoon, I thought of what each student's personality contributes to my day and how much I'll miss them. It feels like when Daniel drowned, like part of me has been cut off.*
>
> *Meanwhile, everyone around me seems to have found the proper place. Starry-eyed couples and new babies abound while I look forward to spending the rest of my days turning into an old maid in my parents' house.*
>
> *Have you had time to take any pretty nurses to dinner? Somehow I can't imagine you in city dress-up clothes.*

Ruth reread her last paragraph several times. Why had she written it? If Theo wanted to tell her about his dates, he would. To eliminate the question, though, she'd have to rewrite the whole page. Folding the paper into her satchel, she decided to think about it later.

She took her time wandering between school and the farm. In a few weeks, this trail would be a shady refuge, but this afternoon buds had not yet begun to form on the dead-looking branches around her. Sunlight streamed between them uninhibited. After months of cold weather and gray skies, she revelled in the bright warmth. For today, at least, she had something to look forward to.

Mom had a way of turning birthdays into full-scale celebrations. Everyone but the birthday person participated in choosing presents, though no one breathed a clue until after the specially prepared dinner. Ruth had chosen chicken pot pie for this year's birthday meal, with egg pudding and canned raspberries for dessert. Her mouth watered at the thought.

In the barnyard, Phillip and Greg leaned on the fence watching Dad work with Star. She noticed how well the horse responded to his direction. The boys flashed her mysterious-looking grins, but said nothing in greeting. The house had a feeling of mystery about it, too. This feeling of suspense enhanced the joy of a birthday, knowing something delightful would happen in a few hours but also knowing there was no choice but to wait. Mom refused Ruth's offer of help in the kitchen. "Go take a nap or something," she advised, pretending to be irritable. "I don't want you here under my feet."

Ruth felt uncomfortable not helping, but did as she was told. The sunshine she enjoyed so much made bright patches on her bed and floor. She stretched out and closed her eyes, but sleep eluded her. The last two sentences she'd written to Theo haunted her. It shouldn't matter what he did with his spare time, but Mrs. Harper's comments wouldn't leave her alone. Ruth thought she wanted whatever would make him happiest, so why her mental tumult? *It's not the marriage part that concerns me,* she told herself resolutely. *It's the thought of him living so far away.*

She retrieved the paper from her bag and then added to the paragraph.

After writing that question, I wonder if perhaps I'm being too nosy. Feel free to tell me it's none of my business. Something Mrs. Kate Harper said the other day just made me curious.

I'm now at home in my bedroom, awaiting my mother's call to supper. I wish you were here to celebrate my birthday with us. Have you ever considered how strange it is that you and I are such friends? A lot of people wouldn't believe a man and a woman could be just best friends.

With spring in the air, I've been watching an example of the other kind of rapport that can exist between men and women, or boys and girls in the cases I'm thinking of. Your sister is one of them. As I'm sure you're well aware, she and young Lionel Spencer are quite taken with each other. She looks like spring sunshine whenever he's around.

I've never felt that way about anyone. Of course, when I was Sara's age, I was becoming a bitter old woman already. Thanks to you and Ida, I've been able to leave that behind.

I still think a lot, though, about the love I always saw in my dad's face when he looked at my first mother. He simply shrivelled up inside when she drowned. Then he met Ida, and his heart shows in his eyes again. Isn't that kind of devotion just too risky? I hope no one ever feels so strongly about me. I know I'd never be able to feel the same, because I'd always be afraid of losing him.

I can't believe I'm writing these thoughts. I've never told anyone else about them, but then I've told you many things no one else knows about. You're a better friend than I ever could have asked for.

I just heard Mom holler outside for the guys to come in for supper, so I'd better close this. Thanks for always caring about what bothers me.

Everyone came to the table in dress clothes. Even little Beth wore her Sunday dress. Mom had prepared sugared carrots to go with the pot pie and had set out a dish of dilled beans. Every time Ruth looked at Greg, he giggled and ducked his head as if he were afraid she'd read the secret in his eyes. Actually, everyone looked more excited than usual. She knew better than to ask, so she concentrated on enjoying the tasty meal.

When everyone had eaten their fill, Mom cleared the dishes away and replaced them with dessert. Ruth looked around for the pile of packages that usually accompanied this part of a birthday dinner. Dad caught her glance. "We've decided to stretch out the suspense a little more."

"That's not nice," she protested.

"We just didn't want age to make you set in your ways," he teased.

Ruth had almost finished her second helping of pudding and berries when Greg and Phillip bolted from the table. After peering out the door, they beckoned to her. "Come look, Ruthie."

Her parents' smiles stretched wider. "Go ahead," her dad encouraged.

She left the table hesitantly, half afraid her brothers had devised some kind of prank. Only an approaching visitor met her gaze. Seated on his magnificent black stallion, Jed Harper rode down the lane at a trot with a sorrel gelding following on a lead rope. The sorrel's flaxen mane and tail rippled as he tossed his head and pranced sideways. Ruth longed to feel his gallop beneath her. Her gasp brought a chorus of "Happy Birthday's." She looked back at Dad. "A horse for my birthday?" she asked in disbelief.

He nodded. "From all of us."

The gift seemed too wonderful to be real. "So that's why the children at school thought I needed a saddle blanket. Pretty sneaky, you two." She grabbed both brothers in a rough embrace, then bolted out to meet her new friend.

Jed relinquished the lead rope. "He's already broke to saddle."

The horse stopped prancing when Ruth stroked his nose. "You're such a pretty boy. I'd like to take you for a run, but I have a party first. We'll go tomorrow all by ourselves." She led him in several circuits of the farmyard, talking quietly to get him used to the sound of her voice.

Dad met her at the barn door. "Bring him in here and see how he likes it."

Ruth tugged gently on the rope, and the horse followed. Dad led the way to a stall with a thick layer of fresh hay. A brand new saddle sat on top of the gate. She looked at Dad with wide eyes. "You shouldn't have spent so much!"

He laughed. "This isn't from us." He pulled a piece of paper from underneath the saddle and handed it to her.

"*Happy Birthday, Ruth,*" the note read. "*We hope this saddle brings you as much joy as you've brought us. Love, Doug, Cynthia, Theo, and Sara Pierce.*"

Happy tears filled Ruth's eyes. "I've always admired Mr. Pierce's leather work. I can't believe he made this just for me."

"You're worth it. Let's turn your friend out into the corral and see if Jed would like to join us in a checkers tournament."

The McEvans had spent many happy hours over the checkerboard. During the winter or on special occasions, the entire family participated in tournaments that could last several hours. Tonight, Beth and Mom played against Timmy, who won. Jed then offered to have a game with the little boy, who won again and went to bed feeling like a genius. With the toddlers asleep, fun began in earnest.

Jed appeared to relax quickly. At first, his few words were directed mostly at Timothy. After awhile, he offered suggestions to help Greg beat Phillip, then moves that helped Greg beat Ruth. Around ten o'clock, he emerged the winner. "Sorry to win and run," he apologized to Mom, "but the stock will be hollering at five tomorrow morning."

"Come again whenever you have the time," Dad offered.

"Thank you, sir." Jed looked at Ruth. "Happy birthday."

"Thanks for bringing the horse over. He's the nicest birthday present I've ever received."

Jed's face turned pink. "Glad to do it."

Ruth lingered at the corral after Jed rode off. Her horse stood at the far side, his golden coat picking up the last glints of daylight. *Sunset.* The term seemed to fit, though some might think it too fanciful. She called him softly. "Sunset." He nickered back and she relished the sound of her very own horse. It seemed unbelievable how so many people had participated in making her day joyous. With such an outpouring of love, why did she still feel so empty inside?

Chapter 5

The next day was Saturday, so Ruth made herself a picnic lunch and saddled Sunset. His excellent training showed in the way he stood quietly for the entire procedure. Dad held the corral gate as she rode out. "You'll stay on our land?" he questioned.

"Yes. I'm going to take him for a run on the road, then we'll come back and be mostly down by the creek."

He nodded, grinning at her eagerness to be gone. "Take care on the road, and don't get too far out. If you're not back by nightfall, we'll start at the creek."

"I want to be back by midafternoon so I'll still have time to go into town to visit Grandma." She waved in farewell and urged Sunset into a trot. Once on the road, she let him have his head. As his stride lengthened, she leaned lower over his neck. "Good fellow. Let me see what you can do." As if in response to her words, his muscles swelled, giving their utmost. His gait was smooth and even, just like a dream horse ought to be. They galloped past the schoolhouse and beyond what she still thought of as Theo's home, a mile and a half west of the school. She slowed Sunset to a trot, then turned him back. Passing the Pierces' farm for the second time, she realized it had been some time since she'd visited Mrs. Pierce. She'd have to take Sunset over to show them how well their gift suited him. *Someday soon,* she promised herself. With her own horse to ride, distance would no longer curtail her activities. But today was hers alone. She directed Sunset down a trail leading to her favorite retreat near the creek.

As the bush thickened, she dismounted and led him carefully through the trail she'd worn over the years until they came to an open area on the creek bank. A large, flat rock lay in perfect position for losing one's self in watching the creek rush or amble by, depending on the season. Today, still swollen with spring runoff, the creek flowed swiftly along. Tying Sunset where he could eat his fill of new grass while she daydreamed, she relaxed on her natural bench with her chin propped in her hands and elbows braced on her knees. Her gaze followed a twig tossing and tumbling on its way downstream. That's exactly how she felt—carried along by forces out of her control, trying her best not to be sucked under by the current of life.

She rummaged in her saddlebag for the book and pencil she carried with her everywhere. Mom gave her a small, clothbound volume with blank pages every year for Christmas. Throughout the year, Ruth filled the pages with her most private thoughts and wonderings. Poems often took shape here, as well as a form of rhythmic prose she knew would horrify any true writer but which expressed feelings she couldn't describe any other way. Settling back on the rock, she began to write the phrases brought to mind by the helpless twig.

Who am I?
   Who do you think I am?
Am I what you'd like me to be?
   I'm just me, not entirely sure who that is.
Sometimes I say the right words, do the right deeds
   Yet feel so empty wanting to know who I really am.
Tired of pleasing
   Wondering if I broke the shell would I still be worthwhile?
Is what I feel the real me
   Or just the me
Moulded by relentless circumstance?
   Why must I follow this stream which changes with each season?
I long for a predictable path
   A future with no uncertainties
A present with no doubts
   A past with no unanswerable questions.
But that's impossible.
   And so, with no other choice
I do my best to keep my balance
   Hoping the rapids I hear ahead won't suck me under,
Praying the waterfalls won't crush me,
   Sensing survival lies not in resisting but in resting,
Trusting that the One who controls the stream will not forget me.

She read and reread what she'd written. The last line especially disturbed her. Where had it come from? Though she could remember kneeling by Mother's knee as a little girl and asking Jesus to be her Savior, she'd been keeping Him at arm's length for a long time. Now she wondered if she might be making a mistake. She closed her book as if to shut out the disquieting thoughts. Other matters needed attention, like how to handle the end of her days in the classroom.

Alone beside the creek, she could finally afford to let her feelings surface completely. Her school represented her place of value in this rural community. In just a few months, her place would be obliterated. She felt as useless as she had the day she'd watched her twin brother repeatedly sucked under by a relentless current. Though logic told her she'd be no less appreciated after the school closed, she still felt rejected and discarded. The future looked bleak because she could see no way of regaining the sense of worth teaching had given her.

What if she accepted Grandmother Carrington's offer? If nothing else, she could at least get her teaching certificate. It shouldn't take more than a couple of years. If she found city living tolerable, she could go on and maybe even get a university degree, perhaps go into nursing. Somehow the ideas stirred no sense of anticipation. At least they offered an option. A firm decision could wait.

Deliberately turning her thoughts to more casual matters, she munched a butter and honey sandwich as her gaze drifted up and down the creek bank. Just beyond a thicket to her left, the creek made several curves before it reached the beaver dam. The swampy area around those curves grew magnificent pussy willows. They wouldn't be ready for cutting just yet, but she'd have to remember to come back next week.

When she finally returned home, voices in the bush just beyond the corral indicated Greg and Phillip were improving their tree fort. This would probably be their last weekend of leisure. Spring planting would start soon, then gardening, and from there one farming activity would follow another until after the snow fell. She wrapped Sunset's reins around a corral rail before taking her pack bag inside.

Mom glanced up from butter churning. "How was your ride?"

"Perfect." Ruth felt a genuine smile creep across her face. "I still can't believe I actually have a horse of my own. Unless you need me here, I thought I'd go into town and visit Grandma."

"That's a wonderful idea. Would you mind taking a few things to her?" Mom always canned and baked more than the family could use so she'd have enough to give away. She rarely let any of her family make a trip to town without sending something to Grandma Lucy.

"How did I guess you'd ask?" Ruth teased.

"I don't know." Mom grinned as she lifted the dasher and peered into the churning crock. "If you're not in a hurry, I'd like to give Lucy a bit of this fresh butter."

"I'll even help you wash it," Ruth offered, using the hand pump beside the sink to fill a basin with cold water. Together they lifted the crock and poured the buttermilk into a large bowl.

Mom scraped whitish lumps of butter off the sides of the crock and plopped them into the water. "Do you think you'll stay for supper?"

"If you don't mind." Ruth mashed the lumps repeatedly with a large wooden spoon until the butter had formed a single large blob and no further milky streaks stained the water.

"Not at all. I think the visit will be good for both of you. You will make sure you're home before dark?"

Ruth chuckled. "You can tell Dad I'll keep Sunset on the road, and I'll make sure we have plenty of daylight in which to come back."

Mom's eyes twinkled. "You know I had to ask so I can tell Dad we did discuss it."

"I know. He's such a worrywart."

"Only because he loves us," Mom assured her unnecessarily. "I think I have everything together. Is this going to be too bulky?"

Ruth surveyed the bulging bag. "I think I can still get it strapped on behind my saddle."

"Then have a good time. I think I'll go rest a bit before the little ones get up from their naps."

With only a little difficulty, Ruth managed to get the burlap bag tied in place. She urged Sunset into a trot, but the bundle didn't slip. Approaching Dawson Creek from the northwest, she reined her horse to a stop. Town always made her nervous. After the railroad had arrived in January 1931, the quiet village had mushroomed into a bustling center of commerce. More people milled about town on Saturday than any other day. At least she didn't have any extra stops to make. Though the boardinghouse sat on one of the town's main streets, a circuitous route would keep her away from the busier areas until the last minute. She nudged Sunset into motion. "Let's go, big fellow."

Once on the main street, she hurried him along the two blocks to the boardinghouse, then around to the back, where she tied him loosely to a ring on the outside of the barn wall. Tapping at the back door, she called out, "Grandma! It's me, Ruth."

Through the screen she could see Grandma hurrying down the hall. "Of course it's you, girl. I saw you riding around from the front. What brings you to town this late in the day?"

"I just wanted to come for a visit. Mom sent this for you and asked me to give you her love." She handed over the bag, then hugged her white-haired friend. "I also wanted you to see my birthday present."

"What is it?" Grandma Lucy's eyes sparkled with interest.

"You have to come see," Ruth said teasingly. "It's outside, so you'll have to put on your mud boots."

Grandma set her bag on the floor. "This can wait. Let's go see this present of yours."

Ruth led the way back outside and around the side of the barn. "There he is."

"Isn't he a beauty?" Grandma breathed, slowly reaching out to stroke the horse's neck. "What did you name him?"

"Sunset." None of her ideas felt foolish when shared with Grandma Lucy.

"What a perfect name! I would guess you spent the entire morning riding him all over the countryside."

Ruth grinned. "Pretty much."

"Well, I'm glad your travels brought you in to visit me. Can you stay for supper?"

Ruth nodded. "I only have to make sure I'm back home before dusk, or Dad will start fretting."

"Well, then, come on into the kitchen and we'll see what your mother is giving me this time. Bless her heart! Bread, her special chokecherry jelly, fresh butter, and some cookies. That girl must think I don't know how to cook." Twinkling eyes belied her fierce words. She used a fork to test something in a steaming pot. "So where did you and Sunset wander?"

"Mostly down by the creek. He munched grass while I scribbled and thought. May I set the table for you?" Ruth felt awkward doing nothing while Grandma Lucy bustled.

"Thank you. There will be six of us. You know where everything is. Do you mind telling me what you were thinking about?"

Ruth laid the plates, cutlery, and glasses in precise position while mentally searching for the right words. She knew from experience Grandma Lucy would wait patiently for as long as necessary. "Mostly about school," she finally confessed.

Grandma Lucy turned from her bread board to face Ruth. "You're having a tough time with it closing, aren't you?"

Ruth nodded without looking up.

"Are you ashamed of hurting?" The gentle tone enveloped the younger woman in compassion.

"No, but I wish I didn't feel this way."

Grandma Lucy didn't say anything, but her intense gray eyes invited Ruth to elaborate.

"I feel helpless. I'm losing a vital part of my life—" Ruth's voice cracked. She swallowed hard. "And there's nothing I can do about it."

"Have you thought about what you're going to do after June?"

"I don't see many options. Even if I had the skills for a different job, it wouldn't be the same as teaching. I can either make the best of helping out at home or accept Grandmother Carrington's offer to go live with her."

Grandma Lucy only faltered a moment in her stirring as she poured canned peas into the pot of creamed potatoes. "Are you seriously considering a move to Toronto?"

"I don't know." Ruth swallowed around another lump in her throat. "In her last letter she offered to send me to one of the fancy schools there or to find me a husband."

"What do your parents think of the idea?"

"I haven't told them. When the letter first came, I just put it away with all the others. Since I lost my job, though, the offer's become more attractive."

"It would be hard for you to live with someone who feels about your dad the way she does."

Ruth abruptly sat down on the chair at the end of the long table. "I hadn't thought about that."

"The day she arrived on the first train, she told everyone within earshot how she holds him responsible for your mother's death and how she intended to rescue her daughter's children from him."

"Every letter I've received from her contains at least one derogatory remark about him. I thought she was just writing those things to try to get me to come live with her."

Grandma Lucy placed the full bread basket and a bowl of butter on the table. Putting a hand on each of Ruth's shoulders, she looked straight into her eyes. "Please just promise me you'll let your Heavenly Father direct your decision."

Ruth wanted to give the answer that would make Grandma happiest, but she couldn't bring herself to say something she didn't mean. Boarders began gathering at the table, relieving her of the need to reply. Grandma stepped away from Ruth, but her eyes promised the discussion would continue later.

While helping put serving dishes on the table, Ruth recalled when Grandma Lucy had looked after only Mom and another boarder named Mr.

Carey. When Mom had lived here, most of Grandma's business had come from farm families who had to stay overnight for various reasons. Since then, the house had been expanded to make room for a total of six residents. Dawson Creek's growth had filled Grandma's house with single men who'd come to find jobs but didn't want to live at the hotel. Gruff Mr. Carey still occupied his room to one side of the large kitchen. Only three others settled around the table, though Ruth guessed the vacancies would fill quickly. All four waited for Grandma to ask the blessing before helping themselves to the steaming chicken and potatoes. After multiple helpings and two pieces of pie each, the men vanished to their rooms or outside.

Grandma submerged a stack of dishes in hot water and Ruth grabbed a dishtowel. Grandma tried to scowl, though her merry eyes marred the effect. "I can handle these. You just relax. I remember what teaching can do to a body. Ida used to come in looking like she'd wrestled a grizzly."

Ruth grinned but didn't relinquish her dishtowel, secretly relieved Grandma had forgotten the earlier sensitive discussion. "That's what I feel like some days. Anyone who doesn't think spring fever exists ought to stop by my schoolhouse this time of year."

"Do you remember how Nettie Harper used to create a ruckus? Your mom used to come home almost in tears."

"It's hard to believe she's married and due to be a mother soon."

Grandma laughed. "Young Jeff Williams is braver than I expected of any fellow his age. Being loved has settled Nettie a lot, though. I expect motherhood will do the rest." She gave her dishcloth a good wringing, then snapped it out of the twist. "Thanks to your help, we're finished already. How about a cup of your favorite tea?"

"I've been waiting all day for one."

"Ida used to love my peppermint tea, too. You remind me a lot of her when she lived with me."

Ruth felt her eyes widen in surprise. "How?"

"She was still making peace with her mother's death. During her first year of teaching, her life took a few unexpected turns, and like you, she felt she had to handle them alone. After awhile, though, she learned to take God's Word at face value when it says all our steps are ordered by the Lord."

As often happened in discussions with Grandma Lucy, Ruth felt like the protective layers around her heart had been peeled back and its secrets revealed. Yet in the process, she also felt thoroughly loved. It gave her courage to say what she couldn't have told anyone else. "My life makes Him look like a pretty lousy planner."

Grandma's rough-skinned hands grasped Ruth's smooth ones gently. "He has given you a lot of heartache, child. I like to think it means He's also given you a capacity for more joy than most people discover. The times we can't explain why His plan is the way it is are our greatest opportunities to trust Him. Nothing brings Him greater joy than our trust even when we hurt."

Ruth dared to look into her friend's eyes. "I don't think I could do that."

A mysterious smile lit Grandma Lucy's eyes. "I've felt that way, too. If you want to hear about it, ask Ida to tell you my story some day. The most important lesson of my life, and one it seems I have to relearn almost every day, is that trust isn't a feeling. It's a choice. It's probably the most difficult decision we ever make. Every time God sends us something we don't understand, we have to choose again."

What she talked about sounded wonderful, but too far removed from where Ruth lived. "It still sounds impossible."

"I know, dear. But if you ask our Father to show you the way, He will." Returning from the stove where she'd put more water on to boil, she pulled Ruth into a long hug.

Ruth let herself relax in the embrace. She thought she heard Grandma whispering, but she couldn't be sure.

Though their conversation moved on to family activities and community events, Ruth's mind returned to Grandma Lucy's "*Trust is a choice*" as she rode Sunset home. Obviously Grandma didn't understand the depth of her problem. God's involvement in the life of Ruth McEvan had been sporadic at best, nonexistent at worst. How could she ask Him for anything? Though she dismissed the idea as ludicrous, something deep inside ached to try it anyway.

Chapter 6

"Dad, may I please be excused?" Greg sat on the end of the bench awaiting release from the supper table. Phillip had already bolted. Reportedly, they had just "two more things" before the tree fort would be perfect.

"In a moment, Son. Phillip, please come back." Dad's eyes glowed with mystery and something else Ruth couldn't define.

Phillip groaned loudly, but returned. "Sorry, Dad."

"You know better than to leave without being excused. But I have something more important to discuss. Please take your seat." He waited until the boys had settled. "Your mom and I have some special news for you. In about four months, you'll have a new brother or sister." He could hardly finish his sentence around his wide grin.

Ruth looked closely at Mom. "Is this why you've been so tired? I was beginning to think you were really sick."

Mom's smile matched Dad's. "I kept telling you it was nothing to worry about."

"Can we go now?" Greg looked bored.

Dad shook his head. "No. I need to explain something."

Ruth knew what was coming. They'd heard the same speech before Timmy and before Beth. Ruth, Phillip, and Greg would have to be sure to help Mom all they could so she wouldn't work too hard.

Dad had only said a few words before Ruth realized the speech had been rewritten. "Boys, I'm going to expect you to help your mother. I don't want her getting overtired. Ruth has enough to do with school, so I'm going to be watching you two. Until this baby is born, I don't want to hear your mother ask you to haul water, bring wood for the stove, or dump the slop pail. I want you to see what needs to be done and do it. No excuses. If I catch either your mom or your sister doing something you should have done or having to ask you to do it, we'll have an immediate meeting behind the barn. Understood?"

"Yes, sir," the boys chorused.

Dad studied Phillip's face for several moments before dismissing the two. "I'm not sure he heard me," he muttered after the door slammed behind them. "But he's going to learn responsibility this summer or else."

Ruth laughed at his determined expression. "His teacher will thank you." She pushed down the familiar feeling of loss.

Her struggles increased as the days slipped away. Young Lionel, David and Tommy Spencer, Teddy Harper, and Phillip disappeared from the schoolhouse to help with planting. Ruth knew she wouldn't see them in her classroom again and had to blink back selfish tears. The students who were left absorbed her mood. By Friday, she realized she had to do something to lift them all from the doldrums. She rang the bell to call them in from lunch recess, but didn't write any assignments on the blackboard. When everyone had settled into their seats, she asked nine-year-old Tabby Spencer, "Do you know what will happen seven weeks from today?"

The girl's blue eyes sparkled from behind the white blond hair that always seemed to hang in her face. "Is that the last day of school?"

"Yes." Ruth tried to make her face reflect their excitement rather than her own heartache. "How would you like to plan a concert for that day?"

"But it's not Christmas!" six-year-old Audrey protested. "We only have a concert for Christmas."

"That's what we've done before," Ruth explained gently, "but we can have a special program any time we want to work hard enough to make it enjoyable for your parents. What does everyone else think about the idea?"

The older girls exchanged glances across the room before Karin Harper, one of the thirteen year olds, asked, "What kind of concert?"

Ruth decided to take a risk. "Any kind you want."

"You mean we can plan it all ourselves?" Clara Spencer asked, her face alight with the challenge.

Ruth nodded. "Every Friday afternoon, I'll leave you to yourselves so you can plan or practice. I'll help as much as you want me to, but you'll have to ask. This will be entirely your project."

"Who will be in charge?" Julie Harper wanted to know.

"Whichever one of the older girls all of you pick." Maybe this part of her plan would prove to be a mistake, but she wanted the entire project to be their own.

After a few moments of silence, Sara Pierce raised her hand. "I think June should, since she's the oldest." Clara Spencer nodded agreement. Karin Harper didn't look so sure, but Ruth often had to mediate squabbles between the two sisters.

She looked at the fifteen year old, whose face showed interest for the first time all year. "Do you want to be in charge, June?"

"Yes, ma'am," the quiet girl replied. "It will be a lot of work, but we can do it."

The rest of the afternoon flew by as the children discussed ideas. Ruth watched in amazement as June diplomatically coordinated everyone's suggestions into a workable plan. Even Greg, the only boy left in the classroom, responded well to her. Ruth tried not to wish they'd be back next year.

After the first Friday, Ruth felt comfortable leaving her students alone under June's supervision. She brought Sunset and a riding skirt with her to school the next week. Just as she'd suspected, the swampy area by the creek had produced some magnificent pussy willows. She trimmed off half a dozen branches, then made her way to the Pierce farm.

"What a pleasant surprise!" Mrs. Pierce exclaimed when she answered Ruth's knock. A stylish printed dress fitted her slender frame to perfection and not a hair had drifted out of its place in the elaborate arrangement at the back of her head.

Ruth held out her gift. "These are from Theo and me."

The lady's eyes misted, though she smiled with delight. "I know for sure it's spring when you bring me pussy willows. You two never forget. Can you stay for tea?" She rubbed one of the puffs against her cheek.

"For a little bit. June Harper is supervising a special project they're all working on, so I try to make myself scarce on Friday afternoons."

"You know you're welcome to come visit me any time you want." Mrs. Pierce put her willow branches in a cut glass vase that reflected sunlight in delicate rainbows and placed the vase in the middle of the dining table in the formal dining room. "You make me feel almost like Theo's home again."

"I miss him, too," Ruth admitted. "Has he written anything to you about when he'll be back?"

Mrs. Pierce filled a small flowered china plate with brownie squares. "He'd hoped to be home for a couple of weeks this summer, but he isn't sure if it will work out. He's now in charge of all the first-year students."

"That's wonderful." Ruth felt so proud of her friend she wanted to cheer. She watched her hostess fill teacups from a graceful silver tea service. "I never doubted he'd make a terrific doctor."

"Me either." The mother's eyes glowed. "Apparently the hospital has also offered him a full-time job in the fall. I've been hoping he'd be able to set up a practice here in town, but I try not to interfere in his decisions. I know he'll make up his mind only when he's sure of what God wants him to do."

Sipping her tea, Ruth searched for an appropriate response. She envied her friend's confidence in God's direction.

"Do you have any plans for after the school closes?"

"Just helping out at home, for now." She tried to sound far more cheerful than she felt.

"Your parents are blessed to still have you around. I've realized lately my daughter will probably be setting up her own home right after she finishes school."

"Are she and young Lionel that serious already?" Ruth suddenly felt aged.

Mrs. Pierce refilled their cups. "I don't know, but he's exactly the kind of young man her dad and I have been praying for. We've prayed for Godly mates for our children ever since they were born."

After sending her students home that afternoon, Ruth lingered at the schoolhouse. Had her parents been praying for her future husband, too? Lately, her thoughts had turned more often to the possibility of marriage. She had no idea what kind of person she'd like to spend the rest of her life with or if she'd ever be given the choice. Theo had been the only boy she'd spent much time with, at least until recently.

Since her birthday, Jed Harper had stopped by the McEvan farm at least once a week. She wondered how he found the time with all of his own responsibilities. The first couple of times, he had helped Dad finish training Star. At the boys' invitation, he had inspected the tree fort and pronounced it a fine piece of work. Mom remained the only one who could beat him at checkers. After awhile, his visits developed a routine. Timmy and Beth would see him coming and run to meet him, knowing he'd have a piece of candy or a whittled toy. Then after he'd visited with the family for a while, he'd ask Ruth to accompany him on a horseback ride. They'd race down the road, Sunset matching Jed's stallion stride for stride. By the time they'd returned, Mom and Dad would have disappeared into their room. Gradually Jed and Ruth's conversations over the kitchen table had become longer. She'd learned of his determination to help his dad make their horse ranch the best in the Peace River Country and of his love for their land. While she hadn't felt comfortable disclosing her inner contemplations, she had found it easy to talk with him.

She swept the floor and tidied the shelves in preparation for Sunday. About a year ago, their Sunday fellowship had grown too large for the one-room cabin at the Spencers' farm, so meetings had moved to the schoolhouse. Families took turns arriving early enough to move desks to the perimeter of the room and set up benches brought from the cabin. Lars Harper had enlarged the top of the woodstove so food could be kept warm until time to eat. One thing hadn't changed—children still outnumbered adults. Grandma Lucy and the Albertsons were the only adults without youngsters. The Millers, on the other hand, had added five between the ages of five and twenty-one to the gathering. Ruth had tried to befriend their eldest, Ellen, but the girl was too shy. She seemed happiest when left alone with the little ones.

Two days later, Dad's question during breakfast surprised Ruth. "Can anyone tell me what special day this is?"

Mom waited a few moments for someone else to speak up, then suggested, "Easter Sunday."

Dad gave her his special just-for-you smile. "Who can tell me what Easter means?"

"It's the day Jesus came alive again," Greg answered as he reached for another piece of bread.

"Phillip, can you tell me why that is so important to us?"

Phillip looked unusually contemplative. "Because only God could make that happen?"

"Excellent answer. Jesus said he was God and that he would live again after he was killed. If he hadn't done so, that would have made him a liar. We would have no reason to trust God and no reason to celebrate today."

There it was again—that idea of trusting God. It refused to leave Ruth alone. She tried to ignore it while she helped Mom dress the little ones for church. During the meeting, one person after another spoke about what Easter meant to him. She simply couldn't share their joyful emotion. As a younger person, the special day had brought her as much delight as anyone. Somewhere in the last couple of years, however, an unbridgeable gap seemed to have formed between her and the One she'd been taught to call Heavenly Father. Real communication with Him had become as remote a concept as flight. She both longed for and feared the awareness of Him she saw in those she met with each Sunday. Mr. Spencer's final "Amen" gave her respite from her mental debate.

Justin Harper appeared just as the ladies were cleaning up after lunch. He smiled charmingly at everyone, then drew Ruth outside. "A friend of mine wants to take a motor trip to Grande Prairie this afternoon and invited me along. Please say you'll come, too."

She shook her head. "We're going on a picnic with the Spencers and Pierces this afternoon. I'm sure you'd be welcome if you wanted to join us."

He snorted. "Sorry. Not interested. Jed's not going to be there, is he?" He glared at his cousin, who was exchanging farm talk with the other men.

She let astonishment show in her voice. "Why should he be?"

"I've heard about you two galloping around the countryside." His tone remained nonchalantly superior. "You must like him a lot if you'll put up with him making you ride a horse."

"But I like to ride," she protested. "Besides, I can't recall it being any of your concern."

"Just wait. One of these days. . ." With that enigmatic threat, he scrambled astride his swayback mount and headed back toward town. She returned inside, hoping no one had noticed the exchange.

"What did that boy want?" Kate Harper's voice seemed to fill the schoolhouse. "How James and Ruby managed to raise such a useless dandy, I'll never know. Ruby keeps hoping he'll move back home, but I always tell her she's lost him for good. Probably should've had more paddlings when he was young. Take my Nettie, for instance. Now there was a difficult child if I ever saw one. But her pa and I never let her get away with a thing, and now she's a married lady with a baby due just any day."

Ruth caught Mom's glance and suppressed a smile. They'd often laughed privately at how much Nettie resembled her mother and how Mrs. Harper turned every conversation toward the new baby. "At least it keeps her out of other people's business," Dad had observed drily. Mrs. Harper tossed a basin of water out the door, then rounded up her husband and sons and departed, keeping up a continuous stream of comments about the joys of being a grandparent.

"It always seems so quiet when she leaves," Ruth whispered to Mom.

Mom grinned. "Kate's actually very warmhearted. She's genuinely interested in other people, though she usually expresses it in words first, then actions. If someone needs help, she's always right there."

"Talking them to death," Dad muttered. "What time are we supposed to meet the Spencers?"

Mom, Mrs. Pierce, and Mrs. Spencer debated the question for several minutes. The other two ladies wanted to make sure Mom had enough time for a nap. Mom didn't want to inconvenience the men's choring routines. Eventually, they agreed to meet at the pasture just behind the McEvans' farm. "That way you won't have to walk far," Mrs. Pierce explained.

Mom protested. "I'm not an invalid."

"Not as long as you behave yourself." Dad put his arm around her shoulders. "Let's get you home so Nina and Cynthia don't get after me for not making sure you get enough rest."

While Mom rested, Ruth put Timmy and Beth down for naps, then prepared the family's picnic. The woodbox stood almost empty, but she remembered Dad's warning about what would happen to the boys if she filled it. Her mind drifted back and forth between Justin and Jed, comparing and contrasting them. Each had become a friend of sorts, though neither knew her as well as Theo. What fun they'd have this afternoon if he were around!

Grandma Lucy and Michael Harper came with the Spencers, increasing the gathering to a whopping eighteen. Grandma and Ruth took Timmy and Beth for a walk by the creek while the other three ladies sat on a blanket and visited. When Ruth and Grandma came back, the men had been lured into playing freeze tag with the older children. Little Audrey even managed to tag her dad and Mr. Pierce. By the time the ladies set out the food, everyone had worked up an appetite.

"This is certainly a nice break from the fields," Mr. Pierce observed. "Who made these wonderful jelly sandwiches?"

"I did." Ruth felt herself blushing. "But Mom made the jelly."

He waved what was left of the sandwich toward Dad. "Your wife's almost as talented as my Cynthia."

"Don't I know it." Dad patted his stomach. "She's fattened me right up."

Talk drifted to recipes among the ladies and seed prices among the men. Ruth let the words float around her, not really listening to any of it. She felt isolated from both the adult conversations and the children's activities. She busied herself gathering picnic remnants and putting them in the appropriate containers to be taken home.

Young Lionel approached his dad. "May Sara, Michael, Clara, and I walk home?"

Mr. Spencer's eyes lit with teasing twinkles. "If you need exercise, we have plenty of rock-picking to do."

Young Lionel blushed. "Dad!"

Mr. Spencer relented. "You'll need an adult with you. If Miss McEvan is willing to chaperon, you may go as far as Sara's place. We'll pick you up there."

Ruth relished the opportunity to do a little teasing of her own. "Sure. I'd enjoy visiting with the girls." Clara and Sara both turned pink. Until this afternoon, she hadn't realized Jed's younger brother was sweet on Clara Spencer. Junior romances seemed to be springing up everywhere.

Her mind turned introspective again as she followed a discreet distance behind the two couples. She'd never felt like looking at anyone the way these kids looked at each other. Though Sara was only thirteen and Clara merely fourteen, Ruth wouldn't be surprised to see marriages in a couple of years. There was an indefinable something shared between each couple that carried a hint of forever. Sort of like the seed form of the way Dad and Mom looked at each other.

It felt strange to be considered a suitable chaperon. The more she thought about it, the older she felt. Why hadn't she ever experienced the springtime love she now supervised? Had she missed an opportunity that would never return? If love had come into her life, she wouldn't now be facing an empty future.

They had just reached the edge of the Pierce farmyard when Ruth heard the rattle of the Spencers' wagon. She declined the offer of a ride home. Early evening sun still provided plenty of light, so Dad shouldn't mind her walking alone.

He was leaning against the corral when she arrived. "Have a good walk?"

"Sort of." She wondered if he'd been waiting for her.

He didn't leave her in suspense long. "Care to talk about what you've been thinking today?"

She leaned against the rails, too, so she wouldn't have to look at him. "Nothing makes sense anymore." When put into words, her feelings sounded ridiculous. "Following those kids home tonight, for the first time ever, I felt old. Isn't that stupid?"

He didn't laugh. "No, Ruthie, it's not stupid. You are older than most young people around here are when they get married. But it's nothing to be ashamed of. Ida was older than you when we got married."

"I know. But sometimes I wonder if I'll be an old maid living with you and Mom for the rest of my life." The words came out almost in a whisper.

He lifted her chin until she looked in his eyes. "If God arranges things so that you never leave us, I'll feel blessed. But I don't think that's what He has in mind. He's made you a unique and precious person, and He's been preparing an equally special young man to be your husband. Until then, don't you dare feel guilty for still living at home. Mom and I thank God every day for loaning you to us as long as He has."

"Really?" He'd said much the same thing after the trustees' meeting, but tonight his words soothed a sore spot deep inside. "I mean, I probably won't have a job next winter, and the house is going to seem pretty crowded when the new baby gets here."

"You'll never make us feel crowded, Ruthie. You bring us joy just by being yourself. Whether you have a job or not doesn't matter. You're family. You don't have to pay your way."

Though she returned his hug, she knew she'd only let him see the surface of her heartache. She couldn't bring herself to tell him how worthless she felt, how much anger she'd harbored since the river, how desperate she'd become in her search for escape from her own feelings. "Do you mind if I go for a short ride?"

"If you don't stay out too long. You don't want Sunset to trip over any dead logs or into any holes."

Once on the road, she urged Sunset into a gallop. Though she hadn't mentioned it to Dad, Justin's remarks had added to her emotional tangle. Should she tell him not to call on her anymore? But then he'd assume she and Jed were getting serious. Why couldn't he be as considerate and uncomplicated as Theo? Though she couldn't find the words for a letter, if there were any way she could actually talk with Theo, she knew he'd help her find a solution.

Chapter 7

Justin made another appearance Tuesday evening to ask Ruth to accompany him Friday to a Shakespeare reading. *This might be a good way to find out if he's really as obnoxious as he seems,* she thought. Except for the ride into town and back home, they'd be among a crowd. Besides, she relished the prospect of hearing classical literature. On the appointed evening, she stood ready and waiting when Justin arrived. She had chosen one of her longer skirts, a navy blue one with pleats, and a long-sleeved cream-colored blouse with a navy and green tie at the neck. A matching scarf held her hair away from her face. Since she wouldn't have to do much walking, she chose her dressy school shoes instead of boots.

"Maybe you should take your coat," Mom suggested. "That gray sky looks like it could get cold tonight."

Ruth grabbed the garment off its peg by the door, blew Mom a kiss, and hurried out to the buggy. For some reason she couldn't define, she didn't want Dad talking to Justin for long. Justin helped her into the buggy, then encouraged the team of horses to navigate the lane more quickly than was necessary. Ruth wondered where he'd borrowed the assemblage. His own horse was a sad-looking creature of indeterminate parentage, offered by a trader who had realized Justin's ignorance of horseflesh and dedication to a bargain. "Guess what I heard today? We're going to start getting mail by aeroplane rather than train. They're saying it will come in once a week regular-like now."

"I thought it's always come in weekly," Ruth ventured, feeling her inadequate knowledge of town routines.

"Well, it's supposed to," he replied in a tone laced with sarcasm, "but you know those trains. If they're not late, they're too full, or some such thing. Aeroplanes are real progress, that's for sure. Another couple of years, and they'll completely replace trains."

Ruth could tell he didn't really know what he was talking about, though it felt good that he wanted to impress her. Before she had time to think of any kind of reply, he launched into a description of the automobile he hoped to buy. "They're so much cleaner than horses," he explained. "Besides, you don't have to feed or water an automobile. Just park it and forget about it until you need it again."

"Isn't it expensive to buy?" Ruth queried.

Justin waved a hand carelessly. "With the kind of money I plan to be earning in the next few years, the cost of a car would be pocket change."

"I didn't realize the telegraph office had become so successful." Ruth now felt genuinely interested. If the telegraph office were prospering, then many other businesses in Dawson Creek would be, too. That would mean better prices for farm produce, which would benefit many families she knew.

"It is getting busier, but that doesn't mean anything to me. I'm looking for a really good job. Hopefully I can get something at the airport and then learn to fly some day. With my own plane I could fly wherever I wanted and get rich doing it." He laughed loudly and slapped the reins to make the horse trot faster.

His arrogance stunned her. He obviously thought life would give him whatever he wanted. She wondered why he wanted to spend time with her.

The reading turned out to be as entrancing as she'd hoped. Two town teachers, Miss Riley and Mr. Bentworth, performed together from several different plays. They read their parts so convincingly Ruth felt as though she were sitting in a city theater rather than a small town schoolroom. Only Justin's obvious boredom marred her enjoyment. He sighed often and fidgeted, finally pulling a deck of cards from his pocket and laying out a game on his leg. She wanted to sink into the floor with embarrassment. When the final applause faded, she picked up her coat and stalked outside. He followed quickly, pleading for an explanation.

As soon as they opened the door, Ruth realized a more serious problem had developed. The gray clouds Mom had noticed had been harbingers of a spring snowstorm. Huge, fluffy flakes drifted thickly out of the sky, driven into swirls of whiteness by a biting wind. Some of the snow had melted already, creating trails of mud where streets had been. Traveling home would be slow and cold.

Justin's face paled when he saw other wagons and buggies struggling through the mud and accumulating snow. "I guess I won't be taking you home tonight."

She looked at him in shock. "What do you mean?"

"I've rented this buggy from the livery. What if I get all the way out to your place and can't get home again? I'll have to pay for an entire extra day." His expression indicated he couldn't believe she hadn't figured it out for herself.

"But, Justin, my parents will worry when I don't come home."

"Nah." He waved again in the careless gesture that now irritated her. "They know you're with me, so you're perfectly safe. They wouldn't expect me to bring you home in this mess. We'd both freeze, not to mention what would happen if the buggy slid off the road."

Ruth didn't trust herself to speak. If she were driving, she knew they'd make it. It would be cold, for sure, but at least they'd get there. However, Justin's pride would never let her handle the reins. With him guiding the horse, they probably would end up stuck along the side of the road. "I don't suppose you'd be willing to ride out to the farm and let my dad know I'm all right."

He shook his head with surprise. "If it's too cold to ride in the buggy, of course it's too cold to go on horseback. It's not a big deal, Ruth. I'll explain everything tomorrow."

But in the meantime, Dad would be half sick with worry. There was no way this selfish oaf would be able to comprehend. "Fine. Go wherever you need to go. I'll walk to the boardinghouse."

"Now, Ruth," he reached for her hands, but she pulled them back. "Don't get yourself all worked up. I'll give you a ride to the boardinghouse since it's on my way to the livery anyway. If your dad doesn't come into town tomorrow, I'll make sure you get home."

His patronizing tone sparked her anger. "Justin Harper, I've had it with you. Don't bother inviting me anywhere ever again. Your selfish arrogance is appalling. As long as we're on the subject, you mortified me in there tonight. If you didn't want to listen like a gentleman, why did you even go?"

He seemed to think she wanted an answer. "Because I wanted to be with you." His tone sounded sulky.

"Then it's time you discover you can't have everything you want. I mean it. Don't come around again."

"At least let me give you a ride to the boardinghouse," he pleaded. "Everyone's going to see you walking alone, and they're going to blame me."

"Which is as it should be. Good night, Mr. Harper." She snugged her coat around her chin and set off toward Grandma Lucy's. Within a couple of blocks, she almost regretted her decision. On the gravelled sidewalks, wet snow lay deep enough to melt into her shoes. When she had to cross the road, mud sucked at her feet, making it almost impossible to walk. The wind whipped snow into her face and numbed her hands. She hadn't seen Justin driving past, so he must have sneaked to the livery by a back way. Angry indignation warmed her enough to get her to the boardinghouse.

The door swung open before she had a chance to knock. "Ruthie, child! Whatever are you doing out in this? Come inside and get warm before you even try to talk. Why, you're just about chilled through. Let's move this chair right close to the stove. Now sit, and I'll take off your shoes. Put your feet here in this pan of warm water. I'll run upstairs and get a comforter to put around your shoulders." Grandma matched actions to words, peeling off Ruth's soaked coat, pouring steaming water into a basin, and tucking the blanket under Ruth's chin.

As warmth seeped into her chilled body, tears began to trickle down Ruth's cheeks. "He wouldn't even ride out to tell Dad where I am." She gulped back a sob of exhaustion.

"Who wouldn't, dear?" Grandma held a cup of hot tea, her antidote for any crisis, toward her. "Drink this, and tell me what happened."

Ruth took a sip of the honey- and chamomile-flavored liquid. "Justin. He asked me to come with him to hear Miss Riley and Mr. Bentworth read Shakespeare." Another sob welled in her throat, but she washed it down with tea. "He spent the entire evening fidgeting like a first-grader. He even pulled out a deck of cards, Grandma! It was so embarrassing, and he didn't even care." The sob made it all the way out this time.

Grandma set the tea on the table nearby and gathered Ruth into her arms. Held against Grandma's loving warmth, Ruth let tears take over. When her weeping quieted, Grandma asked, "How did you end up walking here?"

Ruth pulled back so she could look into Grandma's face. "The storm started while we were inside. Justin said it was too cold to take me home and that he didn't want to get stranded out at the farm because he'd have to pay extra for the horse and buggy he'd rented. I know Dad's just going crazy worrying about me. He always does when I'm out after dark."

"Did he just leave you at the school?" Angry glints showed in Grandma's eyes.

"No. He wanted to give me a ride here because he was afraid people would see me walking alone and blame him for abandoning me. I told him he deserved to be blamed and that I didn't want to see him ever again."

Grandma stroked Ruth's drying curls. "I guess this red hair isn't just for show."

Ruth felt a smile appear. "When he told me my dad shouldn't worry, my temper took over. My reaction wasn't at all Christian or ladylike."

"But it was perfectly human." Grandma handed her the tea again. "Justin didn't treat you with respect, and it's a healthy sign that it made you angry."

"What do you mean?"

"Sometimes a young woman gets so desperate for a husband, she lets a young man treat her inconsiderately. It may be like Justin not caring about your feelings tonight, or it could be more obvious, like making fun of her or treating her as though she can't think for herself. Unfortunately, he'll only get worse after marriage. That's how women end up marrying men who hit them. As long as a man's disrespect makes you angry, you won't marry the wrong kind of person."

"Is there any way to let Dad know I'm okay?" Ruth knew he'd probably begun to pace. The storm had come from the north, which meant it would have hit the farm before town. He'd know exactly what kind of weather she'd been out in.

"Are you goin' to jabber all night, Miz Barry?" The door on the right side of the kitchen opened, and Mr. Carey's rumpled head emerged.

"I don't know, Mr. Carey. Ruth McEvan has been stranded in town and we were trying to figure out a way to get word to her dad that she's with me."

He scowled. "She didn't come in with her family?"

Ruth looked at Grandma, wondering what she'd say. Grandma paused. "A young man brought her in for the Shakespeare reading, but his horse isn't very surefooted in this weather."

"If that Harper boy is the one, the problem ain't his horse. How do you think your horse would manage?"

"Morton's steady in any kind of weather."

"If you let me ride him, I'll take a message out to the farm then."

"Would you really? Oh, Mr. Carey, you're just wonderful." Relief warmed Ruth all the way through. Stepping out of the pan of warm water, she impulsively ran to hug him.

He squirmed away, though his eyes looked suspiciously soft. "Ain't no cause for carryin' on. Just hate to know a man's all worked up over nuthin'."

Grandma Lucy almost hid her grin. "Do you have a good rain slicker? That snow's melting almost as fast as it's coming down and there's a sharp wind. You'll also need a good wool sweater underneath. I can wrap up a jar of hot coffee to give you something warm to drink on the way and—"

Mr. Carey held up his hand. "Just 'cuz I'm offerin' to do Miss McEvan a favor doesn't mean I need you runnin' my life. I wouldn't huv offered if I didn't know what I was doin'." His door shut with an emphatic click.

Grandma Lucy grinned. "Isn't it a shame when a man has to work that hard to be a grump?" she whispered, emptying the coffee pot into a quart jar, which she wrapped in several dishtowels.

Ruth grinned back. "Mom's told me how he's mostly bark and very little bite."

"When it comes to you children, he's a genuine pussycat, if you don't mind a different metaphor." She paused as he came out of his room wearing a wide-brimmed floppy hat and a slicker that reached past his knees.

"Got that coffee ready?" He harumphed when she told him to ride safely and thumped down the hall in his rubber boots.

"Did you know he still talks about the first time you visited here?" Grandma poured the pan of water into her slop pail and handed Ruth a fresh cup of tea.

"I'm not sure I remember," Ruth confessed.

"You and Ida had talked at church, and she brought you home for supper."

Ruth thought she recalled what had happened. "Wasn't that the day we went on a sleigh ride with a man who wanted really badly to impress her?"

Grandma nodded. "Ken Danielson. You were the first guest Ida had invited here. Mr. Carey commented after you left that you had the saddest eyes he'd ever seen. He always asks how you're doing and was pretty mad when he heard your school is closing. I'll bet anything he was eavesdropping and that's why he came out when he did."

"It was really nice of him to offer to ride out there."

"You should have seen the look on his face when you hugged him." Grandma giggled again. "I don't think anyone else could have gotten away with it."

"It's strange that he wants to be so nice to me. It's not like he's known our family for a long time or anything."

"It's not strange at all, dear girl. You and Ida both have gentle hearts that bring out the best in people. That's part of why you're such good teachers."

Ruth felt her cheeks warm at the praise. "At least a dozen times a day, I wish I had somewhere I could teach next fall. I'm still wondering if I could handle living in the city long enough to get my teaching certificate, maybe even a degree."

Grandma filled the teacups again. "You mean accept your grandmother Carrington's offer?"

"Just for a couple of years," Ruth mumbled, looking down into her tea.

Grandma paused. "Why?" Her uncharacteristically short answer surprised Ruth.

"I'm not sure there's anything left for me here," she admitted. "Dad says he and Mom are blessed to have me around, but I don't feel like a blessing. Without a job, I feel useless. Why should they have to support me when I'm supposed to be an adult and they still have little ones?"

"It sounds to me like you're calling your dad a liar. In the process you're also calling God a liar."

Ruth couldn't deny the first part of the accusation, though she didn't see what it had to do with God.

"If you can't trust your dad when he says you're no burden, how do you expect to trust God when He says He's ordering your life?"

"I wish I could," Ruth mumbled miserably.

"May I tell you what I think?" Grandma waited for Ruth's nod. "I think you're still angry with God for allowing your mother and brothers to drown. Until He explains Himself, you aren't willing to give Him more than token trust. You're trying to control your life so well you don't have to depend on Him."

Again, Ruth wished she could contradict Grandma's statement.

Grandma placed her hands around Ruth's tight grip on the cup. "Please look at me, child. God understands your fear of trust. He knows you feel betrayed. But He'll only be your Lord as far as you'll allow Him. If you want to run things on your own, He'll let you until you realize how puny your understanding is compared to His wisdom." She let the words sink in before continuing. "Have you read the book of Job in the Bible?"

Ruth shook her head. "It always looked boring." In all honesty, she hadn't opened the covers of her Bible in months.

Grandma smiled understandingly. "You might not find it so boring now. Job was one of the wealthiest and one of the most righteous men in the world of his time. God let Satan take away Job's entire family, all of his possessions, his health, and his wife's loving support. Scripture says, 'In all this, Job sinned not, nor charged God foolishly,' and later, 'In all this did not Job sin with his lips.' Yet while he didn't blaspheme, he still tried to demand an explanation from God. God let Job yell into the wind as it were until he ran out of demands. Then God finally revealed Himself, but without explaining any of His actions. He merely gave illustration after illustration of man's complete inability to understand or explain God. Once Job traded his demands for an appreciation of God Himself, God rewarded him with twice as much wealth as he had had before, restored his health, and gave him a new family."

Ruth looked at Grandma disbelievingly. "You mean God did all that to Job just to make him trust Him?"

"No, that's one of the strange things about Job's story. What happened to Job was actually a result of Satan trying to prove that Job only loved God because God had blessed him. God knew Satan was wrong, so He let him take away the blessings."

"Did God ever tell Job why it all happened?"

Grandma shook her head. "Not as far as we can tell from Scripture. It's what I find so beautiful about the story. Through Job's experiences, God illustrated the value He places on trust. Trusting God means we have more confidence in who God is than in our ability to understand Him."

"But how can we trust Him if we don't understand Him?"

Grandma's eyes glowed as if imparting invaluable treasure. "We trust because we believe what God says about Himself. He says He loves us. He says He wants only what is best for us. So, even though we can't explain how He accomplishes those objectives through what we see as the bad things in our lives, we have confidence in His ability to do what He says. That's why trust has nothing to do with how we feel. It has everything to do with who He is."

Ruth studied Grandma's face for several minutes. "I wish I trusted God like you do. I've tried, but it just doesn't work."

Grandma's grip tightened around Ruth's hands. "My dear child, trust isn't something you try. It's something you just do. When you get desperate enough, you'll discover how easy it is. Now, let's get you to bed."

Long after she'd been tucked into the big double bed in the room beside Grandma Lucy's, Ruth lay staring into the darkness. Every time she closed her eyes, she could see the river. Against her will, she felt again the sickening thump of their raft hitting a submerged log, then tipping them all into the water. She'd been holding baby Greg, so she swam to the bank and laid him on the grass. She'd turned back to the water in time to see Dad dive in after depositing Phillip. He'd hollered for her to stay put and watch the little ones. She'd watched Mother's head go under just before Dad reached her. Daniel had tried to help, but a piece of the raft struck him on the head and the current carried his limp body downstream. She screamed as she followed on the riverbank, useless to do anything. An eddy sucked him under, taking with him her childhood faith. Nine-year-old Sam and seven-year-old Benjamin also vanished.

She buried her face in her pillow, trying to shut out the horrible memories. Instead, she saw Dad's grief-stricken eyes as exhaustion had forced him to give up his futile search. The look on his face had solidified her anger. It felt as though her heart had iced over. She didn't cry for almost two years. With the first bout of tears came enough healing to help her function again, but the rage hadn't dissipated. The incredible effort of maintaining her schooling while taking care of her family had been a relief. As long as she kept too busy to think, the horrible, helpless feeling stayed in the shadows. Teaching accomplished the same. Except she could no more preserve her classroom than she could have rescued her family.

Rage boiled inside. How could God do this to her again? She had to clamp her lips together to keep the screams inside. If only she were out on a ride with Sunset where she could let it all out. The urge to scream turned into sobs so intense, she felt the bed shake. Scalding tears poured down her cheeks. Only one word filled her brain. "Why? Why? Why?"

Only vaguely, she felt comforting arms scoop her against a warm shoulder. A tender voice gradually subdued her mental roaring, though she heard no specific words. Her weeping continued as though squeezed from her very soul. Gentle rocking finally replaced her tears with sleep.

Chapter 8

Sunlight peeking around the curtains woke Ruth the next morning. She studied the unfamiliar surroundings for several moments before remembering where she was. The reading, the storm, Mr. Carey's trip to the farm gradually came into mental focus. Then those tormenting memories after she'd gone to bed. Her eyes felt sticky and sore and her head felt swollen.

She dressed and bathed her face gently from a basin of cool water on a washstand by the door. Grandma Lucy met her at the bottom of the stairs with a hug. "Did you sleep okay?"

Ruth's still fragile emotions produced more tears. "Yes, once I got to sleep. Were you in my room last night?"

Grandma smiled and nodded. "You fell asleep in my arms. It wasn't a nightmare that upset you, was it?"

"Memories." She saw understanding in the soft gray eyes. "I'm sorry I disturbed you."

Grandma gently brushed tears off Ruth's cheeks. "Please don't be. I only wish I could take away the hurt." After another hug, she asked, "Do you feel like breakfast?"

Surprisingly, she did. She'd just finished her third pancake drenched in cranberry syrup when Dad arrived with Mr. Carey in the mud-spattered wagon with Morton tied behind. The snow had melted, making the outdoors a sea of mud. She ran outside to meet him. He leaped down and hugged her so tightly she couldn't breathe. "I was so worried about you."

Ruth leaned back to smile at him. "I know. I was worried about your worrying."

He gave her a ghost of a smile. If he noticed signs of last night's turmoil on her face, he didn't comment. "We thought sure Mr. Carey had brought us bad news. What happened that Justin couldn't bring you home?"

Ruth gave a sketchy account of the previous evening's events, omitting Justin's behavior during the readings and her angry outburst. Dad's brows drew together in a deepening scowl, so she tried to finish on a positive note. "Grandma Lucy bundled me up next to the stove, and Mr. Carey volunteered to take a message out to you."

Dad didn't change his expression. "Mr. Justin Harper and I are going to have a talk."

Grandma Lucy chuckled. "From what I heard, your daughter already gave him a good dressing down."

"A second one won't hurt," he replied grimly. "I think I'll stop by the telegraph office on our way out of town."

From her vantage point behind Dad, Ruth saw Justin's face pale as they entered the building. He tried to smile charmingly. "I was just going for lunch, but William here will be happy to help you."

"Since you're leaving anyway, how about meeting me outside. I'm glad what I have to say won't interfere with your working time." Dad's voice held an ominous chill. "I wouldn't dally if I were you."

Dad had just helped Ruth back into the wagon when Justin approached hesitantly. "If you'll let me explain, Mr. McEvan. . ."

Dad cut him off. "There's nothing to explain, Mr. Harper. The moment you invited my daughter to accompany you, you assumed responsibility for getting her back to me safely. Since you proved yourself totally incapable of handling that kind of responsibility last night, you will never be permitted to take my daughter anywhere for any reason. Am I making myself clear?"

"Sir, I didn't think you'd want me to bring her home in such dangerous weather."

"And what was your excuse for not riding out to tell me where she was?"

Justin had to think. "My horse isn't very surefooted in mud or snow."

"That's a lame excuse if I've ever heard one. What kept you away from the livery?" The sarcasm in Dad's voice sent shivers down Ruth's neck. When Justin didn't reply, Dad continued. "Your problem, Mr. Harper, is selfishness. You didn't bring Ruth home because you didn't want to make the effort. Don't bother coming around to change my mind. You won't be welcome." He climbed into the wagon and slapped the reins. "Good day, Mr. Harper."

Dad said nothing until they were almost home. "I hope you didn't mind my telling him not to come around again."

Ruth smiled reassuringly, relieved to see his temper abating. "I already told him I didn't want to see him again. He didn't believe me, though."

"He'd better have believed me."

Mom met them at the barn with a hug for each. "Are you okay, honey?"

"I'm probably better than Justin." Ruth grinned. "Dad really let him have it. Grandma accused me of having a redheaded temper, but she should have seen Dad."

Mom ruffled Dad's rusty hair. "If all he did was talk to Justin, he restrained himself admirably. He *was* threatening physical violence. What happened last night?"

Ruth related the story, this time in its entirety. "I don't know why he even took me. He certainly didn't appreciate the readings."

Mom raised her eyebrows. "Who knows? If yours and Dad's combined efforts haven't convinced him not to come calling again, nothing will."

Jed's visit later in the evening helped soothe Ruth's lacerated emotions. He gave Beth and Timmy countless shoulder rides around the house, then let Greg beat him at checkers. Ruth thanked him for his patience after they escaped outside for a walk. "You're even better with the little ones than Greg and Phillip."

A bit of pink tinged Jed's ears. "Teddy arrived just before my tenth birthday, so I learned early how to handle babies. I've always wished I'd grown up in a large family like Uncle James and Aunt Ruby's. I probably ought to get married pretty soon if I want to see that dream come true." He looked at her with odd intensity.

She glanced away toward Sunset galloping across the pasture beyond the corral. "I hadn't realized before how much a part of my life my own horse could become. Isn't his gait just terrific? I enjoy watching him as much as riding him. My dad sure knows how to pick a horse."

He followed the conversational distraction. "You should come over to our farm and see the entire stock. The new colts pick on each other and carry on like a bunch of children."

She turned to lean her back against the rails. "There honestly isn't much about the farm I don't enjoy. Even weeding the—" A plume of black smoke off to the west caught her attention. "What's that?"

Jed squinted for just a moment. "It looks like a fire near the Pierces. I'll saddle up if you'll go get your dad."

Ruth dashed toward the house, yelling long before she arrived. "Dad! Dad, come quick!"

Dad yanked the door open just as she reached it. "What on—" He glanced over her head and saw the smoke. "Oh Lord, please help us!" he prayed aloud, then grabbed his coat and boots. "Ida, it looks like there's a fire at or near the Pierces' place. Jed and I are headed over to help. Phillip! Front and center right now!"

"I'll come, too." Mom reached for her coat. "Greg can watch the babies."

"No." Dad's emphatic response stopped her. He put his hands on her shoulders and gentled his tone. "If you come, you'll try to help and get all worked up. I'd much prefer you stay here. Prayer will do more for us than water, anyway. For your sake and for our baby, please?"

Mom wrapped her arms around him. "You're right. Just keep yourself safe."

He kissed her quickly and joined Ruth outside. "Are you coming?"

"If you don't mind."

"Cynthia and Sara could probably use your comfort." He looked back toward the house and bellowed, "Phillip John McEvan!"

The name had hardly left his mouth when the front door opened. "Coming, Dad. What's up?"

"Fire at Pierces' place. We're going to need your help."

Even Phillip's face blanched. Fire presented a fearsome threat. In moments, a blaze could destroy a farmer's most expensive assets. Even if livestock were saved, hay, feed, and many farming tools usually disappeared with a barn. Despite firefighters' best efforts, flames could easily spread to other nearby buildings. Lumber to replace any structure didn't come cheaply.

Once onto the main road, Dad encouraged the horses into their fastest trot. The fire's glow intensified as they approached the Pierces' farm, confirming their fears for their neighbors. Ruth visualized the lovely home which she knew as well as her own. Would there be anything left of it?

Dad turned the team down the Pierces' lane, providing a full view of the disaster. Huge flames leaped and danced around what had been Doug Pierce's beautiful, two-story barn. Mr. Pierce stood at the well in front of the house, filling buckets as fast as he could pull them up. Jed had already joined the fight, carrying the water across the farmyard. Mrs. Pierce used what looked like a wet sheet to beat at the ground where sparks ignited smaller fires between the barn and the house. Dad stopped the team at the edge of the Pierces' farmyard, tying the horses to a fence rail. Phillip leaped from the wagon almost before it stopped moving and dashed forward to join Jed. Ruth scrambled down and took off toward the well at a run with Dad right behind her. "I'll send Phillip to relieve Doug at the well," he yelled. "You and Mrs. Pierce can help most by keeping buckets full and sheets wet," he yelled as he ran toward Mrs. Pierce.

A large washtub sat beside the well. Ruth grabbed a bucket Mr. Pierce had just filled and dumped its contents into the washtub. Phillip came back with another empty bucket. "Mr. Pierce, Dad says for me to take over from you."

With only a nod, Mr. Pierce snatched the two buckets he'd just filled and ran toward the fire. Jed returned to the well for more water, and Sara approached from the house with an armful of sheets. Instead of crackling comfortably like a bonfire, these flames roared. The noise sounded like it came from all sides. Mrs. Pierce relinquished her battle to Dad and joined Ruth at the washtub. Her hair straggled around her face, while the stylish twist at the back of her head sagged. Soot streaked her face and dress. Though she looked ready to drop from exhaustion, she didn't hesitate before lifting a dripping sheet from the tub and passing it to Dad.

Ruth had never been more impressed with her oldest brother than during that night. He pulled endless buckets of water from the well almost as quickly as they were used to fight the blaze. In sharp contrast to his often indolent attitude toward farm chores, tonight he didn't pause for even a moment in his grueling, yet monotonous task. She emptied yet another pail of water into the washtub. Mrs. Pierce passed dripping bedsheets and full buckets to the men and accepted empties and sooty linen.

"Jed, look out!" Mr. Pierce's shout made Ruth look toward the barn just as what was left of one of the outside walls burned loose from its supports and fell outward. She bit back a scream as Jed barely leaped clear of the deluge of coals and sparks. All three men converged on the spot to prevent the burning fragments from starting new fires.

The close call reminded Ruth how easily this crisis could turn to tragedy. In volunteering to help, Jed had risked his life. Part of her mind focused on the vital task at hand while another part contrasted Justin and Jed. Just twenty-four hours had brought out the worst in one and the best in the other. Though they were close in age, Justin still behaved like a boy while Jed was, without question, a man.

Darkness engulfed them, but they fought on in the light of the flames. Ruth's muscles ached from endless effort. Tension knotted her stomach. Bit by bit, the rest of the barn collapsed. Miraculously, the men kept the fire from spreading across the yard.

Dad appeared beside the washtub, so Ruth thrust another sheet at him. He let it drop. "Thanks, Ruthie, but we've won."

"What?" She turned to grab another bucket from Phillip.

"The fire's out. You can stop."

She looked blankly around the farmyard. Moonlight shadowed rubble, which still smouldered where the barn had been. Jed stood guard, while Mr. Pierce comforted his now-weeping wife. Sara's scared face peered out the door. "What about his stock?"

"He'd just put them out to pasture yesterday. He figures he won't need bedding hay or feed for them until fall. Basically he just lost the barn itself."

Dad draped his arm over her shoulders. "We couldn't have done it without either of you." He grabbed Phillip as the boy headed toward the ruins. "Son, I'm proud of you. You came through like a man tonight."

Phillip just grinned and shrugged away, but Ruth noticed a bit of pride light his face.

Sara thrust a tray of glasses at them. "Cold water?"

"Thanks." Ruth took two. "I'll take one over to Jed." He didn't turn until she called his name. "Jed? Are you all right?"

"Yeah." He drained the glass. "I wish we could have gotten here sooner. A barn's tough to lose."

His empathy for the Pierces intensified the admiration she'd been feeling toward him all night. "Thanks for being here. You came close to getting badly hurt."

"Yah. We do what has to be done."

"I was really scared for you when I saw that wall falling."

He turned to face her directly. "You saw it happen?"

"Yes. I almost screamed."

"I didn't think I'd be able to get out of the way fast enough." He seemed to look for something in her face.

She felt compelled to say something. "I'm glad you made it."

"Yah." He nodded. "I've been thinking about the things I would have missed out on if I'd been trapped."

The intensity and length of the conversation surprised her. He'd never before been so willing to talk. She didn't reply, hoping he'd continue.

He let a pause linger. "I've always wanted a family of my own someday. After tonight, though, someday's not soon enough." He studied her silently until Ruth started to feel uncomfortable. "Um, Ruth," he cleared his throat. "Maybe I'm a fool for asking, but. . ." He kicked at some blackened wood. "I mean, this is probably the worst time possible to ask, but. . ." Gulping air, he spoke his piece in a rush. "What I mean is, do you think you'd ever want to marry me?"

Chapter 9

Ruth peered dumbly though the darkness at Jed. "Are you serious?"

"Yah." Jed's speech had taken on the flavor of his parents' Norwegian background. "It's time I have me a family."

She had an overwhelming urge to laugh and cry simultaneously. She'd despaired of ever receiving a proposal, much less discussing the matter beside the smoking remains of Theo's parents' barn. "Why are you asking me? Why not some other girl?"

He kicked at a charred piece of wood. "Most girls want to get away from farmin'. You said you love it. Besides, Ma has been tellin' me for a long time how much she'd like to have you as a daughter-in-law."

"You've talked to your parents about us?" Ruth couldn't decide whether to feel flattered or insulted.

"Yah. I know I haven't been callin' on you long, but we do get along real well. Pa said he'd give us a few acres to build a cabin on. It wouldn't be much to start, but we'd build on as we could afford it."

Ruth felt as if she were sitting on a runaway horse. What could she say that would neither commit her nor turn away this possibility? It wasn't that she didn't care about Jed. She'd just never thought of him as anything but a friend.

He didn't appear disturbed by her hesitation. "This is too fast, yah? Maybe you should think and tell me later."

She would have hugged him if she hadn't noticed Mr. Pierce approaching. "Thank you."

"I don't know what she's thanking you for, son, but my wife and I are deeply grateful for your help this evening." He gave Jed a hearty thump on the back. "Do you have time to come inside for a little refreshment? We shouldn't have to watch this anymore. No coals could survive in all that water we dumped."

Ruth relished her reprieve from the confusing intensity of Jed's inquiry. She carefully removed her muddy, soot-streaked shoes at the door. "I hope we won't make a mess in Mrs. Pierce's lovely house."

"If it weren't for you, our house might not still be here," Mr. Pierce replied. "Don't worry about it, please." He directed them to the dining room table, where Mrs. Pierce sat with her hands in a bowl of water.

Ruth hurried around Phillip. "How did you burn yourself?"

Mrs. Pierce smiled wearily. "It must have happened when I was helping Doug before you came. I didn't realize until after it was all over how much my hands hurt." She lifted them out of the bowl. Blisters that must have formed early in the evening had been torn open by her handling of the buckets and sheets. Now patches of raw skin lay exposed on both sides of her hands.

Ruth winced. "That must hurt."

"Some." Mrs. Pierce submerged them again.

Mr. Pierce emerged from the kitchen with a pitcher of water and a steaming teapot. Sara followed with glasses and mugs. They both vanished into the kitchen again and returned with cake and small plates. "Let's thank the Lord," he suggested. "Heavenly Father, thank you for keeping us all safe tonight and that the fire didn't spread beyond the barn. Thanks especially for these friends who saw our need and came to help. Bless them as only You can do. I also ask You to ease the pain in Cynthia's hands and bring quick healing. In Jesus' name, Amen."

Ruth felt bone-deep exhaustion set in while she ate. Yawns threatened to escape each time she opened her mouth for another mouthful of cake. Mrs. Pierce ate or drank little, preferring to keep her hands in the cool water.

"Do you have some ointment and soft cloths?" Ruth asked softly under cover of the men's conversation. "I could bandage your hands for you before I leave."

Mrs. Pierce's lovely, gracious smile appeared again. "I'd appreciate that. Doug tries to be gentle, but he doesn't always succeed. Sara," she caught her daughter's attention. "Would you please bring me the burn salve from the kitchen and the cloth strips from the upstairs cupboard?"

Obviously pleased to be able to do something for her mom, Sara hurried back with the supplies. Ruth spread the salve as tenderly as she knew how.

"Ooh, that feels nice," Mrs. Pierce breathed. "It's taking the sting out already."

"Where did you get it?" Ruth studied the unfamiliar container carefully, thinking it would be handy to have around their farm.

Mrs. Pierce turned her hands so Ruth could complete her ministrations. "Theo sent it soon after he started medical school."

"I'm glad it works," Mr. Pierce observed. "I think we'd better see if we can find someone to help you around the house for a week or so. I'd rather you didn't try to do very much until those burns heal."

"I wish I could disagree, but there isn't much I could do alone." The injured woman looked at her husband as though drawing invisible strength from him.

"I'll help," Sara protested.

Her dad hastened to reassure her. "I know you will. I'd just like to have another adult around. You have to keep up with your studies, and your mom's going to need a lot of personal help as well as housekeeping."

Ruth glanced at her dad, who nodded slightly. "I'd be glad to stay with you for awhile, if you'd like. I'll be at school during the day, but I'm usually home by four in the afternoon."

Mrs. Pierce's eyes lit up. "Would that work, Doug? She and Sara can leave lunch for you on the stove. I should be okay on my own while they're at school."

Doug smiled. "I think what my wife is trying to say is that she can't think of anyone she'd rather have. If you're willing to come, we'd both be grateful."

"When would you like me to move in?"

Mr. and Mrs. Pierce looked at each other in the wordless communication Ruth had often seen her parents use, then Mr. Pierce spoke. "How about late afternoon tomorrow? Bring your whole family over and we'll have tea. Jed is welcome, too."

Dad nodded agreement while pushing himself away from the table. "If Ida's feeling up to it, we'll be here."

"How's Ida doing these days?" Mrs. Pierce wanted to know. "I've not been able to visit with her as much as I'd like."

"She's still tired and not eating much, but she assures me she's fine. I won't rest easy until the baby's born."

"Isn't that the way it always is?" Mr. Pierce grinned and draped a protective arm around his wife's shoulder. "This business of having babies is pretty terrifying from our angle." Ruth remembered Theo telling about the three babies who had died between his birth and Sara's and how close his mother had come to death when Sara was born.

"True enough," Dad agreed. "She wanted to come with us, but I asked her not to."

Mrs. Pierce nodded. "I'm glad you did, Timothy. Fighting a fire is no job for a woman in her condition. We'd have had a hard time forgiving ourselves if anything had happened to your baby tonight."

"You're sure she can spare Ruth?"

Dad smiled directly at Phillip. "Absolutely. She'll have two strong boys who've already promised to help as much as they can. We'd best be on our way. My wife isn't a worrier, but she won't go to bed until we're home."

The clock indicated an hour past midnight by the time they unharnessed the horses and stumbled into their own house. As Dad had predicted, Mom had waited up for them. She had hot bath water waiting and insisted on inspecting each of them for burns. "How are the Pierces?" she inquired as Phillip stripped off his shirt and disappeared behind the curtain that turned their kitchen into a bathing area.

"Cynthia burned her hands pretty badly before we got there," Dad responded. "She won't be able to do much for the next week or two, so Ruth volunteered to stay with them until her hands have healed."

"Bless you, Ruth!" Mom looked at her with shining eyes. "Your generosity makes me so proud and even makes me feel I'm doing something to help by extension. You're a daughter to make any mother proud."

Despite Ruth's weariness and the warm bath, sleep did not come easily. Her thoughts wouldn't turn off. What kind of answer would she give Jed? He wouldn't wait forever. What would the future hold for her if she said no? It almost felt as if she had to say yes if she didn't want to be dependent on her parents for the rest of her life. Hardly any chance existed of a man more dependable than Jed coming into her life. She certainly didn't feel about him the way Mom did about Dad. Maybe she just needed to make the commitment and love would follow.

Not a besotted kind of love, she told herself firmly, pulling on her housecoat for a trip on tiptoe to the kitchen. *Just a steady, comfortable affection.* She sat at the table and sipped milk, willing her whirling thoughts into stillness. Instead, they turned to last night's conversation with Grandma. Who was the Bible character she'd talked about? *Job.* Ruth resolved to read his story sometime. Maybe next fall when she no longer had a classroom. Perhaps she'd be married by then. A sigh from her soul sounded loud in the silent room.

"Troubles?" Mom's whisper startled Ruth. Her slippers shuffled against the plank floor as she moved around the table to sit beside Ruth.

"Did I wake you?"

Mom hugged Ruth's shoulders. "No, you didn't, but thanks for asking. My bedtime snack seems to have given me indigestion. I didn't want to wake your dad with my discomfort. What's keeping you up?"

Ruth looked down at the table, trying to decide which of her mental puzzles to put into words. "Jed proposed tonight."

Mom moved her hand to rub up and down Ruth's spine. "You don't announce that like a young woman who's in love."

"I don't think I ever will be, regardless of who might want to marry me."

"Why do you say that?"

"You and Dad love each other so much, it's like you're two halves of the same whole. If anything goes wrong with one of you, the other one hurts. I'd rather not be so tangled up with another person."

"Ruthie, that's what makes marriage such a joy! I wouldn't have married your dad if I hadn't known we'd become one in spirit as well as in name. The pain of oneness makes its joys even greater."

Ruth felt her tense neck muscles relax under Mom's tender massage. "Is that why Dad frets about you so much?"

Mom kept her chuckle barely louder than Ruth's question. "He worries because he's afraid of losing us. Love is a lot easier when one trusts the care of an omnipotent God."

"God doesn't always protect loved ones."

"I know." Compassion echoed in Mom's voice. "I'd still rather love completely while they're here."

One of the things that had drawn Ruth to this lady years ago had been Ida's loss of her mother just a few months before coming west. Her dad had died in 1917 during the Great War. Ruth had felt Ida understood her pain as no one else could. Tonight she realized they had very different perspectives. "I wish I could feel that way."

"Ruthie," Mom placed her hand around her daughter's, "you can't go on holding God accountable for events only He can explain. You'll just become miserable."

"Grandma told me the same thing last night." Ruth returned gentle pressure. "She said God wants me to trust Him most when I can't understand Him."

"Scripture calls that faith and says without faith, we can't please God."

In that case, Ruth knew it would be a long time before she'd be pleasing to God. Trusting Him until she understood why He'd taken so much away presented too great a risk. "I think I can sleep now. Besides, if I keep you up any longer, Dad will have my hide."

She felt Mom's smile as loving arms closed around her. "I'll keep praying for you."

"Thanks." She wasn't sure prayer would do any good, but it couldn't hurt.

Morning came far too quickly. Gentle shaking awakened her and she tried to force gritty eyes open. Mom's face hovered over her. "I'll be serving breakfast in about twenty minutes."

Ruth knew she dare not stay in bed even a moment after Mom left, or she'd fall asleep again. Why did she feel so sore and exhausted? Memory returned with increasing detail. Would Jed expect an answer today?

∞

Church made her feel like a hypocrite. She mouthed words to hymns, listened dutifully to testimonies, and bowed her head for prayer while wishing she didn't feel so detached.

She risked a glance across the room at Jed. He appeared totally involved in the worship service. Finally, Mr. Spencer closed with a blessing on their meal. Ruth kept a smile glued to her face as she helped the other ladies move lunch from the stove to the outside table.

"—a big, healthy boy," Kate Harper was saying to anyone and everyone. "Her Jeff came to get me about ten o'clock, and by three, it was all over. My Nettie didn't so much as whimper. She just buckled down and got the job done. They've named him Aaron Lars after his two grandpas. He definitely has his mother's chin—"

"We weren't the only busy ones last night," Jed observed, settling beside her on the bench. "How do you feel after working so hard?"

"Pretty good," Ruth lied. "How about yourself?"

"Not bad, though I won't be able to visit the Pierces with you this afternoon. Mom wants us to take a family trip over to see the baby." He grimaced. "She and Nettie are going to expect me to say how cute he is. I like children, but only after they pass the baby stage."

She managed to laugh while noticing how closely Ellen Miller watched Jed. She waited for the stab of jealousy that never came. It wasn't that she felt secure in his affection. She simply felt. . .nothing. Forcing her attention back to Jed, she predicted, "Just wait until the first time he calls you Uncle."

"We'll see." He didn't appear convinced. "It looks like Ma's already packing up to leave. I wanted to let you know I won't be around much this week. We've got two fields to seed and half a dozen colts to start breaking. But you're welcome to come over any time. If you need me for anything, send one of your brothers over with a message and I'll make time." His unspoken message came through clearly.

Meeting his gaze directly, she smiled genuinely for the first time. "Thanks, Jed."

He lifted his hat in salute and swung himself up into his parents' wagon. Her lunch had lost its appeal somewhere in the conversation. She sidled over to the slop pail where scraps were collected each week for the Millers' pigs and discreetly cleaned her plate.

The afternoon kept her too busy to think. While Mom napped, Ruth filled two pillowcases with clothing and underthings. Comb and brush set followed, along with her nightgown. Her Bible also went in as a final after-thought. She tied each cloth bag closed.

When Mom awoke, she insisted on assembling a crate of food. "It will make things easier on all of you if you and Sara don't have to do any baking right away," she informed Ruth, setting three loaves of bread on top of a paper bag full of cookies, several jars of canned vegetables, and two jars of chokecherry jelly. "At least you know you can serve Doug jelly sandwiches for any meal and he'll be happy."

Ruth answered with a laugh. "You're going to get everyone in the area addicted to your jelly."

"As long as you and your brothers bring me plenty of berries in the fall, we won't have a problem." She wedged a final jar into place. "I think we're ready to go."

The family piled into the wagon. Ruth followed on Sunset, who would help her get to and from school much more quickly than if she had to walk. At least that's what she'd told Dad. Her real reason lay in the feeling of freedom and independence the animal gave her. He remained the single element in her life that didn't prompt disquieting thoughts and uncomfortable questions.

Chapter 10

Monday brought one of Ruth's most frustrating days in the classroom. Sunshine streamed across desks and tempted her students to restless behavior. She searched in vain for the inner well of patience on which she'd come to rely. Instead, irritated reprimands left her mouth before she thought. Lunchtime brought an immense feeling of relief as she sent everyone outside and put her head down on her desk.

She had to get control of herself. Taking her inner turmoil out on her students was unforgivable. Tears seeped out from under her eyelids as she wondered how to make amends. A rustling at the door caught her attention. A folded piece of white paper protruded from between the door and its casing. Wiping her eyes, she crossed the room to investigate.

"*To Miss McEvan,*" read the outside. Ruth unfolded it. "*Dear Miss McEvan,*" the short note began. "*I love you and wanted you to know. Sara Pierce.*" Tears coursed down her face in earnest. The gentle words eased her troubled spirit and gave her an idea for making up for this morning. For starters, she'd give the class an extra twenty minutes of lunch break.

Everyone seemed subdued when she called them in. Once they'd settled into their seats, she spoke softly. "Class, I'm sorry for being such a grouch this morning. Will you please forgive me?" Their ready agreement threatened to crumble her composure, but she held on. "Thank you. I think maybe we should do something different this afternoon." A rustle of excited whispers swept the room. "In case you didn't know, Mr. and Mrs. Pierce's barn burned down Saturday night. Mrs. Pierce burned her hands trying to put the fire out. Would you like to write pretty notes to tell her we hope she gets well soon?" Seven of the eight heads bobbed excitedly. "What's the matter, Greg?"

He mumbled with embarrassment. "Boys don't make pretty things."

Knowing her brother's handwriting, Ruth didn't dispute the issue. "Is there something you'd rather do?"

He pondered the matter. "I could make her a rock collection."

Karin Harper snickered derisively, but Ruth silenced her with a look. "If you arrange them nicely and write her a note telling her something about each one, I think she'd find it a very nice present. Don't bring too many, all right?" She couldn't imagine a young boy's rock collection anywhere in the gracious Pierce home, but she'd resolved to make this afternoon as enjoyable as possible for her students.

"I know." Greg nodded as he dashed out the door.

Clara Spencer's hand went up. "May we talk while we work?"

Ruth smiled, thinking this could turn out very much like a ladies' sewing club. "Let's arrange your desks in a semicircle in front of my desk, so we can all visit while we work."

"Are you making a card, too, Teacher?" Tabby Spencer wanted to know.

"I wish I could." Ruth wrinkled her nose in a mock grimace. "But I really should grade some arithmetic papers."

"That sounds boring," Tabby pronounced.

"Won't we make it hard for you to conc'ntrate?" Julie Harper folded her sheet of white paper in half.

Ruth smothered a laugh. Actually, their chatter would make her least favorite job bearable. "No. I'll enjoy listening."

"You could just mark them all 100 percent so you could draw with us." Tabby's suggestion sounded like something Phillip would have thought of.

Ruth marked a red X beside two of her brother's incorrect answers. He knew his multiplication tables well, but often did his quizzes in such a hurry he made careless mistakes. "What do you suppose would happen if you took the paper home and your dad noticed I'd let you get away with incorrect answers?"

"My dad wouldn't even notice." June drew colored curlicues around the perimeter of her creation.

"Why do you say that?" Ruth put her pen down to concentrate fully on the girl's answer.

She looked up frankly. "He doesn't notice any of our schoolwork. I don't know why he makes us go when Jim is the only one who matters."

Ruth couldn't think of a good reply. She suspected James Harper Sr. probably didn't make a fuss over his children's schoolwork because he didn't understand what they'd done. Jed's mother had once mentioned that James hadn't gone to school beyond the third grade. But explaining this to June would only antagonize her further. "Does your mother talk with you about your work?"

"Nah. She's too busy. It doesn't matter. I think school's boring anyway. I'd rather be married and have babies like Patricia."

Her sentiment gave Ruth no feeling of surprise. Keeping the girl in school this year had taken a combination of encouragement from her teacher and insistence from her parents.

"I just tell Mama what we've done while we work," Julie offered, coloring a large orange sun at the top of her paper.

Ruth noticed June's eyes flash. She hastened to intervene before a family feud broke out. "I'm glad you've been here this year, June. The concert you're organizing is going to be the best we've ever had."

The compliment did the trick. Conversation shifted enthusiastically to details of the program. Karin and Julie planned to sing "A Mighty Fortress Is Our God" together. "We have to practice in the barn right after school so no one hears us before the concert," Julie explained as she cut shapes out of colored paper. "I'm singing melody and Karin is learning to sing something else."

"I listen to Mrs. Pierce on Sunday and try to copy her," Karin explained, her cheeks turning pink.

"Would you mind singing for me?" Ruth asked, curious to hear what the two had done.

"We have to stand up," chatterbox Julie informed her.

Ruth nodded. "That's fine."

Julie moved to stand beside her teacher. "First we hum, like Mrs. Pierce showed us in music class." The two hummed in unison, then Karin's voice moved to a tentative harmony and the hymn began. Their blended voices sounded almost identical when in unison, and enhanced each other in harmony.

"That's beautiful," Ruth enthused when they finished. "You both have lovely voices."

"Do I sound all right?" Karin's penchant for perfection brought worried wrinkles into her forehead.

"You have a real talent for music," Ruth reassured her. "Not many people could learn how to do that just by listening."

Karin still looked disturbed. "There are a couple of parts that don't sound right, and I can't figure out what's wrong."

"Maybe you could come home with me some afternoon," Sara offered. "Mom could help you and Dad would drive you home afterward."

Karin's face glowed. "Your mom wouldn't mind?"

Ruth blessed Sara for thinking of it. Even this morning, Mrs. Pierce had already begun to fret about feeling useless. She wouldn't be able to play the piano, but her ear for music could help the girls without an instrument. Ruth turned to June. "If anyone else wants to sing, I'm sure we could arrange for Sara's mom to help them, too."

June basked in the recognition of her leadership. "I'd kind of like all of us to do something like that together at the end of the play, but I don't know what."

"A play? I hadn't heard about this." Delight at their initiative tingled through Ruth.

The "director" beamed. "Sara and Clara wrote one together. It's about Queen Esther in the Bible."

"You did?" Ruth looked at the two girls. "That's terrific! Who is playing the men's parts?"

Both girls blushed, and June giggled. "They talked young Lionel and Michael into doing the King and Mordecai. When Phillip heard about it, he asked to be Haman."

Ruth groaned. "That sounds like Phillip. Is everybody in it?"

A chorus of agreement answered her.

"How have I not noticed what you were doing? I must have been totally unobservant."

"We kept it a secret deliberately," Sara hurried to reassure her. "We wanted to have it all planned before we told you so you wouldn't worry about it."

"Me? Worry?" Ruth tried to sound disbelieving. "Where are you getting the costumes?"

June turned pink this time. "Mrs. Spencer is showing me what to do with the scraps she, Ma, and Aunt Kate found for us."

"Do they know what's happening?"

"No." She shook her head emphatically. "At least Ma and Aunt Kate don't. We just told them we needed stuff for a surprise. I had to tell Mrs. Spencer so she could help me plan what everyone needs."

"You ladies amaze me." Ruth's students beamed under her praise. "Your initiative has made my day."

Six-year-old Audrey piped up. "What's 'nishutiv?"

"In this case, it's figuring out how to do something by yourself. You've shown initiative by making such a pretty picture without copying anyone else's." Ruth examined the youngster's drawing of a mass of brightly colored flowers. "Is everyone else finished?"

"Almost." "I will be in a minute." "As soon as I draw one more thing." The chorus indicated a unified conclusion.

Ruth remembered her only male student. "Where's Greg?"

"Here." The boy appeared in the doorway, his pockets sagging from their dense cargo and his hands holding a quart jar full of twigs, new grasses, and even a bit of moss. His shirt had come untucked from his pants, which showed evidence of close contact with mud, and his hair contained small bits of the same material he held in his jar. His eyes glowed with triumph. "It took me a long time," he explained unnecessarily, "but I found just the right stuff."

Ruth knew from experience how important "the right stuff" was to him. "What are you going to do now?"

He dumped his treasures on her desk. "Mom gave me this jar a long time ago, and I kept it in my fort for something special. See, if I turn it on its side like this, put the twigs in it like this and the moss like this, then the rocks look real nice on top. You'll have to be real careful, though." He looked at her with concern. "If you don't carry it right, it will get messed up."

She had to admit her brother had created an intriguing arrangement. It actually looked pretty, but she knew better than to say so. "I'll carry it properly and not let Sunset run while I'm taking it home."

"Do I still have to write sumthin'?" He looked at her hopefully.

"I would like you to at least make a note for Mrs. Pierce telling her who this is from and why you made it for her."

He wrinkled his forehead in thought. "I guess I can do that. As long as it doesn't have to be long."

Ruth shook her head with an indulgent smile. "First, though, I'd appreciate it if you'd clean off my desk and wash your hands. You don't want to get your paper smudged."

His expression didn't look as though he shared her concern, though he did follow instructions. While the girls tidied up after themselves and put the desks back in order, Greg sat hunched over his project. Finally, he looked up with an engaging grin. "Is this good enough, Ru—I mean, Miss McEvan?"

She stifled a grin of her own. Even after three years, her brothers still slipped up occasionally when addressing her. Dad had been the one to insist they call her "Miss McEvan" just like the rest of her students.

"Miss McEvan is your teacher, not your sister, when you're in that building. I don't want to hear of either of you trying to take advantage of her," he had informed them sternly at the beginning of each school year.

He won't have to make that speech this fall. She pushed aside the glum thought to examine Greg's work. The letters had obviously been formed carefully, in contrast to his usual scrawl.

Dear Missus Pierce,
> *I made this rock colekshun for you since Miss McEvan sed you was hurt. I hope you get well soon.*
>> *Greg McEvan*

"That's very nice," she approved. "Since everyone else is finished, shall we sit outside while I read another chapter in *Tom Sawyer*?"

A stampede for the door answered her suggestion. She rummaged on her desk for the book she'd begun reading aloud at the beginning of the year. Saved for special occasions, it looked like the story would last until the last day. She'd hoped to follow it with *The Adventures of Huckleberry Finn* next year.

Why does every day remind me of what I'll lose in just another six weeks? she wondered as she rode to the Pierces' two hours later with Greg's project carefully balanced in front of her. The students had gone home happy an hour ago, but she'd stayed to catch up on the never-ending quiz and composition papers. Her insides churned in turmoil. The school's closing still felt like a monumental loss. Her uncertain future now looked more complicated than ever. She felt uneasy about accepting Jed's proposal. Yet a negative response would turn away what most likely would be her only chance to choose an alternative to spending the rest of her life as Timothy McEvan's old maid daughter. Unless, of course, she accepted Grandmother Carrington's offer.

She had started to guide Sunset toward the small pasture near the house when she noticed Sara sitting on the back porch. The girl didn't look upset, but Ruth felt a prickle of concern. Idleness simply didn't come naturally to Sara. "Is everything all right?" she called out, halting Sunset near the porch steps.

Sara's cheery smile reassured Ruth more than her words. "Perfectly. Mom's sleeping, so I didn't want to do anything noisy inside. You'd probably have time for a ride before she wakes up."

Tempted by the suggestion, Ruth felt compelled to protest. "What about supper?"

"Dad came in about half an hour ago and said we ought to plan for a late one and just let Mom sleep as long as she can. He said she hasn't rested well the last couple of nights."

"If you're sure—" Ruth still hesitated, not wanting to appear irresponsible.

"Go away." Sara's blue eyes twinkled as she waved a small hand toward the pasture. "If my brother were here, he'd say you need some time by yourself. I'll even take your things inside for you."

Uncanny perception must be a Pierce family trait, Ruth mused to herself as she handed over Greg's gift and her school satchel. A ride over some of the trails she and Theo had discovered together should at least quiet her tumultuous emotions enough to enable her to think clearly. She dismounted to open the gate into the pasture where the occupants of the former barn now grazed contentedly, led Sunset through, then fastened the gate back into place. Over in one corner a dark gray horse stood alone. The black splotch on his forehead exactly matched the color of his mane and tail. He turned his head toward the newcomers and nickered a greeting. As Sunset wandered toward the gray, thoughts of Theo came to the forefront of Ruth's mental tangle. Shadow, as Theo had named the horse, had taken the two of them on countless jaunts around the countryside. He and Sunset touched noses, and she leaned forward to stroke his head. Closing her eyes, she remembered the feel of galloping across a field, her arms wrapped around her friend, her cheek pressed against his back. The memory only intensified her futile wish to be able to talk everything over with him. She turned Sunset toward a trail that was just barely visible in the bush bordering the pasture. Aching for a long, hard gallop yet mindful of Dad's many warnings, she firmly held Sunset down to a walk. Neither she nor her horse knew this area well enough to hope to avoid the holes and low-lying soft spots that could cause a running animal to stumble. She'd never be able to forgive herself if her own carelessness hurt her horse.

On the other side of the bush line, the trail turned uphill, then flattened out at a small meadow. Ruth could see where the trail continued beyond this rise to another taller hill, but she turned back. The meadow provided an excellent view toward the Pierces' farm and the schoolhouse just a bit to the northeast. She'd joined Theo and his family on many Sunday afternoon picnics at this spot. The landscape below had changed since her last visit here. Mr. Pierce had managed to clear another pasture area out of what had been a poplar stand, and one of his pastures had been plowed into a field. She smiled to herself, feeling quiet contentment that contrasted sharply with the day's emotional upheaval. She loved the way the farms and homesteads could alter the Peace River Country, yet leave it the same. She and Theo had often sat up here and discussed how the cycle of land development had a rhythm similar to the seasons, always predictable yet never identical. Both offered a reassuring sense of continuity. How had he endured six years of isolation from this world they both cherished? She tried to imagine seeing people instead of trees, houses instead of barns, well-tended yards instead of freshly plowed fields. According to Grandmother Carrington, Toronto offered the best in city living. Could it provide anything as satisfying as this view?

The question touched too closely to the thoughts she'd come here to escape. She nudged Sunset with her heels. "Let's go back, fellow. It's probably time to start working on supper."

Twilight had already begun to encroach on the evening by the time

Ruth and Sara put the meal on the table. Mrs. Pierce apologized for sleeping so late, but her husband quickly reassured her. "You needed the rest, sweetheart. It hasn't hurt us a bit to wait a couple hours for supper."

Mrs. Pierce didn't look convinced, so Ruth added her own encouragement. "Besides, it gave me a chance to go exploring like Theo and I used to do. Remember that meadow where we used to go on family outings?"

Sara nodded. "It's been ages since we've been up there."

Teasing twinkles lit her dad's eyes. "You've appeared more interested in the view from the Spencers' farm lately."

Sara blushed, but didn't lose her smile. "You're just jealous because I bake more cookies for Lionel than I do for you."

Mrs. Pierce grinned. "I think she has you there, dear."

"That's okay," Mr. Pierce replied. "I noticed Mrs. McEvan took pity on me and sent some of her jelly over. As long as you ladies keep me supplied with bread, I won't need cookies."

Now the teasing twinkles showed up in Sara's eyes as she stood to clear dishes from the table. "In that case, I'll just bring you a couple slices of bread for dessert, and the rest of us will enjoy the spice cake I made this afternoon."

"Why can't I have both?" He pretended to pout.

His wife patted his arm. "I'll give you part of my cake."

Ruth reveled in the banter, so much like her own family's antics. Mom often said humor made the difference between simply coping and actually enjoying life. Her ready laughter had been a welcome addition to the McEvan family after almost two years of unrelenting sadness. Now Ruth wondered if her first mother had laughed much. She'd been only twelve when the river had changed her life. Why couldn't she remember clearly anything before it?

"Mmm. That was well worth the wait. Thanks, girls." Mr. Pierce pushed back from the table and kissed his wife. "I have a couple more things to take care of before nightfall, so I'd better get back at it."

Mrs. Pierce sat in the dining room quietly looking outside while Ruth and Sara cleaned up after the meal. Sara had just let the last of the dirty dishwater out of the kitchen sink when Ruth remembered her class project. "Did you give your mother her gifts?" she whispered.

Sara shook her head. "I thought you'd like to. I put them upstairs in your room."

Ruth ran upstairs to the pretty guestroom and returned to the dining room with Greg's jar in one hand and the cards in the other. "My students wanted to let you know they were thinking about you this afternoon." She set the jar on the table in front of Mrs. Pierce, and laid the cards out side by side so her friend could look at them without having to pick them up. "Greg made this instead of a card, and the girls each made you a card."

With the edge of a bandage, Mrs. Pierce opened each card with damp-eyed delight. "How thoughtful of you to suggest they cheer me up! This is something your mother would have thought of. You're more like her all the time, you know."

Ruth paused in the doorway, afraid to voice the strange question that had come to mind. "Which mother?" she asked softly.

Her companion's gaze lifted from the pile of get well wishes. "I meant Ida, but now that I think of it, you're much like Janet, too."

"How well did you know my first mother?"

Mrs. Pierce stared out the window again, remembering. "I'd say we were friends. Why?"

Ruth forced her hands to stay busy wiping the already clean table. "I don't remember much about her anymore. I can't even recall things we used to do as a family before—" Her voice broke.

Mrs. Pierce let her collect herself before reminiscing in her gentle, cultured voice. "We didn't have long to become acquainted with your family before the tragedy happened, but since we were neighbors we helped each other quite a bit. My Doug helped your father clear the area where your house was built, and your dad helped clear our upper pasture in return. Janet was about your height with dark auburn hair. I guess you didn't have a chance at any other color with two redheaded parents." She coaxed a smile from Ruth with one of her own. "Her eyes sparkled with enthusiasm for everything and she never seemed to run out of energy. Most of all, she had a contagious love for God. She talked to Him and about Him like He was her best friend. I'm sure she's just as tickled about being in Heaven as she was with being alive down here."

The quiet words only increased Ruth's heartache. *Why would God have done such a terrible thing to someone who loved Him so much?* She dared not voice the thought. "I don't remember my brothers much, either. Even Daniel, my twin. I wish I had that much left of them."

Mrs. Pierce gestured with a bandaged hand toward the sitting room. "Please sit with me a moment. I'd like to tell you something I don't discuss much." Ruth obliged, and with pain-shadowed eyes the lady continued. "You've heard our family's story from Doug when he shared it with our fellowship group."

Ruth nodded, remembering the snowy Sunday at the Spencers' farm.

She'd cried for the first time since the river, and Ida had been there with tears of her own and hugs of comfort. It had marked the beginning of a kind of healing, though she still felt far from whole.

"Each baby who died took a piece of me. I thought their little faces would be imprinted in my memory forever. I struggled to imagine what they'd be like as they grew. The first time Sara called me 'Mama,' I cried because I'd never heard it from my three babies. Doug let me weep for awhile, then ever so gently pointed out my grief was robbing me of the joy of Sara's important moments. I had to learn to release my little ones to the Heavenly Father whom they now know better than I did. While I can't tell you anymore what the babies looked like, I remember how their short lives brought me happiness." She smiled through tears. "If our memories remained vivid forever, our pain probably would, too, and that would be unbearable."

"Do you think she knows how we've felt and what's happened to us since she died?" Ruth whispered.

"Hebrews says we're surrounded by a cloud of witnesses made up of those believers who are already with God, so I think she does. She probably watches you even more closely than she did while she was here."

Ruth looked into the blue eyes in which compassion had replaced pain. "Why do you say that?"

"While she was alive, she loved you with a purely human love. Now she sees and understands you the way your Heavenly Father does and loves you just as much." She patted Ruth's leg softly with a bandaged hand.

The back door opened. "Cynthia, do you feel up to a walk?" Mr. Pierce called. "The sunset's really beautiful tonight."

Mrs. Pierce hurried to join her husband with the same delighted expression Mom wore when offered time alone with Dad. Ruth wandered up to her room feeling more unsettled than ever. She'd hoped happy memories of her mother would replace the horror-filled images that had plagued her at Grandma Lucy's. Instead, her quest had led her back to the nagging issue of her attitude toward God. If Mrs. Pierce were right, Mother knew Ruth wanted to keep God at a distance. She must be terribly disappointed. Yet if God had left well enough alone, Ruth wouldn't be questioning Him.

Chapter 11

After nearly a week, Ruth had reached a decision. The more she'd thought about it, the less life with Grandmother Carrington appealed to her. At least if she married Jed, she'd be able to remain near those she loved and in a familiar, comfortable environment. Yet she felt in no hurry to communicate her decision to him. Whenever she saw him next would be soon enough.

As she explained in a letter to Theo, *"At least this way, my future is secured. Jed is a pleasant companion and I'm sure we can enjoy as many comfortable years together as life allows us. With a wedding to look forward to, the end of school won't seem so bleak."* For the first time in their long friendship, she wondered if she was being completely honest with him.

Music practices were as successful as Ruth had hoped. The evening after the first one, Mr. Pierce met her at the edge of the pasture where she was saddling Sunset for an evening gallop. "Thanks for helping my wife. Bringing the girls over this afternoon lifted her spirits more than you can know."

She tugged on the saddle to ensure its straps were fastened securely and hurried to give due credit. "It was actually Sara's idea."

"But it wouldn't have happened without your encouragement." He stroked Sunset's pale mane. "How's the saddle working?"

"Perfectly." This was one subject about which Ruth could feel genuinely enthusiastic. "It's one of the nicest things anyone has ever done for me."

"You're more than worth it." He moved away from the fence. "Enjoy your ride."

She directed Sunset to the road before urging him to a full gallop. They thundered westward, past the turnoff toward home. Just before they reached the edge of Lars Harpers' freshly plowed land, she turned back. Tonight didn't feel like the right time to talk with Jed. With plenty of daylight still left, she decided to visit her favorite place by the creek and hoped her family wouldn't be offended that she'd been so close to home but hadn't stopped by. The water level had gone down quite a bit since her last visit. Its flow now seemed easy and peaceful. Too bad her life hadn't followed the same pattern. She began to fill another page in the book she'd left untouched since her last entry here at this very place.

> *I'm stretching, reaching for something I can't see.*
>> *I don't know what's just beyond my fingertips*
>>> *but I can almost touch it.*
> *There are some who see my helpless efforts,*
>> *who sense my restless spirit.*
> *They know what's out there.*
>> *Patiently, they watch me search, question, and sometimes react.*
> *They've already found.*
>> *Why can't someone pass the secret on to me?*
> *Why must I reach?*
>> *What will I grasp?*
> *They say trust is the key*
>> *But I don't understand.*
> *How can I depend on something which makes no sense?*
>> *Maybe someday I'll see it, touch it, claim it for my own.*
> *I can always hope.*

With her future at least partially arranged, she found school less heart-wrenching than usual. Remembering what Mrs. Pierce had said, she made a point of enjoying each day in the classroom as much as possible. The throbbing ache in her heart had disappeared, replaced by a kind of emptiness. Even questions about trusting God didn't plague her so much. Yet something Grandma Lucy had said wouldn't leave her alone. "You're trying to control your life so well you don't have to depend on Him. God will let you run things on your own until you realize how puny your understanding is compared to His wisdom. When you get desperate enough, you'll discover how easy it is to trust."

Ten days after the fire, she moved back home. Mrs. Pierce had held her in a long embrace as Ruth had prepared to leave. "Thanks for coming," she'd whispered. "You're a treasure."

Ruth wished she felt like a treasure instead of a bundle of confusion. She'd thought making a decision about Jed would unravel her feelings. Perhaps telling him what she'd decided would help.

Her entire family met her in the barn with hugs and exclamations of welcome. "Don't go 'way, never 'gen," Beth instructed, wagging her chubby baby fingers.

Mom laughed. "She's asked about you every day. I finally had to ask

Greg not to talk about school when she could hear. You should have seen the tantrum when she discovered he saw you every day and she couldn't. Then I had to keep her and Timmy home Sunday because they had the sniffles. I was not the world's most popular mother."

"I've missed you guys, too." She revelled in their welcoming affection. "Greg, would you ride over to Jed's for me and ask him if he can come over tonight?"

Dad's bushy eyebrows lifted. "You're not in a hurry to see him, are you?"

Ruth felt a flush stain her cheeks. "The night of the fire, he asked me to marry him. I still haven't given him my answer."

Her parents waited until Greg had gone and Phillip had disappeared to his fort before pursuing the subject. "So are you going to let us in on the secret or keep us in suspense?" Dad inquired as they sat around the table enjoying cups of tea. Mom's knitting dropped to her lap as she watched her daughter intently.

The question made Ruth uncomfortable, but there was no reason not to answer. "I'm going to tell Jed yes."

A shadow passed over Mom's face. "Are you sure about this?"

Ruth felt sure she'd chosen her only real option. "Yes. He treats me with respect and will be a good provider." Even to her ears, the words sounded defensive.

Dad studied the tabletop before looking up with a false smile. "Congratulations! Have you set a date?"

Apprehension briefly knotted Ruth's middle. Choosing a wedding date would move her decision from the realm of contemplation to reality. For the first time, she realized she was about to make a commitment that would change her life. "We'll probably discuss it tonight."

Mom laid her handwork aside. "I'll go get the little ones into bed, then whip up a cake so we can celebrate."

Dad and Ruth sat in uneasy silence. She'd never felt restraint with him before. When their gazes finally met, she saw her uncertainty reflected in his eyes. He reached out for her hand and cleared his throat. "You don't have to do this, Ruthie."

"I know." She tried to speak with conviction. "I'm doing it because I want to."

"But why?" He seemed to search her inner thoughts. "I don't think you love Jed. That won't make for an easy marriage."

She shrugged. "Love will come as we live and work together."

He cleared his throat again. "Ever since you and Daniel were born, I've dreamed of the day when you'd look at some wonderful young man the way your mother looked at me on our wedding day. Why don't you wait until you know you love him?"

"Because I don't want to." She knew her words would hurt him, but if she didn't make him understand, he'd talk her out of her tenuous decision. "I don't want to feel about anyone the way you and Mother felt about each other. If something happens to Jed, I want to be able to go on. Jed isn't madly in love with me, either, so it's not like I'll be taking advantage of him. Besides, if I don't marry him, who else is there?"

Pain filled Dad's eyes, though it seemed to be more for her than for himself. "You're shortchanging yourself, little girl." Hoofbeats in the yard caught his attention. He gave her hands a final squeeze. "I just want to see you happy."

"I will be." She stood. "It's plenty light out, so we'll probably wander around outside for awhile, but I'll make sure Jed comes in before he leaves."

To her intense relief, Jed didn't try to kiss her when she gave him her news. He just enfolded her hand in his large, calloused one. "You've made me very pleased."

She let him hold her hand for awhile before tugging it loose to point at a nest near the top of a tall pine. "Do you have any idea what kind of bird is building up there?"

He squinted upward for a moment. "Can't say I do. It's probably not good for eating or dangerous to the stock, so I don't pay much attention."

Ruth's parents had encouraged her to find out as much as she could about the plants and creatures with whom they shared the land. They'd praised curiosity and tried to help her find answers. "Don't you ever want to know about something just for the fun of finding out?"

Bafflement spread across his face. "Learnin' never was much fun for me. If it don't help me run the farm better, I don't need it clutterin' up my head."

What a boring way to live, Ruth thought, but kept it to herself. This man would become her husband. She had to learn to accept his way of thinking even if it differed from her own. "When do you think we ought to get married? Dad and Mom were asking if we'd set a date."

"It depends on whether you're set on takin' a trip." His tone, though pleasant enough, indicated he didn't feel much enthusiasm for the idea. "We'd have to wait until after harvest in that case."

She wanted to be settled into her new home by the time school started again. "Then we'd be travelling in snow and cold. I don't think we need a trip."

"Then let's get married near the end of June. The first hay crop won't be ready to come off until mid-July."

"Shall we go in and look at Mom's calendar?"

He nodded approval and reached for her hand again. She didn't pull away. Dad and Mom would notice if there weren't some show of affection.

Whatever their reservations, they welcomed Jed enthusiastically. Dad shook his hand and thumped his back. "Welcome to the family, Son."

Jed's blush deepened when Mom hugged him. "You'd better get used to it," she teased. "I don't plan to treat a son-in-law any different from my other sons. Hugs are routine around here."

Phillip and Greg appeared from their room to see what the fuss was all about. "Ruth and Jed are getting married," Dad informed them.

"When?" Greg looked uncertain.

"We actually came in looking for a calendar so we can decide just that." Ruth looked at the page tacked up on the kitchen wall. "What about June 27th? That will give me two weeks to get ready after school is out."

Mom pulled a pan from the oven. "Come sit, everybody. Who wants coffee and who wants tea?"

Greg and Phillip both asked for coffee along with Jed and Dad and were actually given some. Mom and Ruth sipped tea. "Do you know yet where you're going to live?" Mom asked.

"Pa's given me a few acres just across the creek. We'll probably stay in the big house until I can get a cabin built. Ma's really lookin' forward to having Ruth around."

Ruth avoided looking at her mother, their previous conversations about Kate Harper replaying in her memory. Could she handle sharing a house with the incessant talker?

"May I have the honor of announcing your plans this Sunday?" Dad asked. "If you don't mind, I'll see if we can get a cabin-raising organized for the weekend before the wedding. You young folks ought to have a place of your own from the start."

Jed shifted uncomfortably, his ears reddening. "I'd rather not be beholden. This is a busy season for everyone."

"Then perhaps you ought to postpone the wedding." Dad spoke conversationally, but Ruth heard a subtle challenge. "Adjusting to marriage is challenge enough without having to continue living with one set of parents or the other."

Evidently, Jed heard it, too. He met Dad's gaze directly. "I guess folks wouldn't come if they didn't want to."

A smile softened Dad's expression. "Just like you wouldn't have helped fight the fire if you hadn't wanted to. We all need each other from time to time. That's what pioneering's all about."

Dad's announcement on Sunday brought cheers and applause. Every man present promised to help with the cabin raising, and Mr. Albertson offered to supply windows "as our wedding gift to the kids."

Kate Harper hurried over to Ruth with a beaming smile. "I'm so proud I could burst," she exclaimed unnecessarily. "My Jed's one of the most responsible men in the Peace River Country, and you're the finest young woman I know. It will be wonderful having you as neighbors just across the creek. You're sure you don't want to get married a little sooner?"

"Don't be rushing them, Kate," Nina Spencer intervened. "Ruth has a school year to finish first."

"Didn't this work out fine?" Mrs. Harper's enthusiasm continued un-abated as she and Mrs. Spencer approached the food-laden table together, her voice carrying well. "I was beginnin' to wonder if she'd ever get married, bein' so attached to her teachin'. Not that it wasn't good for our children to have such a devoted teacher, but gettin' married and havin' babies is what girls her age are meant to do. Most girls settle even younger. Take my Nettie, for instance. Why, she was only sixteen when she and Jeff married. Little Aaron will be four by the time she's Ruth's age. Did I tell you he's already—"

"I hope you don't mind my mother." Jed approached with two laden plates. "Since she kinda had you cornered, I took the liberty of getting you some dinner."

"Thank you. That's very thoughtful." Ruth's smile came from her heart. If today was any indication, coping with her future mother-in-law would not be easy. Her suspicion strengthened into conviction a week later.

Mrs. Harper sent Teddy to the schoolhouse with a message for Ruth on Friday afternoon. "Ma says to ask you to come for dinner tomorrow night and to come as early in the afternoon as you want."

Ruth saddled Sunset shortly after four Saturday afternoon. Though she felt nervous about time alone with Mrs. Harper, she didn't want to insult the lady by not accepting the invitation to come early. This way, they'd only have an hour or two before the men came home from the fields.

Mrs. Harper seemed to have been watching for her. "Just take your horse to the corral and leave your saddle on the fence. The men will take care of it later," she called from the door.

Ruth followed instructions, though she felt uncomfortable about it. "If you can use something," Dad always said, "you can put it away properly."

Dumping her saddle on the fence rail certainly didn't fit that description, but neither could she simply hang it anywhere in the barn. Sunset certainly needed to be brushed down after the ride, but it also seemed rude to help herself to the Harpers' tools. She patted his neck. "I hate to do this to you, old pal, but I don't have a choice. I'll make it up to you when we get home."

Mrs. Harper met her in the yard. "I was hoping you'd be able to make it early, but I know how busy you must be with school and helping your ma and all. How is she feeling? The first few months are always so hard when one's in the family way. My Nettie thought she'd die. She and Jeff will be here in about an hour. That'll give you and me a chance for a real good visit. Now just sit there at the table and relax while I finish this cake I've planned for dessert. Jed loves spice cake. I'll have to be sure to give you all his favorite recipes, though I hope you two will feel free to just pop over here for a meal anytime you like. I envy you, being able to start your marriage so close to family. Lars and I moved out here right after our wedding so I had to learn everything by myself. He's an easy man to please, my Lars is, and Jed's pretty much the same." She poured the batter into a pan and placed it in the oven.

Sitting across the table from Ruth, she continued. "Did I ever tell you how Lars and I met? His family moved to the prairies from Norway when Lars was thirteen and James, ten. The boys had to work just like men right from the start, so neither finished school. Lars knew hardly any English when I met him. My parents had also come from Norway when they were children, so I'd learned enough Norwegian from them to help Lars learn English. He was twenty-one and I was sixteen when we married in a double ceremony with James and Ruby. Then the four of us moved out here. We started on a single homestead in Lars' name, then two years later James and Ruby started over on their own land. They got their lean-to finished just two weeks before James Jr. was born. I'll never know why they had to go and have seven children. I mean, your folks have six, but that's two families. No one expected Ida not to have babies just because your dad already had you three."

Ruth involuntarily thought of the days when her other brothers had been alive, then moved her thoughts to the six Spencer children. Large families were more common around here than small ones, but she wasn't given an opportunity to volunteer her opinion.

"Let me show you around our house real quick before I have to get dinner on the table. The men should be back soon."

Ruth followed her future mother-in-law throughout the two-story house, murmuring appropriate admiration when they reached the parlor.

"When Lars decided to build us a regular house to replace our old cabin seven years ago, I told him I wanted a parlor. He thought it a foolish idea, but built it anyway. Our bedroom is here at the back, and the children's bedrooms are upstairs. Of course, Nettie's is empty now, and Jed's will be at the end of next month." She smirked sideways at Ruth. "But it won't be long before we'll have grandchildren all over the place, and the rooms will be put to good use."

Ruth willed the heat out of her cheeks, wishing Mrs. Harper wouldn't be so plainspoken. She didn't want to think about having children just yet.

But her thoughts took a completely different direction when Nettie and Jeff arrived, bearing baby Aaron. "Let Miss McEvan hold him," Nettie instructed her husband, a short, blond young man with friendly brown eyes.

"I think since we're going to be sisters, you might as well call me Ruth," the former teacher requested, holding out her arms for Jeff's tiny burden.

"It may take me awhile to get used to being so familiar-like, but I'm real glad we're going to be family. If you don't mind keeping watch on the baby, I'll help Ma. There's Pa and the boys coming now, Jeff. They'll be glad of a hand with chores." Nettie obviously had not lost her childhood powers of organization.

Ruth sat with her back to the table, silently savoring Aaron's weight in her arms. She'd loved holding Timmy and Beth when they were tiny, but this felt different. What would it be like to hold a child of her own? He lay sleeping, a perfect picture of peace, totally undisturbed by the chatter and clatter created by his mother and grandmother. The vague desire she'd carried for months abruptly became full-fledged yearning. She fervently hoped she wouldn't have to wait long for her own baby.

He awakened just before the men came inside, so Nettie hustled him off for a feeding. "Go ahead and start without me," she instructed her mother. "I'll join you after Aaron's finished."

To Ruth's relief, the men had plenty to discuss as the food dishes passed from hand to hand around the table. Who knew what Mrs. Harper would say if talk moved to more general matters? She didn't have to wait long to find out.

"I'm sure Ruth's not interested in dirt and weather." She looked at Jeff. "I don't guess we've formally introduced you two. This is Ruth McEvan, one of Nettie's former teachers and Jed's fiancée. They'll be getting married at the end of next month."

"Congratulations," Jeff commented politely. "Will you be buying land nearby?"

Mrs. Harper didn't give Jed or Ruth a chance to answer for themselves. "Oh, no. They'll be building just on the other side of the creek so Jed can continue helping his pa on the farm."

Teddy used his fork to stab a piece of bread in the basket near the center of the table and lift it to his plate while grinning mischievously at Ruth. "You'll have a longer walk to school next year."

"She won't teach after she gets married," his mother informed him, "and ask for things to be passed. Ruth will think we've raised you in the barn."

From her experiences with the boy in school, Ruth recognized the glint in his eyes. He'd reached across the table just to get a reaction from his mother. She squelched the urge to wink at him.

"What's this I hear about consolidation?" Jeff asked, passing the mashed potatoes to his wife, who'd just sat down. "I haven't gone to any of the meetings since everything will probably change again before Aaron gets to school."

Mr. Harper explained what he knew of the plan from his role as trustee. *If Mrs. Harper hadn't just put a piece of pork roast in her mouth, she probably would have answered,* Ruth thought uncharitably. Her hostess's comment had struck a tender spot that still hadn't quit throbbing when Jed helped Ruth saddle Sunset for the ride home.

"Thanks for coming," he said. "Ma was real happy to have you over."

Ruth hid her feelings behind a smile. "It was nice to meet Jeff. I'll see you tomorrow?"

"Maybe I'll ride my black to the service and we can go for a ride together after lunch." He appeared eager to do something that would please her.

"That will be fun." She nudged Sunset with her heel. "Good night."

He opened the corral gate and waved her out.

Her future mother-in-law's comments continued to rankle while Ruth rode home. It felt as though she would be expected to meld into the family without even a ripple of independence. Mrs. Harper even seemed to think Jed and Ruth would be a mere extension of her household rather than a new family on their own. For the first time since accepting Jed's proposal, Ruth allowed herself to wonder if she'd decided wisely.

Chapter 12

Two weeks later, on a Tuesday afternoon, Dad stopped by the schoolhouse. "Had to go to town for a new bridle for Star and picked up the mail. I thought maybe you'd like to read this here." He held out an envelope addressed in Theo's writing.

The tension in Ruth's shoulders eased a little. "Thanks."

"Have you told him about Jed?"

"I sent a letter to him the day after I decided."

"Does Jed know about your correspondence?"

Her gaze met his in surprise. "Does it matter?"

He lowered himself to one of the desktops. "Maybe not to Jed. Personally, I wouldn't take too kindly to your mom writing regularly to another man."

"But Theo's my best friend!"

"He has been a good friend," Dad agreed gently. "That will have to change, though, honey. You and Jed are preparing to commit yourselves to each other for life. If any man is your best friend, it should be your husband."

Ruth tried to imagine telling Jed some of the things she wrote to Theo. "Jed's not that kind of person."

Pain flickered in Dad's face. "Then maybe you should reconsider about marrying him."

His words resembled the feelings Ruth had been trying to ignore. "I can't do that, Dad. I gave him my word. Besides, people have already started giving us stuff, and the cabin raising is already scheduled."

"Ruthie, please listen to me." His voice deepened to a rumble and he waited for her to look into his eyes. "There is absolutely no valid reason for you to marry Jed unless you want to. You can return gifts. The cabin building can be cancelled. Once you say 'I do,' you're in it for life. After that, you can only make the best of what you have. Until June 27, however, you are free to change your mind. It's better for both you and Jed to suffer a little embarrassment now rather than spend a lifetime together in a marriage you're not happy in. If you're not happy, he won't be either."

She felt entangled in a web of her own making from which there seemed to be no escape. "I don't know what I should do anymore."

"Have you asked your Heavenly Father about it?"

How could she tell him how she felt about God? "I think I'm too scrambled to pray coherently."

"God doesn't care how fancy we talk. He only wants to know that we want what He knows is best for us. If we're willing to listen, He's willing to show us the way."

"Then ask Him to show me what's right," Ruth whispered, afraid she'd start to cry.

Dad hugged her against himself, his shirt smelling like dirt, sweat, and horses. "My wonderful daughter, your mom and I bring you before the Lord first thing every morning and last thing every night. We won't stop even after you're married. Please don't be afraid to talk with us if we can help."

She enjoyed the secure feeling of resting against his muscled strength. "You're pretty wonderful yourself."

He pulled back with a grin. "Your brothers aren't going to think I'm so wonderful when I return and put them back to work. I'll see you tonight."

Long after the clump of his boots faded away, she sat staring at Theo's unopened letter. Dad was right. As much as it hurt to consider, her friendship with Theo would have to develop distance if she went through with marrying Jed. If she broke her engagement, she and Theo could stay friends, but only until he married. Then she'd be left without a husband, a job, or a friend. She slowly slit the edge of the envelope, savoring what would probably be her last letter from him.

My dear friend,

I read your latest letter with more concern than joy. You didn't write like someone preparing to share her life with a man she loves. I wish I could be there to look into your face and see that my fears are groundless.

I hope I'm not out of line to encourage you to pray carefully about your upcoming marriage. Make sure you're making the wisest decision, not just grasping at straws because your future looks uncertain. No one who matters will blame you for changing your mind if you need to. Even though Jed would probably be hurt, if he's the man I think he is, he'd rather have you back out now than make a mistake that will affect his life as much as yours.

My future is looking rather uncertain, as well. Plans had almost been finalized for me to return to the Peace area and set up my practice.

However, something has come up that will delay those plans, if not change them altogether.

This will probably be my last letter to you. Though I'll always consider you my very dear friend, continuing our correspondence wouldn't be doing right by Jed. I'll miss your letters and continue to pray for you with all my heart.

Please tell Jed I congratulate him on his choice of a fine wife. I hope the two of you will be very happy.

Tears streamed down her cheeks as she returned the letter to its envelope. Her heart felt torn out by the roots. Theo's friendship had been her strength for more than ten years, even during those horrible grief-blackened days that still haunted her. She thought she'd endured the ultimate in pain then, but she knew now how wrong she'd been. At least she'd had Theo to lean on. She had to face this alone. She felt utterly abandoned.

By the time she walked home, her tears had dried into quiet agony. Dad must have told Mom about their discussion because she said nothing about Ruth's reddened eyes or her request to remain in her room while the family ate supper. Not only had her appetite vanished, but she couldn't bear either kindness or curiosity from anyone just now. Besides, she had to pull herself together. Jed would arrive in just a couple of hours. She either had to mask her feelings or explain them to him. Lying face down on her bed, she dozed fitfully. At the last minute, she forced herself upright, returned her hair to tidiness, and pasted a smile on her lips as she pulled on her long riding skirt. She'd ride to meet Jed. If she had to visit with him under her parents' knowing glances, her hard-won composure would shatter.

Jed's face lit with a delighted smile when he saw her. "This is a pleasant surprise. How was your day?"

"Not bad," she murmured. "How was yours?"

"We're almost finished seeding, and three different buyers stopped by to look at horses. One of them is interested in my colt out of the sorrel mare by my black. He offered an incredible price if I'll have him broken to bridle by fall." If he noticed her lack of response, he didn't comment.

They continued riding west in silence for several miles. On impulse, Ruth urged Sunset into a gallop. Rather than holding him back as she usually did when riding with Jed, she let him go. Jed's black kept up for a while, but Sunset gradually began to pull away. It made Ruth feel as if she had shed his mother's confining expectations, the heartache of Theo's letter, the burden of trying to force herself to feel the way a bride-to-be ought to feel. Sunset's labored breathing finally caught her attention. She reined him down to a trot.

"What was that for? If I didn't know better, I'd think you was tryin' to make me and my black look bad."

Jed's faintly accusing voice made her turn Sunset to face him. Veiled hurt showed in his eyes. His black was their prize stud. Though she'd sensed for awhile that Sunset could outrun the black, she hadn't known for sure. As a horse breeder, his horse's superior speed was part of his professional reputation.

"I'm sorry." She gulped down the urge to correct his colloquial grammar, which only reminded her of Theo's precise speech and wide vocabulary. "I didn't realize. . . I didn't know. . ." Her voice trailed off.

"Just don't tell anyone. I can't have folks knowin' my wife's horse is better than mine."

"I'm not your wife." The unwise words shot from her mouth before she could stop them.

"You will be, unless of course you're thinkin' of changin' your mind."

She plucked at Sunset's mane, unwilling to reveal her doubts but unable to reassure him.

"C'mon, Ruth." He slid from his horse and held out his arms to her. "We can't talk like this. Come down and we'll walk for a while. The horses could use the rest, anyway."

Dismounting without his assistance, she ignored the subtle accusation. She wrapped the reins around both hands.

Jed noticed. "What is it? I don't think it's such a bad thing for me to want to touch you. We're engaged, so we should be gettin' used to each other."

His words intensified her guilt. If she really loved him, she'd welcome his touch. If she didn't love him, why was she pursuing this sham? How long before he saw through her act?

"Ruth, please talk to me. I know something's not right. Since the Saturday after our engagement, you've refused to visit our farm again. Sunday's the only chance my ma has to get to know you, but you avoid her. I know she's not the easiest person to visit with, but you have to get used to her pretty soon. She'll be your closest friend durin' most of the summer. You're going to be too busy helpin' her to go ridin' off elsewhere, and me and Pa are goin' to be busy from dawn till dark."

Ruth couldn't stop tears of frustration. "That's just the point. You and your ma both assume because I'm marrying you I'm going to become just another Harper. She's mentioned several times how blessed I must feel to be marrying you rather than having to find another job. Why can't I be married to you and be a teacher, too? What's wrong with that?"

He looked puzzled. "But I thought you said awhile back you wouldn't be able to find another school."

"Even if I could, though, your ma wouldn't want me to take it."

"I wouldn't either, but it's not a question. So why fret about it?" His voice remained deliberately calm.

She stopped walking and looked directly into his face. "Can't you see that *is* the question? You're not paying any attention to the kind of person I am inside. Learning and teaching have been my life for seventeen years. Why must I abandon it simply because I'm marrying you?"

"But your school is closing, so it doesn't matter."

"Yes, it does, Jed." Frustration sharpened her voice. "You don't know there's any life beyond your fields and your horses. I'm not like that. I'm curious about the outside world. I like to learn and to teach. I have to have more than endless days of cleaning, gardening, and cooking."

He shrugged. "I s'pose we could subscribe to the town paper, if you like, and Ma'll be glad to teach you to knit."

She couldn't decide whether to laugh or cry. "You can't understand, can you? It's not what I do that matters. It's the kind of person I am."

"But Ma really likes you. In a few months, you'll get used to us."

Maybe he'd understand if she explained her feelings differently. "Jed, you told me a bit ago I couldn't tell anyone Sunset's faster than your black. That doesn't make any more sense to me than my teaching does to you. Why does it matter if my horse can run faster?"

Embarrassment tinged his face. "Because you're my wife, or will be next month," he quickly amended.

His reply stung. "And what difference does that make?"

"Can't you see it, Ruth? If another man breeds a better horse, that's business. If a woman breeds a better horse, that's business. But for my wife to ride a better horse, I'll be a laughingstock! I won't take him back. Since he's gelded, he wouldn't be much practical use to me anyway. Just, please, don't let on he's faster than my black."

"You've forgotten an important point about Sunset." Ruth fought back hysteria. Jed's attitude on the heels of Theo's letter had stretched her nerves almost to the breaking point. "My parents bought him as my birthday present. When, or if, I become your wife, Sunset remains mine. Do you hear that? Mine! I may have to give away part of myself to marry you, but I'm not handing over my horse."

"I still don't understand." Jed looked more betrayed than hurt.

She swallowed hard to calm herself. "Jed, do you realize how different I am from your mother and sister? I could become fond of your ma, but I'm not ready to let her or you run my life."

"Then perhaps you shouldn't be marrying me."

His inability to see her perspective had pushed her past the point of caring about his feelings. "Perhaps I shouldn't."

"I'd like to change your mind, Ruth." He looked at her with sad brown eyes. "But I don't want you to become my wife because you feel you have to. I'll ride with you back to your farm, but I won't come to see you again unless you ask. If you haven't sent a message to me by Sunday, I'll call off the wedding."

Ruth turned her back to him. "Please just leave me alone. I'll make it back by myself."

"If that's the way you want it." His black's hoofbeats made the only sound as he rode away.

She wrapped her arms around her horse's neck and buried her face in his mane. "What have I done, Sunset? I'm so confused I don't know anything anymore." A fresh torrent of tears dimmed her eyes as she hoisted herself into the saddle. "I can't become the kind of wife they expect. But in another month, I won't be a teacher anymore. I have nothing left." Scarcely noticing where Sunset took her, she let weeping take over. She rode and cried until exhausted. Should she write Theo about what had happened? If she didn't write back, she wouldn't have to endure the pain of breaking off their letters when he married. She didn't think she could endure this afternoon's grief again.

Her thoughts drifted back to the evening Justin had abandoned her in town. Jed now probably felt similar to the way she'd felt that night that seemed so long ago. Her fierce independence had hurt them both. What if she had chosen trust as Grandma Lucy had suggested?

"God, I'm tired," she found herself praying. "I don't know what You would have had me do differently, but I wish I'd tried to listen to You. I don't know if You're even listening to me anymore. You obviously aren't going to tell me why You let my family drown. Will You at least make sense out of the mess I've created? If it's not too late for me to learn, I want to find out how to trust You." The tears that flowed this time finally brought release.

Dusk had begun to fall when she finally took stock of her surroundings. They'd wandered off the road into a pasture she thought might belong to Doug Pierce. At least she hoped so. She'd hate to be caught trespassing on someone else's land. If she didn't return home soon, Dad would worry. Her heels prodded Sunset into his long, easy gallop. She glimpsed the Pierces' home off to the left, which meant the road should be not far ahead. How they'd wandered so far, she couldn't explain. Her head hurt. Leaning low over Sunset's neck, she closed her gritty eyes. He stumbled once, then twice. She only had time to wish she'd heeded Dad's warning not to gallop in unfamiliar fields before she felt her body launched into the air.

Chapter 13

Ruth squinted her eyes open. Judging by the sunlight streaming painfully around the edge of the curtain, she figured she must have overslept drastically. She tried to sit up and swing her legs over the side of her bed, but pain knifed through her left leg as gentle hands pushed her shoulders back onto the pillow. "Quiet, Ruth. Don't try to move."

The voice sounded like Grandma Lucy's. What was she doing here? Why did she hurt all over? She tried to remember. *Theo's letter.* Grief clogged her throat again, though it didn't explain why she was trapped here in bed. Her leg remained immovable.

"What happened?" Her voice sounded croaky. She tried to focus bleary eyes.

"You've broken your leg and have a nasty bump on your head. Dr. Watson says you're not to get up for at least another day. He'll be by this afternoon."

"How? What about school?" More questions than answers flooded her mind. Why couldn't she remember?

"Your mother's taken your classes. Just rest." Grandma placed a cool cloth on her head.

Ruth pushed it away. "No. I have to know what happened. I can't remember."

Grandma's smile brought no reassurance. "I'll get your dad. He's the one who found you." She left the room quietly.

Found her? Where had she been? The pain in her body felt insignificant compared to her hurting emotions. Why did she feel so awful?

"I hear you're awake." Dad's face slowly came into focus. He looked like he'd been up all night. Something sad hid in his eyes.

"I think so." Ruth reached for his hand and tried to smile. "If I'm dreaming, I hope I wake up soon. I hurt all over."

He lowered himself onto the bed. "You and Sunset fell."

She remembered crying into Sunset's mane. "Where? Why?"

"I don't know why you were in the Pierces' pasture. We just found you there early this morning."

219

The Pierces' pasture. She recalled seeing their house off to the left. In a horrible rush, it all came back. She and Jed had argued. She'd told him she couldn't marry him. Sunset had stumbled. "Sunset?"

Dad's eyes told her wordlessly.

She tried to turn away, to bury her sobs in her pillow, but the weight on her leg kept her helplessly in place. "It was my fault. I didn't mean to, but I wanted to come home. I killed him." Though it hurt to cry, it hurt more to try to stifle it.

Dad lay down beside her and cradled her head against his shoulder. "It's all right, Ruthie. Hush, honey. It's all right, little girl." His endearments continued until her sobs quieted.

Her head ached too much to think anymore. Nestled in his comforting embrace, she let sleep claim her again.

Dad still lay beside her when she awoke. He lifted himself up to look down into her face. "How're you doin'?"

Her memory hadn't faded this time. Tears filled her eyes again, but Dad's comforting presence made the sorrow bearable. "Awful."

"Do you feel like talking?"

Her attempted nod set off drumbeats in her head.

"Jed stopped by to tell us the wedding is off." He searched her eyes for a reaction.

"He didn't tell you it was my fault?"

Dad traced her cheeks tenderly with calloused fingers, wiping away tears. "No. He just said he wanted us to know where you were and that you'd asked to be alone."

"I can't marry him."

"I know, Ruthie. I'm just glad you found out before it's too late."

"Sunset—" As soon as she said his name, she remembered. "He's dead."

Dad's hand cupped her cheek comfortingly. "His leg broke when he fell. I'm sorry."

"It's my fault. You told me not to let him run except on the road. You gave him to me and I killed him." Weeping took over once more.

"Ruth!" Dad's voice sharpened. He shook her shoulder.

Her throbbing head halted the hysteria.

"Ruth, listen to me." Absolute authority replaced tender sympathy in his voice. He lowered his head so she had no place to look but directly into his eyes. "We know you made a mistake last night. Sunset paid part of the price, and you're paying for it with a headache, a broken leg, and a hurting heart. But Ruthie," his voice softened, "we still love you. Sunset was just a horse. We can't afford to replace him right away; however, as soon as we can, we will."

Shutting her eyes against the pain, she whispered, "I don't want another horse."

"Get her to drink this," Grandma's voice suggested.

Ruth felt her head and shoulders being lifted by Dad's muscled arm and a cool glass pressed against her mouth. "Please drink, honey," he softly commanded. With her eyes still shut, she obeyed. It was an unfamiliar taste, but soothing. Welcome blackness enfolded her.

The next time she woke up, the sunlight didn't seem nearly as bright. Her head still hurt. "Dad? Grandma?" She felt Grandma's soothing presence even before the beloved face leaned over her.

"Right here, child."

"Where's Dad?"

"He's in the fields today. If you need him, I only have to blow the whistle he left." She gently brushed Ruth's tangled curls back from her face.

"Today? But he was here when I went to sleep." Her mind still refused to function clearly.

Grandma laughed gently. "That was yesterday afternoon, dear one."

"Who's taking care of your boardinghouse?"

"Nina, and before you ask, Clara's plenty big enough to cook for her family while Nina's helping me. Anything else you want to worry about?" she teased.

Ruth didn't feel like smiling. "So many people. . .messed up. . .because of me." She had to swallow hard between each phrase.

"Now that's enough of that, young lady," Grandma spoke sternly. "Self-pity is not allowed in my presence. I'm here because I love you, Nina's where she is because she loves both of us, and the change is good preparation for Clara. Can you remember my verse?"

It took a moment, but the words gradually filtered into her memory, bringing profound reassurance. "The steps of a good woman are ordered by the Lord." She lay silently, savoring the peace. Why did it feel so newly familiar? Something had happened before she had fallen, even before she'd foolishly urged her horse to run. Pushing back guilt, she forced herself to remember each detail. "Grandma?"

"Yes?" She hadn't left Ruth's side.

"I remembered something good about last night." She corrected herself. "Or I guess it was night before last, since I slept all day yesterday."

"You needed it," Grandma soothed. "What's the happy memory?"

"I asked God to teach me to trust." The simple words caused unbelievable peace to seep into her spirit.

Grandma's reply was barely above a whisper. "I'm so glad, child. It looks like He's given you plenty of time to practice."

Denial rose abruptly to her lips. Her present situation resulted only from her own stubborn choices. "This has nothing to do with Him."

"Nonsense. He didn't quit being God just because you were ignoring Him."

"How did you know I was ignoring Him?"

Grandma chuckled. "How do you know when your brother is upset with your dad? When you love two people, you just know."

"I still don't know why Mother and the boys had to drown." Even as she spoke, the answer didn't seem nearly as important as it had.

"And you probably never will know." Grandma sat beside her and stroked the back of her hand. " 'Why' is one question God often leaves unanswered. I like to believe its answer is simply too complex for our finite minds. We just aren't capable of seeing from God's perspective yet. Until we can, we have to leave the question with Him."

Ruth felt sleep creeping up on her again, but she fought to finish the conversation. "It used to be too hard."

"God's wonderful that way. Sometimes all we have to do is let Him know we're willing, and He does the rest. Go ahead and sleep now. It's the best thing for you. I'll still be here when you're ready to talk again."

By the third day, Ruth's body no longer demanded endless hours of sleep. "I'm already awake," she announced when Grandma tiptoed through the door, then laughed at the lady's startled expression.

"My, aren't we chipper?" Grandma's eyes crinkled with the affectionate smile that always made Ruth feel uniquely loved.

"I doubt I'm ready to go rock picking, but my head doesn't feel like a woodpecker lives inside anymore."

"In that case, how would you like a sponge bath and a hair wash?"

It sounded heavenly. "Could we really?"

"Absolutely. A clean body always feels healthier than a dirty one. But first, do you mind if the little ones come in to say hi? They've been fretting themselves sick because we wouldn't let them in here."

"Sure." She suddenly realized how long it had been since she'd seen any of her family other than Dad. Remembering his comforting presence filled her eyes again. "I'll see if I can keep from crying for a few minutes."

"Don't fight it, child." Grandma patted Ruth's shoulder. "You've been through a lot emotionally and physically. Tears are God's way of helping us cope."

Her kindness caused Ruth's eyes to overflow. With a lacy, sweet-smelling hanky, Grandma dried Ruth's cheeks. "Now," she announced briskly when the shower had passed. "Let's prop you up on a couple of pillows and bring the babies in."

Ruth heard Beth's squeal and Timmy's running footsteps before Grandma even opened the bedroom door. Both stopped abruptly when they saw their sister in bed.

"What dat?" Beth pointed a pudgy finger at the huge lump that was Ruth's leg.

Ruth pulled the blankets back so they could see. "Dr. Watson put this hard stuff on my leg so it won't hurt so much."

"How did you get hurted?" Timmy wanted to know.

She pondered for a moment before deciding on an explanation. "I did something Daddy told me not to do."

"You were dis'bedient?" His tongue had difficulty forming the word often used by their parents before a spanking. His wide eyes expressed disbelief that his big sister could have done such a thing.

"Yes, I was."

"Me kiss it better," Beth offered, lifting a short leg to clamber onto the bed.

Grandma grabbed her quickly. "Let me hold you and you kiss Ruthie that way. It will hurt her if you make her bed wiggle."

Beth accepted the explanation, planting a wet kiss on Ruth's cheek. "All better," she pronounced, then wiggled out of Grandma's arms. "Go play now." Timmy followed enthusiastically.

Grandma chuckled. "I think your cast impressed him more than his most recent spanking. Are you still up to getting your hair washed?"

"Yes, please." She felt grimy and rumpled.

By the time Grandma had shampooed her hair, administered the sponge bath, and helped her into a clean nightgown, Ruth felt more than ready to relax against the pillows. This gave her a clear view of her cast, which extended from the middle of her foot to her upper leg, propped on several folded blankets. Her curiosity rippled to life. Too bad Theo wasn't here to explain. He'd told her about the various bones in her leg, and he would probably know which one she had broken. He would also ramble on at length about the substance from which her cast was made, who discovered its use in helping broken limbs mend properly, and what had been used before. They had often laughed together about how much they enjoyed discovering facts other people found boring or useless.

Shifting her gaze to the sunny day beyond her window, she wished he were still only a mile and a half away. He'd know how to help her make sense of her tangled thoughts and how to help her escape the horrible feeling of guilt over Sunset. Not only had she failed her horse, she'd let her parents down. They had worked hard and saved carefully to be able to buy him. Ever-present tears overflowed.

"You're looking better." Dr. Watson's cheery voice roused her. "How do you feel?"

She swiped at her cheeks, hoping he hadn't noticed. "Not bad, all things considering."

He leaned over her head, probing around the large lump over her left ear. "Does your head hurt much?"

"Not a lot unless I move it quickly."

"Do you remember tripping over the water bucket at school?"

Puzzled, she corrected him, struggling to keep her voice steady. "I didn't get hurt at school. This happened when my horse fell."

His eyes twinkled as he backed away from her. "I just wanted to see how much you remembered. How many brothers do you have?"

"Three."

"Sisters?"

"One."

He pulled the covers away from her leg. "Let's look at this. Hmmm." She tried not to wince as he ran a finger around the inside of both ends of the cast. "The swelling seems to be going down well. I'd like you to stay put for the weekend. Monday we'll look at replacing the cast, since this one's getting too big. Once we have your leg stabilized, you can start getting around. I'll bring a pair of crutches next week."

"How soon can I go back to school?"

"I'd like you to wait at least another week." He looked at her soberly. "Your fall gave you a serious concussion and we have no way of knowing when your head has fully recovered. Even after you're out of bed, you'll tire easily. You'll be much better off at home, where you can rest whenever you need to."

When she tried to suggest otherwise to her parents that evening, they supported Dr. Watson. "There's no need for you to push yourself," Mom said firmly. "There's only one week of school left, and we're spending most of the time practicing for the concert anyway."

"What about you having to push yourself? You haven't been feeling well, either."

"I'm not sick. I'm just expecting a baby. Being in a classroom again is great fun." Mom's sparkling eyes verified her words.

"But it's my last chance!" Ruth wailed, feeling the aggravating tears pushing through again.

"Last chance for what, honey?" Mom asked.

Ruth sniffed, trying to form a coherent reply. "I don't know. I just want to be there for the last day."

"I think I understand." Mom smoothed Ruth's hair away from her face. "It's hard to know your final day as a teacher passed without your being aware, isn't it?"

As usual, Mom's perception defined Ruth's feelings precisely. She nodded, not trusting herself to speak.

Dad knelt beside her bed. "Ruth, I know how important this feels to you, because your health feels the same to me. All I want is for you to recover completely. We'll make sure you get to the school for the concert, but I can't help you disregard Dr. Watson's instructions."

Only the love in his voice silenced her protests. Missing this last week with her students would be one more entry on the list of negatives resulting from her own poor choices.

Chapter 14

Saturday dragged by. With Mom home, Grandma Lucy had gone back into town to give Mrs. Spencer a break. Ruth could hear Timmy and Beth chattering while Mom did household chores. She watched Dad and the boys working around the farmyard. Every once in a while, one of them would look toward her window and wave. During meals, the sounds of her family's conversation drifted to her room. A feeling of helpless isolation threatened to overwhelm her. Looking around her room for something to distract her thoughts, she noticed her Bible on her dressing table where she'd put it while unpacking from her stay at the Pierces'. How long had it been since she'd opened it for personal reading? *Months. Maybe even over a year.* She easily recalled the anticipation with which she'd read as a young girl. Some days it had felt like a particular Scripture passage had been written just for her. Would it happen again?

Unfortunately, the table sat in the opposite corner from her bed. She moved her good leg to the edge of the bed, then tried to get her cast to follow. It wouldn't budge. She pushed the covers to the side near the wall, grasped the white mountain with both hands, and placed it as close to the edge of the bed as possible. She lay back against the pillows at an awkward angle, breathless from effort. Her strength seemed to have drained to nothing. After several moments' rest, she tried again. Bracing her good foot on the floor, she lifted the heavy leg. Too late, she realized how precarious her seating had become. She toppled helplessly off the side.

Mom came in a rush. "Ruth! Are you all right?"

Both her head and her leg had begun throbbing again. Her pride also stung, not helped by the tears she couldn't hide. "I just wanted my Bible," she whimpered.

"Why didn't you ask?" Mom helped her to a sitting position on the floor, then braced her so she could lift herself back onto the bed. The extra pair of hands made maneuvering the cast much easier. Mom plumped the pillows behind Ruth's shoulders, smoothed the covers, and placed the Bible on the edge of the bed. "I wish you would have called."

"I didn't want to bother you."

"Helping you get well is not a bother." Mom kissed her forehead. "You must be getting pretty bored. Shall I send the little ones in to entertain you?"

"I'd like to see them, but my head is pounding again," she admitted sheepishly.

"Sleep is probably the best thing for you. Next time, call me, please?" Mom shut the door softly behind her.

Ruth slept restlessly. Theo's face drifted in and out of her dreams. When she called out to him, he disappeared. She awoke with wet cheeks. While she regretted hurting Jed's feelings, Theo's withdrawal had created the deepest wound. She wanted desperately to restore contact, but that would only postpone the pain. Sooner or later, he would fall in love with the nurse who could enhance his practice. Ruth wished she had decided to learn nursing. Dad's arrival with the checkerboard made a welcome distraction.

The next morning, Grandma Lucy showed up while the rest of the family was eating breakfast. "I've come to keep you company while everyone's gone," she announced to Ruth. "How are you feeling?" Her piercing gaze defied the younger woman to be less than honest.

Ruth didn't even try to fool her. "Frustrated and confused."

Grandma smiled understandingly. "You mean you're arguing with your Heavenly Father again?"

Denial rose and dissipated quickly. "I guess you're right. You did tell me this would be a perfect place to learn trust."

Grandma pulled the rocking chair close to Ruth's side. "What's the trouble?"

"I feel like I've wrecked everything and have no way of putting it back together." Grandma's silence encouraged her to continue. "Jed told me if he didn't hear from me by today, he'd make the announcement canceling our wedding. Mr. Albertson has already bought windows for us, and the Millers have hauled a load of lumber out to the Harpers' for the new cabin. I've made life pretty embarrassing for Jed."

Grandma didn't contradict her. "He'll survive."

"But I feel so badly."

"You'd feel worse if you'd gone through with it. Will you choose to trust his Heavenly Father to take care of him?"

She weighed the question, pondering its significance. "It seems unfair to expect God to make up for my mistakes."

"The Bible is full of illustrations of God doing just that. Jesus' death on the cross was nothing more or less than God's ultimate atonement for mankind's biggest mistake."

"I'd never thought about it that way."

Grandma's gaze never left Ruth's face. "You're not alone. It's easy to think we have to fix or hide our failures rather than coming to our Father just as we are."

"I feel like I've failed my schoolchildren, too. If I hadn't gotten so messed up over Jed and Theo, I'd be able to finish the school year with them."

Grandma stopped rocking. "Theo?"

Ruth's face warmed. Mentioning him had been a slip of the tongue she'd immediately hoped Grandma would miss. Hesitantly, she told about the letter and her feelings since. "I miss him so badly it hurts."

"May I ask an impertinent question?" She waited for Ruth's nod. "What would you say if he asked you to marry him?"

Shock numbed Ruth all over. She finally managed a protest. "We're just best friends!"

"There's no better way to start a terrific marriage," Grandma declared firmly.

Ruth refused to let her mind dwell on the possibility. "I wouldn't be the kind of wife he needs."

Humorous twinkles appeared in Grandma's blue eyes. "Wouldn't it be better to let God decide that one?"

"It always comes back to trust, doesn't it?"

"Now you're catching on. Shall we pray about all this together?" She clasped Ruth's hands. "You start and I'll finish."

At first Ruth didn't know what to say. Other than her desperate appeal while riding Sunset, her prayers had been as nonexistent as her Bible reading. She began hesitantly. "Heavenly Father, I'm sorry I've been so stubborn. Because I refused to trust You, I've affected a lot of people." With the admission, her thoughts seemed to flow much easier. "I'm asking you to make up to Jed for the hurt I've caused him. Please help me continue to trust You with my future, and bless my students even though I can't be with them on this last week of school. Give Mom strength as she takes my place. I ask for patience for myself and for Your help in learning whatever You want to teach me." Her voice dropped to a whisper. "Please bless Theo, Lord."

Grandma's voice took over comfortingly. "Father, I ask for Your comfort for Ruth. While I know You don't always show us Your working in others' lives, would you please let her see what You're doing for Jed while he adjusts to their decision not to marry. I also sense You're not finished with her and Theo, despite the way circumstances look now. Please bring peace and healing to Ruth's heart and give her an assurance of Your will. Thank you for Ruth. She's brought much joy to many of our lives and we look forward to seeing the joy You bring to hers. Amen."

They sat hand in hand in comforting silence until Ruth ventured, "I wish trust were as easy to learn as the multiplication tables."

Grandma smiled. "It's harder because your emotions fight so hard against it. But in some ways it is just as easy. The only way you learned your multiplication tables was by practice. I'm still having to practice trust, to choose between trying to figure things out myself or waiting to see what God does."

"It's hard to remember to choose."

"Have you read the book of Job since we talked about it? Chapters 38 through 41 present an awesome picture of God as He describes Himself. You should read them sometime, along with Psalm 139. The struggle isn't nearly so hard when you begin to get a glimpse of Who it is you're trusting."

"I was going to do some Bible reading yesterday, but got sidetracked." Ruth giggled as she told of her mishap.

"You wonderful, stubbornly independent woman!" Grandma exclaimed through laughter. "I don't suppose you thought of how badly you could injure yourself."

"Not until I was on the floor in a painful heap."

"You won't try getting out of bed on your own again until Dr. Watson gives you leave, right?"

Ruth shook her head. "Though it is frustrating to have to call for somebody for something as simple as using the chamberpot."

"I know." Grandma patted her hand comfortingly. "I spent several months in a hospital in England before I met Mr. Barry. Humility is no easier to learn than trust." She picked up Ruth's Bible from where it lay on the floor beside the bed. "May I read aloud to you?"

"Sure." Ruth snuggled into her covers, prepared for a treat. As she expected, Grandma turned to the chapters to which she'd referred earlier. With each thunderous question from the Almighty, Ruth felt her own foolishness at demanding an explanation for anything. Then with barely a pause, Grandma swished a few pages and continued reading. "O Lord, thou hast searched me, and known me. Thou knowest my downsitting and mine uprising, thou understandest my thought afar off. . . How precious also are thy thoughts unto me, O God! how great is the sum of them!" The words wrapped Ruth in a comforting cocoon. The fog of confusion lifted, and all at once she understood what Grandma had repeatedly tried to tell her. God didn't choose to withhold explanations about His ways just to be difficult. His plan was simply too overwhelming for her to comprehend. Rather than offering a defense of His ways, He extended the assurance of His unfaltering love, His continuing presence with her through both easy times and hard.

Her eyes slid shut as she continued to explore these unfamiliar ideas. Because of what God said about Himself, trust was more than hoping for an invisible safety net. It represented her confidence in God's faithfulness to His own character. The fear she'd carried for seven years retreated as she realized she no longer had to be afraid of loss. Heartbreak wouldn't come her way again unless by Divine plan. Though she still couldn't comprehend why He might permit such pain, He'd help her endure it. A delicious sense of freedom made her tingle all over.

She opened her eyes to see Grandma watching her with a loving smile. "It finally makes sense," she whispered.

Grandma's grin widened. "I wish you could see your own face. You look like you just discovered gold."

"I wish I could feel this way forever."

"You won't, though," Grandma stated matter-of-factly. "That's why you have to rely on what you know, not what you feel."

"How do you do it?" Ruth wished for an easy formula.

"I never let myself forget what God says about Himself. Since He cannot lie, His words form an indestructible foundation for our faith. Sometimes I remember easily. Other times it's a struggle. I have to get alone and read passages like Psalm 139 aloud. I've never been sorry for choosing to trust Him, even when it's hard." Pounding on the front door broke the contemplative silence. Grandma hustled off to respond.

Ruth glanced out the window to see if she could figure out who'd come, then looked again. A black stallion stood tied to the corral fence. Before she had time to panic, Jed appeared in the doorway, turning his hat around and around in his hands. "May I come in?"

"Sure." Ruth gestured toward the rocking chair, wondering why Grandma hadn't followed him.

"I was real sorry to hear about your accident." He finally quit worrying the hat and set it on his knees. His fingers drummed on the arms of the chair.

"It was my own stupidity," Ruth assured him, inwardly wondering where the oppressive sense of guilt had gone. She felt no less responsible for what had happened, just ready to leave it in the past.

"It was partly my fault." Jed's words came out quickly before she could interrupt. "You were right about us not being suited. I can't explain why. This morning I just realized we'll be better off as friends. I told folks this morning that the weddin's off. Mr. Miller and Mr. Albertson both told me to keep the buildin' supplies, anyway. I wanted you to know I'm not upset, and your dad said I could come see you before they got home."

"Thank you." The words barely fit past the lump in her throat. "I'm sorry I didn't say no when you first asked."

"I prob'ly wasn't too smart for askin', but mistakes is part of livin'. I hope you won't mind if I come around once in awhile."

His poor grammar made her feel like a cat who'd been rubbed the wrong way, but she focussed on the meaning behind it. "You'll always be welcome. When you discover the right girl, I hope you let me meet her."

"Sure." The familiar pink tinged his ears. "I best be goin'. Thanks for seein' me."

Grandma reappeared with a lunch tray shortly after Ruth heard the front door close behind Jed. "I hope you're hungry."

Ruth pretended to glare at her. "What if I had needed moral support?"

Grandma snorted. "The poor boy was so nervous he could hardly walk straight. If anything, *he* needed the moral support."

Ruth accepted a jelly sandwich and briefly related their conversation. "I would have expected him to never speak to me again."

"Jed's made of finer stuff than that," Grandma Lucy contradicted. "Besides, didn't I tell you God would straighten things out?"

Ruth just grinned, silently hoping He'd work as quickly to make sense of her relationship with Theo.

Chapter 15

D r. Watson waited until Wednesday to release Ruth from bed rest. Grandma Lucy continued her daily trips from town to keep the McEvan household running smoothly.

As promised, Dad made sure Ruth was able to attend the end-of-the-year concert. She'd never felt more proud of her students. The entire program flowed smoothly, showing the hours of practice they'd invested. No church choir could have produced better music than Julie and Karin's duet.

After a month, Dr. Watson finally consented to remove the cast. Ruth spent the next week exercising her leg as much as she could tolerate. At long last, she managed the short distance between the farm and school. She'd asked Mom to let her do the final cleaning and clearing up. It was something she simply had to do alone. She pushed open the door, noticing the large pot of steaming water on the warm stove. Dad must have come by earlier to build a fire and put the water on to heat. This last month would have been unbearable without his and Mom's continuous loving gestures.

Seeing the empty desks brought back her last afternoon as teacher, when she'd sat at the front of the room crying as she read Theo's farewell letter. She'd made the right decision, she reminded herself firmly. The pain of separation would come eventually. Better to face it now than later.

One by one, she washed the desks carefully. The town school board had offered to buy them, along with anything else this building no longer needed. Each swipe of her cloth brought back a different memory—each youngster she'd taught, their strengths and weaknesses, charms and moods. Julie's desk had been emptied; she'd obviously even washed it out before leaving. Phillip's, right behind, remained stuffed with scraps of paper as well as a collection of leaves, sticks, rocks, and other items Ruth didn't want to identify. By the time she reached the back row of desks, her thoughts had drifted even further to her own years as a student. She'd used this desk, with Theo right behind her.

They had shared only one year of formal schooling before he had left for the city, but on that first day he had waited for her to choose a seat, then selected the one directly behind her. She wiped the wood caressingly. It had taken wrong and foolish decisions to make her aware of the love that had grown between them. Even her dislike for the city wouldn't hold her back if he asked her to marry him.

But it wouldn't happen, she knew. He still thought she wanted to marry Jed. If he had acquired the position in the hospital of his choice, he wouldn't be able to come home until Christmas at least. Maybe things would change then, though she wouldn't build her hopes on it. If nothing else, the past weeks had taught her to entrust each of her moments to her Heavenly Father. Her recovery time had given her hours on her own to read Scripture. She still found some passages dry, but others seemed written just for her—like the one she'd found in Isaiah. "In quietness and in confidence shall be your strength."

She found herself humming snatches of hymns as she continued her farewell to her precious classroom. Misplaced mittens and lost pencils showed up in the strangest places, like behind the bookshelf from which she removed used textbooks to add to the rapidly filling crates. Her damp cloth removed pencil marks and sticky spots. Her leg was throbbing by the time she'd completed everything she wanted to do. Even the large teacher's desk at the front had been emptied and cleaned in every corner of every drawer. She dipped and wrung her rag one more time and hobbled to the chalkboard. If her leg would hold her up for just a couple more minutes, everything would be spotless. She reached for the highest corner, trying to keep most of her weight on her right leg. Overbalancing, she would have fallen had not a pair of masculine arms grabbed her from behind.

"I don't think your doctor would approve of this activity," his familiar voice chided.

Shock immobilized her for a moment before she turned in his arms to hug him ecstatically. "Theo! Where did you come from?"

His beloved chuckle rumbled beside her ear. "Where do you think? Come, I can tell it's long past time for you to sit down." He guided her gently to her chair and hoisted himself onto her desk. Without removing his gaze from her face, he remarked, "You could have really hurt yourself again, you know."

Was the warmth in his brown eyes for real or just the product of her hopeful imagination? Since she'd seen him two years ago, he'd grown a beard, which most attractively added a few years to his appearance. He looked more filled out than she remembered. The boy she recalled had unquestionably become a full-grown man. "I'd like to know how you happened to be right behind me at that precise moment. I didn't even hear you come in."

"I meant to sneak up on you." That wonderful smile parted his beard. "Your humming made it easier than I expected."

Her cheeks warmed. "I hadn't counted on anyone being close enough to hear it."

"I'm glad I did. You sounded and look happy."

"I am." The words sounded far too simple for the contentment she'd found in the past couple of weeks.

"I can tell. You look like it goes all the way through, too." His gaze searched hers with comforting intensity. "You're not fighting your Heavenly Father anymore."

Her smile felt like it came from the deepest part of her heart. "I finally realized it's stupid to resist Him when He loves me so much. But I can't believe you're actually here. From your last letter, I figured it would be months, if not years, before you made it back. Did you get your job in the city?"

"No." The single word came out tersely. His gaze travelled slowly over her face, then returned to her eyes. "I decided I didn't want it after all. But if you don't mind, I'd rather talk about you. Mom said you'd broken your leg and given yourself a concussion. What happened?"

She wondered how much to tell him, since much of the story involved her feelings for him. A pang of regret knifed through her. Not so long ago, she wouldn't have even considered weighing her words.

"Hey, this is Theo," he reminded, leaning down to clasp one of her hands. "Good old Theo. You can tell me anything."

Rather than pulling away, she wanted to snuggle back into his arms. She began talking to keep herself from acting on the impulse. "Everything happened that day. Dad brought your letter by here on his way home and pointed out I probably shouldn't be writing to you anymore. Your letter told me the same thing." Theo's grip tightened compassionately, but he didn't interrupt. "I couldn't stand the thought of losing my best friend simply because I'd agreed to marry Jed. Then Jed invited me to go riding with him later that evening, and we had words."

"Because of my letter?" he asked with regret in his eyes.

"No. I don't think he was ever aware of our correspondence. It actually started because Sunset outran his black stallion. I'd never let it happen before, but that evening I was too upset to pay attention. Our conversation, or argument, or whatever you want to call it, gradually included everything from his mother to my teaching. By the time he suggested I might not want to marry him, I agreed readily." She smiled up at her friend. It felt so good to be confiding in him once again. "He's a really nice fellow and will make some woman a terrific husband. Just not me. He needs someone who finds the farm as all-absorbing as he does."

"And someone who won't disagree with him much," Theo supplied with a twinkle.

She giggled. "That, too. He's so goodhearted, though, I still sometimes feel like a wretch for breaking our engagement."

"Don't." A mysterious light in his eyes accompanied his whispered advice.

"I keep telling myself the same thing. Anyway, he offered to escort me home, but I told him not to bother. I have no idea how far Sunset and I rode that evening, but when I finally stopped crying enough to realize where we were, we'd reached your dad's east pasture. I put Sunset into a gallop, he stumbled and fell, and next thing I knew, I was in bed with a sore head and a huge leg."

"I'm sorry." His quiet sympathy wrapped around her heart.

"Me, too. There's so much I wish I could go back and undo."

"Like what?"

"Like deciding I wouldn't depend on God for anything because He wouldn't tell me why He hadn't made things happen differently at the river. If I'd been trusting Him all along, I wouldn't have panicked when they told me the school was closing, and I'd have told Jed no the night he proposed."

"You're sure about that?"

"About Jed?"

He nodded.

"Absolutely. I wish I didn't have to be totally dependent on my parents, but I'm willing to wait and let God work that out."

A delighted smile lit his face. "You've come a long way since your last letter."

"You're probably wondering why I didn't write to you again."

"Not really. If I can still read you as well as I used to, the potential change in our friendship shook you up as badly as it did me." He still retained his hold on her hand. "Remember what I wrote about something changing my mind about setting up a practice here?" She nodded, unable to tear her gaze from those wonderfully soft, dark eyes. His voice dropped to a ragged whisper. "That something was you and Jed."

Hope silently overflowed inside her, though she tried to still her racing heart. His doctor's fingers would detect it in a second.

Though his thumb rubbed her wrist ever so gently, he made no comment about her pulse. "I've known since we were both still in school you were the one I wanted to marry. I didn't say anything before I left for fear of scaring you off. Did I do you wrong?"

She shook her head, while trying to absorb both his words and the overwhelming affection in his gaze. Even a month ago, she would have been so intimidated by this much caring she would have pushed it away.

The worry wrinkle disappeared from between his eyes. "I've been hoping and praying I did the right thing. When you wrote to me about accepting Jed's proposal, I realized I'd waited too long. Distance didn't give me an option other than praying something would happen to change your mind." His eyes offered her the same heartfelt devotion Dad's showed when he looked at Mom and young Lionel's held for Sara.

Strangely, rather than being frightened of the intensity, she felt like her heart had finally come home. She spoke the first coherent words that came to mind. "I thought you'd marry a nurse."

His laughter eased some of the tension hovering between them. "Several of them tried so hard, it was embarrassing. None of them came even close to replacing my best friend." He walked around to the front of her desk and paced back and forth. "I couldn't believe it when Mom wrote that you and Jed had called the wedding off. When I read you'd been hurt, it was all I could do to finish out my contract at the hospital. I wanted desperately to rush home and take care of you myself."

"I wished for you," she assured him. "Dr. Watson did as much as he could for my leg and my head, but he couldn't make my heartache go away."

He finally quit pacing. "Because of my letter?"

"Sort of. Even if we did start writing again, I figured I'd have to give you up again when you found the girl you wanted to marry."

"Dear little friend." He pulled her from the chair into a wonderfully possessive embrace. "The girl I want is right here. Will you please marry me?"

"Yes," she whispered against his shoulder.

"Did you just say what I thought you said?"

She leaned back to smile into his eyes. "Yes."

Joy filled his eyes as he leaned down to kiss her tentatively. When he lifted his head, she reached up a hand to pull him down for a second, more thorough kiss. He looked as dazed as she felt when they finally looked at each other again. "You'd better be Mrs. Theodore Pierce the next time you do that," he warned shakily, "because I'm not sure I'll behave responsibly. Come. I want to show you something." When they reached the doorway, he stood behind her, arms around her waist. "What do you see?"

His horse, Shadow, grazed near the edge of the bush beside a delicate-looking bay filly. White patches above each of the filly's hooves looked like socks, contrasting with her dark mane and tail. No horse could have looked more different from Sunset yet just as striking. "She's beautiful," Ruth breathed.

"I had a bit of money saved up. When I heard about Sunset, I thought this filly would make a good bribe in case you weren't sure about marrying me."

She turned to look into his eyes. "Is she really mine?"

"Only if you marry me."

She brushed her fingers down his beard. "I've missed your weird sense of humor."

"Who's laughing? You'd better marry me after that little display back there by the desk."

"Who started it?"

He grinned, tightening his arms around her. "I've missed you, too." His expression sobered. "I came so close to losing you. Is it my imagination or did you really say you wanted to marry this small town doctor?"

For answer, she laid her head against his chest in another hug. As a boy this person had proved his friendship. As a man he offered his love. Nothing she'd imagined or hoped for had come close to the fulfillment of committing herself to him for always. In trusting her Heavenly Father's direction of her steps, she'd found her heart's desire.

Winding Highway

To Phyllis Pettigrew:
with whom I've dreamed, cried, laughed, and prayed;
whose path has taken unpredictable turns but whose faith
remains a beacon for mine.

Chapter 1

For the umpteenth time in less than an hour, Jerusha Porter stirred vegetables bubbling in a stew pot and checked baking powder biscuits in the bread warmer near the stovepipe. Her brother could be so exasperatingly concerned about others, even to the detriment of his own health and home life! He had seen a firelike glow coming from Stein's warehouse six blocks away in the downtown area of frontier Dawson Creek, and even though she had just started serving up supper, he had insisted on "going to see if I can help."

His patient, gentle explanation didn't ease her irritation. "That building used to be livery stable, so the upper story is full of hay. If it's really on fire, the boys are going to need help getting it out."

"The boys!" she muttered derisively, pushing a couple of loose bobby pins more firmly into the twist of black hair at the back of her head. No matter how hard she tried, she couldn't think of the ever-present American army troops as anything but heathens. David, on the other hand, seemed determined to be a personal friend to each of the thousands of soldiers camped on the hill beside Dawson Creek. *This isn't the only area of contrast in our ideas about ministry*, she reminded herself.

"The ministry" had been a prominent concept in both their lives as far back as she could remember. Their parents, Nathan and Mary Porter, had met each other on a mission station in Kenya, and David and Jerusha had been born there. When Jerusha was ten and David eleven, the family had returned to Winnipeg on furlough and the children had been enrolled in a local school. Their parents departed for a new mission assignment only six months later, leaving David and Jerusha in the care of Mary's sister and brother-in-law, Cameron and Vivienne McDonald. Jerusha could count on the fingers of one hand the number of times she'd seen her parents since. Though they returned to Canada for year-long furloughs every four years, some crisis always sent them back to "the field" after a mere month or two.

Peering out the kitchen window, Jerusha could see men and vehicles moving quickly toward the center of town. For once she felt grateful their parsonage and newly constructed church hovered on the edge of the equally new Alaska Highway. She would be able to keep track of what was happening as effectively as the crowds now streaming in the direction of the warehouse. *Fools! Why would they want to bundle up against subzero temperatures just to watch a fire being extinguished?* The glow of the fire lit the early evening darkness so she could see trees bending in the wind. What an uncivilized country! As if forty-below-zero wasn't enough, the wind never stopped blowing.

A thundering boom assaulted Jerusha's eardrums. Then the parsonage shuddered as if struck by a gigantic hand. Suddenly she wanted to be outside. Where was David? How could she help him if she didn't know where to find him? A siren screamed not far away, then another joined it. Even from her vantage point of relative distance, she could see the fire had spread. Another shock wave, smaller this time, shook the building. What was happening? Knowing her brother, she figured he had probably charged into the middle of the disaster. What would she do if he were injured?

At least she'd have a valid reason for returning to Winnipeg. Answering the call to pastor in Dawson Creek had been David's idea. His face had glowed as he'd shown her the letter his Bible college dean had given him. "It's from a group of about a dozen families who've been an informal fellowship for about fifteen years. They feel they're now able to support a full-time, formally trained pastor, so they're asking the college to recommend a graduate. Dean Pauley said he thought immediately of me. What an opportunity!"

Much as she loved her aunt and uncle, she couldn't bear the thought of being separated from her brother. Besides, it wouldn't do for her to be the only member of the Porter family not involved in The Ministry. She'd volunteered to accompany him as housekeeper and parsonage hostess. How often in the past six months had she wished for the opportunity to choose again! Their parents' example didn't obligate Jerusha to follow her brother to the end of the earth, did it? She'd often wondered what her life would have been like had Mary Porter chosen motherhood over the mission field. Uncle Cam and Aunt Vivienne had been wonderful guardians, but Jerusha still had to force aside resentment at her parents' absence from her life. One of these days, God would surely punish her severely for not admiring their sacrifice as her aunt so verbally did. She wondered what her mother would think of this boomtown at the end of the rail line, its population swelling daily even in the grip of midwinter. Of course, what would be left when the men finally gained control of the fire? Maybe the destruction would be severe enough to push David back to civilization.

Not a chance. Jerusha felt her lips tighten in frustration. For some reason, David loved this town with its overabundance of military personnel, its fortune-seeking opportunists, and its slow-moving farmers. Should fire reduce the buildings to rubble, he'd feel invigorated by the challenge of rebuilding. She mentally pictured his blue eyes sparkling with excitement, his black hair standing on end from his absentminded rumpling, and his tall, lanky body bent forward as if he couldn't get to his destination quickly enough. What if fire destroyed the church and parsonage he'd built practically single-handedly? He'd probably say something ridiculous like, "The Lord gives and the Lord takes away," and start planning a new building. She really should plan how to rescue their few belongings if the fire spread this far. Looking around the sitting room, she evaluated what should be preserved. A cloth-covered bench along one wall caught her attention. The steamer trunk she'd covered to make a seat for David's ever-present visitors. It would make perfect storage and protection. She dragged the trunk to David's study corner and quickly piled his books into it. Then she hurried up the ladder to his loft-bedroom to collect his one good suit and his work clothes. Next, she went to her bedroom for her Sunday frock and her three day dresses, gathered her aprons from the kitchen, and took the bedding from the shelves by her room. Cooking utensils could be stuffed into the burlap grain bag by the back porch. She reached for the bag as the back door shook from heavy blows. Should she open it or pretend not to be home?

The blows came again, this time sounding as though the door were being kicked, while a heavily-accented voice called, "Open up, ma'am. I've got the reverend here. He's been hurt. I can't help 'til I put him down."

With a gasp, Jerusha jerked the door open to admit a soldier in a blood-covered uniform and crookedly placed combat helmet. Used to her brother's skinny height, she noticed immediately this man's relative shortness. In fact, he stood only a few inches taller than her own five foot three. A red cross on a white square emblazoned on the helmet's center announced his medical knowledge. Blood oozed from a horrible-looking bump on David's head, which lolled off one of the medic's arms. His legs dangled off the other, one of them at an awkward angle.

"He'll be all right, ma'am, but I have to lay him somewhere." The soldier spoke reassuringly, yet with authority.

Jerusha tried to focus her thoughts. There would be no way the soldier could carry David up the ladder to his own room, nor would it be easy for her to care for him up there. Yet she didn't want him in the sitting room where visitors could disturb him at all hours.

"Let's put him in here." She led the way to her own room, flipping the electric wall switch to light the room and swiftly pulling down the blanket covering her bed.

"Do you have an extra sheet?" The soldier didn't relinquish his burden. Jerusha nodded, wishing he'd just hurry and fix David.

"Fold it in half widthwise and lay it in the middle of the bed. I'll put the reverend on top of it so we don't have to change all the bedding when I get him fixed up. He's your brother?"

She answered his question aloud while she grabbed two sheets from the trunk. She and David looked enough alike to be twins, so the American's observation came as no surprise. Did he really know what to do for David, or was he just acting? She folded the two sheets and laid them end to end on the bed.

"Thanks, ma'am." The soldier set David down gently. "I also need hot water, clean rags, and fresh clothes for him."

Jerusha hurried to the kitchen stove, where she dipped steaming water from the built-in boiler into a metal washpan, then rummaged through her rag bag for a couple of soft cloths. She delivered the items, then scampered up to David's room for his pajamas. Somehow she hadn't thought about packing them. What if they still had to escape from the fire? How would she move him?

"David told me to be prepared for evacuation if the fire came this way," she said when she re-entered what had become the sickroom. "How am I going to get him out?"

"I don't think you'll have to, ma'am." The soldier lifted his gaze from his quick-moving hands to direct another reassuring smile at her. "Everything seems under control at this point." He bent back over his patient, giving her a clear view of wide, well-muscled shoulders. His stockiness emphasized the gentleness with which he attended David.

Silence hovered while Jerusha watched him wipe soot, blood, and dirt from David's face. Her brother remained unconscious. How soon would he wake up, or would he? She suddenly felt the need to touch him. Only his leg was close enough for her to reach without getting in the way. The movement attracted the soldier's gaze.

"He'll wake up soon enough. Something hit him on the head hard enough to knock him out, and I hope he stays out until I get that leg set. Could I trouble you for his razor? I'd like to shave a little of his hair away from this bump so I can make sure it's clean."

Glad to have something to do, Jerusha went in search of the razor. When she came back, David's shirt was off and his rescuer had another request. "Do you have anything to make cloth strips from?" He pulled the bed away from the wall into the center of the small room.

She thought for a moment. "The Winnipeg Ladies' Aid sent us some worn-out sheets in our most recent missionary barrel. Would that work?"

"Perfect. Could you tear them the long way into four-inch strips, and I'll call when I'm ready for them." He smiled again before turning his attention back to David.

The barrel stood in a corner of the kitchen where David had put it yesterday. Thankfully, the lid was still loose and the sheets near the top. She quickly ripped them as instructed, realizing how tactfully she'd been banished from the sickroom while the soldier changed David's clothes. She wished she could think of a tactful way to find out the stranger's name. In less time than seemed possible, she heard him call, "I'm ready for the bandages whenever you can bring them."

David had begun to stir and the soldier's relaxed manner vanished. "We don't have long before he comes to. Can you quickly find me something to use for a splint?"

"There are a few boards left over from the church benches David made this morning. Would they work?"

"They should, at least until we can find something better if we need it. Where are they?"

Jerusha led the way through a door in the sitting room to the meeting area. Turning on the lights revealed an array of building supplies littering the floor. It only took the soldier a couple of moments to find what he needed.

"These are perfect." He picked up two narrow pieces and a third wider one. "In fact, more than I'd hoped for. Can I get you to hold him still while I work? If he's waking up, he may fight back when I grab that leg."

David moaned when they entered the room. "I'm not sure I'll be much help," Jerusha admitted, looking at her brother's thrashing frame.

"I've learned a bit about controlling these big dudes. Size isn't everything, you know." The soldier grinned and showed Jerusha how to brace herself against the bed, then hold her arms across David's body to still him. He pulled on the broken leg. David struggled, then abruptly went limp.

"Good. He's out again. Would you please hand me a couple of cloth strips?" He wound the material snugly around David's leg, then positioned the wider board underneath with the narrower boards on the sides. "Hopefully these bandages will keep the leg from chafing against the wood. Now for more strips to secure the splints." He worked quickly and confidently. "You'll probably have to cut off one leg of his pajama bottoms to get them over the splint, but he shouldn't have any trouble with his underclothes. Now for that bump on his head." He folded one of the strips to form a pad that he held in place with another strip wrapped around David's head. A couple more strips finished the bandage. "I'll turn him on his side if you'll fold the extra sheets toward him. Good. Now we'll change sides, and I'll roll him the other way and you can pull them out from under him. Easy as sliding off the road, wouldn't you say?" He grinned, once again relaxed.

"What do I do with him now?" Jerusha couldn't imagine how to care for her brother without help. She'd never felt so helpless, so frustrated.

"He'll sleep for a while, probably until tomorrow sometime. For the first couple of days, he'll be pretty quiet while he recovers from the head blow. After that, the hard part will be keeping him still long enough for the leg to heal. I'll try to check on him at least once a day, and I'll see if I can bring something in case the pain gets to bothering him."

"Are you a doctor?" The question popped out before Jerusha could think about its propriety.

A pair of eyes as blue as David's twinkled when he grinned again. "Sorry I haven't introduced myself. I'm Corporal Keith Sutherland, U.S. Army medic, at your service, ma'am." He swept his combat helmet off in an elaborate bow, revealing a blond crew cut.

"Pleased to meet you." Jerusha didn't know how to respond to his breezy humor. "I'm Jerusha Porter. How did you know where to bring David?"

"He visits us army boys often, as I'm sure you know, and made sure we're all aware of where he lives in case we want to drop by."

"How did he get hurt?" She blinked away threatening tears.

"The warehouse had dynamite and percussion caps stored in it. The fire set it all off, which sent the downtown area flying. You've never seen a mess like we've got over there now. I hate to rush off, ma'am, but I've got to get back. I'll check in again tomorrow." Another bright grin, a wave, several quick thumps of his boots, and he was gone into the firelit night.

Chapter 2

Jerusha felt silence close in behind Corporal Sutherland's departure. Then commotion from downtown overwhelmed it—more sirens screaming, army trucks roaring, people yelling, and it seemed she could hear the fire crackling. She noticed wet spots left by snow melting off the soldier's boots onto the wood plank floor and black smudges where soot had rubbed off. What to do next? Weariness suddenly made her limbs feel heavy, though her mind still raced. The clock showed only thirty minutes past eight. She should at least get the stew into a bowl to stay cold in the back entry area that served as mudroom, storage room, and cold room. Maybe egg gravy for breakfast would make the biscuits edible. She'd wait until morning to unpack the trunk. . .just in case. Where should she sleep? David rested quietly in her bed. She could use his bed, but she might not hear him if he awoke, and the ladder would make getting to him quickly difficult. Maybe a pallet on the floor in the sitting room would be the best idea. Thank goodness the Winnipeg Ladies' Aid had seemed to believe bedding to be their most pressing need. Jerusha had laughed derisively when David had first opened the barrel to reveal blankets and sheets in abundance.

"They must think we're running a hospital, not starting a church," she had grumbled, recalling the bedding showered on them before they left. "Too bad all these sheets couldn't make me a housedress or a new shirt for you."

"Don't fret, Rushi." David laughed with genuine amusement. "I know it's frustrating to feel our people back home don't understand what we're doing here, but God never sends us anything we don't need. I'll keep this lid on loosely, and we'll wait to see what He has in mind for His bedclothes."

With a small amount of gratitude, Jerusha now extracted enough blankets to make a soft pad, then a couple of sheets and another three blankets to keep herself warm on the cold floor. She'd have to make sure she stoked the fire well, both in the barrel stove and in the cookstove. Not only did they need extra warmth in this frigid weather, but she wasn't sure she could start the fires again should they go out. She filled each stove with as much wood as it could hold, then pulled the dampers shut to keep the wood from burning too quickly.

Too tense for sleep, she decided to indulge in a quick sponge bath and a cup of warm milk before bed. She turned out all the lights in the house so she wouldn't be visible through the curtains, dumped her soiled dress onto the pile of David's clothing left by the medic, and pulled her flannel gown and wrapper from their pegs beside the door. Though the damp cloth on her skin caused her to shiver, the feeling of cleanliness combined with the cozy warmth of her nightgown did bring relaxation. She thought about turning a light back on before she dumped the soiled water, but decided against it. The sky's red glow lent enough light that she wouldn't bump into things, and the semidarkness was soothing. She tiptoed into the sickroom for the pan of water used by the medic, then carried it and her own washpan to the back door and flung their contents across the snow. Theoretically, their house was tied into the city drainage system, but she knew from experience how unreliable the system was. When the water drained at all, it went down so slowly as to leave her sink unusable for at least half an hour. As it was, dirty water from the pipes often bubbled up through her drain to fill the sink. She'd never had the sink overflow, but she knew it would happen some-day. Just one more problem in this town that had mushroomed from seven hundred people to more than four thousand civilians in less than a year.

She wondered again what had drawn so many people to this desolate place. For some reason she had yet to discover, the U.S. Army had decided to build a highway from Dawson Creek, British Columbia, to Fairbanks, Alaska, as part of the war effort. Locals were outspoken in their disdain of what they saw as an impossible project, which seemed totally unrelated to the carnage in Europe. Some even went so far as to declare that the men and money being utilized in highway building could be much more effectively used where the war was actually taking place.

However, construction had brought prosperity of sorts to what had been simply a frontier village. With Dawson Creek being the northern ter-minus of the railway, all army and construction supplies and personnel were funnelled through the tiny community. Carpenters, truckers, laborers, and opportunists from all over had come to join the action. The army paid their contractors well, and those who couldn't get work for the army directly could easily make a living at the myriad of services needed by the mushrooming boomtown. One of David's parishioners, a white-haired woman named Mrs. Barry, had doubled the size of her boardinghouse and said she had every room filled every night. Sometimes she and her niece, Maisie, even had to double up in her room to provide more space for guests. Jerusha couldn't imagine allowing those uncouth types into the house, much less cooking and cleaning for them, too. She shuddered at the thought.

Back in the kitchen, she scooped two tablespoons of milk powder into a cup and added a tablespoon of honey. Here was another symbol of this uncivilized place. Who could possibly be fooled into thinking this powder mixed with water would replace real milk? Six months ago, she hadn't been able to tolerate its taste. Unfortunately, the farms around this community couldn't keep up with the demand for milk, butter, and cheese. Such products could be brought in by train, but were too expensive for the Porters' budget. So she had learned to first accept, then even enjoy, the powdered milk beverage, as long as it was hot. She wrapped her hands around the warm cup, wishing it had been that easy to adapt to other changes in her lifestyle.

For one thing, money had become almost nonexistent. Having grown up in relative comfort due to Uncle Cam's successful business ventures, Jerusha found herself continually frustrated by David's limited and irregular salary. Over the winter, his pay had often come in the form of food and firewood. Even so, she'd been forced to take in laundry from the boardinghouse to earn necessary income. Though the job only included bedding, she still felt demeaned.

She pulled the pins from her hair. Mother and Aunt Vivienne had never cut their hair, so neither had Jerusha. Her fine, thin strands refused to style as gracefully as theirs, but cutting it would be giving in to worldliness. As she brushed, she felt it catch on the roughness of her fingers. Her hands had once been her single private vanity. Days of lifting sheets from soapy water and hanging them outside in stinging wind had reddened and cracked them. Their condition both mortified and continually reminded her of what she'd given up to remain at her brother's side. As she inched into her makeshift bed, she wished yet again he'd just give up and take her back where she belonged.

It seemed she had only slept a few moments when she heard a knock at the back door. Who could it be at this time of night? If it were someone with evil intent, they wouldn't bother knocking. She belted her wrapper snugly around her and hurried to the entry. Before she could inquire, a somewhat familiar voice called, "It's Corporal Sutherland, Miss Porter. May I talk to you about something urgent?"

With a small sigh of relief, she switched on a light and opened the door. "Come in."

"Sorry to disturb you so late, or should I say so early. It's this way, Miss Porter. The hospital is full up with people injured when the dynamite blew.

It's against regulation to bring civilians into the army hospital, and we still have wounded lying on the boardwalks and in the streets closed off from traffic. I noticed your meeting room is fairly large as well as being close by. Would it be possible for us to use it? An army team will take care of the medical end of things if we can just get the patients out of the cold."

She didn't have to wonder what David would say. He wouldn't hesitate. Besides, the barrel in the corner of the kitchen still contained innumerable blankets and sheets. Could this be why it had been sent? In any case, no good minister or his family ever refused to be helpful.

Corporal Sutherland sensed her hesitation. "I doubt we'll be noisy enough to disturb the reverend. In fact, it will keep me close by in case he needs help." Another charming grin erased some of the weariness etched around his eyes.

"I'm sure my brother would be delighted to make the room available. The front doors are unlocked. Shall I make up beds on the floor or on the benches?"

"Maybe we'll push three benches together for treatment areas and pallets on the floor for sleeping patients. I wish we could bring cots over from the infirmary, but the trucks wouldn't be able to get through the mess downtown. God bless you, Miss Porter. We'll be back shortly." He lifted his combat helmet and vanished again.

Jerusha hurried to the meeting room, where she quickly stacked the short pieces of lumber against one wall. The long pieces were too difficult to lift without entangling her long gown. She hoped she could get the area cleared to her satisfaction before the men showed up. It wouldn't do for the reverend's sister to be seen in her nightclothes in the company of soldiers. She decided to unload the blankets and sheets from the barrel, then go change. The church would be turned into a hospital, so she, the minister's sister, would have to be on hand to help.

She'd just pulled on a dress when thumps from the meeting area announced the beginning of the rescue effort. She quickly fastened the last buttons on her dress, tied on a white apron, and hurried into the makeshift first aid station. Two soldiers had already begun carrying lumber outside, and another two, wearing helmets that matched Corporal Sutherland's, were pushing benches together, padding each "bed" with a blanket, and covering each with a carefully folded sheet. One of the medics looked up as she entered.

"Hello, ma'am. The corporal said to thank you again for your generosity." Smiling her acknowledgment, Jerusha reached for a blanket with which to make up a floor pallet. The gratitude made her feel guilty, since the offer hadn't been her idea or even her choice. She'd simply done what any good minister's sister would do, regardless of her personal feelings. Familiar resentment churned inside as she worked. Unbidden, she mentally heard her aunt's voice praising her mother's dedication. She reminded herself that she wasn't doing this only for David, but also for her family's reputation. She couldn't belittle her parents' sacrifice by cringing from her duty. The thought didn't change how she felt about the hardships of this town, the rough company, and now being forced into nursing duty simply because she was David's sister.

"Miss Porter." Corporal Sutherland's voice broke into her introspection. She looked up, unaware he'd come in.

He stood beside a makeshift bed, a thrashing child in his arms. "Would you help me soothe this young man? I can't do much for him until we get him quiet."

His apparent confidence in her ability warred against the nervousness she always felt around children. "I don't know how much good I'll do." She stood slowly, rubbing her hands in her apron.

"Kids usually respond better to women. All we can do for any of these people is try." He smiled encouragingly and put the child on the bed.

Jerusha instinctively reached for the boy's hands while murmuring whatever came to mind. "Calm down, young man. We can't help you if you won't let us. That's it. Lie still, now. It won't hurt as badly if you don't move." To her surprise, the thrashing stopped.

"Looks like you have the touch, Miss Porter. Keep it up, and I'll have him bandaged in no time."

She never knew what kept her going until the first rays of sunshine created a murky dawn through the heavy smoke still blanketing the town. It seemed the procession of injured people would never end. Head wounds, broken bones, unconscious people without visible injuries, and cuts and scrapes in abundance. Corporal Sutherland's unending gentle humor and continuing energy amazed her. He seemed genuinely contented and appeared to want to help these people. She wished she could feel that "want to." It would be so much easier to be the proper minister's sister if she had the emotions to go along with the part.

"I think that does it for now." Corporal Sutherland motioned for another medic to help him lift a patient with a sprained ankle to one of the last three pallets. "Shall I look in on the reverend before I report back to the base?"

"Yes, please." Jerusha felt like she'd been run over by a truck and hoped fervently no one would decide to visit until she'd been able to grab some sleep. But then who would keep watch over the wounded who littered the church? She sighed wearily, ignoring memories of her luxurious bed and quiet, spacious room in Winnipeg.

"I'll see if I can get a couple of my men assigned to our little first aid station here so you can catch some rest. I'm sorry we've imposed on you so severely." Concern showed past the exhaustion imprinted on his face.

"The church isn't much good unless it's used for more than social gatherings," Jerusha replied automatically, quoting one of David's favorite sayings.

"It's too bad more people don't believe that." Corporal Sutherland followed his comment with enigmatic silence. Jerusha wondered if he saw through her act of dedication. She shook her head, trying to clear the guilt. She was just tired. What would he care, so long as she helped? He was just one of those military heathen, anyway.

Corporal Sutherland placed a squarish hand on David's forehead at the edge of the bandage. "No fever, and he seems to be resting well. When he wakes up, he'll probably want to get up right away. If you can, keep him still and feed him as lightly as he'll allow. Porridge would be a good idea, or light soup. Make sure he doesn't try to walk on that leg."

"Thanks for the help, Corporal." Jerusha clutched the edge of the doorway to steady herself in a world that suddenly seemed to tilt and spin.

"Pleased to—Miss Porter!" She heard alarm in his voice and firm hands grabbed her arms just as she felt herself falling. "Here, sit down." He unceremoniously pushed her onto the bed and shoved her head between her knees.

The stench of unwashed bodies and stale blood in her apron threatened to overturn her stomach, though her head cleared. She straightened slowly, working to keep the room in focus. "I'm sorry. I'm not in the habit of fainting."

"Don't apologize, Miss Porter. Lack of sleep and food combined with a night of hard work will do that to anyone. Do you have some soup I can warm for you?"

Jerusha couldn't find the words to refuse him politely. "On the shelf in the back entry. It's frozen."

"I'll find it. Don't go to sleep on me. I'll be right back."

She felt far too light-headed to stand up. She forced herself to focus on David's face, then on the fire-tinged sky outside her window. It seemed only moments until the medic returned with a steaming bowl. "I'll hold it if you think you can handle the spoon." Again his smile encouraged her while he knelt on the floor.

Gradually, clear thinking returned while the soup's warmth spread throughout her body. She felt almost ready to handle the new day without sleep.

"If smell is any indication, you must be a pretty good cook," Corporal Sutherland observed.

Jerusha grinned at the obvious hint. "I must be some sort of beast to eat in front of you. Help yourself before you leave."

"Since I don't want to pass out getting back to camp, I'd better accept your offer." Humor twinkled from his exhaustion-ringed eyes.

They both stood, but a sound from the bed stopped their departure. "Rushi." The corporal lifted an eyebrow at Jerusha before stepping past her to David's side. Slowly, David's eyes opened. "Rushi?" He called again.

"Right here, David. How do you feel?" A dizzying feeling of relief weakened her knees again.

"What's with my leg? My head. I shouldn't be sleeping—"

The medic quickly interrupted what was turning into a restless tirade. "I think you should, Reverend. I found you under a couple of wooden beams near the co-op store. You have a nasty bump on your head and a broken leg. Sleep's the best thing for you."

"Keith?" David seemed unsure of what he saw.

"That's me, Rev. The boss of this here temporary first aid station."

"May I eat?" David's buoyant good humor asserted itself as he became more alert.

"If you'll promise to be quiet and absolutely no trouble to your sister. She's been up all night helping us in your meeting room, which we've turned into a recovery area."

"Thanks, Rushi." David's gentle gaze told her he realized the struggle she'd been through. His uncanny perception both reassured and intimidated her. He looked back to the medic. "If you can help me take care of a little personal problem, Corporal, I think I'll be able to rest a lot better."

Jerusha felt her cheeks flame as both men chuckled. "I'll have soup waiting for both of you when you're ready."

Chapter 3

By Wednesday morning, the last of the invalids had been moved to the hospital or taken home. Dr. Pierce, a tall, smiling man and one of David's most faithful parishioners, stopped by the parsonage that evening.

"Sorry I couldn't come earlier, Miss Porter," he apologized. "Since Keith found him, I knew he'd been well taken care of, and I've been so busy my wife has almost forgotten what I look like." He grinned. "Keith wanted me to double-check his work, though."

"Thanks for coming." Jerusha directed him to the bedroom. This made the second time Jerusha had heard Corporal Sutherland referred to with respect. Generally, civilians held the army in distrust, and soldiers kept mostly to themselves. Somehow this medic had reached beyond the barriers to earn a rapport with civilians. He'd certainly gained her confidence. She yanked her thoughts back to the real doctor, whom she heard conversing with his patient in the sickroom.

"Couldn't have looked after him better myself," Dr. Pierce smiled when he came out. "Your brother's head wound is healing nicely. I would have liked to have set his leg in plaster, but we're fresh out. The reverend should be okay with the splints if you can keep him still. Good day, ma'am." He left chuckling at his own joke.

"Rushi." David's call brought Jerusha running. He had already pushed himself into a sitting position. Obviously, keeping still didn't rank high on his list of priorities.

"David!" She tried to keep her voice calm and rational.

"I'm being careful." His grin ruined the reassuring tone of his voice. "I just can't handle lying here anymore. Keith brought me some crutches this morning, and I'd like to try them out before this evening's service."

The urge to shriek at him almost overpowered her. "You're still planning church for tonight?"

"Why not? The hard part will be getting to the meeting room. Nobody will mind if I don't stand at the pulpit, and you can help me prop my leg on a chair. But first, I need presentable clothes and some practice with the crutches."

Jerusha glared at him. "Why not just cancel the service?"

"Our people need encouragement." Laughter had disappeared from his eyes, replaced by a gentleness and something else she couldn't define.

"But they would understand if we cancelled just for tonight. Besides, they'll probably all be busy and won't come anyway." She tried to push him back onto the pillows, but he enveloped her hands in his own.

"They will come, Rushi. Disaster shows people how much they need each other and God."

She tried to pull away. "They can find God at home. They functioned for years without you. There's no need to drag yourself out of bed."

"I'll be fine, little sister. I need them as much as they need me."

Jerusha brought his clothes, helped him dress, walked with him while he practiced with his crutches, then busied herself tidying up the meeting room while he slept, all the while contrasting his words with her feelings. She thought of this town as a mission field, its people as heathens, its Christians as converts. How could he feel he needed them when he'd come to help them? She remembered his eyes as he'd spoken of them. Their expression certainly bore no resemblance to her own sense of duty.

To her surprise, their meeting room began to fill early. She noticed several people who hadn't attended before, as well as a few who usually came only for the Sunday service. David sat at the front of the room, his injured leg positioned on pillows on a chair in front of him. Each person who came went straight to him before finding a seat. Jerusha watched him carefully for signs of fatigue. Instead of becoming tired, though, he seemed more invigorated with each hand he shook. He inquired after the women's homes and families, ruffled the children's hair, and swapped stories with the men. Occasionally, his hearty laugh filled the room with joy. She wished she'd been able to clean more thoroughly, instead of just pushing the benches into place, moving the bedding to their own sitting room, and sweeping the floor.

"He loves these people, doesn't he?"

The deep voice near her ear caused Jerusha to jump. She turned to glare at its owner, but her gaze was met by a pair of sparkling blue eyes. "Corporal Sutherland!"

"At your service, ma'am." As he swept a low bow, she noticed his freshly pressed uniform, carefully knotted tie, and the cloth hat he held. His presence added to her discomfort.

"I'm sure the reverend will be pleased to see you here."

He sobered as he looked at her, but his eyes retained their twinkle. "A few of the guys in my outfit have the night off and decided they'd like to come here. Funny how disaster makes people think of God." He moved off toward David.

She stared after him. He'd echoed David's earlier comment. What made him and David so different from her? She sensed they truly loved the people around them. She cared about some of them, too, she defended herself, seeing Maisie Clarke follow Mrs. Barry through the doorway. She'd become acquainted with the plump young woman soon after arriving, and their friendship had grown mostly because Maisie refused to leave Jerusha to herself.

"Jerusha! I'm so glad you weren't hurt, too. How is the reverend?" Maisie's round face wore its usual sunny smile.

"He insisted on being here tonight, even though I think he should have stayed in bed."

"He probably needed to see his people." Maisie studied him for a moment. "I think we needed to see him, too."

"He said the same thing." Where had it come from—this mysterious bond between her brother and these strangers?

"And we have visitors tonight! Do you know who they are?" Bubbling interest turned Maisie's eyes to green twinkles.

"The shorter man is the medic who brought David home, but I don't know who the others are."

More familiar arrivals distracted Maisie from the strangers. "And here come Lewis and Sheila Murray! He doesn't often come into town on a weeknight."

The two women waited eagerly for the couple to come inside. Sheila formed a third in their trio of friendship, as equally determined to include Jerusha as Maisie.

"I'm so glad you came! How are you feeling?" Maisie studied Sheila carefully, though her friend's small frame had yet to make her pregnancy visible.

"Jist fine, and that's the truth of it." Sheila smiled as easily as Maisie, her Irish brogue thickening as she talked. "And how is it you are, Jerusha? Lewis told me you were in the thick of it t'other night."

"We just did what needed to be done." Jerusha felt uncomfortable under her friends' scrutiny. "At least the bedding in the missionary barrel came in handy."

"Lewis will be coming to town tomorrow. How about if I come help you with the cleaning up?"

"And I'll come, too," Maisie eagerly added. "Auntie won't need me until supper time, so we'll get everything tidied in no time."

Jerusha's pride wanted to refuse the assistance, but she knew if she tried to do it alone, she'd fall behind in her other laundry. "If you want to help, I won't complain."

Singing began at the front of the room, so the ladies seated themselves quickly, Maisie with Mrs. Barry, Sheila with Lewis and their two small sons, and Jerusha in her usual place on the front row. To her amazement, Corporal Sutherland led the music with a pleasant, strong voice. After several hymns, he motioned for everyone to sit down.

"If y'all are like me, you feel a special sense of gratitude tonight, just being alive and unhurt, except for our preacher, here."

Jerusha didn't miss his possessive tone.

"Let's sing a verse of 'What Wondrous Love,' and then we'd like to hear your story of God's protection Sunday night."

Usually "testimony times" were slow at this little church. She'd often noticed how reluctant people seemed to be to share anything about themselves in public. She identified with the sentiment. But tonight, the singing halted for a full hour as one person after another told, some with shaking voices, how they had experienced Divine protection during the disaster. Even Lewis Murray spoke about being in town during the explosion and seeing men on either side of him thrown across the street by the blast, while he huddled safely against the side of a building. Mrs. Barry told about the large window in her kitchen being blown to bits without harming either her or her boarders. A young couple whom Jerusha hadn't seen before gave thanks the fire had been stopped just two houses away from where they lived. Ruth Pierce, the doctor's slender, dark-haired wife, thanked God for protecting her husband while he worked with the injured. David expressed his gratitude for the corporal being nearby when he'd been hit by flying debris.

Corporal Sutherland made his own contribution. "I'm sure many in our community are grateful for this church and for the generosity of the brother and sister who pastor us. In case you didn't know, the room where we're meeting tonight was an emergency aid station until this morning."

Jerusha wished her feelings came closer to those a "generous pastor" should feel. She felt no kinship with these people as they rejoiced. Stories of inexplicable happenings abounded, even outside the church. More than one man had staggered away from the heart of the disaster, while the person beside him had been killed. She'd heard more than twenty people had been killed. The parents and wives of the dead men probably weren't talking of God's protection. It had been a freak accident, making victims capriciously.

Thankfully, none of these pious people could read her mind. She wondered briefly if even God knew how she felt, then gave thanks He probably didn't care. She was doing her best to be the kind of person she should be. What would it matter to Him if her emotions didn't agree?

Chapter 4

Jerusha pushed herself off her floor pallet shortly after five o'clock Thursday morning. She had slept uneasily, feeling like she'd been in a wrestling match all night. Though she still felt tired, sleep required more effort than getting up. She moved quietly around the piles of bedding still littering the cabin floor, trying not to disturb David. After discovering the freedom of crutches yesterday, who knew what he'd attempt today. She'd had a friend in Winnipeg who had been permanently crippled by improper healing of a broken bone. Jerusha feared for David's leg if he didn't take care of it. Being crippled wouldn't send him home, but it would make his work much more difficult. She tiptoed to the kitchen to check the stove. She'd need lots of hot water for the massive laundry project today. Having specific, direct action made it easier to get away from her thoughts.

"Mornin', Rushi."

Jerusha jumped, dropping the stove lid, and whirled around. "David! You're supposed to be sleeping."

Still in his pajamas, he grinned. "I slept enough yesterday for the next week. Besides, Keith and a couple of guys are coming over today to chop firewood and help clean up the meeting room."

"Who? What?" Jerusha wished she hadn't said anything the minute she heard her snappish tone.

"Hey, they're just coming to help. I know you're busy, so we'll stay out of your way."

She took a deep breath to steady herself. "I know, it's not a problem. I'm just tired."

"It's been a rough four days for you, eh? Keith's told me at least twice a day how much help you were in the aid station." He put a hand on her shoulder, and she heard a crutch clatter to the floor.

"Wouldn't be much of a pastor's daughter if I couldn't help people in trouble, now would I?" Bending down, she smiled tightly.

"You're more than a pastor's daughter, Rushi. You're my sister and a wonderful woman." Balanced once again, he leaned forward and kissed her cheek.

Jerusha hid her surprise behind a not entirely phony scandalized tone. "Reverend!"

"Whatsamatter, kid? I'm your brother, remember?" He grinned mischievously and clumped back to the bedroom. A series of bumps and grunts indicated he must be getting dressed. Jerusha sighed. Keeping him still would be harder than she thought. She probably ought to get dressed, too, before anything else happened.

She folded her nightclothes inside her floor pallet, which she folded in half and set in the corner behind a chair. The piles of bedding looked to be pretty well sorted, so the next step should be putting water on to heat. She might even get a couple of loads done before Maisie and Sheila arrived. Usually, she heated laundry water by setting the tubs directly on the stove and filling them there. However, David wouldn't be able to help her carry the tubs to the porch. She'd better use several large pots. It would be more cumbersome, but it remained the only solution available.

The bedroom had become silent. Had he returned to bed? Should she fix him breakfast or wait for him to appear again? Peeking in the doorway, she saw he was fully dressed and sitting on the bed with his legs stretched out in front of him and his back against the wall. His Bible lay open on his lap and he stared out the window. His lips moved slightly. An expression of almost tangible peace covered his face, varied only by his small smile and the happy crinkles around his eyes. *He is definitely demented,* Jerusha thought. What was there about this place, about his situation, to make him look so utterly contented, even happy? Yet she couldn't tear her gaze away from him. Maybe if she watched long enough, she'd figure out his secret.

He turned his head. "You're welcome to join me. I'm just telling our Father how glad I am He's brought us here and also how grateful I feel that He sent you with me."

"David!" She wasn't sure whether she objected to his familiar way of talking about God, his joy at being in Dawson Creek, or his gratitude for her.

"Would you sit with me for a while? I'm sure the water won't scorch in your absence." His gentle teasing drew her to perch on the edge of the bed facing him. "You're distressed, aren't you, sister?"

She wondered what he'd think if he knew the complete truth. But if he knew, maybe he could help her discover how to find what he had. She settled for, "I'm concerned about you."

"And I'm concerned for you, so I guess that makes us a matched pair, eh?" His infectious chuckle stretched her mouth into an answering grin. "How am I worrying you?"

"What if your leg doesn't heal properly? Both the medic and the doctor said you have to keep still. If you don't, you could end up like Susannah Blake."

His forehead wrinkled in concentration. "Susannah—oh, you mean the little girl from next door you used to play with?"

"She was crippled, David, because she broke her leg as a small child and it didn't heal properly."

"I remember her having a bit of a limp, but not crippled."

"She couldn't walk normally, and that's crippled in my book." Jerusha's voice sharpened involuntarily. "How would you like to be like that?"

"If that's the way things turn out, I'll learn to live with it. But it doesn't mean I have to stop living now."

"But pastors aren't supposed to be common laborers!"

"Hey, Rushi." His voice expressed gentle surprise. "We're in a frontier town. We all have to do things we're not used to, pastor included. That's part of building anything, be it a road, a church, or a town." When she didn't answer, he continued. "Don't waste energy resenting anything or anyone on my account, Sis. God called us, and He'll provide the help we need."

She couldn't swallow back the reply springing to her tongue. "He can't provide if people don't cooperate."

"They've got farms to tend, families to feed, and businesses to take care of. They give what they can. Just look at all the food they bring in for us."

"But vegetables, eggs, and milk alone won't finish the meeting room or give you decent clothes. They shouldn't have called you out here if they couldn't support you or even help you build the church they say they want."

"Rushi, the church isn't the building. It's the people I'm learning to know and love, who provide support in ways money can't measure. Think of all the visitors we had last night and the concern everyone expressed for people whose loved ones were killed this weekend. They could have just sat around being grateful it wasn't them. Besides, Keith and a couple of his men are coming to help today."

"So a bunch of army Yanks have to take care of us."

He spoke intently, but without rebuke. "If it weren't for an army Yank, I might not be here." He paused, then asked almost in a whisper, "Rushi, what's really making you unhappy? It's more than my leg and more than the church. Can you tell me?"

"I don't think God will do anything about it." She expected him to withdraw at her blasphemy.

Instead, he put a hand on her arm and asked tenderly, "Why not, kid?"

"Because I can't be the kind of person He expects me to be." The words came out defiantly.

"What do you mean?" Still no condemnation colored his tone.

"I hate being here! It's cold, dark, uncivilized, and lonely. Why couldn't God have called you somewhere safe and cultured? Why the edge of civilization in a dirty town overrun with heathen?"

"So you don't like Dawson Creek. That doesn't make you anything more or less than a human being with an opinion."

"But you actually enjoy it! What will people think of the church if they find out I hate this place?"

"Rushi, please look at me. You came because you felt you should, right?" She nodded.

"Now that you're here, Dawson Creek is God's will for you, and Philippians promises He works in us to want to do His will."

"Then I must be doing something wrong."

"With our Heavenly Father, the issue isn't our doing, but our being. One of His delights is helping us learn to enjoy being the people He's made us to be."

"I don't think that's possible for me." She stood. "What do you want for breakfast?"

He looked at her for a moment, profound sadness in his blue eyes. Gradually, peace returned. "How about some of your marvelous coffee cake? We'll use the leftovers for snacking so we don't have to disturb you ladies."

Jerusha had already fed the second load of sheets through the wringer by the time Lewis, Sheila, and Maisie arrived. "They stopped by the house and offered me a ride. Who was I to refuse?" Maisie pulled her eyebrows up with mock innocence.

"Looks like you've been busy, and that's the truth," Sheila observed. "Shall I take these out to the clothesline?"

"Let me do that," Maisie interrupted quickly.

"Then I'll pump some more water for the stove."

This time Jerusha interrupted. "I just filled them."

Sheila's brown eyes twinkled with amusement. "All right, girls. 'Tis in the family way I am, not dying. I came to help. You have to let me do something."

Jerusha's gaze met Maisie's. Keeping Sheila from overexerting herself would be difficult. "Let's pile the next load on this bench, and you can put them in the washtub without bending too much," Maisie suggested.

"Worse than Lewis, you are," Sheila declared with a saucy shake of her head.

The three worked companionably, Jerusha and Maisie making sure Sheila took only the lightest jobs. She often protested, but without resentment. Midmorning she came up with her first idea the other two didn't override. "How about if I make some soup and cornbread for lunch? The menfolk will be hungry, and I don't think peeling carrots would be too much."

"If you sit down," Maisie and Jerusha chorused, then laughed at Sheila's disgusted appearance.

"Like a couple of mother hens, you two. But I thank ye. It's only for me best you're concerned."

"You're special," Maisie declared, "and so's your little one."

She and Jerusha managed to wash, wring, rinse, wring, and hang two more loads of blankets before the men trooped in from the meeting room ready for lunch. Jerusha was astounded to see half a dozen soldiers with the corporal as well as at least that many men from the church. They loudly praised the soup and cornbread, making Sheila's cheeks flame. Jerusha studied David's face carefully for signs of fatigue, but could only see how much he had enjoyed the activity.

"I'm making sure he doesn't overdo," a male voice whispered close to her as she set a stack of bowls in the dishpan.

She looked at Corporal Sutherland, who only winked and moved toward the door. "Let's get back at it, guys."

By midafternoon, the last of the bedding had been hung on the lines outside, and the first load had been brought in to thaw and finish drying. Conversation turned inevitably to the explosion.

"You should see the shop next to the warehouse," Sheila declared. "Nothing left but a pile of rubble."

"I noticed one of the hotels is pretty well flattened, too. The boardinghouse will be busier than ever, which means even more laundry for me." Jerusha sighed.

"I've heard the army is setting up temporary shelter. Did you know there are military patrols downtown every night?" Maisie's eyes sparkled.

"Whatever for?" Sheila didn't look nearly so thrilled.

"So many stores are missing walls, windows, or doors that the powers that be are afraid of looting. As soon as it gets dusk, the soldiers are out, and they don't leave until the sun's fully up."

"Which means from midafternoon to midmorning," Jerusha muttered to herself.

"And that's the truth." Sheila missed Jerusha's grumbling tone. "Makes me glad we're out on the farm."

"Where are the boys?" Maisie never missed an opportunity to hug and visit with the two youngsters.

"Lewis left them with a neighbor. He said I didn't need to be taking care of them and helping here, too."

"Not a bad idea." Maisie's eyes twinkled with new interest. "Is the baby to be a boy or a girl?"

"Lewis says it doesn't matter." Pain flitted across Sheila's face.

"And you?" Jerusha wondered.

A tear trickled down Sheila's cheek. "Only a boy."

Jerusha didn't know what to do. Undisguised emotion made her uncomfortable. But Maisie didn't hesitate. She moved quickly to Sheila's side and wrapped her arms around the woman. "What is it, Sheila?"

"You'll not tell anyone else, not even the reverend?" She looked at Jerusha.

"Of course not." Her answer came out more roughly than she intended, but Sheila seemed reassured.

She gulped a couple of breaths. "I'm so afraid this baby won't be a boy because I want one so much."

"Why a boy?" Maisie asked gently.

"I want Lewis to love me."

The quiet words hung in the air, almost drowned by chopping and hammering sounds beyond the walls. Jerusha opened her mouth to object, but Maisie's quick glance stopped her.

"Are you sure he doesn't already?"

Sheila shook her head forlornly. "How could he? I've done little but make mistakes since I came. I can sew cute outfits for his sons, but I can't cook a good meal. Now I'm in the family way, I can't even help him with the chores. Well, I could," she amended, "but he keeps asking me not to. If something happens to this baby, he'll never forgive me."

Her words baffled Jerusha. She'd assumed the boys were Sheila's as well. "You mean this is your first baby?"

Sheila's damp gaze regained a bit of humor. "Ye've not heard my story?"

Jerusha shook her head.

"Let's sit a spell while you tell it," Maisie suggested. She dished out squares of leftover coffeecake and poured coffee as if they were in her kitchen. Jerusha felt grateful for her sensibility and understanding.

"I grew up in Ireland, in case you couldn't tell," Sheila began with a chuckle, "the daughter of a dressmaker. Times were always rough, and Mum died when I was just thirteen. Too much work and not enough food. Dad had died when I was a baby. My older brothers found work in the factories, and I hired out as a dressmaker's apprentice. The lady who hired me treated me like a charity case. Anything I learned was by accident, as she felt I wasn't fit for anything but sweepin' floors. Then one day I saw a bit in the paper about farmers in Canada who were lookin' for wives. It said they'd pay our way if we'd just come. I slipped away in the night and made it to the shipping office. Lewis Murray met me at the station in Edmonton. His wife had died a couple of years before in birthin', and he wanted a mother for his little sons. Here I am, but it's not a very good wife I've been." Tears welled in her eyes again.

Though their situations were different, Jerusha felt Sheila's pain. She had those same feelings about her role. She squeezed the woman's hand. "I'm sorry."

Sheila smiled faintly. "At least he hasn't shipped me back."

"And he won't, I'm sure," Maisie declared firmly. "You mustn't worry so much, for the babe's sake. Have you prayed about it?"

Sheila's eyes glowed. "If it weren't for the Heavenly Father, I wouldn't have made it this far."

"Let's talk to Him again," Maisie suggested.

The two bowed their heads while Jerusha stared unseeingly past them. Both sounded so confident that Someone took a personal interest in their concerns. She felt on the outside of a precious secret, something she needed to know but couldn't find.

Chapter 5

By the time Jerusha went to bed Friday evening, life felt almost back to normal, except for David still occupying her room. He tried to encourage her to sleep in the loft, but she didn't want to try the ladder. She'd become accustomed to sleeping on the floor even though real sleep remained elusive. As soon as she'd drift off, images would fill her mind—blood-stained people filling the meeting room, David lying limply in the corporal's arms, Winnipeg's culture and comfort, and most frequently, the peaceful expressions worn by David, Maisie, Sheila, and the corporal. She'd tried to be the right kind of person all her life. One of her few memories of her parents was kneeling by her mother's knee asking Jesus to forgive her for being a sinner and to help her be His kind of girl. She could still feel the trust in Him and love for Him she'd felt at that moment and in the months afterward. Eventually, though, an awareness of her responsibilities as a Christian replaced those childish emotions.

So she tossed her way through the night, waking only marginally refreshed. Two huge cloth bags of soiled bedding had been delivered the day before from the boardinghouse. She should be able to get the work done tonight so it could be delivered first thing Monday morning. The familiar frustration made her feel like screaming. Why should the pastor's sister have to work incessantly on public laundry? Granted, none of the church people seemed in the least offended, but that wasn't a mark in their favor. Church members with the proper respect for their pastor should be ashamed that his family would have to stoop to such work.

She lay in the early morning darkness, thinking of their pastor in Winnipeg. He had lived in one of the nicest homes in the city, and his wife's hands had never been as red and rough as Jerusha's. Mrs. Phillips had been one of the most refined ladies Jerusha knew, seeming to move through any situation with cultured detachment. How would she have handled the events of the past few days? Certainly Reverend Phillips never would have shown himself to his congregation with his leg swathed in boards and rags. Jerusha recalled the eagerness with which people had gathered around David. She couldn't remember seeing that kind of affection demonstrated for their minister. He, the pastor, stood on a pedestal, separate from their everyday lives. It occurred to her that Mrs. Phillips probably didn't have the kind of friends Jerusha had found in Maisie and Sheila. In fact, Mrs. Phillips would probably have been horrified by their frank discussion of emotions and family life. Jerusha scrambled out of bed wondering if she'd ever find a resolution to her frustrations. Thank goodness there was still work to keep her occupied.

David slept longer this morning. Jerusha heard no movement from his room until close to seven o'clock. "Good morning, sleepyhead," she greeted him as he thumped toward the kitchen where she was scooting pots around to get laundry water heated.

He flashed a bright grin. "Good morning, yourself. I thought you said something yesterday about wanting me to rest more."

"So I did. You're learning."

He watched her carry several bucketfuls of water from the pump to the stove. "Guess that's easier in the washtub, isn't it?"

"Don't even think about it. This works just fine."

"Have I ever told you how much I appreciate your laundry work? I know it's not what you bargained for coming out here with me."

Jerusha laughed self-consciously. "I was wondering this morning what Mrs. Phillips would say if she saw me."

"I hope you don't feel you have to live up to her."

She didn't answer, concentrating instead on preparing oatmeal along with toast spread with David's favorite apple butter.

"How are your clotheslines holding up out there?"

"Just perfectly. They're a lot tighter in this cold than they were when you put them up, but not one has broken yet."

"I like that 'yet.'" He laughed. "Guess there's not much I can do to help, is there?"

"Just keep out of the way, and don't try to get too active."

By the time she had the washtubs filled, he had settled himself on the trunk bench along the wall, his leg propped in front of him and his Bible and notebook in his lap. "This okay, Mom?" he teased. "Figured I'd better have a sermon ready for tomorrow."

"At least you're sitting still for a change," she grumbled.

He only winked at her as he opened his books. Jerusha pushed the sheets down into the water with a specially made laundry plunger, forcing water through the fabric without getting her hands wet. After twenty minutes of washing, she used a long-handled wooden spoon to fish part of one of the sheets out of the water far enough to cool so she could touch it. Turning the handle of the wringer with one hand, she carefully fed the steaming sheet between the rollers, squeezing out soapy water. Mounted on a wooden frame between the two washtubs, the wringer fed the sheet into the hot rinse water. Only ten minutes of "plunging" were required for rinsing. She placed a board over the washtub, put her laundry basket on top of it, then directed the sheets back through the wringer into the basket. Three loads usually got the water so grimy, she had to empty the washtub, using a hose attached at one end to a hole in the bottom of the washtub. When not in use, the hose hooked over the edge of the tub. She drained the tub into a small metal pail, carrying each pailful outdoors and dumping it several feet away from the porch. A patch of icy brown snow showed where the wash water had been dumped on previous occasions. A few soap shavings and a bit of bleach turned the rinse water into fresh wash water, and she filled the empty tub with clean scalding water for rinsing. Periodically, David would say, "Listen to this, Rushi," and would read a portion of Scripture. His eyes always lit up like he'd made a wonderful discovery. Jerusha only heard long-familiar words that held little meaning.

Shortly after noon, the back door shuddered under strangely familiar blows. When she opened the door, Corporal Sutherland entered with a grin. "The Rev awake yet?"

She couldn't help smiling in reply. "Since seven o'clock, though he did sleep in a bit."

"Told you I'd take care of him." He removed his boots and stepped into the sitting room.

"Howdy, Preach! Thought your woodpile looked a little scrawny and figured I might be able to help."

"Much obliged. My sister's been rather hard on the supply with this laundry business of hers."

Jerusha was unprepared for the look of admiration on the soldier's face. "You do laundry as a business?"

She nodded.

"That's hard work! Who do you work for?"

"Mrs. Barry's boardinghouse. Any more than that and I don't think I'd have fingers left." She tried to laugh, wondering irrelevantly what her mother's hands looked like.

"Where do you dry all this stuff?"

As if to emphasize her point, she reached for her parka and winter boots.

"Outside. It freeze-dries."

"I thought your hands looked rather rough and sore the other night. No wonder, with hanging wet laundry in this cold."

"I've become used to it." She didn't mean to sound rude, but his concern made her uneasy. She hoisted the basket of wet blankets onto her hip, grabbed her bucket of clothespins, and hurried out the door. Just because she'd found tolerance for the job didn't mean she liked it. Before she'd finished hanging the blankets, she heard the rhythmic ring of the axe achieved only by an expert. Was there anything this man couldn't do well?

He chopped wood all afternoon, coming in periodically to warm up. David continued studying and reading portions of Scripture aloud, only getting up to make another pot of coffee for the corporal's next visit inside. Jerusha had just emptied the last tubful of wash water when he asked, "Mind if I invite Keith for supper?"

"I was only planning to have leftover stew and biscuits."

"Sounds great to me, but if you're bothered, I won't ask."

She could tell he really wanted the soldier to stay. "If you don't mind things being a little late, I could even throw together a dried apple cobbler."

"Thanks, Rushi." He looked straight at her with his special big-brother grin, the smile that said he knew her well and accepted her completely, the look that always made her wonder what he'd think if he knew how she really felt.

Settling dusk forced Corporal Sutherland to quit at the chopping block. He looked quickly at Jerusha before accepting David's invitation. "You've been pretty busy today. Sure you want to feed another hungry man?"

His consideration drew another smile from her. "Of course. David needs the company."

The two chatted nonstop while she made biscuits. She heard David telling how he'd heard about Dawson Creek and decided to come. Over supper, he asked their guest how he'd arrived.

"Though I feel war is the greatest insult possible to human life, I knew I either had to join the army voluntarily or get drafted."

David reached for another biscuit. "Why not register as a conscientious objector?"

"It didn't seem like the direction I was supposed to take. I'd received a bit of emergency medical training and checked into becoming part of the medical personnel. Next thing I knew, we were setting up camp here in Dawson Creek."

"Where did you grow up?" David's question echoed Jerusha's thoughts.

"On a farm in the northern part of the state of Colorado. The country's a lot like this area."

"Can't be as beautiful."

"You bet it is."

Both men spoke with conviction, and Jerusha wondered briefly if they'd lost their minds. She hadn't seen a single attractive aspect about this sprawling, half-built town, and goodness knew, she'd tried.

David had another question. "What are the people like there?"

"If you can believe it, a lot like people here, though more easily excited. I've found Canadians take a comparatively relaxed approach toward life. But in general, they're the same types, hardy farmers, dedicated to families, good neighbors, polite, not much tolerance for rowdy behavior."

"I know what you mean. I think Dawson Creek's still reeling from the arrival of the American hordes." David's grin took any sting out of his words.

"And I know as well as anyone what some of my countrymen can be like when they get a bit too much to drink."

"Anyone figure out yet what caused Sunday night's explosion?"

Corporal Sutherland studied his bowl for a few moments. "The army's not saying. The rumors I've heard indicate either someone was smoking too close to the hayloft at the livery stable or perhaps sabotage behind the area where Oman-Smith Company and Miller Construction had stored a bunch of dynamite that was supposed to be shipped out Monday. The livery went up in smoke before anyone realized what had happened, and by then it was too late to save the dynamite. Next thing we knew, BOOM!"

"Quite a few guys killed, I heard."

"That's even more hush-hush than the cause. Army's saying five civilians, but I don't see how that can be true. There were just too many people hurt. There had to have been at least a dozen right in the building trying to stop the fire, not to mention the crew chain-handling the dynamite away from the storage area. I don't see how any of them could have made it when it blew. Of course, I'm not saying that as an army man."

"Just the stories we heard at prayer meeting the other night make you realize how close this whole town came to going up in bits. Do you have any idea how this is affecting army-civilian relations?" Typically, David appeared most concerned about keeping the peace.

"I guess town officials asked the army to set up martial law Sunday night, and the army's offered to bring in town planners to assist with reconstruction." A chuckle quivered in the corporal's voice.

Jerusha couldn't restrain an incredulous, "Town planners? Whatever on earth for?"

"It's not such a bad idea," David soothed. "I've heard the downtown block is pretty messed up, so what better time to rebuild it so it looks attractive, not to mention scientific in its organization."

She snickered. "It will take more than a couple of planners to bring scientific order to this place. I've never seen so much stuff piled on every square inch of unused ground—lumber, pipe, mechanical supplies, ammunition, not to mention jeeps, trucks, and tents."

Both men roared with laughter at her derision. "You'll have to excuse my sister," David gasped around his guffaws. "She's used to Winnipeg's well-ordered streets."

The corporal managed to bring his mirth under control. "I know the feeling, Miss Porter. Some days I feel like I'm just groping around in a vast outdoor warehouse, myself. But maybe this will make you feel better. The army has also decided to give Dawson Creek a new water and sewer system."

"You mean running water and drains that don't back up?" Jerusha thought of the unused pipe intended to carry wastewater out of their house.

"Those in the know say the hordes that have moved to Dawson Creek or been stationed here have put such a load on the town's existing system as to make it unusable. Part of the army's compensation for Sunday night will be running water and working drains." He grinned at her expression.

"I'll believe it when I see it."

The conversation carried on while Jerusha cleared the table. The men set up a chess game in the sitting room, and she brought their dessert to them there. They discussed various people they knew who'd been directly affected by the fire or the explosion. Their caring for this town and the people in and around it sounded almost like a foreign language.

David invited Corporal Sutherland to stay for a devotional time, as well. They discussed several Scripture passages as though they'd made new discoveries that would make daily life more delightful. Jerusha listened half-heartedly, wishing she could share their enthusiasm. After a brief time of prayer, the corporal stood.

"This has been a most enjoyable evening, Reverend and Miss Porter. But I promised someone I'd help take good care of you, Rev, so I'm leaving before I keep you up too late." He grinned and David grimaced. He bundled into his coat and boots, then departed, leaving behind the same silence Jerusha had noticed Sunday night.

Chapter 6

David finally disappeared into the bedroom for a nap on Monday afternoon just when Jerusha had begun to think he'd be up all day. He'd been on the go all day yesterday, preaching both in the morning and the afternoon, as well as visiting with the steady stream of guests who passed through their sitting room on Sundays. Jerusha had hoped he would need a nap today so she could slip out to deliver the clean laundry and pick up the next bag of soiled linen. David would object strongly if he knew, but she felt she had no choice. There was no way he could do the job for her.

She paused beside the bench outside Patterson's Men's Wear. Half a dozen blocks didn't seem that far until one had to lug an unwieldy bag the distance. She looked around at charred buildings and heaps of rubble. Others' reports hadn't been able to accurately convey the devastation. What she remembered of the area a week ago seemed civilized compared to the present destruction. It took a few moments to catch her breath, and she reached for the bundle again.

"Well, if it isn't the Reverend Porter's sister. And how is our minister feeling these days?"

Of all the people she could have met on this excursion, why did it have to be Sylvia Irvine, daughter of Dawson Creek's most prominent banker? Jerusha tried not to envy the young woman's woolen wrap trimmed in fur, her fashionable matching bonnet, or the mink muff expensively encasing her hands. "My brother's doing very well, thank you. He should be back on his feet in a couple of weeks."

"That must be a relief for you. I know I'd be just mortified having to carry laundry through town. I mean, it's bad enough if people guess what you're doing. But to be obliged to confirm their gossip! I guess spinsters learn to endure all kinds of disagreeable experiences." She tittered shrilly.

Jerusha ignored the inner voice that verified Sylvia's comments and squelched the urge to slap her. "I imagine we've all had to do disagreeable things since last Sunday."

A spark of anger replaced condescension in the young woman's blue-eyed gaze, but her voice remained silky. "That must have been just terrible for you, your brother being hurt like that and then having our beautiful little church invaded by American soldiers. However did you endure it?" Her expression implied only a woman of inferior sensibilities could have refrained from hysterics.

Jerusha mentally reached for her friendliest smile. "It's amazing what one can do when people need help."

Sylvia glanced over Jerusha's shoulder, her expression barely betraying surprise. She tittered again, this time nodding regally. "I look forward to seeing you and your dear brother this Sunday."

Jerusha reached for the laundry bag, only to feel it slip from her grasp. She whirled to face Corporal Sutherland. "It's you! I wondered what frightened her away."

"Frighten? No." He solemnly shook his head, his lips pressed into a thin line, though his eyes looked friendly enough. "She'd just been so busy taunting you she didn't realize I was standing behind you the whole time."

She felt ready to sink through the boardwalk or hide in the nearest snowbank. Sylvia's attitude had been humiliating enough without this man being a witness. "May I have my bag, please?"

"No." This time his lips smiled, too. "I agree with Miss Irvine that you shouldn't be carrying this, but only because it's far too heavy. I think your willingness to work hard right along with your brother is admirable. I can guess where you're going. Have you heard Dawson Creek's downtown is going to be built with brick and stucco buildings?"

"Won't they look kind of out of place with the buildings we still have?" The trivial talk restored Jerusha's sense of balance, though she wondered why she felt so comfortable visiting with him.

"I think the present buildings are either going to be replaced or get new false fronts." He glanced around them. "Isn't winter a gorgeous time of year? The way it snows around here reminds me so much of home. But I do miss being on the farm and looking out over fields covered in soft, undisturbed white. Towns and army camps make winter look dingy and depressing."

Dingy and depressing. Those were just the words Jerusha would have chosen to describe winter, at least in Dawson Creek. In Winnipeg—she stopped herself. She simply had to quit comparing the two places.

The corporal interrupted her mental treadmill. "Have you ever been cross-country skiing, Miss Porter?"

"The only winter sport I've tried is skating. The skating parties back home used to be the big youth social events of the winter."

"I've heard there are some wonderful trails around here where it would be easy to learn to ski. How do you think David would feel about a youth ski trip?"

She had the uncomfortable feeling David would think it a terrific idea. Why she didn't agree, she couldn't say. She only wished heartily this man wouldn't be so. . .she searched for the right word. . .so *interested* in them. "I'm not sure what David would think, since neither of us have skis."

"That could be rectified easily enough." He grinned at her as though he realized her objections had nothing to do with equipment.

With relief she saw the boardinghouse across the street. "Thanks for helping me with this bag. I'm sure David will thank you, too."

"Is there another bag to be picked up?"

She'd been wondering how she would get the bag of soiled linen home, since crumpled sheets filled a bigger bag than folded ones. Though she wanted strongly to cut this encounter short, she knew she couldn't carry the laundry alone. "Yes."

"May I help?"

The twinkle in his gray eyes made her feel like he wanted her to try to refuse. She lifted her chin a notch. "I'd be obliged, Corporal."

"My friends call me Keith," he growled, then kept up a steady flow of conversation until they reached the parsonage. Though his words and tone stayed light and cheerful, Jerusha felt there was more to this man than she could see, something that both attracted her and made her feel uneasy.

David had awakened and sat waiting in the sitting room when she returned. She'd barely opened the door when his don't-interrupt-me tone greeted her. "Jerusha, I know where you've been and you knew I wouldn't approve. We don't need both of us injured. Besides, downtown can be a rough place for a woman alone these days, especially with all the army personnel hanging around. You know I'm not all strung out on appearances, but sometimes a little discretion is advisable."

Corporal Sutherland had touched her shoulder briefly as soon as the tirade began. His wink silenced her defense. He remained out of sight until David's words ran out. A long pause ensued until David asked, less sure of himself, "Jerusha?"

The corporal stepped through the doorway between the porch and sitting room. "She's been with me, Rev."

If Jerusha had been an artist, she would have immediately reached for pencil and paper to capture David's expression. Frustration, relief, and embarrassment vied for dominance until humor won out. "Well, I guess that serves me right for getting so uptight. I shouldn't have jumped to conclusions."

"Oh, you weren't entirely wrong," the corporal assured him with a reproving glance at Jerusha. "I just managed to interrupt her stubbornness before it got her in trouble."

"How far did she get?"

Being discussed like a small child only added to Jerusha's discomfort with her rescuer and her lingering humiliation at Sylvia's hands. "I made it just fine to Patterson's. While I appreciate the corporal's assistance, I don't see I had any other choice. I've been hearing ever since I came about how people on the frontier do what they have to do. Well, I did it. If it upsets you so much, you can ship me home where I belong." To her further mortification, a sob escaped on the last word, and she fled to her room without thinking. The sound of the door slamming behind her brought small relief. She lay face down on the bed, feeling her tears wet the pillow. Though she felt embarrassed by her emotionalism, somehow weeping brought release. Her pride wanted her to get up and face the men immediately as though nothing were wrong, but profound weariness kept her in place.

Eventually, a quiet tap on her door roused her. When she didn't reply, she heard crutches thump near her bed and felt David sit beside her. His hand gently massaged the back of her neck. "I'm sorry, Rushi. I overreacted. Keith told me about Sylvia Irvine. I wish I could have spared you that. I know Dawson Creek is nothing like what you're used to, and I'm sorry I haven't told you more often how much I appreciate your being here with me. I know it's not easy, but you handle it well. I love you, Sis. I wish I could help you accept yourself just as you are. You don't have to live up to anything or be anything other than yourself."

His quiet murmuring managed to reach the always painful place inside her that had become so inflamed since the explosion. She felt unworthy of his words, yet they were a healing balm she couldn't refuse. She turned to look at him with a watery smile. "Thanks."

He extended a paper-wrapped package to her. "Keith asked me to give this to you."

Puzzlement wrinkled her forehead. Why would he be leaving a gift for her?

"Go ahead and open it. I'm sure it's not dynamite."

She sat up and cautiously pulled the paper away. Two bright yellow pieces of fruit lay within the folds. "Lemons?"

"Yeah. He said if you use a thin slice to smear the juice on your hands after laundry, it will help keep your skin from getting so dry and sore."

She wanted to take offense at the corporal's notice of her most embarrassing feature, but something whispered that he hadn't meant to offend. In fact, it appeared he might even care about her as a person, not just as David's sister. "Lemon juice seems like a strange skin tonic."

"Maybe next time he stops by, he'll tell you why it works."

"Maybe so." She stared at the fruit, not sure what to do with the feeling of being the object of concern.

"Rushi?" David's quiet tone made her look into his face. "I think Keith Sutherland wants to be your friend as well as mine. Will you please let him do so, for my sake?"

She didn't feel comfortable with the suggestion. "Why for your sake?"

"Because I'd like you to have someone you can trust besides me."

"You're not planning to hurt yourself again, are you?" Only with her brother did she feel comfortable enough to tease.

Though his eyes twinkled, his face remained serious. "I'd just feel more comfortable knowing there was someone else you could turn to if you needed help."

She thought she understood what had prompted his request. "I'm sorry I worried you this afternoon."

He smiled. "I shouldn't have let myself get so upset, just like I'm not going to let you evade the question. You'll let him be your friend, Rushi?"

Though she couldn't bring herself to look directly at him, she nodded. How else could she respond to his uncharacteristic plea?

Chapter 7

The following Saturday, Jerusha found herself among a group of excited young adults in horse-drawn wagons headed for some snow-covered fields beyond the town. David had eagerly endorsed the corporal's idea of a skiing excursion, and word had spread quickly. Some of the young adults from the church had invited friends, and several of the single men from Mrs. Barry's boardinghouse joined the party. Corporal Sutherland was accompanied by a dozen soldiers. Sylvia Irvine quickly made conquests of at least half of the young men. Jerusha planned to spend the afternoon sitting by the campfire with David.

The wagons turned down a rough road between some low-growing trees. Before Sylvia had a chance to complain, they creaked to a stop. In an unbelievably short amount of time, the young men had a bonfire crackling and several makeshift benches set up around it. Jerusha watched her companions quickly strap on their skis and slide away. Corporal Sutherland made sure David had a place to elevate his leg and plenty of blankets. Jerusha turned to find Maisie, but she'd already been whisked away by an eager soldier.

"Ready for your first skiing lesson, Miss Porter?" the corporal teased.

"I told you I have no skis." She tried to smile away the harshness of her words.

"Never underestimate an American soldier." He grinned and slapped a pair of skis onto the snow in front of her. "I even found a pair of ski boots that I think might be your size."

Jerusha only gaped at him, not believing the circumstances that had put her in this embarrassing position.

"Don't wait around on my account, Rushi," David offered from nearby. "Once you get the hang of it, you'll have a great time."

She glared at her brother, who only smiled back encouragingly. His wink reminded her of their conversation concerning this unsettling man.

"Boots off." The corporal's voice discouraged argument.

Reluctantly, Jerusha unlaced her boots, suddenly grateful David had bullied her into wearing a pair of his pants, ridiculous though she felt. She'd insisted a pastor's sister had no business wearing men's clothes, and he'd insisted no sensible human being would venture out for an afternoon in the snow with only a long woollen skirt for warmth. No sooner had she removed one boot than the corporal replaced it with a ski boot. Before she had time to protest further, he'd slipped skis under her feet and snapped them into place.

"Let's go." He grasped both her gloved hands to pull her to a standing position. The skis started to slip out from under her, but he firmly held her upright. "Don't tense up. Just stand for a couple of minutes and you'll get used to the feeling. Keep your knees loose."

Jerusha had no idea what he meant, but found she had no time to contemplate it. She wanted to dispose of his arms around her as quickly as possible. That meant learning to stand on these slippery boards. It turned out to be only a little more difficult than standing on ice skates.

He released her long enough to hand her a set of poles, then reached for his own. "Don't try to fight the way the skis slide. Try to move with it. Like this." He skied a little ways from her, then back. "You'll balance best if you move your right arm with your left foot and vice versa. Sounds weird, but you'll get the rhythm."

Gradually, they worked their way toward the trees and away from the fire. Jerusha could hear laughter from the crowd ahead and wondered what they thought of her alone with the corporal. As her concentration wavered, so did her coordination. The skis started to slide faster than she could keep up.

"Whoa, there." The corporal quickly steadied her so she could pull her feet back under her control. "Shouldn't try to worry and ski at the same time," he advised with a grin. "Skiing was meant for relaxation."

"Then why don't you go relax?"

If he wondered at her sharp tone, his face didn't show it. He only grinned again. "Because this is more fun."

She laughed sarcastically. "You can't be serious. Why would you want to spend the afternoon teaching me to ski?"

He looked at her intently for a moment, then replied quietly, "Because I'd like to get to know you."

Jerusha didn't know how to answer. *If he does, he'll wish he hadn't.* Yet, she'd promised David. Her companion didn't try any more conversation until they had rounded a group of trees and were working their way back toward the campfire. She let her gaze drift toward Sylvia, who'd removed her skis and now hovered around David, rearranging his blankets.

"You agreed with what she said to you on Monday, didn't you?" He asked the question gently, omitting any hint of criticism.

Jerusha's gaze snapped to his face, where compassion hovered in his eyes. "How did you know?"

"I didn't. I just guessed. But I'd like to know why you left Winnipeg."

"David was called here to pastor the church."

"Were you called, too?"

"Of course. I'm his sister." Her tone sharpened at the gentle probing near her most painful emotions.

His forehead wrinkled momentarily, then he continued skiing slowly enough that she could keep up. "Any family back home?"

"Just Uncle Cam and Aunt Vivienne. She's frightened David's going to get married and I'll be stranded out here." She chuckled, relieved he'd moved his inquiries to safer ground.

"She's a worrier?"

"Not really, but propriety is very important to her."

"What were your pastor and his wife like?"

She pondered for a moment. "Well-educated, also concerned about appearances, refined, almost aristocratic. I admire them both."

"I can tell." He smiled encouragingly. "What did he teach about God?"

"I can't remember him ever talking much about God, except at revival time. Most of his sermons were about maintaining Christian testimony or how wonderful the Bible characters were. God always seemed kind of remote." She almost gasped at her statement, hardly believing that she, a minister's offspring, had dared say such a thing. "I didn't mean—"

He smiled again, this time reassuringly. "I think I know what you meant. Don't worry, I don't think anyone else heard you." He winked. "Just between us, what do you think of God?"

Jerusha felt alarm prickle all over her. "What do you mean?"

"Some people see God as a benevolent grandfather type, always wanting to make us feel good. Others view Him as a dictator, waiting to strike us down if we do something wrong. To my way of thinking, He's a loving Father, Who carefully manages the details of my life so as to bring me the most joy."

Jerusha felt almost dizzy. The God he described bore no resemblance to the One she tried so hard to serve. Was this man crazy or incredibly wise? He was watching her expectantly, waiting for her reply. "I don't. . .uh, I mean. . ."

"Hot chocolate's on!" Maisie's call from the bonfire interrupted the conversation.

"Let's go get it before they drink it all." The corporal seemed not to notice she hadn't answered his question.

Jerusha's fear of falling hampered her impulse to hurry. She never should have allowed this conversation to take place. She should have been where Maisie stood now, handing out steaming cups, making sure everyone was comfortable, keeping an eye on David. As soon as the corporal showed her how to release her boots from the skis, she hurried to her friend's side. "What can I do to help?"

Maisie smiled brightly. "Absolutely nothing. This is your afternoon to relax and enjoy yourself."

Jerusha smiled weakly, wishing she hadn't let herself be pushed into this. Maybe she should have just stayed home. Fortunately there was an empty place on the bench beside David.

"What's skiing like, Sis?"

The corporal's questions had completely distracted her, but she couldn't tell David that. "It's not skating, but it'll do."

He hugged her shoulders. "I hope you're having a good time."

A shrill titter warned of Sylvia's approach. "How nice to see you out here with us, Miss Porter! You've been working so hard lately, I haven't been able to visit with you nearly as often as I'd like." She giggled and fluttered around in front of David.

Jerusha looked at David appealingly, but his expression indicated he noticed nothing amiss. He actually smiled at Sylvia. "How are you enjoying skiing, Miss Irvine?"

"I've never been as robust as your sister, so I find too much exercise quite fatiguing. However, the company is extremely pleasant. You must be bored to tears here all by yourself."

Jerusha looked around for Maisie, needing desperately to get away from Sylvia. The girl's affected manners aroused both Jerusha's envy and disgust. The veiled insults pushed her perilously close to tears. Maisie still stood by the bonfire, surrounded by laughing people, refilling cups. Jerusha looked around the group of young people wondering why she felt so uncomfortable while everyone else was obviously having fun. A pair of gray eyes on the other side of the bonfire stopped her gaze. A bold wink preceded a smile, then the corporal stood and walked toward her.

"How about another lesson? I promise I won't ask any questions this time."

If she didn't know better, Jerusha would have thought he knew how she felt and was trying to cheer her up. She pushed the tempting thought away, accepting his offer as simple courtesy. "Thank you, Corporal."

Rather than releasing her hand when she stood, he tucked it into the crook of his elbow. She tried to pull away, but he held on firmly. "I'm not letting you go until you promise to call me Keith, as do the rest of my friends. Only army folk call me Corporal, and I've never liked the sound of Mr. Sutherland." His eyes twinkled down at her.

"I can't do that!"

"Why not?" He appeared to enjoy her discomfort.

"It's not proper. Now please let me go."

"Life's not nearly so formal out here. No one will even notice, I'm sure."

She couldn't tell whether he meant his holding her hand or the form of address he'd requested. Either way, her answer remained applicable. "It's inappropriately familiar."

He released her hand when they reached the bench where he'd left their skis and poles. "If I thought you were truly as offended as you sound, I'd apologize. Instead, I'm going to propose a contest. If I get my skis on and am standing first, you call me Keith. If you win, you may call me anything you like."

His ridiculous proposal startled her into laughter, something she hadn't felt like doing in months. The challenge in his eyes made her banish thoughts of propriety. But she wouldn't win if she didn't take control of the situation quickly. "It's a deal. Go!" She gave the command and reached for her skis at the same time. The right boot didn't want to fit easily into the binding, but she jammed it in place. She grabbed her poles, but found the other ends of them trapped in the snow by a large boot.

The corporal sat watching her, his shoulders vibrating with silent laughter. "I didn't think you had it in you."

Jerusha couldn't stop the grin that pulled at her lips. His enjoyment was too infectious. "You haven't even started."

His grin faded. "I didn't think you'd take me so seriously. Besides, I want you to consider me your friend because that's what you want, not because I've insisted."

"Thank you, Corporal." She hated to see the disappointment in his eyes. But she didn't feel ready to consider him a friend, despite her promise to her brother. He'd already come too close to perceiving the person she still tried to hide from herself.

She expected him to ski away and join the others. Instead, he put his skis on and slowly led to the area where she'd been practicing earlier. For the rest of the afternoon, he stayed close to her, though not close enough to make her uncomfortable. When it came time to return to town, he was on hand to help her into the wagon. She couldn't be positive, but it seemed he made sure she and David were the last two in their wagon group to be dropped off.

"Hope you didn't get too chilled today, Rev," he said as he stopped the horses beside the parsonage.

"Not a chance." David's voice held a gentle smile. "I was well taken care of."

Jerusha immediately pictured Sylvia hovering, rearranging blankets, making small talk. David couldn't possibly think her pleasant company!

"I enjoyed the day, too, thanks to your sister," Corporal Sutherland commented. "She's getting quite handy on those skis."

"I could never beat her on skates, so it doesn't surprise me." David laughed, leaning on the corporal until Jerusha handed him his crutches. "Would you like to come in for a snack?"

The corporal looked at Jerusha for a moment before replying. "Thanks for the offer, but I have a couple of things I need to take care of back at camp."

David nodded and clumped into the house. Jerusha didn't follow him immediately, though she couldn't have explained why. She looked uncertainly at Corporal Sutherland.

His gaze met hers. "How are the hands?"

"They stung pretty badly the first couple of times I tried it, but the juice seems to be helping." She felt glad her gloves covered the subject of discussion.

"I figured it might hurt to start with, since your hands got so cracked. It's actually the soap residue left on your hands that dries them so badly. The lemon juice cuts through the soap. They should be healed up in no time."

She didn't feel in a hurry to end the conversation, despite the cold. "Where did you find lemons in this town?"

"Never underestimate the army." He grinned briefly. "I really did enjoy spending time with you today."

"I had fun, too."

His eyebrows twitched with amusement. "You don't get as much fun as I think you need. I'd like to fix that if I may."

"Building a church takes a lot of work." She smiled to show she didn't mean to be ungracious.

"But God's the One who invented laughter." He studied her silently again. "I'll be back, and in the meantime, I'll be praying you meet His love."

He jumped up into the wagon and guided the horses down the street. She watched his departure, feeling again the prickly alarm from his questioning, accompanied by a strange sense of anticipation.

Chapter 8

David's leg mended quickly. A little over a month after the explosion, he walked with only a slight limp. The town recovered more slowly. Most storefronts had been restored, though the livery barn remained a burned-out pile of rubble. The army's official word still held the casualty count at only eight soldiers and no civilians, but rumors placed the total anywhere between two dozen and two hundred soldiers and civilians. The army's reluctance to discuss the matter increased Dawson Creek residents' continuing distrust.

"It's just not right," eighteen-year-old Greg McEvan declared one evening when a number of young people gathered at the parsonage for an informal social. His red hair lay in disarray from his vigorous head shaking, and his gray eyes flashed with indignation. "If the army hadn't been here, the explosion never would have happened in the first place."

"I heard it happened because of a fire in the livery barn. That could have happened regardless," David suggested quietly.

"But the explosion caused the damage, and it happened only because the army insisted on storing the dynamite here in town instead of at Mile Eight where they're supposed to."

Maisie refilled Greg's coffee cup. "Mr. Skillings at the telegraph office said the drivers needed a special permit to haul it out of town and had to wait overnight."

"Like I say, those Americans have to make everything so complicated. What's wrong with taking the stuff straight to Mile Eight?"

"There's nothing we can do about it now, son," Mrs. Barry soothed. She had accompanied Maisie as she often did and was welcomed by the young people like a beloved grandmother. She turned to Jerusha. "This cake is delicious! How do you find time for baking with all the laundry we've had to send you? I've worried about working you too hard."

Jerusha wondered briefly why she found Mrs. Barry's questions unoffensive and Sylvia's painful. "I appreciate the business, and with David back on his feet, we're managing."

Dr. and Mrs. Pierce had also stopped by for a quick visit. Dr. Pierce cleared his throat. "I wish for both of your sakes we could afford to pay our pastor a full salary. It would be nice if you didn't have to 'manage,' as you put it, Miss Porter."

She couldn't ignore the genuine affection on their faces. It seemed incomprehensible that these people should actually love her. Ministers' families traditionally received respect, but love? "I've noticed everyone out here works hard. I don't think the minister's sister should be an exception." She tried to smile graciously while she carried away empty plates and cups. All of life since the explosion seemed designed to make her uncomfortable, unsure of herself and her role. As if the conversation had taken place earlier in the day, she unwillingly recalled Corporal Sutherland's words during the skiing party. "I see God as a loving Father, controlling the details of my life to bring the most joy to me." She bid the Pierces good-bye, expressing hopes they would stop again soon, served more tea and coffee, and started dishes, all the while embroiled in her own thoughts. *Joy.* Not a dominant element in her life, she realized. But then love wasn't a concept she readily associated with God, either. Duty, responsibility, sacrifice, good works, proper behavior—those were the qualities found in good Christians. She could almost picture God with a checklist, evaluating her and finding her lacking.

Maybe that explained why Corporal Sutherland hadn't been around since the skiing party. She'd tried not to notice his absence from church, as well as from their sitting room. Had he evaluated her and also found her wanting? She recalled her reluctance to answer his question about God. What did she think about God, anyway, and why did wondering make her so uncomfortable?

"May I help with the dishes?" Maisie's voice startled her.

"Only if you want to." Jerusha studied her friend's face. "I can handle it if you'd rather visit."

"Of course I'd like to help you. How about if I wash? Then you can put things away in their proper places instead of hunting for them until next week."

Jerusha couldn't think of any light conversation. Maisie didn't seem to mind the silence, though she looked quizzically at Jerusha from time to time. Before she realized what she was doing, Jerusha spoke her thoughts. "Maisie, what do you think of God?"

Maisie looked momentarily startled, then her face softened and a smile lit her eyes from deep inside. "I'd say He's my Friend. Sometimes He's like a loving Father to me, but mostly a Friend who knows me better than I know myself. Why do you ask?"

Jerusha didn't know how to explain herself. What would Maisie think if she knew her doubts? "I don't know. People out here seem to think of Him differently than the people back ho—in Winnipeg." She hoped Maisie hadn't noticed her slip.

"Can you give me details?" Maisie looked genuinely interested. Though Jerusha examined her face closely for condemnation, she found nothing but friendly concern.

"Like the day you and Sheila helped me clean up after the explosion. You prayed for her baby, and it seemed like you really believed God cared. Sheila said that day she didn't think she would have survived what's happened to her if it hadn't been for God. Back home, no one talks much about Him. Prayers are for church. I've never heard anyone pray before about personal things. After the explosion, people talked like God really did protect them."

"You don't think He did?" Again, Maisie's face held no criticism.

Jerusha looked straight into her eyes. "This may be shocking, but I don't know. My mother told me about Jesus dying on the cross when I was little. I remember asking Him to be part of my life at that time, and for a while, I felt like I knew Him. But my awareness of Him faded with childhood. Now, He just seems distant and hard to please."

"Have you talked to your brother about it?"

Jerusha studied the dishtowel in her hands. "No. What kind of a minister's sister am I if I don't even know who God is?"

"An honest one. I don't know nearly as much about the Bible as the reverend, but I don't think God minds if we ask questions. I know my dad never got upset with me for asking questions, and I'm sure God has more patience than my dad." Maisie dried her hands and wrapped her arms around Jerusha. "Whatever the case, Jerusha, I only think of you as my friend. You could tell me you didn't believe in God at all and I'd still love you."

Tears filled Jerusha's eyes. She awkwardly returned Maisie's hug, wondering what to do with the strange emotions she felt. Did Maisie really mean what she'd said? Though the sentimental moment passed, and they joined Mrs. Barry and David for a game of dominoes, Jerusha's mind continued to contemplate possibilities.

After losing the third game, David stretched and yawned. "I'm not sure I can handle getting beaten again. You ladies play a tough game."

Mrs. Barry smiled at Jerusha. "We really should be going. We have a long day tomorrow, since Saturday's our cleaning day. Thanks for a lovely evening."

David reached for his Bible. "Would you stay long enough to join us in evening devotions?"

Mrs. Barry nodded. "We'd be honored."

David raised his voice to talk above the noise of the dozen or so young adults still visiting and playing checkers. "Mrs. Barry needs to leave soon, but I've asked her to stay for our devotional." He handed his Bible to her. "I'd like to hear you read my favorite passage, if you would, Mrs. Barry. Romans chapter five, verses one through eleven." The room quieted almost instantly as people found places to sit and turned to face David.

Jerusha had often heard a strange love in David's voice when he read Scripture. Tonight, she heard the same affectionate anticipation in Mrs. Barry's reading. Then the words themselves captured her attention. " 'But God commendeth His love toward us. . . ,' " Mrs. Barry read on, but the phrase replayed itself in Jerusha's mind. Though it had been years since Scripture reading had meant anything more than religious words, tonight the single sentence felt like a refreshing drink to her thirsty soul. She waited impatiently for David to finish praying and for the guests to leave so she could ask David about her discovery.

Well over an hour later, he closed the door behind the last group. "What is it, Rushi? Your eyes have lit up like candles."

She laughed self-consciously. "I heard something tonight, and it sounds almost too good to be true." Suddenly she felt tongue-tied. How could she explain her thoughts to her minister brother? "I've been wondering about God." She waited for his shocked exclamation.

"Have you reached any conclusion?" He lowered himself onto the bench, his gaze remaining lovingly on her face.

She had to ask a question of her own before she could answer his. "Aren't you ashamed of me for even wondering?"

His face softened with a gentle smile. "No. Actually, I've been praying you would start asking questions."

"Why?"

He patted the seat beside him. "Come sit and I'll try to tell you."

"Do you want coffee or more cake?"

"Not now, Rushi." He patted the seat again. "I just want you to relax with me for awhile." When she seated herself, he put his arm around her shoulders and leaned against the wall. "It started a long time ago, soon after you became a teenager. I've watched your gentle love for Jesus be replaced by a compulsion to live up to what you think you should be, what you think our mother is."

She gasped at his accuracy, never having faced her own feelings so bluntly. "What's wrong with wanting to be like Mom? Aunt Vivienne has told us often what a wonderful woman she is."

"But you've forgotten Mom is human. I remember how much she loves God, but also how much she loves life. I remember her laughing with us kids, helping us play jokes on Dad. She isn't perfect, Rushi. I also have memories of her getting flaming mad at Dad, impatient with people in the church who didn't share her enthusiasm for missions. Then time would calm her down, she'd ask forgiveness of people she'd spoken unkindly to, and she'd spend time talking the matter over with God and accepting His forgiveness. Somewhere you've been handed the idea you have to be something Mom never was, and in the process you've lost the awareness of God's love Mom tried so hard to teach us."

The Scripture passage played through her mind again while she considered her response. Part of her felt betrayed by his recollections while another part wanted to hear more of what he remembered. *"But God commendeth His love toward us. . ."* Could it really mean what it sounded like? She decided to be blunt. "That's what I've been wondering about. Corporal Sutherland said something while we were skiing about how he thinks of God as a loving Father. Maisie said she sees Him as her Friend. You obviously think of Him as a Friend, too. Somehow I just can't share your perspective."

"How do you see Him, Rushi?"

She thought for several minutes, still not sure she wanted to reveal exactly how unpastoral her thinking had become. But then again, what did she have to lose? He couldn't very well kick her out of the house. But would he still love her? "I don't know. I guess kind of like some sort of faraway person Who keeps track of how well I'm living up to what He expects."

"And what do you think He expects?" David's voice had lost none of its gentle affection.

"To be the right kind of pastor's sister and daughter. I guess like Mrs. Phillips. Always saying the right thing, always looking my best, never upset by anything, always eager to help the people in our church. . ." Her voice trailed off as she realized the enormity of her expectations.

"What about what Jesus said about the whole law being wrapped up in two commandments, to love God and to love our neighbor as ourselves?"

"I don't measure up there, either. Some days I don't even like the people around here, much less love them. And God seems too remote for me to love." She turned so she could see his reaction.

His gentle eyes met her gaze. "Have you thought about how much He loves you?"

"I've wondered how He can when I'm so far from the kind of person He wants me to be. But one of the verses Mrs. Barry read tonight said He loved us when we were sinners, or did I hear it wrong?"

A gleam of joy lit his eyes. "That's the point exactly, Rushi. His love for us has nothing to do with what we do or how we behave. He just loves us."

She shook her head, unable to reconcile David's words with her mental image of a Supreme Being with a checklist. "It sounds too good to be true."

"God solves that problem, too." David grinned. "According to Him, it doesn't matter what we believe or don't believe. He tells us how it is in Scripture, and that's the way it is. Most of our difficulties come from our efforts to reconcile our own ideas with what He says about Himself, rather than simply accepting—"

A loud pounding at the back door stopped him. He hurried to respond. "Lewis Murray! What can we—"

Mr. Murray's panic-stricken voice interrupted. "Hello, Reverend. I need your sister. My wife's in labor and she's calling for Miss Porter."

Overhearing the conversation, Jerusha gasped and ran for her coat. Concern for her friend thrust her questions out of her mind. Without a miracle, Sheila's baby would be born far too early to survive.

Chapter 9

Jerusha could think of nothing to say as Lewis threw her small overnight bag into the back of his old truck, then assisted her into the cab. What if Sheila lost her baby! The thirty-minute ride to the Murray farm seemed interminable.

The truck had barely stopped when both Lewis and Jerusha threw the doors open and ran for the small, two-story log farmhouse. Even from the porch she could hear Sheila's cries of pain.

"I left my boys with the neighbor." Lewis seemed to be trying to explain something. "They love her so much." He turned abruptly, striding off the porch into cold darkness.

Jerusha pushed the front door open, uncertain of where to find her friend. The next cry seemed to come from the back bedroom. She tiptoed to where Sheila lay in the middle of the big bed, which showed evidence of her intense thrashing. Tears ran from her closed eyes down her cheeks. Jerusha had never seen a birthing before. She felt as helpless to provide emotional support as medical assistance. Why had Sheila asked for her rather than Maisie? Another spasm gripped Sheila, and this time she screamed. Jerusha lost her uncertainty in desperation.

She smoothed the wet, tangled hair away from her friend's face, then reached for the young woman's hand. "I'm here, Sheila, just like you asked."

"Jerusha?" Sheila looked around the room.

"Right here. What can I do for you?"

"Make it stop." The tears poured down her face again. "I'm going to lose the baby, and he's never going to forgive me."

Jerusha didn't know where the words came from. She just started talking. "It's not your fault, Sheila. Sometimes babies just come too early. Lewis cares for you, and he still will after this is over."

"But I wanted to give him another son, and now I'm losing it." Hysteria edged her voice.

"Sheila, please calm down. For now, don't think about Lewis. Concentrate on keeping as relaxed as you can."

"But it hurts. And my baby's going to die!" Another spasm squelched her sobs. She grabbed Jerusha's hand so hard it hurt. Her back arched with pain, emphasizing her gently rounded abdomen. Another moan came through her clenched teeth.

"Can I help?" The ragged whisper came from the doorway where Lewis's white face looked as agonized as his wife's. Sheila heard the whisper and began sobbing again.

Jerusha had a feeling his presence would only make his wife worse. She gently steered Lewis away from the bedroom. "Have you called Dr. Pierce?"

"Yeah. He's at the Andersons'. Louise is having her baby. Ours wasn't supposed to come yet!" The normally quiet farmer slammed his fist onto the nearby kitchen table.

"Only God can stop a baby once it decides to come." Jerusha felt like an idiot, but what else could she say?

But the words seemed to calm the tall man. "I'd forgotten He cares, too." He leaned against the wall with his head bowed for a few moments. Then he looked Jerusha in the eyes. "Please tell me what to do."

She didn't know how to say it. "Sheila's pretty upset. Um. . . well, maybe if you didn't. . .I mean. . ."

He was already nodding. "I'll try to stay away from the room. Can I bring anything for you?"

His understanding overwhelmed her. For someone who didn't love his wife, this man showed an amazing amount of compassion. "I want to try wiping her face with a cool cloth. If we can get her more comfortable, she might relax."

"Jerusha!" The scream pulled Jerusha back to Sheila's side. Now the young mother was curled in a ball, hugging her knees. Jerusha rubbed her back until she relaxed. She seemed more comfortable on her side, so Jerusha positioned a pillow between her knees and another at her back. She felt a cloth pressed into her hand, but when she looked up, Lewis had already disappeared.

The night passed slowly. At times, the pain would disappear and Sheila would sleep. But just when Jerusha had begun to hope, Sheila would awake with a cry of agony. Jerusha tried to keep the bedclothes smoothed, Sheila's face cooled, and her hair pulled away from her face. It seemed to be all she could do. Lewis kept Jerusha supplied with fresh cloths and hot tea. Jerusha remembered the last time she had worked through the night: the night of the explosion when she'd helped Corporal Sutherland. He might know what to do here. But his absence of late made her reluctant to send for him. Dawn's gray light announced another day in progress and Sheila slept again.

Jerusha heard a curious clatter outside the room and tiptoed to investigate.

Lewis had set up a small table with two chairs. Steaming cups of coffee perched beside plates of scrambled eggs and perfectly browned toast. "Thought you might like to eat while she rests," he whispered.

Jerusha smiled her thanks, realizing how hungry she felt. She couldn't believe this man had cooked such a perfect-looking meal.

He seemed to read her thoughts. "I spent almost a year as mother and father both to my boys. I learned." A shadow passed over his face.

In her exhaustion, she spoke before she thought. "Do you still miss her so much?"

His eyes widened in surprise. "Who?"

"Your first wife."

He looked intently at Jerusha for several moments, then his expression softened. "Her death caused me grief, but I had to let go of her long ago. With two small boys and a farm, I had no choice. I actually got used to being alone before God sent me Sheila." His voice took on a note of wonder. "Maggie will always be a special memory, but Sheila's my heart now. I couldn't bear it if—" His voice broke. He strode abruptly out of the house.

Jerusha felt like a sharp blow had taken her breath away. She couldn't believe she had asked such a personal question, and the answer surprised her even more. She recalled the strange words she'd spoken in comfort the night before. "Lewis cares for you." She'd had no idea where they'd come from, but they were more true than she could have guessed. How could Sheila have missed it?

Moans from the bedroom indicated Sheila's agony had awakened her again. This time the pain didn't pause. Shortly after noon, her water broke, sweeping away any hope that the baby might be saved. Jerusha was still trying to change the sheets in between Sheila's spasms when the doctor arrived. When he saw Sheila, his exhaustion dropped like an unwanted blanket, replaced by tense concern.

Lewis appeared and Jerusha heard their whispered conversation outside the room. "I can't do anything for the little one."

"What about my wife?"

"She's had a good nurse, and we'll do what we can from here."

She had no time to relish the praise. Sheila's pain intensified. Jerusha's hands felt crushed from her squeezing. Then quiet moans replaced the screams. Her grip grew less strangling, and she merely moved her legs instead of thrashing across the bed. Jerusha looked at the doctor. Was this good or bad?

The doctor put his face close to Sheila's. "Don't give up, girl. We need your help to do this right. Push."

Was it an hour or minutes later when the tiny stillborn boy appeared? He fit easily in Dr. Pierce's hand. Without a word, Lewis carried his infant son's body from the room.

Jerusha breathed a sigh of relief that the struggle was over. At least for Sheila. Jerusha felt a wave of rising anger. She'd begun to believe God might actually care. *If He honestly loved Sheila, why had He broken her heart?* Maybe He didn't care as much about the details of life as people had led her to believe.

"Towels, quick!" The doctor's shout snapped Jerusha back to reality. A bright red stain spread rapidly under Sheila, who appeared to be sleeping peacefully. Not even knowing where to find towels, Jerusha ran from the room to search for anything that might work.

Lewis met her at the bottom of the stairs, his arms full of the precious linen. "Is she in trouble?"

Jerusha couldn't answer, but he must have seen the answer on her face. He followed her to his wife's side. "How bad is it, Doc?"

"If you've ever prayed, this is the time for it. But make some tea out of this while you're at it. Not too hot, so we can feed it to her." Without looking up, he reached into his bag and handed Lewis a small paper-wrapped package. Lewis ran from the room.

"Let's get her feet up." The doctor reached for pillows and wrapped them in a soiled sheet. Jerusha automatically lifted Sheila's legs.

Lewis returned with the tea. Brushing aside Jerusha's help, he tenderly lifted his wife's head with one hand and held the cup to her lips with the other. "Don't give up on me, love. I need you." He murmured desperately to her until the cup was emptied.

"Good. Be ready to do that again in five minutes. I need more sheets." The doctor fashioned another cushion and placed it under Sheila's hips. He looked at Jerusha. "Keep her warm. The way she's losing blood, she's going to get chilled. We don't need that, too."

The three worked together in a desperate rhythm, replacing linen, making tea, and keeping Sheila's body protected from chill. Jerusha wondered how much longer Sheila could stand the drain. Surely God wouldn't take Lewis's second wife, too.

"I think it's slowing," the doctor finally whispered. "Give her another cup of tea." He and Jerusha watched.

Lewis held another cupful to his wife's lips. "Just a bit, my girl. I'll pour some in, now swallow. Come on, swallow. Sheila, my heart, please swallow. You have to, if you're going to stay with me. Good girl. Now again. Come on, sweetheart, one more time." He set the empty cup on the floor and wrapped both arms around Sheila. "Don't leave me, girl. I need you too much. Our baby's gone. I won't let you go, too." His voice dropped to a broken whisper. "Can you hear me, Sheila? I love you. Please hang on, for my sake. Fight, my girl. Just fight a little bit, and I'll help you do the rest." He buried his face in her damp, tangled hair.

Jerusha had to leave the room. She couldn't remember ever seeing such naked emotion. Its intensity brought tears to her eyes. Could God's love be anything like it?

Chapter 10

With Lewis by her side, Sheila pulled through the night. For the next twenty-four hours, Jerusha and Dr. Pierce alternated their watch, while Lewis refused to move. By the third day after Jerusha had been summoned, the doctor declared their patient out of danger.

"But she still needs lots of rest. I'd like you to stay on here for a while, Miss Porter, that is if Lewis doesn't mind." The doctor looked from one to the other.

"I'd be grateful if you could." The farmer looked appealingly at Jerusha.

She thought of David and the piles of laundry. "I'd like to, but—"

The doctor cut her off. "Would you let me talk with the reverend about it? I know you have responsibilities in town, but I'd feel a lot better if there were another woman here to keep an eye on Mrs. Murray."

Jerusha nodded her consent. It felt strange, the intensity of her desire to stay. She hadn't even considered what the proper response might be. She simply wanted to do whatever she could to help this couple she suddenly cared about deeply.

"I'll be back this afternoon, then." The doctor lifted his hat to Jerusha, then turned to Lewis. "Your prescription for today is at least four hours' sleep. Anything you think needs doing can wait." A blast of cold air filled the room as he opened the door, and they heard his pickup rumble to life.

Lewis rubbed his puffy eyes. "I guess I'm under doctor's orders. You'll call if she wakes up?"

"I promise." She felt limp from tension and lack of sleep.

He shook his head wearily. "I don't know what I would have done if we'd lost her."

"But we didn't, Lewis. Just go sleep, please." She didn't realize until he started upstairs that she'd used his first name. It had just seemed right. In fact, formal address would have been insulting after what they'd experienced together.

Sheila still slept soundly. Jerusha pulled a chair from the kitchen into the bedroom. Maybe she could catch a light nap. Sitting up, she shouldn't sleep soundly enough to miss something if Sheila awoke.

Midafternoon dusk had already darkened the outdoors when Jerusha opened her eyes. It took her a few moments to recall why she'd fallen asleep here. Her shoulders and neck ached from the awkward position in which she'd slept. She looked over at the bed in time to see Sheila's eyes flutter open.

"Jerusha?" Her voice was a weak whisper.

"I'm glad you're awake." Jerusha couldn't tell how much of the past two days Sheila remembered or what she needed to hear.

Sheila stretched out a hand trembling from weakness. "I'm glad you're here. I feel so tired."

Jerusha tried to smile reassuringly. "You've had a difficult time."

"The baby?" Sheila's eyes filled.

Jerusha instinctively folded her into a hug. "You're going to be okay."

Sheila's sobs were little more than mild tremors, but Jerusha could feel her grief. Eventually, the young mother quieted enough to ask another question. "Lewis?"

"He's been worried sick about you." Jerusha pulled back to look into Sheila's eyes. "He went half crazy when we almost lost you."

"Was he in here with me?"

"Yes, from Saturday night until this morning."

"Did he hold me?"

Jerusha only nodded.

"I remember hearing him begging me not to leave him. I think he told me he loves me. Did he really?" Sheila's eyes lit with hope even though her voice had faded to the softest of whispers.

"Yes. He was really frightened for you." Tears filled Jerusha's eyes at the memory. "Don't try to talk anymore. Just rest. I'll bring you some soup."

Sheila seemed to slip back into sleep, a smile hovering around her pale lips. Jerusha opened a jar of canned chicken, then added some water to make a light broth for her friend's next meal. A creak on the stairs turned her attention from the stove. Lewis descended the stairs slowly, his hair and clothing still rumpled from sleep. He looked questioningly at her.

Jerusha didn't have to ask what he meant. "She woke up a few minutes ago, but I think she's sleeping again."

"Did she say anything?"

"She asked about the baby."

"You told her?"

"She guessed. She doesn't know it was a boy." Jerusha wondered how much to tell this bearded man who, just a week ago, had been little more than a stranger. "Lewis?"

He'd been headed toward Sheila's room, but he turned back.

"Maybe this isn't my place, but I think I need to tell you something."

He nodded understanding and pulled out a chair near the table.

Jerusha twisted a towel in her hands, afraid she was making a mistake, yet compelled to let him in on what she knew. "Remember when Sheila came to help me with laundry right after the explosion?"

He nodded again.

"She told Maisie and I then she really wanted this baby to be a boy." She paused, not knowing how to continue.

"Why?" Lewis's voice was a ragged whisper.

She studied the twisted towel. "She hoped it would make you love her." Once the words were out, she could look at his eyes.

He moved his mouth, but made no sound. Tears ran down into his beard. Finally he croaked, "Do you know why?"

As had happened last night, her answer seemed to come from nowhere, words that gripped her heart while they appeared to touch the feelings of the man across from her. "Some people just have a hard time feeling loved, no matter what others tell them." Could that be why she couldn't find God's love? Maybe it was there, just like Lewis's had been for Sheila, but she hadn't believed it.

"What do I do? How do I convince her how precious she is? If I'd lost her. . ." He buried his face in his hands.

"I know." She surprised herself by putting a hand on his arm, knowing he needed the comfort of physical contact. "She remembers you holding her last night, begging her not to die. Maybe she needs to be held again so she doesn't think it was a dream."

Lewis laid one of his roughened hands on hers. "Thanks, Jerusha." He rubbed his thumb across his eyes. "I think I'll get cleaned up so I'm not so grubby when she wakes up."

When Dr. Pierce arrived, his face had lost its haggard exhaustion. "You look like you've rested a bit," he greeted Jerusha. "I talked to your brother and he says he can manage fine if you want to stay for a while."

"What about the laundry?"

The doctor chuckled. "The reverend said you'd ask and said to tell you Miss Clarke and Mrs. Barry have volunteered to take care of things for as long as you have to be gone. It seems word of the trouble out here spread quickly."

Jerusha could barely believe her ears. It sounded as if they wanted to help her as much as she wanted to help Lewis and Sheila. "That's good of them," she said lamely.

"You and the reverend have put a lot of caring into this town. I figure it's time you got some back." He cleared his throat roughly. "Where's Lewis?"

The voice spoke from the stairs. "Right here." With clean, combed hair and fresh clothing, he looked almost like a different person.

"Isn't it amazing what a nap and a bath can do for a man?" The doctor laughed. "You look a thousand times better. This morning I wasn't sure you'd make it."

Lewis shook the doctor's hand. "Thanks for being here."

"I'm glad I was. How's our patient?"

"She woke up a bit earlier, then went right back to sleep," Jerusha explained. "I've got some broth ready for the next time she wakes up."

"She probably won't be awake much over the next few days, which is just right. Warm broth is the perfect food. Any kind of hot liquids she wants are fine, but go easy on the solid food for a while. I'll go take a look." He followed Lewis down the hall.

Jerusha finished putting the broth on to simmer, then began peeling vegetables for an evening meal. The doctor didn't linger in Sheila's room.

"I assume you're willing to stay for a while?" he asked, accepting a cup of coffee.

Jerusha nodded.

"Good. They're both going to need you, especially when the boys come home. Sheila's not out of the woods yet, and the least bit of overexertion could start the bleeding again. I don't want her even out of bed for two weeks. Lewis is so relieved she's still alive he doesn't realize yet how long it will take her to recover." He blew on his coffee for a few moments. "He tells me she asked you about the baby."

"She knows he's. . .that he didn't make it." Jerusha tried to swallow back the tears.

"I think she's going to have a rough time adjusting. I don't mind telling you I've rarely seen a woman as distraught as she was when I first got here."

"She'd calmed quite a bit by then."

"That's what I was afraid of. It's going to take a lot of love to pull her through. She's a believer, isn't she?"

The question surprised her. "Yes. She told me once she wouldn't have made it to Canada without God."

"She's going to need reminding of His love." He smiled at Jerusha's wide-eyed surprise. "That's an unusual prescription, isn't it? But I can't imagine doctoring in these parts without Him. We all need Him for whatever we have to do, I guess. Well, I'd best be on my way. Please tell Lewis I'll be back tomorrow."

Jerusha felt stunned by his comments. It seemed like every direction she turned, she was reminded of a love she still wasn't sure of. She'd like to ask Keith about it, if he ever showed up again.

Life slowly settled into routine. Lewis brought his boys home Tuesday morning. Jerusha found herself longing for the ease of her laundry business after three days keeping track of Colin and Bradley. Colin was five and Bradley, three. Rarely a morning or afternoon passed without one of them creating a mess somewhere, usually involving a fresh change of clothing. She barely had time to clean up from one meal before it was time to prepare another, not to mention endless loads of laundry and an infinite number of questions.

"Where are birds in the winter?" from Colin, who seemed fascinated by the seasons.

"Why is the stove hot?" from Bradley, whose favorite questions always began with why.

"When does spring come?"

"Where is your mommy?"

"Does the snow go away in spring or summer?"

"Why can't cows feed themselves?"

Despite the frustrations, she found herself developing an affection for the boys. She had always thought of herself as awkward around children, but Colin and Bradley didn't give her time to be uncomfortable. After a couple of days, they weren't content to go to bed until they had hugged Daddy, Mommy, and "Auntie 'Rusha." She had no words for the delight their enthusiastic love brought her.

Caring for Sheila proved to be a light load. Lewis did his chores in record time, spending every available minute with his wife, whether she was sleeping or awake. Every time Jerusha went to do something for her friend, she found the job already done and Lewis sitting on the bed holding Sheila in his arms as she rested. Sheila's eyes took on a shine Jerusha had never seen before. Though she cried periodically over her baby, she didn't encounter the despair Dr. Pierce had feared.

One of their rare moments together came when Sheila asked to have her hair washed. "I want to be fresh and as pretty as I can when Lewis comes back from feeding the livestock," she explained. Then while Jerusha brushed out the wet locks, she quietly commented, "This sounds terrible, but Davey's death may have been good for me."

"What do you mean?" Jerusha had been wondering how her friend felt about the loss of the son she had wanted so desperately.

"I thought a son would make Lewis love me. If Davey had lived, I might never have believed Lewis loves me for myself. But what I felt was my failure has been what I needed to enable me to see how much he cares. His love is almost too good to be true."

"It's for real, all right." Jerusha recalled again the agony in Lewis's eyes as the three of them had struggled together to stop Sheila's bleeding. She helped settle her friend back against the pillows, her clean hair spread out behind her head.

"Hmmm. This feels good. I didn't do anything, and I'm still tuckered out." Sheila snuggled under the comforter and closed her eyes.

Jerusha tucked the blankets in around the edge of the bed to prevent drafts. "Dr. Pierce says it will take you awhile to get your strength back."

Sheila opened her eyes a bit. "Thanks for being here, Jerusha."

"I wouldn't want to be anywhere else." She intended to reassure her friend, but the words she chose surprised her. Amazingly enough, she really was doing exactly what she wanted to do.

Chapter 11

Bradley and Colin had finally settled down for their naps, much to Jerusha's relief. Sheila was now strong enough to move from the bedroom to the sitting room, though she often tried to do more. Once the boys fell asleep, Sheila would also rest, and Jerusha would be able to catch up on bread baking and the ever-present laundry. She measured milk, honey, and yeast, then stirred in the flour. A few minutes of kneading and she could put the bread to rise on the far corner of the stove while she washed a couple loads of work clothes and little boys' play clothes. Good thing there weren't diapers to rinse, too. Jerusha smiled at her thoughts. A month ago, diapers would have been the furthest thing from her mind. These two small boys had entwined themselves in her heart, making her wonder what it would be like to have sons of her own. A sharp rap on the door startled her. She looked quickly out the window, but only saw a green army jeep. Could it be? But why would he come all the way out here?

She opened the door to greet the face that had intruded on her thoughts all too often in the past month. "Corporal Sutherland! Come in."

His eyebrows pulled together and he growled something under his breath. By the time he shed his parka and stepped out of his boots, his face had cleared. "Your brother told me I'd find you here. Word has it you've been doing a great job of being both nurse and mother."

The heat spreading across her face had little to do with her proximity to the cookstove. "You're not looking for Lewis? He's out in the barn."

"I'm glad he's outside, because that means you have to visit with me. You look like you're enjoying being out here."

"I am." The statement seemed too terse, but she didn't know how else to explain her feelings.

His gaze became more intent. "Your eyes look brighter and happier than I've ever seen them. I'm glad."

She silently handed him a cup of steaming coffee and a piece of last night's leftover cake, not sure what to say next.

"Thanks." He grinned and took a large bite of cake. "The cooks sure don't produce anything like this at the chow hall. I hear you had a close call with your patient."

Jerusha nodded. "I wished for you to be here."

"Why? I'm just a medic, not a doctor." His eyes widened in surprise.

"I'm neither and Dr. Pierce was busy delivering a healthy baby over by Rolla."

"You honestly thought of me?" His smile indicated he was teasing, but his gaze probed hers intently.

"I've thought of you a lot in the last month. I was afraid I'd offended you." She studied the wood grain of the table.

"Offended me? How?"

His shocked tone pulled her gaze back to his face. "When we were skiing and I wouldn't answer your question about God. I'm not the kind of Christian you are."

"Wait just a minute." He set his cup on the table with a thump. "Are you saying you think I didn't come visit because I was upset with you?"

She nodded, wondering why she'd even opened the subject.

"I'm really sorry." His voice dropped to comforting softness. "I was out of town. I get sent up the road periodically to relieve other medics further north. They shipped me out the day after the skiing party, and I just got back this morning. I'm so accustomed to the way the army works, I never dreamed you wouldn't know. Can you forgive me?"

She smiled, wondering why she suddenly felt so much lighter, almost like dancing across the kitchen. Instead, she refilled his coffee cup and reached for the bread bowl. "I'm glad it wasn't me. What's it like up the highway?"

He watched her sprinkle flour, then dump the bread dough on the table. "Pretty rough. They're trying to hack this highway out of frozen ground, and most of the troops have never encountered this kind of cold. There's lots of frostbite and injuries from guys trying to work without gloves. Their hands get cold and clumsy real quick. Or should I say very quickly. I'm picking up soldier talk."

"I've never understood what this project is all about anyway. Why does the American army need to build a Canadian road?"

"That could be a loaded question. We need to get supplies to an American army base in Alaska."

The bread dough was getting sticky, so she sprinkled more flour and continued kneading. "I didn't know there was one there."

His mouth tightened. "There isn't, but we're trying to get one there as fast as we can. That's why we need the road."

"What's the rush?"

"Does the name Pearl Harbor mean anything to you?"

"Isn't that where the Japanese made a vicious attack on the Americans?"

"That's it. The Japanese have been basically cleaning up on us ever since. Before we know it, we could find them on our shores."

"Like here in Canada?" She knew little about the Japanese, but she'd always heard the word uttered with tones of dread.

"Could be. We're doing our best to fight them back, but we haven't been too successful so far."

"And this new road is supposed to help?" She couldn't figure out how a trail hacked through the wilderness could make any difference in a war between foreigners.

He slid his chair back and stood. "We're hoping it will help us at least prepare for an attack on this continent, if not launch one ourselves. And speaking of attacks, I'd better get back to base or my CO will launch one on me." His grin looked just like Colin's when Lewis tried scolding him. "Thanks for the cake."

She wanted to ask when he'd be back, but the question felt improper. She settled for, "I'm glad you stopped by."

With another charming grin, he slipped into his parka and boots and left only a blast of cold air and an empty coffee cup as evidence of his visit.

To her surprise, he dropped by the next day and the next. By the time Jerusha had been with the Murrays for a month, he'd become a regular visitor, usually around suppertime.

"I've heard you army guys'll do anything for a home-cooked meal, but a twenty-minute drive?" Lewis teased one evening, handing the corporal a plateful of hot stew.

Corporal Sutherland only raised his eyebrows innocently in reply, then winked at Jerusha. She focused on getting the boys' plates filled and cooled, while their chatter eliminated what could have been an awkward silence.

"Are you really a soldier?"

He smiled at young Colin's enthusiasm. "No, I just take care of hurt soldiers."

"So you don't shoot people?" The boy was clearly disappointed.

"No, son, and I'm glad."

"Why?"

" 'Cause I don't like hurting people."

Now Bradley jumped in. "But if they're bad guys it doesn't matter."

Corporal Sutherland looked at Lewis, who only shrugged his shoulders, indicating he, too, waited for the corporal's reply. "It's like this, boys. Does Jesus love everybody or just a few people?"

There it was again—God's love out in the open where Jerusha couldn't ignore it. She mashed harder on Bradley's vegetables.

"Everybody," Colin proudly declared.

"So if I love Jesus, should I love everybody or just the people I like?"

Colin's enthusiasm was waning. "I guess everybody."

"Do you kill people you love?" Corporal Sutherland's manner remained gentle, even though he emphasized the point.

Bradley knew the answer to that one. "My mommy says Jesus wants us to be kind to ev'body."

"That's right, Bradley. That's why I only help hurt people. I guess I'm not a real soldier."

"But you're nice, anyway," Colin assured him. "That's what my mommy told Daddy."

The adults laughed, each self-conscious for a different reason. "How about eating, boys," Lewis suggested, with the father tone of voice that left no room for discussion. "If Mommy's still awake when you get finished, we'll go in and talk to her for awhile."

Jerusha recognized the blatant scheme to leave her alone with the corporal. For some reason, she felt almost grateful for it.

"How's Mrs. Lewis doing?" Corporal Sutherland asked quietly when the other three left.

"Better than the doctor predicted." She didn't know how much to tell. If she started talking about Sheila and Lewis's marriage, she'd probably stumble into her own still uncertain feelings about God.

"Sometimes tragedy carries wonderful discoveries with it." He stacked dishes and brought them to the cupboard, where she filled wash basins with hot water. "You're surprised I said that."

His perception made her nervous. "I just wondered how you guessed."

"We men are more observant than you think." He smiled teasingly, then sobered. "It just seemed to me Mrs. Lewis worked pretty hard at trying to please someone who already thinks she's wonderful. Kind of like we do with God sometimes."

His comment touched too close to her feelings. She concentrated on cleaning the stack of dishes, waiting for him to change the subject.

He pulled a chair close to where she worked. "You know, Miss Porter, you never did answer my question at the skiing party. Have you thought any more about it?"

She looked directly into the gray eyes watching her with such concern. "I've thought of little else. No sooner do I think I've found an answer than something happens to make me lose it."

"Want to talk to an old soldier about it?"

"Actually, David and I were discussing it a bit when Lewis came to get me." She took a deep breath for courage, then related David's comments that evening and her own feelings. "The verse Mrs. Barry read made me think maybe I haven't understood God at all. It seems to say He loves us no matter what we do. But that just doesn't make sense."

"Why not?"

"If He's so perfect and holy, how can He love such imperfect people?"

"Because He's God."

She looked at him in confusion while she wiped biscuit crumbs off the table.

"Let's try it from this angle. If we have to be perfect in order to be loved by Him, then what was Jesus' death all about?"

She had never thought about that. In recent years, Calvary had become a religious historical event, without any personal meaning. She remembered the verse that had started this train of thought: "While we were yet sinners, Christ died for us." There seemed to be a comforting message there, if she could only hear it through the confusion of her own thoughts.

"Jerusha." His gentle voice drew her gaze to his face. "It seems to me you're trying to figure God out. Faith is simply accepting that He is who He says He is."

"But the God you talk about is so different from what I've always thought He is! Sometimes it just doesn't make sense."

"I feel if I could explain God, He wouldn't be God anymore, just a creation of my imagination. What makes Him so wonderful is that He's Who He is, yet He chooses to love us finite, imperfect humans."

She shook her head at him. "I wish I could feel the way you do."

Whatever she had been planning to say further was cut off by the attack of a small body. " 'Night, Auntie 'Rusha."

"Good night, Bradley." She detached his arms from around her legs and picked him up for a tight hug. "You could have called me from upstairs."

"But Daddy said not to 'sturb you. I thinked if I comed in here, I wouldn't 'sturb you, but you'd hafta hug me."

She kissed the boy's soft cheek. "Where's Colin?"

"Here." A quiet whisper came from the stairs. "I couldn't sleep without a good night hug."

She carried Bradley to the stairs and hugged his older brother. "Didn't your daddy hug you?"

"Yeah, but I wanted one from you."

"Boys!" Lewis called from Sheila's room. "I thought I sent you upstairs."

"Auntie 'Rusha wanted to hug us. We didn't 'sturb her, Daddy," Bradley explained quickly.

Lewis approached the stairs, the twinkle in his eye indicating he guessed what had really happened. "Okay, now git!"

"Kids are special, aren't they?" the corporal commented when she returned.

"At least those two are." She grinned self-consciously while rinsing the last few dishes. "They've found a soft spot in me I didn't know I had."

"I noticed it the night of the explosion. As soon as you picked up that hurt boy, a new gentleness showed. I like it." His smile seemed almost intimate.

She sought for safer conversational ground. "Have you been around children much?"

"My sisters each have three, and I love spoiling all of them. After the war ends, I hope God allows me to have my own family." Unfamiliar shadows darkened his eyes.

She studied his face. This was an unfamiliar side of him. "Why wait for the war?" She hoped the impulsive question wasn't offensively personal.

He sat silent for so long she wondered if he'd decided not to answer. She set a cup of hot coffee on the counter beside him, then pulled a chair closer to the stove—and to him.

"I'd never ask any woman to marry an army man."

If she thought before she spoke, she would have bitten her next inquiry back. "Why?" Then good manners took over. Her face heated. "I'm sorry. I shouldn't pry."

He reassured her with a brief smile. "Remember I told you the other day about the base in Alaska? That's supposed to be a jumping-off place for an offensive into Japan. As soon as the Alcan Highway is complete, I could get shipped up there and then maybe to Japan. It would be unfair to leave a wife and children behind to wonder if I'd ever come home again."

The thought of him leaving never to return left a little cold spot in her middle. *Surely God wouldn't permit someone who loved Him so much to be killed! But then Sheila's baby hadn't even had a chance to decide for or against God.* She studied his sober expression, usually so cheerful. "Does it bother you to think about God letting you get killed?"

Surprise covered his face. "I'm doing what I feel He wants me to do, so it's up to Him whether or not I survive. Why do you ask?"

"If He really loves you, why wouldn't He keep you safe?" she whispered, not sure how her friend would respond. Maybe even God would be offended by the thought.

The corporal sat silently for several minutes. "I wish I could explain why God allows the things He does. Like this war. He could have prevented it, but that would have meant overriding the wills of men and nations. People being hurt and killed is part of war. All I know for sure is that He is God, and He's in charge."

Jerusha couldn't make sense of his gentle words. The familiar resentment churned in her stomach again. She thought of her often-absent parents, pursuing God's will while she cried herself to sleep at night. Her own attempts to follow God's will had dumped her in this revolting boomtown.

"Jerusha?" the corporal called softly. When she looked at him, he continued. "This isn't really about what might or might not happen to me, is it?"

Jerusha wiped the clean counter again to avoid his gaze.

He wouldn't let her shut him out. "Would you mind telling me what God's done to make you question Him so harshly?"

Again, she felt punched in the stomach. "What makes you think that?"

"Your anger at Him is written all over your face." The words carried no hint of accusation. "Will you tell me why?"

She whirled to face him, feeling like the lid to her seething emotions had been pried off. "My parents have been missionaries all my life. All I've heard about them is how wonderful, how dedicated, they are. When they'd come home on furlough, I'd try to be as good as I knew how so they'd love me enough to want to stay. But they always went back, usually sooner than they'd planned, because they said God needed them. Why didn't God realize I needed them, too? If He loved me, He sure had a strange way of showing it." To her dismay, tears poured down her face.

He merely held his arms out to her, tears glistening in his eyes. When she didn't move, he took a couple of slow steps toward her until he was close enough to embrace her. His hug broke the last fragments of her reserve. She sobbed into his shirtfront, feeling like a small girl again. Years of grief and anger poured through her tears. He simply held her close, saying nothing until her shoulders stopped shaking.

"Every time they left, it felt like personal rejection, didn't it?"

The rumble in his chest as he spoke brought as much comfort as his words. She nodded against him, wondering why she'd never been able to describe her feelings so well.

"Rushi, God never asked them to choose between Him and you." Large hands rubbed her neck and shoulders. "His will isn't some arbitrary decision He makes without regard for our feelings or the feelings of those we love. I can't explain why God allowed things to happen in your family the way He did, just like I don't know why God allowed Sheila's baby to come so early. But I do know He's hurt with you all this time, just like He's cried with Sheila and Lewis."

She pulled back to look into his face. "But I've blamed Him for everything!"

"Some of Jesus' best friends did the same thing. When Lazarus died, the first thing his sisters said to Jesus was, 'If you'd been here, this wouldn't have happened.' He didn't defend Himself or try to explain anything. In fact, the Apostle John said He saw their grief and was troubled. He shared their grief, even though He knew He would raise Lazarus to life." He rested his hands lightly on her shoulders. "He doesn't expect us to be stoic. He knows we'll weep and rant at Him. He just waits until we're ready to listen so He can show us all over again how much He loves us."

Jerusha felt half-ashamed of the question, but she had to ask. "Why doesn't He at least tell us why He lets things happen the way they do?"

Keith's eyes softened with a compassionate smile. "I don't know, Rushi. Lots of people in Scripture asked Him to explain Himself."

"What did He say?"

"Most often, He simply showed them Himself."

The warmth of his hands on her shoulders suddenly felt too personal. She moved away, studying his face for clues to the mystery. "You mean He never told them why, and they just decided everything was all right?"

"Any revelation of God includes His love. When they saw God as He revealed Himself to them, they realized He can do nothing outside His fathomless love for us, the people He's created for fellowship with Him. His love is the essence of who He is, which enables us to love Him in return. When we know His love, we don't need explanations."

"I wish I could." She shook her head sadly, looking away from him. The darkness outside the kitchen window looked like what she felt inside.

"You will."

"How do you know?"

"Because since the night of the explosion, I've been asking Him to make it so."

Chapter 12

The next day, Dr. Pierce gave permission for Sheila to start taking up the care of her household again. "But go carefully, now, Mrs. Murray. At least one nap every day, and don't lift anything, not even your sons."

Jerusha expected to see pain on Sheila's face at the reference to her sons. The children under discussion were actually her stepsons. Her own son lay in a shallow grave already covered by a snowbank. Instead, Sheila gave Lewis a glowing look and turned back to the doctor. "My guardian angels here don't give me a chance to misbehave." She smiled at Jerusha. "I haven't even been allowed to wash my own hair."

"Which is as it should be," Dr. Pierce pronounced. "I know I'm leaving you in expert hands." He reached for his coat and bag. Lewis remained behind with his wife, but Jerusha followed the doctor. His hand was on the door when she finally found the courage to address him.

"Dr. Pierce, I need to ask you a question, if you have time."

He immediately put his bag on the floor. "I have all the time you need. What is it?"

Her discomfort increased, but she knew she felt driven to find answers. "You mentioned that Sheila might have a hard time adjusting to her baby's death."

He nodded, watching her with kindly brown eyes.

"She hasn't. Is she just pretending to be okay, or is there something I've missed?"

"Have you asked her about it?"

"No. I've had little time alone with her. Lewis hovers around her like a mosquito in the dark."

"What a romantic simile." The doctor chuckled. "But I know what you mean, and it could be the answer to your question. Maybe just realizing she's loved provided the healing she needed."

Jerusha shook her head. "It doesn't make sense."

"Love often doesn't, Miss Porter. God's love is incomprehensible, and human love is supposed to be a reflection of Him. I'd recommend you talk with Mrs. Murray. Since she's experienced it, she might be able to help you understand." He pulled his hat flaps down over his ears, picked up his bag, and departed in a gust of chilly air.

Jerusha puttered around the kitchen, wiping clean counters, straightening tidy cupboards, stoking an already-crackling fire. Anything to avoid talking with Sheila just now. Should she face her friend immediately, Sheila would be able to see her conflict. Somehow it didn't seem right for a person of Jerusha's background to be struggling so intensely with the love of the One she proclaimed to serve. She heard Lewis's clumping steps coming from the bedroom.

"I'll probably be out until supper time," he said from beside the door, where he donned layer after layer of warm clothing. "Now that my wife's on the mend, I need to get caught up out in the barn. I'd like to be able to be on hand for the first couple of weeks after you leave." His lips twitched in the half-smile that was Lewis Murray's version of a grin.

His expression lingered in her memory while she peeled vegetables to add to the roast already cooking. Lewis could easily seem unfriendly, even surly. She'd never seen him grin like Keith, much less laugh. He didn't talk easily, either. Now that she had spent time around him and his family, she knew his gentleness expressed itself in his actions rather than his words. If one watched closely, hints of his emotions showed in his eyes—brightening for his sons, softening for his wife. What a contrast to Sheila's easy expression of her feelings! Could her feeling unloved have been no more than not understanding Lewis's ways of communicating? A scuffling sound from the direction of Sheila's bedroom interrupted her thoughts. She plopped the last handful of carrots in the roasting pan and hurried to investigate.

Sheila looked up guiltily as Jerusha peered into the room. "I'm staying warm," she announced from where she stood next to the partially made bed.

Jerusha duly noted the quilted robe encasing her friend from shoulders to ankles. The scuffling sounds had come from Sheila's rabbit-fur moccasins as she had moved from one side of the bed to the other, straightening the covers. A pile of linen near the door indicated Sheila had changed the sheets before being discovered. Jerusha tried to look stern. "Dr. Pierce said no lifting."

"Sheets aren't heavy."

"But it's hard work tucking them around the edge of the mattress. Why didn't you ask for help?"

Sheila beamed. "It just feels so good to be out of bed!"

"If you're not careful, you'll end up right back there and Lewis will have my hide!"

Sheila giggled delightedly. "It's so wonderfully fragile and carefully cherished he makes me feel." She lowered herself back onto the bed. "I do need to sit and catch my breath a bit."

Jerusha studied her carefully. Somehow she looked years younger than she had even a couple of months ago. After her harrowing experience, she should still look drained and tired, or at the very least, sad.

Suddenly it felt like the perfect time for questions. "What's made the difference, Sheila?"

She didn't pretend not to understand. "All the hours Lewis spent with me right after the baby came showed me how many faces love wears. I kept looking for words and completely missed Lewis's more subtle ways of caring. Lying here, I had nothing but time to watch him and think. Now I know what to look for, I see his love for me in everything he does."

"But what about the baby?"

Sheila's face shadowed. "What do you mean?"

"Maybe I shouldn't have brought it up." Jerusha backed toward the door.

"Don't be afraid to talk about him, Jerusha. He's still my baby, and I still wish I could have held him and watched him grow." Tears misted her eyes, though she smiled encouragingly.

"You wanted him so badly. Even Dr. Pierce predicted you might have a hard time adjusting."

Sheila leaned back against the pillows. "I've cried lots." Drops sliding down her cheeks verified her statement. "But so has Lewis, and somehow that makes it easier. He loves me so much he's willing to hurt with me. We've become best friends since we lost the baby. I'm not glad Davey died. But if he hadn't, I might never have discovered what his daddy is really like." Now Sheila studied Jerusha. "It's hard to understand, isn't it?"

Jerusha nodded. She still couldn't see the baby's death as anything less than tragedy.

"It's kind of like my relationship with God," Sheila continued quietly. "He always seemed remote to me until life got hard after my ma died. I'd cry myself to sleep at night, and I'd feel His presence in my dreams. The seamstress I worked for would scream at me, and I'd feel inside me how much God loved me in spite of the horrible things she said. And coming over on the ship, when I felt like I'd die from either fright or sickness, I knew He'd take care of me. I guess it takes the difficult times to make me sensitive enough to realize what He's really like." Gentle silence followed.

"I think I smell the roast burning." Jerusha hurried to the kitchen, glad for an excuse to escape the mood created by Sheila's words. She'd barely closed the oven door when pattering feet on the stairs announced the boys' awakening from their afternoon naps. Shuffling slowly, Sheila met them at the bottom.

"Mama!" they chorused, delight shining in their big brown eyes.

Jerusha watched carefully as Sheila hugged the boys, then guided them to the rocker in the sitting room. "Colin, if you'd fetch me a book, we can read a story. Bradley, pull up that stool for you and one on the other side for Colin."

"But I want to sit on your lap." Bradley's lower lip trembled convincingly as he lifted a sad gaze to his mother's face.

Well accustomed to his clever theatrics, Jerusha intervened before Sheila's tender heart overrode common sense. She hurried to kneel beside the boy. "Bradley, your daddy needs you to help take care of your mommy for awhile."

"She doesn't look sick." Curiosity replaced Bradley's pout.

"That's because her hurt is inside her body where we can't see it. But if she does things the doctor said not to do, it could make her even more sick. That would make your daddy very sad." Jerusha glanced at Sheila, whose eyes twinkled with merriment.

Bradley looked seriously at Jerusha, then at his mother, as if to verify Jerusha's comments. "Did the doctor tell her not to hold me?"

Jerusha nodded solemnly.

"And if she does, Daddy might spank her for dis'bedience, right?"

Again she nodded, trying to keep laughter from escaping. From the corner of her eye, she could see Sheila's arms shaking with suppressed giggles.

Colin returned just in time to hear his younger brother's comment. "Daddy wouldn't spank Mommy, silly! They're adults, and adults don't get spankings."

Bradley looked back at Jerusha. "Then what will happen if she holds me?"

Colin knew that answer, too. "You'll get spanked, 'cause Daddy already told us not even to ask her. She's sick and we have to take good care of her so she gets well again."

"I guess that settles it, then." Sheila opened the book, and the boys settled on either side.

After a couple of stories, they were ready to go outside to play. Sheila and Jerusha helped them into heavy pants, sweaters, mitts, hats, and coats, then wrapped scarves snugly around each face.

"They won't be out more than twenty minutes before they'll be wanting in again." Sheila laughed, watching through the window as they tumbled over each other in the snow like a couple of puppies. "While they're out, would you help me do my hair?" When Jerusha nodded, she released the lightly twisted bun at the back of her head. "I want tonight to be a special supper to celebrate my getting well. Moose roast is Lewis's favorite meal, and I'll make him an apple pie when I finish with my hair."

"How about letting me handle the pie?" Jerusha suggested, wrapping a heated towel around Sheila's shoulders. Over the weeks of Sheila's recovery, they had devised a system for getting her hair cleaned quickly, yet thoroughly. Sheila lay across her bed facing the ceiling, her long hair hanging into a small washtub Jerusha had set on a stool.

"This is a lot easier now that you're able to help." Jerusha used a cup to pour the warm water through the dark, curly hair.

Sheila's voice softened. "I haven't told you how much I appreciate you coming out here. Lewis has mentioned often how we couldn't have made it through this without you."

The praise made Jerusha uncomfortable. "I'm glad to be able to help, though you and Lewis would have survived fine without me. You're both strong people."

Sheila turned her head abruptly to look into Jerusha's face. "Part of what makes us strong, Jerusha, is having friends like you."

Jerusha concentrated on working lather into the ends of the hair close to Sheila's scalp, then carefully rinsing away the suds. She wrapped a towel around the wet hair, helping Sheila to sit up.

Sheila watched her carry out the washtub, then the stool. Still silently, she let Jerusha comb out her wet hair. The job was almost finished when she commented, "You've changed since you've been out here. In a good way, I mean."

The comment caught Jerusha completely off guard. "Wh-wh-what do you mean?"

"Like your joking this afternoon with Bradley. Three months ago, you hardly even spoke to the boys. You've handled them like family lately."

"I guess being around them so much has made me more comfortable with them."

"And maybe love is teaching you not to be afraid of being yourself."

Jerusha dropped the comb with a gasp. "Love?"

"You've had little part of a real family, haven't you?" Sheila asked gently.

Jerusha thought immediately of Uncle Cam and Aunt Vivienne. "My aunt and uncle were like parents to us since our own were overseas so much."

"But you've always seemed to me to be trying to live up to someone else's expectations of you. You've been afraid to let anyone know you or love you just as you are. That's what I've found so wonderful about children. Their little minds are too busy discovering the world to worry about what other people think. They either love people or they don't. It's quite a compliment that our two have fallen so hard for you. They're going to miss you when you go back."

Jerusha visualized the tidy parsonage, unruffled by crying, scattered toys, or spilled food. "I'll miss them, too."

"I'll bring them around lots so you don't forget what love is like. I imagine that army fellow will also do his part."

Voices at the front door rescued Jerusha from reply. "Can we come in now, Auntie 'Rusha? It's cold."

She hurried out to help the two snow-covered figures. "Yes, but shut the door so your mommy doesn't catch a chill." She hung the now-wet winter clothing on chairs around the kitchen stove to dry while she made the pie. The smell of cinnamon and apple had begun to fill the house when Sheila finally came out of her room again, fully dressed this time.

"How do I look?" She twirled in front of the stove.

Jerusha tried to look stern. "You look like you've put in a lot of work. Sit down."

Sheila sat, eyes glowing. "But do I look like an invalid?"

"Definitely not." Jerusha hugged her, then backed up to look at her again. Sheila had braided her dark hair in a coronet around her head, then donned a soft pink dress with a gathered skirt and a high ruffled neck. The full sleeves ended in ruffles at the wrists. The pink in her dress emphasized the returning glow in her cheeks and deepened the color in her shining eyes. "I think you'll take his breath away."

"Good. Now, would you mind getting the fancy dishes off the top shelf? I'll see if I can find the lacy tablecloth in the linen closet."

Jerusha stopped her with a firm hand on her shoulder. "I don't mind if you sit here and give orders. The best way to end up back in bed is to do too much your first day up."

Sheila sighed in resignation, but the twinkle in her eyes didn't disappear. "Okay, boss. Can you find the dishes?"

In a remarkably short amount of time, the simple kitchen table had been transformed into a dining area fit for Winnipeg's finest home. Under Sheila's direction, Jerusha had also found two hand-carved candleholders and two store-bought pale pink candles. The china had a fine, pink-flowered design enhanced by the lacy tablecloth. Then Sheila sent the boys upstairs for specific pants and shirts "so we can look extra-special nice for Daddy tonight." Neither child looked excited about dressing up, but the novelty of having Mommy help encouraged cooperation.

"Now you," Sheila announced, looking at Jerusha. "I don't want you looking like our kitchen maid."

"But I didn't bring any fancy clothes with me," she protested.

"Which is why it's a good thing we're much the same size. Come with me. The pie won't burn if you hurry."

Feeling helplessly caught in the tide of Sheila's enthusiasm, Jerusha followed. Sheila reached toward a wooden peg behind the curtain that hid hers and Lewis's clothes from view. "I made this while still in Ireland, but the color doesn't suit me. I think it will look marvelous on you." She held up a dress made from a soft woolen fabric the color of Aunt Vivienne's darkest roses. Jerusha had never thought of wearing any color other than "discreet" browns, grays, and blues, but she now wanted nothing more than to try on this beautiful garment. Cloth-covered buttons closed the dress from the waist up to a wide collar. The sleeves buttoned halfway between elbow and wrist, and the skirt hung in gentle folds around her calves.

"It looks even better than I thought it would." Sheila clapped her hands delightedly. "Now here's an apron to keep you clean until supper is served. May I try something a little different with your hair? I won't take long."

Jerusha didn't object as Sheila loosed her tight bun. "You have lovely hair. Why do you keep it pinned up so tightly?"

"Just to keep it out of the way, I guess." Jerusha tried to laugh, wondering why a different hairstyle should make her feel so uneasy.

"I'll show you how hair like yours should be worn, and it won't be in the way, I promise." She combed, twisted, and pinned. "There. You can feel what I've done, but touch it gently."

Jerusha reached exploring fingers to the back of her head. Her hair felt loose along the sides, yet it didn't fall into her face. It had been pulled back gently, then tucked into a soft roll. The looking glass on a nearby wall revealed the overall effect of softness.

"I can't believe this is me," Jerusha giggled. "I look almost pretty. Is that vain?"

Sheila hugged her. "Not at all. You look just as I've always thought you'd look if you let yourself be more a woman and less a preacher's sister. Too bad your army friend won't be here."

Still looking in the mirror, Jerusha saw herself blush. "He's not *my* army friend. He's actually more David's friend than mine."

Sheila wisely said nothing. Feeling more defensive than ever, Jerusha hurried back out to the kitchen to check on the pie. Hopefully Lewis would come in before the roast overcooked. She had just decided to try to keep it warm on the back of the stove when she heard boots stamping on the porch. It sounded like someone had accompanied him.

"I invited this stray for supper." Lewis stopped as soon as he stepped inside, looking first at his wife in the rocking chair reading, then to his dressed-up sons, then at the fancy table, then at Jerusha. "Looks like you picked the right night, Keith." He moved to the side so both men could remove parkas and boots.

Jerusha felt intense heat from her neck to her hairline. Sheila stood quickly and filled what could have been an awkward gap. "I'm glad you came, Corporal Sutherland. We're just celebrating my release from the sick-room. I hope you like parties."

"Yes, I do, ma'am. I hope you'll excuse my not being in dress uniform." His gaze strayed back to Jerusha, who stood as if glued in place.

Sheila laughed. "It's the company, not the clothes, that make the party. I've always thought men looked more handsome in work shirts than suits, anyway."

Jerusha willed her feet to move. Another china plate for the table, along with cutlery and a glass. *Continue slicing the roast. Make gravy. Potatoes and carrots in a bowl.* She had finished talking herself through the rest of the preparations by the time Lewis reappeared, washed and wearing a clean shirt. The boys chattered excitedly while Lewis asked Sheila quiet questions about her afternoon. Only Corporal Sutherland and Jerusha had nothing to say. She felt a strange happiness that he should see her at her feminine best, yet uncomfortable with her new appearance as well as the memory of last night's embrace. What must he think of her for allowing such contact? Her tears made the memory even more embarrassing. Every time she glanced at him, his gaze had not wavered from her.

Lewis asked a short blessing over the food, including a heartfelt thanks for his wife's recovery. When Sheila reached for the serving dishes to begin filling her sons' plates, he stopped her with a gentle reprimand. "No lifting, wife. Jerusha and I can help the boys." Glad for activity, Jerusha concentrated on mashing Bradley's potatoes and cutting his meat. Sheila plied the corporal with inquiries about his work. With his attention distracted, Jerusha felt her tension easing.

By the end of the meal, Sheila had begun to look weary. Lewis noticed immediately. "Boys, how would you like to help me put Mommy to bed?

You can find your favorite books and we'll read her some stories." Excited chatter indicated his sons' approval. He looked to Jerusha. "You don't mind being left with dishes?"

"I'll be glad to help her," Keith cut in.

"But you did that last night!" Jerusha's protest came instinctively. She hoped he wouldn't leave right away, but she didn't want to be left alone with him again. Or did she?

"It's a biblical principle that a man's got to work if he wants to eat. I just managed to get to the eating before the working." He grinned, and Lewis nodded agreement.

Jerusha helped Sheila to her room while Lewis got the boys into their nightclothes. She reached for the buttons on the back of her dress. "I'd better change out of this before I start cleaning up. I'd hate to ruin it."

Sheila touched her arm to stop her. "I think the corporal would like it better if you didn't."

An unfamiliar quiver of pleasure tugged at Jerusha even though she continued her protests. "That's not a good reason."

"Why not? It looks to me like he's falling in love with you."

Jerusha took a deep breath to steady her voice. "I don't think that's a possibility. Besides, I came to Dawson Creek to help David, not find a husband."

Sheila raised her dark eyebrows. "Who knows what could happen? Hand me my nightgown, please. If I'm not in bed when Lewis gets back, he probably won't let me have my bedtime story." Jerusha laughed at her friend's foolishness, then helped her get comfortable.

When she returned to the kitchen, the table had already been cleared.

"I don't know what to do with this stuff." Keith gestured helplessly at the leftovers. "You ladies always make it look so easy, but when I tried to do it at home I could never find the right size dish."

Jerusha chuckled in spite of herself. "I'm glad there's something you're not good at."

He winked. "I guess I just need lessons."

She felt her face heat again and wished desperately she could get over her intense responses to him.

"I can see it's a good thing I came out tonight," he offered quietly.

For the first time during the evening, she looked him straight in the eyes. "Why?"

"I thought our conversation last night might have left you uncomfortable. You don't have to be embarrassed at letting me see the person you are inside, Jerusha. I think you're pretty special, and I'm honored you'd trust me with what you think."

She shrugged, wishing she could regain her previous detachment. Emotions didn't get embarrassing when she kept her distance.

"I mean it, Rushi."

His use of David's nickname and his hand on her shoulder unsettled her too much. She jerked away.

"Hey!" His voice dropped almost to a whisper. "What is it?"

She backed further from him. "I wish you wouldn't touch me." She could feel his gaze on her face, though she concentrated on pouring gravy into the dish of potatoes.

"Jerusha, please look at me." The pleading in his voice reached her more intimately than a physical touch. "Please don't feel upset over last night. It's not weakness to need comfort. You're dealing with a lot of pain, and I believe God invented hugs to get us through those hard times. I'm glad I was the one He chose to help you."

She couldn't believe she'd heard him correctly. It seemed like he always saw her at her weakest emotionally. Was it possible he didn't despise her for accepting his comfort so readily?

"Please come sit down." He pulled the chair away from the end of the table. When she perched on the edge of it, he straddled the bench to her left so he could face her. "I hadn't intended to tell you this, but I feel you need to know. You've become a very special person to me, Jerusha. Though I'm not free to develop the kind of emotional bond with you I'd like to, I want to be your friend. I'll never judge you for being honest with me, and I'll never criticize you for not being the kind of person you think you ought to be. You're precious to me, and to God, just the way you are. Will you let me be your friend?"

She searched his eyes for hints of mockery or disdain, but found only compassion that seemed to come from the most tender places in his soul. She nodded.

"Will you promise not to shut me out even when you don't like the way you feel?"

The warmth in his eyes wrapped her in a blanket of safety. Maybe she didn't have to be perfect to be loved. All at once, God's love as he'd described it seemed possible. She could respond to that hope only with honesty. "I'll try."

"Good girl." The grin that always brightened her day lit the kitchen. "Now let's see what we can do about these dishes."

Chapter 13

Sheila continued to gain strength daily. Within two weeks, Dr. Pierce and Lewis deemed her hardy enough to manage without Jerusha. Not surprisingly, Keith showed up to take Jerusha back to town. She tried to ignore the conspiratorial twinkle in Sheila's eyes while she gave final instructions. "Don't you dare try laundry on your own for at least another month. I'll come out on Saturdays to help with that. Leave major cleaning for then, too."

"Yes, ma'am." Sheila ducked her head in pretended submission.

"I'll stick close to the house to make sure she behaves," Lewis reassured Jerusha with his small smile.

Keith held her overnight bag while she fastened her boots and heavy coat. She turned to say good-bye to the boys, who had seated themselves on the stairs.

"Why are you leaving, Auntie 'Rusha?" Bradley arranged his features in his most pathetic look.

" 'Cause she has to help the preacher. He's her brother, you know," Colin informed him wisely.

"Will you ever come back?"

Colin awaited the answer as expectantly as Bradley. Jerusha felt their sad gazes tug at her heart. "Come here, both of you." She knelt on the floor so she could wrap them both in a hug. "We love each other, right?" They nodded solemnly. "Then that means we're always together even when we can't see each other. I'll be thinking of you with loving thoughts, and you'll be thinking of me. Besides, your mommy and daddy will bring you to church on Sundays, and I'll come out often to make sure your mommy isn't working too hard." Grins lit both faces, and two pairs of chubby arms wrapped themselves around her neck.

"Okay, boys, let Auntie 'Rusha go home now so she can come back sooner," Sheila encouraged.

Keith and Jerusha made the trip back to town in silence. David greeted her with an enthusiastic hug, then invited Keith to come in for coffee. "This is going to feel like a regular party after weeks of silence," he commented.

"Silence?" Jerusha raised her eyebrows disbelievingly. "What happened to the unending stream of 'Reverend, could you please. . .' "

"It's not the same as family." He gave her another rough hug, then held her away from him at arms' length. "You've changed, little sister."

Jerusha felt the blush creeping up her face. No reply came to mind. David filled coffee cups and the three sat down at the table. He looked intently into her eyes.

"Have you perchance found answers to the questions you were asking the night you left?"

She looked quickly at Keith, wondering what his reaction would be to her honesty. Nothing showed in his gaze but the gentle concern to which she'd grown accustomed. She sighed deeply. "I don't know."

"You look more peaceful."

She forced herself to look directly at David. "I feel like I'm barely touching the edge of something wonderful, but I can't quite find it."

The enthusiastic twinkle in David's eyes softened to encouragement. "Do you know what you're looking for?"

Jerusha nodded. "God's love. Sheila and I even talked about it some. All of you know what it's like. It just doesn't make sense to me."

A pause ensued. Keith looked down at the table, his lips moving silently. Finally David spoke. "You're closer than you think you are, Rushi. I can see it in your eyes. Don't try to live up to whatever you think His love is. You don't have to chase God. If you really want what He has to offer, He'll catch up with you." After a few more minutes of silence, the conversation moved quietly onto other topics. Eventually, a knock at the back door interrupted.

"Silence?" Jerusha asked David teasingly.

He just shrugged. She noticed he hardly limped at all as he moved toward the door.

She looked back at Keith. "Thanks for the ride."

"I was glad to help." The side of his mouth twitched with a suppressed grin. "Besides, if I hadn't come, I might not have learned about the problem here at the parsonage."

"Problem?" She wondered what she'd missed.

"You heard the preacher say it gets too quiet around here. I guess I'll have to keep a close eye on you two."

A lovely lighthearted sensation inside made her smile, though she didn't offer any comment. Maisie called from the entry, "Jerusha? Are you really home?"

Jerusha hugged her other friend delightedly. She'd missed Maisie more than she'd realized. "I'm really here, ready and willing to take all that laundry off your hands."

Maisie laughed. "It's not been that bad. Your lemon-juice trick kept my hands from aging before their time, though I had to use vinegar. Besides, your brother has helped a lot, or wasn't I supposed to tell her that?" She grinned at David.

"Now that the secret's out, I guess I'll have to keep helping. I've gained a whole new appreciation for your little enterprise, Rushi. Leaving already, Keith?"

The corporal zipped his jacket. " 'Fraid so. The army seems to like to see me around on a regular basis. Would it be okay if I brought a few of the guys over tomorrow evening? We have a growing number of new believers who'd like some place to go other than the bars."

"Is that too soon for you?" David asked Jerusha.

Not if it means Keith will come, too, she thought silently. Aloud she only said, "I think that will be fine."

"How about if I bring snow ice cream?" Maisie offered.

"The guys and I will find some popcorn, and we can have a regular party. But we don't want you to make any special preparations for us." He looked directly at Jerusha, giving her the feeling she'd just been given an order from a superior officer. At her nod of acknowledgment, he opened the door. "Until tomorrow night, then."

Jerusha spent the rest of the afternoon with Maisie, catching up on town chatter while they sorted laundry, cleaned the house, and prepared supper.

"Ruth Pierce told Mrs. Barry and I the doctor's quite impressed with how you helped Sheila, especially the day she lost the baby." Maisie's eyes glowed with pride for her friend. "You should have seen David's face when I told him. You'd have thought someone just declared you queen."

Jerusha shrugged. "I just hope I never have to live through another night like that."

"How's Sheila doing? About losing the baby, I mean."

Jerusha's hands ceased their scrubbing on the floor as she contemplated. "I don't understand it, but she's peaceful. She's even found something to be glad about."

Maisie said nothing, watching Jerusha closely.

"She said she might never have realized Lewis loves her for herself if she hadn't lost Davey."

"You sound confused."

Jerusha looked at her friend directly. "It's like what you and Keith and

David keep telling me about God. You say He loves me, but I always feel like I have to be something special to be worthy of His love. I wish I could feel about God's love the way Sheila does about Lewis's."

"If we could be good enough on our own for God's love, it wouldn't be such a miracle, would it?"

"David said the same thing. I just can't feel like it's true."

"That's where trust comes in, Rushi. Feelings often tell us something different about God than what He tells us about Himself in the Bible. We have to choose whether we're going to believe our feelings or believe Him."

The glimmer of hope Jerusha had felt since talking with Keith grew brighter. She silently resolved to do more Scripture reading. Maybe she could find something to show her whether God was like her imaginings or like her friends' descriptions.

Ever sensitive to others' feelings, Maisie quietly changed the subject. "Did I tell you what Kevin Pierce said to Mrs. Barry last week? It seems he's been learning about family relationships. He knows Mr. and Mrs. McEvan are his grandparents because they're Ruth's parents, and Mr. and Mrs. Pierce are his grandparents because they're Dr. Pierce's parents. But he couldn't figure out why they call Mrs. Barry Granny B. He decided it's because Mrs. Barry doesn't have a husband. 'You have to have a Grandpa to be a Grandma,' he told her. 'But you're just as nice as if you were a Grandma instead of a Granny.' "

Jerusha laughed, thinking how much the comment resembled something Colin would say. "What does he think of having an aunt and an uncle younger than he is?"

"I think the family has tried to prevent him figuring out the details of his family relationships. It's confusing enough to the rest of us."

"Mrs. McEvan doesn't look old enough to be Ruth's mother."

Maisie laughed. "She's not. I guess that's another Dawson Creek story you haven't heard."

"This town is full of unusual stories." Jerusha wrung out her scrubbing rag for the last time. "Do our drains work yet?"

"They're saying sometime in the spring. Since we're finished with the kitchen, how about a cup of tea while I tell you about the McEvans?"

"Sounds good." Jerusha threw the water out the back door as usual, vaguely aware she didn't feel nearly as bothered by useless drains as she had a couple of months ago.

"Would you like to try one of Mrs. Barry's dried apple muffins?" Maisie already had the tea water heating, cups and saucers on the table, and she was reaching for small plates for the muffins.

Jerusha revelled in having someone else provide refreshment. "Sounds tasty."

"Any of Mrs. Barry's cooking is marvelous. Can't you tell by my waistline?" Maisie giggled, unembarrassed by her roundness. "Anyway, about the McEvans. Mrs. McEvan came to Dawson Creek in the early thirties to teach in one of the country schools that used to be all over around here. Ruth and Phillip McEvan were in her school, and she took quite a shine to them. Apparently, their mother and three of their siblings had drowned in a river crossing a year or so previously. Little Greg was just an infant when it happened. The kids fell in love with Ida, and their dad followed suit. Theo and Ruth married only a month after Rachel was born, so Ruth's two boys fit between Ida's three youngest in age."

"What an incredible story!" Jerusha wanted to say romantic, but the word felt strange even in her thoughts. "How does Mrs. Barry come into it?"

"Mrs. McEvan lived in the boardinghouse before she got married. Neither of them will say much about it, but I get the feeling the wedding had a lot to do with Mrs. Barry's matchmaking skills. I think the dear lady has someone picked out for every unmarried person in Dawson Creek." Maisie giggled again, a faint blush darkening her cheeks.

"I hope she's found someone other than Sylvia for my brother."

Maisie's eyes widened. "What brought that on?"

Jerusha shook her head. "It's just that Sylvia seems to have decided David's her latest conquest, and whatever Sylvia wants, Sylvia gets."

"Are you sure it's not just David's lack of interest that's attracting her?"

"I don't know whether he's uninterested or not." Jerusha felt the worry twisting her stomach again. She could think of nothing worse than having Sylvia Irvine as a sister-in-law. "I've never seen him give her anything but the same friendly interest he gives everyone."

"Isn't that a good sign?"

"Sylvia appears to see it as a personal challenge. She's going to get him to fall in love with her if he doesn't watch it. I have no idea what she's been up to since I haven't been in town."

"Jerusha, don't you think your brother can take care of himself?" Maisie put a comforting hand on Jerusha's arm, her voice carrying no reproach.

"He's just so interested in people, I'm afraid he's going to get taken advantage of."

"He also loves God too much to fall in love with someone who doesn't love God, too."

Jerusha filled her teacup thoughtfully. Part of her evaluated David's ability to withstand Sylvia, while the other part wondered what Keith would think. Would he also avoid someone who didn't love God as he did?

The conversation replayed itself in Jerusha's mind during the next evening. So many young adults showed up, the gathering moved to the meeting room. Maisie's ice cream disappeared in short order, along with the snacks brought by various other girls. The soldiers brought popcorn, as promised.

"May we use your kitchen to make this stuff edible?" Keith asked Jerusha.

She extended her hand for the bag. "I can do it."

"I know you can, but I already promised this impromptu party wouldn't make any extra work for you. Just show me where to find a large pan and some bowls." His eyes twinkled at her.

Recognizing the futility of argument, she did as he asked, then wandered back into the meeting room. Several games were already in progress, Maisie was playing the piano for a group of singers, and an intense discussion of military strategy was underway. David concentrated on a game of chess while Sylvia hovered nearby. She noticed Jerusha come in.

"Miss Porter, I'm so glad to see you. David's cup is empty, and I wouldn't have a clue where to find the coffeepot." She fluttered her eyelashes at David, who looked at Jerusha with an understanding smile. "If you have any cocoa on hand, I'd love a cup of hot chocolate," Sylvia continued. "I'd understand, though, if you haven't been able to afford any."

Jerusha snatched David's cup without replying. If she didn't leave the room quickly, her ungracious feelings would burst out of hiding.

Keith started to grin at her when she re-entered the kitchen, but his expression quickly changed. "You look ready to cry or kill."

Jerusha tried to laugh. "It's Sylvia again. She's too helpless to refill coffee cups herself, then announces she'll understand if we can't afford to give her a cup of hot chocolate."

A muscle along Keith's jawline twitched. Though he smiled, his eyes looked cold as the winter sky. "Good thing I had some cocoa on hand from Mom's last care package. How about if you let me take the drinks out, and I'll let you finish the popcorn?"

"You'll let me?" Jerusha felt like laughing, surprised at how his understanding turned her anger into more pleasant feelings.

Keith's eyes softened with her laughter. "Pretty high-handed, aren't I? Guess it comes from too long in the army."

By the time the guests finally left, Jerusha couldn't believe how she'd enjoyed the evening. Keith seemed always on hand to make her laugh or draw her into another game. He and Maisie were the last to leave.

"This was a great idea, Rev," he said. "We should do it more often."

"I'll agree to anything as long as it includes Miss Clarke's ice cream," David replied.

Keith's eyes took on what Jerusha recognized as his teasing twinkle. "Which means I don't have to bring popcorn next time?"

"Not so fast. The popcorn fills people up so there's more ice cream left for me."

Maisie blushed and grinned. Jerusha noticed for the first time how pretty her friend looked, especially when her eyes glowed. A strange silence gripped the four briefly.

Keith cleared his throat. "Miss Clarke, may I escort you back to the boardinghouse?"

"Thank you. Mrs. Barry gets irritable when I come home alone."

Keith reached for her coat, but David beat him to it. "Thanks again for helping Jerusha yesterday, Miss Clarke." He settled the coat on her shoulders with an unfamiliar expression on his face.

A wink from Keith caught Jerusha's attention. "Was it my imagination or did you enjoy yourself tonight?"

Her smile felt like it came from the happiest part of her heart. "I did, thanks to you."

"I'm glad you didn't let our resident fly in the ointment spoil your evening." He patted her shoulder. "See you soon. Don't work yourself too hard, or I'll have to take your brother out behind the woodshed."

David's chuckle blended with Maisie's laugh. "You should know by now, Corporal, how hard it is to slow my sister down when she has the working bit between her teeth."

Keith grinned. "Take care of yourself, too, Rev."

Long after the cold blast of Keith and Maisie's departure had vanished, a strange quiet lay over the parsonage. David had quickly bid Jerusha good night and vanished up to his loft bedroom. She noticed his lamp still burning even after she'd finished dishes and straightened the meeting room. Though glad to be alone, she didn't feel sleepy yet. Maybe this would be a good time to rediscover her Bible, which had sat untouched on the shelf by David's desk since they'd moved to Dawson Creek. A small piece of paper protruded from the top edge. She opened carefully to the place marked, only to see handwriting on the marker.

Jerusha,

    I've been expecting you to turn to Scripture soon. Nothing anyone says about God can replace what He says about Himself. I John is a good place to start. I'm praying for you.

                           Keith

Chapter 14

Lewis arrived shortly after breakfast on Saturday morning to take Jerusha out to the farm. Thankfully, he seemed content to ride in silence. She found her mind occupied with Keith, trying not to be disappointed he had not appeared this morning to give her a ride. *He's already told you he's not interested in romance,* she reminded herself. *Besides, he can't just leave his army duties whenever he wants. Even if he were romantically inclined, he'd want someone like Maisie who shares his faith.* This brought her thoughts around to the Scripture passages she'd been reading whenever she found time. She'd followed Keith's suggestion and discovered a wealth of hope in the little book of I John.

Once at the farm, she found herself too busy for any kind of thinking. Colin and Bradley were so excited to see her, they wanted to be wherever she was. That slowed her cleaning and laundry considerably, but their endless chatter made the routine tasks more enjoyable.

"Auntie 'Rusha, Daddy says we can get a puppy when spring comes," Colin informed her with bright eyes.

"What's spring?" Bradley asked.

"It's when the snow melts," Colin informed him disdainfully.

Bradley wasn't impressed. "I asked Auntie 'Rusha. What's spring, Auntie 'Rusha?"

She looked over at Sheila, who watched her sons' antics with a grin. Sheila just shrugged her shoulders. Jerusha knew if she didn't handle the question just right, she'd have one or both boys highly displeased.

"Well, Colin's mostly right, Bradley, but there's more to spring than just melting snow. Spring is when the sunshine feels warm enough that you don't need a coat to go outside. There's usually lots of mud, which little boys like but mommies don't."

"Do aunties like mud?" Bradley had developed a love for impossible questions.

Jerusha smiled at him. "This one doesn't."

"Why?" Colin's curiosity had been aroused.

"Because everything gets dirty, and I like clean." She continued scrubbing the floor around the cookstove.

"Mommy does, too." Colin's face showed his disgust. "She even wants us clean, so she scrubs our faces and makes us take baths."

Both Sheila and Jerusha laughed. "I think your daddy likes clean," Jerusha pointed out.

"But he works in the barn!" Bradley seemed to feel the two ideas were incompatible.

"What does he do first thing when he comes inside?"

"He kisses Mommy!" Now the boys giggled in unison.

Jerusha grinned at Sheila. "Then what?"

The two thought for a moment, then the disappointing light dawned. "He washes his face and hands," Bradley said.

Colin's mind had already jumped to a new conclusion. "Does that mean I have to like clean when I get big?"

"I wouldn't worry about it too much now," Jerusha reassured him, picking up the bucket to dump the dirty water outside.

"How is the town drainage system?" Sheila asked when Jerusha came back in, shivering from her coatless exposure to winter.

"Still as useless as ever." Again, she noticed her strange resignation rather than irritation.

"And running water?"

"We have a well and an indoor pump, so I don't notice. But Maisie says the water system's just as bad as the drainage. Apparently the army is predicting improvement in the spring." She moved pots of heating water around on the stove. "Colin, would you bring me your dirty clothes from upstairs?"

"I can do it, too," Bradley asserted.

"All right. That would be a big help."

Strutting importantly, the two scrambled for the stairs. "Any errands for me?" Sheila's face took on an innocent expression.

"Not a chance," Jerusha said firmly. "Rest while you can."

She paused in her laundry to make some soup and biscuits for lunch. The work went more quickly after Lewis sent the boys upstairs for naps.

"A short sleep probably wouldn't hurt you, either," he told Sheila, brushing her cheek gently with his fingers.

She gave him the gentle smile that always left a hollow feeling in Jerusha's middle. "I'd rather visit with Jerusha."

He nodded and clumped back out to the barnyard.

"So tell me the news." Sheila turned her rocking chair to face Jerusha's laundry tubs.

"I'm sure I'm not the best source for news. I don't have much contact with people outside the church." Jerusha scrubbed at some food stains on the front of a small shirt.

"I know you're always busy, which is one reason why I'm so grateful you've come. What do you do, besides laundry, I mean?" Sheila's laughter made Jerusha smile.

"David always has a steady stream of visitors, so I try to keep lots of bread on hand, and other goodies when I have time. Meals, regular house-keeping, and I've been doing some reading lately." All at once, she wanted to tell Sheila what she might have found.

"Reading? Like what?"

"The book of I John."

Sheila waited so long to reply, Jerusha looked up to see what she might be thinking. A brilliant smile rewarded her. "I'm so glad! Is it making any sense?"

"Some. It talks about God's love as if it were a fact, just like the sun coming up in the morning."

" 'In this was manifested the love of God toward us, because that God sent his only begotten Son into the world, that we might live through him,' " Sheila quoted softly. "Are you remembering what the next verse be saying?"

Jerusha nodded, turning the handle on the wringer while she pushed socks and shirts through to the rinse water. "It seemed so strange to me when I first read it, it stuck in my memory. 'Herein is love, not that we loved God, but that he loved us, and sent his Son to be the propitiation for our sins.' I had to ask David about the propitiation part."

"And?" Sheila's face was alight with interest.

"He said it has to do with turning away God's wrath by offering a gift. In other words, God was angry with man's sin, so He sent His Son Jesus to die and become the sacrifice that would turn His anger away."

Sheila's voice was hushed. "Sure, and that's a lot of love!"

"You'd think I wouldn't have any more questions, wouldn't you?" Jerusha concentrated on scrubbing the dirt out of Lewis's work pants.

"Maybe. What are you thinking?"

Jerusha pushed a pair of pants through the wringer before replying. "The book of I John seems to be divided equally between reassurances of God's love and statements about how we'll act and feel if we know God's love. I no sooner feel hopeful about it than I read one of those verses that shows me how far away I am."

Sheila walked over to where Jerusha bent over the scrub board and placed an arm around her friend's shoulders. "Those verses aren't there to be telling you what you need to be in order to be loved by God. They are for telling us what we'll be like when we know God's love for ourselves. The first step is to be believing what He says about His love. Sure and the rest will come."

Jerusha smiled her thanks for the reassurance and kept scrubbing. It still sounded too easy, yet at the same time, impossibly difficult.

Sheila let her work in silence for several minutes, then asked another question. "Has your army friend been visiting lately?"

Jerusha felt her cheeks warm. "He brought a bunch of army guys over a few nights ago for a party. We had a lot of fun."

"Sure, and is this Jerusha Porter I hear talking about fun?" Sheila's voice sounded playfully scandalized, her Irish brogue thickening. "He's good for you, I'm thinking."

"He has been a good friend." Jerusha made the statement more for her own benefit than her friend's.

"Friend? Aye. He was feeling a way more than friendship the night I dressed you up, 'tis sure!"

Jerusha tried to ignore the hope fluttering through her. "I'm sure it wasn't, Sheila."

"And why must that be?" Sheila's voice was heavy with Irish disapproval.

"He told me he'd never ask any woman to marry an army man. Besides, I'm not the kind he'd love." She dropped wet clothes into the clothesbasket with more force than necessary.

"Faith, girl, and why not?"

To her annoyance, tears stung her eyes. "He'll choose someone sweet and gentle, someone who sees God like he does. I didn't come out here to get married, anyway."

"Jerusha, you're for trying to make yourself good enough for him, just like you are for God. Love doesn't come with a measuring stick. It just comes, surprising you with the joy of it all. He is saying he wouldn't ask a woman to marry him, but I'm thinking he never counted on meeting a pretty little preacher's sister with a kinder heart than she knows and a true desire to know God."

Any hope generated by Sheila's encouragement dribbled away as weeks passed without any word from Keith. Though she didn't want to, Jerusha found herself thinking more frequently of the compassion in his kind, gray eyes, the infectious grin that made her want to laugh, even the way he looked shorn right after he'd visited the army barber for another brush cut for his blond hair. Maybe he got sent overseas as he'd feared. Perhaps he'd realized how incompatible their ideas of God were and asked for a transfer so he wouldn't have to explain. *That's not the kind of man he is,* her heart told her. *He'll be back.*

Her tension grew. Her Bible sat beside her bed, once again neglected as she kept herself too busy to think. Mrs. Barry's boarders seemed to use more linen than ever, and countless guests consumed her baking as fast as she could make it. When she went to bed in the evenings, fragments of Scripture chased each other through her mind. She wondered if the God she was beginning to find would vanish, too. Even Saturdays at the farm seemed difficult. Such a Saturday brought her to the breaking point.

As usual, the boys had hung around her knees, asking questions, telling stories, and generally getting in the way while she worked. She'd just finished scrubbing the kitchen floor when Bradley came running over to show her a picture he'd drawn. He tripped over his own feet and grabbed the laundry tub to steady himself. The hose came loose from the tub, pouring filthy, soapy water all over.

She didn't see the apologetic little boy. She only felt the effects of sleepless nights and unrelenting tension increased by a messy job she didn't want to do. "I wish you would stay out of the way! Look at the mess you've made." She hated the sharpness in her voice as much as the tears sliding down her cheeks. Clamping her lips together, she concentrated on wiping up the water.

Bradley retreated to his mother's arms. Jerusha heard Sheila explaining that Auntie 'Rusha knew Bradley hadn't meant to make a mess, but that she was tired today. She hated herself for having taken out her frustrations on the small boy. Yet if she softened enough to apologize, she might start crying uncontrollably. The boys stayed clear of her work area for the rest of the afternoon. Thorny remorse prevented her from appreciating the peace. She made their favorite oatmeal cookies while preparing supper for the family and hugged them both extra tight before she left.

Bradley's lower lip trembled. "I'm really sorry, Auntie 'Rusha."

She forced herself to smile. "I'm sorry, too, Bradley. I know it wasn't your fault."

"It wasn't your fault, either." He wrapped his chubby arms around her neck and squeezed again. "Are you coming back sometime?"

"I think Sheila ought to be able to help next week," Lewis offered. "Then after that, I'll help her so you can have your Saturdays back."

Jerusha felt no better. Back at the parsonage, she prepared and served David's supper in a fog of preoccupation. Having spent so much time in

Sheila's kitchen where the drain worked, she unthinkingly dumped her dishwater down the sink. Thirty minutes later, it still hadn't drained, and she burst into tears. "I hate this horrible place! I just want to go home!" She collapsed at the table and burst into tears.

"Rushi!" David hurried from his desk to her side. "What is it, Sister? I thought you were becoming happy here."

"I was," she sniffed. "But lately, everything's going wrong."

"Like what?" He rubbed her neck in his familiar comforting gesture.

She related her experience with Bradley, and Lewis's comment about next week. "He didn't say it, but I feel like they don't want me around anymore."

"That's not true, Rushi," David replied calmly. "They were talking to me Wednesday night about how much you've helped. They have been concerned that you've been working so hard lately, though, and asked me if I felt two more Saturdays would be too much. But that's not all. You miss Keith, too, don't you?"

She wanted to deny any such emotional attachment, but the mention of his name made her sob even harder.

"Hey, Rushi, it's all right. He'll come back." David's gentle tone made the words more than glib assurance.

"What if he doesn't?"

"I can't answer that. Have you tried talking it over with our Heavenly Father?"

Jerusha shook her head, looking at her brother through her tears. "I'm still not sure how I feel about God."

David dried her cheeks with the backs of his fingers. "Maybe that's the heart of your struggle. You're trying to figure Him out instead of simply letting Him love you."

"I've been trying to feel His love, but it doesn't work."

"Love and trust go together, Rushi. You can't have one without the other. You've been reading Scripture. You know He says He loves you. If you trust what He says, then you can simply accept His love as fact. Until you decide to trust His word, you'll continue trying to live up to an impossible dream of what you ought to be. I would think acceptance is much easier." He smiled gently. "May I pray with you?"

When she nodded, he grasped both her hands in his and bowed his head. "Father, You know we've both come to Dawson Creek because we felt You called us here. You also know how hard it's been for Jerusha to adjust. She's been searching for Your love, Father. I know You're just waiting for her to accept what You offer. I'm asking You tonight to show her how real You are and what Your love is really like. Give her peace, Father, and please protect Keith wherever he is. In Jesus' name, Amen."

To Jerusha's relief, he didn't release her hands immediately. His words and his prayer had rekindled the spark of hope she'd felt before Keith left. She felt if she didn't acknowledge it verbally, she might lose it again. "God, it seems strange to call You Father since I've not really known what a father is like. But You've shown me in the Bible that Your love is real and that I don't need to do anything special to deserve it. I accept Your love, Father. Please teach me how to know You like David and Keith do. David says trust and love work together, so I'm telling You that I choose to trust You. Amen."

David squeezed her hands so hard they hurt. When she looked up at him, tears spilled from his eyes. "You don't know how long I've prayed for this, Rushi. Keith's got to come back just so he can find out how our prayers have been answered."

She didn't feel sure anything significant had taken place. No blinding flash had taken away her doubts. But she did agree with him about Keith's return. A strange spark of hope told her he would be back.

Chapter 15

Jerusha woke Sunday morning feeling more refreshed than she had in months. She expected to hear birds singing outside her window until she remembered it was only the first week of April. Though snow was beginning to melt, she'd been told spring didn't come to this country until late May. Why, then, did she feel so lighthearted? Slowly, last night's conversation and prayers returned to memory. It seemed incredible her simple prayer could have made such a difference. David wouldn't be ready for breakfast for awhile yet. Maybe another look at I John would explain things. She opened her Bible and read until the eighth verse of the second chapter. "The darkness is past, and the true light now shineth." That exactly described her feelings—like someone had turned on a warm, wonderful light inside her.

This would be a perfect morning for David's favorite breakfast, dried apple coffeecake. While she worked, she hummed a tune from her days in Sunday school. "I am so glad that Jesus loves me, Jesus loves me, Jesus loves me. I am so glad that Jesus loves me. Jesus loves even me." Somehow it actually made sense this morning. Of course, she didn't have to live up to anything to receive God's love. If she could earn it, it wouldn't be Divine love. She still wasn't sure how a holy God could love an imperfect human such as herself, but somehow it didn't really matter anymore. He said He loved, and for Jerusha, His assurance had become enough. An unfamiliar delightful emotion bubbled in her—kind of like contentment, but with lots of happiness mixed in, though more than happiness. She remembered something Sheila had said. "Love just comes, surprising you with the joy of it all." Was this joy? Whatever its definition, Jerusha wanted to feel it forever.

Sheila had actually been talking about Keith, she recalled. The familiar wondering anxiety encroached again. Jerusha felt her elation withering. *But I promised God last night I'd trust. Maybe I should trust Keith, too.* It wasn't easy, overcoming a habit of worry developed over years, but the simple resolve to try lifted her spirits again.

When their congregation gathered for worship, Jerusha experienced more unfamiliar emotions. She no longer felt threatened by the people gathering in the meeting room. She saw on their faces a bit of the joy she'd been

333

revelling in all morning. In fact, she wanted to hug each one of them, even the ones she had resented for not doing more to help David. When Maisie arrived, she couldn't help herself. She wrapped her friend in a joyous, strangling embrace.

When she could breathe again, Maisie laughed. "I don't believe I know you anymore, Miss Porter. What's happened to my favorite uptight Miss Minister's Sister?"

Jerusha grinned, suddenly embarrassed by her display, glad only a few folks had arrived yet. "Last night David and I prayed. I decided to quit trying to figure God out and simply accept His promise to love me."

"Oh, Rushi, I'm just delighted!" This time Jerusha received the bone-crushing hug.

" 'Tis good news over here, I'm thinking." Sheila's familiar Irish lilt interrupted the girls' happy conversation.

"The best," Maisie assured her. "Jerusha discovered last night God's not her enemy."

Sheila hugged both her friends ecstatically. "No wonder your eyes be sparkling. Now if we can get your army friend back in town!"

Jerusha felt her cheeks warm, but her heart didn't droop. "It's okay if he doesn't."

"Sure, and he won't be able to stay away." Sheila winked, then joined her husband and sons who were already seated.

Maisie nudged Jerusha. "Look over there. I think a couple of little people want your attention."

Bradley and Colin were both waving as enthusiastically as they could without attracting a reprimand from their dad. Jerusha's eyes stung. She still felt badly for yesterday's scene, but it appeared both boys had already forgotten it. She smiled and waved back. Rather than sitting in her customary place by herself at the end of the first row, she joined Maisie and Mrs. Barry a little further back. To her delight, she found some of the hymns exactly expressed her emotions. When members of the congregation gave testimonies, she no longer felt like she was listening to meaningless prattle. And David's sermon! It seemed like he'd written it just for her, though she knew he wouldn't embarrass her that way.

His text was Romans 8:15–17. "For ye have not received the spirit of bondage again to fear; but ye have received the Spirit of adoption, whereby we cry, Abba, Father. The Spirit itself beareth witness with our spirit, that we are the children of God: And if children, then heirs; heirs of God, and joint-heirs with Christ." He looked around at the congregation with joy lighting his eyes. "I've come to realize in recent weeks how often our perceptions of God stand between us and all He has to offer. We often get the idea that we have to earn His love. Yet He says here that He gives us His spirit, which causes us to come to Him like little children do to their daddies. Kevin, are you afraid of your daddy?"

Kevin Pierce turned bashful, simply shaking his head and snuggling closer to Dr. Pierce.

"How about you, Colin?"

"Only if I make Mommy work too hard, 'cause then I know I'll get spanked."

The congregation laughed, Sheila blushed, and David continued. "But after the spanking, you're not afraid anymore, are you?"

"Nope." The answer came emphatically.

"That's the kind of relationship God wants with us as His children," David explained. "There are times our sin gets between us and Him, but Jesus' death is the solution we need. His sacrifice so fully atones for our sins—past, present, and future—that God is able to write them off as if they didn't exist.

"But there's more. Verse 17 says we're joint-heirs with Jesus. That means everything He has is ours. Ephesians 2:14 says He is peace, so we have peace. Other scriptures tell us of His righteousness, so we are righteous. Now look at the last five verses of Romans 8. Paul makes an incredible list of circumstances and events that could, in our minds, keep us apart from this incredible love. Yet he ends the chapter by saying none of those things will be able to separate us from Him. We may choose to live like it isn't there, but our decision can't affect His reality. When we're ready to accept it, He's still waiting to bestow His wealth on us."

The remainder of the day continued in the same marvelous theme. Maisie and Mrs. Barry stayed for lunch, and for once, Jerusha simply enjoyed having company. A collection of young people showed up later in the afternoon. Without any sense of inadequacy, Jerusha offered them refreshments. She felt like she'd been miraculously released from a prison built from her own expectations.

She filled the coffeepot for what seemed like the hundredth time. How long would this joyous miracle last? The thought briefly clouded her mental landscape. Squaring her shoulders, she decided to handle it if and when it happened. For now, she'd enjoy the euphoria. While waiting for the coffee, she prepared popcorn. There were a few baked goodies left, and Mrs. Barry had given them a couple dozen of her muffins that could be cut in half to go around. After passing around the food, she refilled cups.

"You're handling this well, Rushi!" David commented quietly as she leaned over his shoulder to pour him more coffee.

A joking retort popped into her mind and slid out her mouth before she realized what she'd said. "And what would you do if I weren't around anymore?"

His eyes widened for a moment until he realized she was teasing, then he teased right back. "I'd just have to find a pretty girl and marry her."

Sylvia Irvine and a couple of soldiers arrived at that moment, increasing the comment's significance in Jerusha's mind. Her better sense told her David wouldn't even consider falling in love with Sylvia, but the old obsession didn't die easily. She feared Sylvia more than any of the other girls, perhaps because the banker's daughter had a way of making Jerusha feel like a mere servant girl in spite of her honeyed words. Jerusha stayed by the stove, watching the crowded sitting room. Sylvia had taken up her customary position as close to David as possible. David smiled at her, and she fluttered her eyelashes at him. He started visiting with her, so she beckoned one of the soldiers into the conversation so she could flirt with both men at once. Just when Jerusha thought she could stand no more, David's sermon came back to her. "No circumstance or event can keep us apart from God's love." *Not even Sylvia?* she asked herself. From somewhere deep inside she felt reassured. Not even Sylvia could touch the deep joy she'd found.

To Jerusha's amazement, the joy continued. One of the hotels asked her to fill in for a week for their laundry lady who had sprained her wrist. While David and Maisie helped as much as they could, Jerusha still wondered if there would be enough hours in each day. Yet, the work got done. She even had time in the evenings for Scripture reading with David, a treat she anticipated throughout the day. His sermon from Romans 8 had drawn her from I John to Romans. In the mornings, she read by herself and in the evenings discussed with David what she'd read. She felt an unquenchable thirst to know more. Her awareness of Divine love still felt tenuous. Maybe finding out more about God would strengthen her hold on His reality.

David exuded more enthusiasm than usual. Members of their congregation were beginning to invite others to the services. Both Sunday and Wednesday services had filled the meeting room almost to capacity last week. The increased congregation meant more visitors to the parsonage and more demands on David's time, but Jerusha no longer battled resentment. She hoped everyone who came would encounter the same God she'd found.

One of their rare evenings alone made Jerusha wonder if her newly ordered world had begun to unravel. David asked a quiet question from where he sat at the table while she washed supper dishes. "What would you think of my getting married, Rushi?"

Images of Sylvia moving into the parsonage filled Jerusha's mind. Just as quickly, she knew it wouldn't work, and she tried to envision a steady stream of visitors in and out of a fancy house like the Irvines'. That didn't seem feasible, either. "It would depend on who you wanted to marry." She kept her eyes on the dishes.

A long pause followed. Then, so quietly she almost didn't hear him, David replied. "I'd like to ask Maisie Clarke to become my wife."

Jerusha whirled around in surprise, the soapy plate she held slipping to the floor. "Maisie?" she squeaked.

"I'm not trying to take your friend away, I promise. In fact, I thought it might be easier for the three of us to live together since you two are so close." An unfamiliar blush tinged his face.

The blush calmed Jerusha's shock, pushing her to tease him a bit. "You mean you decided you wanted to marry her just so your wife and your sister would get along?"

He reddened further, even while his twinkling eyes acknowledged her humor. "No. I love her more than I thought possible. I just don't want you to feel pushed out of either of our lives if she says yes."

"You haven't asked her yet?"

He shook his head. "I wanted your opinion first. I hoped it would give me the courage to put my feelings into words."

David lacked courage? The thought didn't fit in Jerusha's mind. "Does she have any clue how you feel?"

"I hope so." He traced circles on the tabletop. "We spent a lot of time together while you were out at the Murrays' and I was helping her and Mrs. Barry with laundry. I discovered her tender heart, her marvelous sense of humor, and most of all, her passionate love for God. It wasn't until after you came back, though, that I realized I love her. I've gone over to the boarding-house several Saturdays while you've been out at the farm, and I think she returns my feelings. But I won't know until I ask her straight out and the mere thought gives me the trembles."

The sight of her brother trembling at the thought of proposing to her best friend almost gave Jerusha the giggles. She tried to recall anything Maisie had said or done that she might be able to use to encourage him. But it seemed she'd been so involved in her own turmoil, she'd missed any hint of this developing romance. "I wish I knew what to say, David. I was so afraid you were falling for Sylvia Irvine I never even thought of you being interested in anyone else."

His head snapped up. "Sylvia Irvine? Why would I fall for her?"

Now Jerusha felt embarrassed. "Because she tries so hard to get your attention. Besides, she always looks so beautiful and acts like such a lady."

"Fine clothes are well and good in their place, but they can't cover a person's heart." He walked over to put his hands on Jerusha's shoulders. "Even if Maisie turns me down, I want you to know I'll never consider any woman who isn't kind to my sister. I won't abandon you, Rushi."

She blinked away unwanted tears, wrapping her arms around her brother in the first hug she'd initiated toward him in years. "Thanks, David. You don't know how much that means to me." She pulled back to look into his eyes with a grin. "But for tonight, I think you have more important business than settling my feminine fears. Go get your preachin' suit on, or should I call it your courtin' suit, and get out of here."

He didn't return for several hours, which Jerusha took as a good sign. Intuition told her Maisie would accept his proposal. But where would they put a third person in this tiny cabin? Would she and Maisie be able to work together harmoniously? Maybe she should consider taking Maisie's place at Mrs. Barry's. Would she ever have the opportunity to make the decision Maisie was making? If not, would she live as an old maid aunt with David and his wife forever? What if his wife got tired of having her around all the time? *Nothing "shall be able to separate us from the love of God. . ."* The fragment of Scripture calmed her tumbling thoughts, though she wished she could answer all the questions. She finally gave up waiting for David and went to bed. As she fell asleep, the verse played through her mind like a lullaby. *Nothing "shall be able to separate us from the love of God. . ."*

David's glowing face the next morning told her Maisie's answer, though he seemed to feel an explanation was needed. "She said yes, Rushi! I can't believe how blessed I am. Mrs. Barry wants to throw an engagement party here tonight during the youth meeting, and she said to tell you she'll bring everything. I stayed so late because we just had so much to talk about." He chattered on while Jerusha served breakfast.

She bent over his chair to hug him, delighted for his happiness. "I'm excited for you, David. Now, will you please hush and eat?"

He grinned self-consciously and consumed three bowls of oatmeal, then decided he needed to take a walk "to clear his mind." Jerusha giggled to herself as the door shut behind him, relieved he was getting out of the house. She wanted to give it a top-to-bottom cleaning. In his present mood, he'd only get in the way. She worked steadily, pondering life's changes. Like the contentment that now filled her days instead of the resentment of not so long ago. What a miracle her simple prayer had brought about! Yet another simple prayer remained unanswered. As she was learning to do each time she thought of Keith, she asked again for Divine protection for him.

Hunger rumblings brought her work to a halt about midafternoon. When she realized the time, she wondered briefly why David hadn't returned. *He probably "wandered" by the boardinghouse and stayed for lunch*, she told herself with a grin. Tonight would be a good time to serve a special meal. After putting her lunch dishes by the sink, she rummaged through the box of wrapped meat that sat frozen in the coldest corner of the porch. Gratefully remembering the members of their congregation who kept them supplied with meat from their own herds, flocks, and hunting expeditions, she found a chicken. It had been a long time since she'd made fried chicken, David's favorite dinner. She still had enough potatoes to make mashed potatoes, all creamy and fluffy like he liked them. Some canned corn would also be nice, and how would dried apples work in apple pie? Feeling reckless, she decided to try it.

David finally returned around four. "Sorry I was gone so long, Rushi. I just stopped for a moment at the boardinghouse, and Mrs. Barry invited me for lunch. Then I got to helping Maisie with some cleaning, and I forgot the time."

Jerusha just laughed at him. "I'm not expecting your brain to be in working order. Did you happen to notice whether the ladies mentioned what time they'll be arriving tonight?"

He looked faintly embarrassed. "I invited them for supper. I hope you don't mind."

She could only laugh again. "Not at all. I just hope you guys haven't planned a long engagement. Six months of this could get stressful."

"June 8," he announced, climbing the ladder to the loft.

It took Jerusha a moment to realize he'd told her the wedding date. Supper was an hilariously happy affair. None of the four could stop smiling, though Mrs. Barry and Jerusha found their conversation more coherent than David and Maisie's. Maisie tried to include the others, but her eyes kept looking back in David's direction. His gaze never wavered from her face. Mrs. Barry shooed them into the sitting room after dessert. "Neither of you is good for anything tonight, so just go somewhere out of the way. Now, dear," she addressed Jerusha. "I think I can find my way around in here if you'd like to go change into something festive."

Jerusha started to protest that she had nothing, then remembered the burgundy dress Sheila had given her. "Thanks. I'll be right back."

"There's no need to rush." Mrs. Barry's smile looked purely maternal.

Jerusha intended to slip into the dress quickly, tie on an apron, and return to the kitchen. Instead she found herself sitting beside the dress on the bed, remembering the first time she'd worn it, the way Keith's gaze had followed her as David's did Maisie. Whether or not he loved her, he'd promised her his friendship. She sent up another fervent prayer for his return, at least so she could tell him how she'd changed. Once she had donned the dress, she realized her hair wouldn't do at all. She combed it out carefully, then tried to arrange it as Sheila had. The small mirror on her wall twenty minutes later indicated the time had been well spent.

"What a beauty!" David whistled when she came back to the kitchen.

She hid her feelings behind a laugh. "I didn't think you'd even notice!"

"Of course I notice. My fianc—" He choked on the word with a silly grin, then tried again. "My fiancée will be the most beautiful woman here tonight, and my sister will be a very close second."

Maisie beamed. "You do look gorgeous, Jerusha."

Guests started arriving less than half an hour later. Mrs. Barry had outdone herself with a lavish spread of goodies.

"Where did you get the sugar for all this?" Jerusha asked, thinking of how often she'd tried unsuccessfully to buy the sweetener. The local stores seemed unable to keep it in stock for more than a couple of days. It was just one more challenge that accompanied living in an overcrowded town.

"I have my ways." The older lady's eyes twinkled. "Some of the squares are made with honey from my son's farm."

Though David had planned to keep his announcement for later in the evening, his and Maisie's faces gave the secret away. The word spread as quickly as people shed their coats and boots. Sylvia's eyes looked like little bits of blue granite when one of the soldiers gave her the news, though she kept a smile firmly in place. "Maybe you should offer Miss Porter your job at the boardinghouse so you can have the preacher all to yourself," she suggested to Maisie with a shrill titter.

"Never!" Maisie declared, with a harsher expression on her face than Jerusha had ever seen. "I wouldn't let her leave us for anything other than a husband of her own."

Jerusha looked quickly to David, who winked and smiled. *He really did mean what he said about marrying someone who would love me, too.* The thought restored her earlier sense of well-being. Though the details might not be easy, she could feel enough love among the three of them to overcome the challenges.

Mrs. Barry had even brought extra glasses, which she now handed around. "I thought lemonade would be a nice treat for tonight. Please don't take a drink until everyone gets a glass." She continued passing the glasses around, taking the final glass for herself. "The world uses alcoholic beverages to drink a toast for special occasions. I'd like to propose a blessing to which you can agree by raising your glass and saying 'Amen.' David and Maisie, we all wish for you God's best as you build your home and do the work He gives you. We pray He'll give you many years together, each marked with a love more mature than the year before."

Jerusha echoed "Amen" with the others, feeling a tightness in her throat as she looked at her brother and her friend, their eyes filled with love for each other. Someone cracked a joke she didn't quite hear, and the ensuing laughter almost drowned out a knock at the door.

Chapter 16

A cold blast just before she reached the entry told Jerusha their visitor hadn't waited to be invited inside. Her eyes had barely registered the delightfully familiar grin and gray eyes under a khaki hat before she was engulfed in a cold bear hug. "I've missed you!" a welcome gruff voice declared.

Her arms wrapped themselves around him instinctively. "Keith! Welcome back!"

He pushed her away to study her face, then smiled into her eyes. "You look like you're doing wonderfully well. What's the noise about?"

Jerusha laughed joyously. "David's engaged to Maisie Clarke. Mrs. Barry threw a party for them tonight." Slivers of pain dimmed the happy twinkle in his eyes. She looked for words to ease his hurt, hoping she hadn't caused it. "He'll be so glad you managed to be here!"

Keith dropped his gaze for a few moments, then his eyes cleared when he looked at her again. "I'm glad, too. Let's go help them celebrate."

The merrymaking continued, taking on the joyous sparkle Jerusha remembered from youth gatherings right after she returned from the farm. It was well after ten when the last guest departed.

Keith slapped David's back. "There's no need to ask if you're sure about this, Rev. That goofy grin tells it all."

With an arm around her shoulders, David hugged Maisie closer to him. "You know what Proverbs says, Keith. 'Whoso findeth a wife findeth a good thing. . . .' "

"Yeah, I know. I'm glad for you both." He grinned at them while picking up cups to take to the kitchen.

Jerusha wondered if anyone else heard the strangling sound in his voice. She wanted to wrap her arms around him and take his pain into her own heart, even though she had no idea what weighed on him so intensely. She absentmindedly wiped dishes as Mrs. Barry washed.

"There. We have your kitchen back in order," Mrs. Barry announced. "Amazingly enough, they didn't eat all the cake or apple muffins, so I'm leaving them for you and David, though I get the feeling I'll be cooking for him more often than you will." She fixed Jerusha with a direct look. "Promise me if you get to feeling abandoned or left out, you'll invite yourself to the boardinghouse for dinner."

Jerusha's eyes stung from unexpected tears. The affection offered by this perceptive lady seemed too good to be true. She nodded. "I promise."

"I'll be doing what I can to keep her from getting too lonely, Mrs. Barry." Keith's hands came to rest lightly on Jerusha's shoulders.

Mrs. Barry's eyes twinkled with understanding and something else Jerusha couldn't identify. "I'll hold you to that, soldier."

"I recognize that tone of voice, Mrs. B.," Maisie called. "Are you matchmaking again?"

"Of course not," the older lady declared indignantly while Jerusha felt her cheeks warm and Keith's hands tremble on her shoulders. "I'm just making sure Jerusha doesn't feel forgotten while you and the reverend wander around with your heads in the clouds. Reverend, I think I'm ready to go. I'd appreciate it if you'd escort us home, though you're welcome to use my parlor as long as you like."

Now Maisie's cheeks turned pink. "She means she wants to get home, but she doesn't want us to feel in a hurry to say good night. Subtle as a tank, isn't she?"

"Mrs. Barry, you're a jewel." David hugged her shoulders. "Of course I don't mind taking you home, though I might tie up your parlor for quite awhile."

Maisie swatted his arm. "You'd better. We still have a lot of planning to do."

The three teased each other all the way out the door. Jerusha could hear David's laugh echoing from outside.

"I've always been afraid marriage would take him away from me," she mused aloud. "But he's so happy right now, I don't care anymore."

Keith leaned against the counter, facing her. "Have they talked with you yet about your plans?"

She laughed. "They're not at the practical stage yet. However, they've both told me how much they want me to continue living here after they're married."

Keith looked around the cabin. "This little place could get crowded."

"We'll manage," she reassured him with a smile.

He looked at her intently. "Rushi, what's happened to you?"

"What do you mean?"

He took her hand and drew her toward the sitting room, where he pulled her onto the padded bench against the wall. "Before I left, you would have been in a panic about David's getting married, with a thousand questions about the future." He chuckled softly. "I kind of think you might even have been talking about hopping the first train back to Winnipeg. Instead, I find you smiling and at peace. What's happened?"

She didn't know how to begin. His absence had been one of the most insistent issues pushing her toward surrender, but she couldn't tell him so. "Do you want just an overview or all the details?"

He slouched back against the wall, his legs out in front of him, and gave her the incredible grin that had brightened her memories. "I've got the rest of the night if you need it. All the details, please."

She told him about continuing to help at the Murrays and the additional laundry workload she'd picked up. "You weren't around anymore, and I kept thinking you'd been sent somewhere dangerous. When I tried to sleep, all my questions and fears and wonderings about God and life in general muddled my brain, so I'd just lay there staring at the darkness. I'd been reading in my Bible, and everything I read contradicted so many things I thought were important. Finally, a couple of Saturdays ago, I lost my temper at Bradley over something he didn't mean to do. I realized I had to change something before I fell apart completely. That night David and I talked about it and he helped me see my problem was in trying to figure God out rather than simply taking Him at His word. He prayed for me and I told God how I felt. It felt like somebody had finally turned on a light after I'd been stumbling around for ages in darkness. Every time I start to feel overwhelmed, I remind myself God loves me and choose to trust Him. It's worked every time so far."

"And it won't ever stop working. That's the basics of faith—knowing who God is and choosing to believe. Peace looks good on you, Rushi." He shifted on the bench, but retained his gentle grip on her hand. His smile held something that made Jerusha's heart pound and left a trembly feeling in her middle. "Your discovery is an answer to my most heartfelt prayers. It also makes what I want to tell you and ask you easier. Though it's what I came for tonight, I don't think I could go through with it if I didn't know you'll have Divine love supporting you."

Her throat constricted. Was this good-bye? She forced herself to take a deep breath and hear him out.

He seemed to sense her apprehension and reached for her other hand. His felt chilly. "I have to apologize again for leaving without telling you. Unfortunately, that's the way the army works—everything happens right now unless, of course, you need it right now. In that case you have to wait at least a month."

He smiled tightly at his own joke. After a heavy sigh and a long pause, he continued. "Though nobody's supposed to know this, we're in a series of false maneuvers designed to confuse the Japanese. The end of the maneuvers for all of us will be Alaska, and from there, probably overseas."

Jerusha couldn't stop the whimper of surprise, which she tried to cover with a smile. "When do you leave?"

"Day after tomorrow." He didn't look at her now. He still held her hands, stroking her fingers with his thumb. "Jerusha, I think I fell in love with you that night you almost fainted by David's bed. I've alternately analyzed and ignored my feelings because I didn't want you to be hurt further by what may or may not happen to me. I thought we could just be friends, allowing me the pleasure of your company without any painful emotional ties." He lifted his gaze to her eyes, revealing infinite tenderness shadowed by an agony for the future. "Rushi, you've become part of my heart. The joy in your eyes makes me wonder if I can ever love you any more than I do right now. Much as I'd like to do differently, I won't ask for a commitment right now. I'd have to be some kind of cad to ask you to love me, then disappear, maybe forever. However, if I'm still alive when this horrible war is over, may I come looking for you?"

A million thoughts and images went through Jerusha's mind while she looked into Keith's eyes, drinking in the unfathomable love she saw there. This seemed too sudden, too intense. How could she live up to his kind of faith? He could get killed, and how would she ever know? It didn't make sense. It didn't even feel proper. She could get her heart broken, feeling like this. Yet the certainty remained—she loved him as he loved her. "Please do. I'll make sure I'm not hard to find."

The pain in his eyes receded behind a joyous glow. "You don't know what it means to me, Rushi." He hugged her tenderly, and she knew she'd be forever content in that embrace. "I wish I knew for sure whether I'll come back. I'll send your address to Mom tomorrow, so you'll be notified if—"

She pulled back to put a hand on his lips. "Don't say anymore, Keith. You've told me we can trust God to take care of even the smallest details. He won't make a mistake on something this important."

Moisture filled his eyes, though only a single tear escaped. "You really believe, it, don't you?"

"Yes," she whispered, still clinging to his gentle gaze.

"Don't ever give it up, no matter what you hear." He tenderly touched her lips with his.

She wrapped her arms around his neck when he kissed her a second time, wishing she could hold him there, yet knowing the God she'd recently discovered could care for him far better than she.

"Another kiss like that and I won't be able to leave," he whispered, brushing his fingers across her lips.

She lay her head on his chest, soaking up the security of his presence. Would she miss him more or less now that they'd put their feelings into words?

His fingers explored the edges of her hairline. "I like what you did with your hair tonight."

"Sheila showed me how."

His chuckle vibrated against her cheek. "I remember that evening. You looked both stunningly beautiful and absolutely terrified."

"Hmmm." She remembered all too well.

"Ever since then I've wanted to see your hair down," he whispered. "Would you mind taking your pins out?"

Without lifting her head, she released the style she'd worked on for about half an hour to get just right. He ran his fingers through the locks as they tumbled down her back. "Have you ever cut your hair?"

"No. Mom and Aunt Vivienne always said short hair on women is a sign of rebellion."

"What do you think?" His fingers maintained a caressing rhythm, smoothing out tangles.

"I don't know. This is the way it's always been, so I don't think much about it. Maisie has short hair, and David doesn't seem to mind."

"I hope you never cut it."

"Why?"

He tipped her chin up so he could look into her eyes. "Because I think it's beautiful." He planted another kiss on her lips.

"Is it vain of me to be so pleased to hear you say so?"

His grin reached into the places of her heart where insecurity still lingered. "Not at all, my proper little worrywart. And to prove it, I'll tell you again. I think you're beautiful. Not just your hair, but all the way through. You're a lovely person both inside and out, Miss Porter." A kiss confirmed his words.

Gentle silence enveloped them. She would have thought his impending departure would make them want to discuss everything they could think of. Instead, she felt like too many words would mar the bliss of these last moments together.

David returned home. Though a smile lit his eyes when he saw them, he said nothing. He rummaged in the kitchen for a few moments, then returned carrying a small kerosene lamp he'd lit. Still without a word, he placed the lamp on the crate they used as an end table, turned out the electric light, and climbed up to his room.

"Hmm. Your brother's a clever man," Keith murmured with a hint of a chuckle in his voice.

Jerusha had her answer ready. "Of course he is. He told me a long time ago I needed to let you be my friend."

He looked down into her face again, the flickering kerosene flame reflecting in his eyes. "Did he really?"

"Um hmm." She laid an arm across his broad chest in a half hug. "He was right."

He embraced her closer, and the comforting silence enfolded them again. She felt him lay his cheek against the top of her head. At long last he stirred and lifted his watch to the light. "I hate to do this, Rushi," he whispered, "but I'm on duty in a couple of hours."

Setting a light kiss on her lips, he sifted his fingers through her hair one more time. "I wish I had words to tell you what it means to know you'll be waiting and praying for me." Pulling her up to stand beside him, he looked into her eyes for several long moments.

She cupped his face in her hands. "God will keep us both."

He nodded and backed toward the door, zipping his parka without breaking eye contact. "I'll be back as soon as I can."

Chapter 17

Keith stopped by once more before he left. "Here's something I ordered for you, and it's finally arrived." He offered a large, paper-wrapped package.

Jerusha fumbled with the string, finally unveiling a dozen lemons. Tears sprang to her eyes. "How did you get so many?"

"Connections." His grin didn't stretch beyond his mouth. "I wanted to make sure you'd have enough until I can get you some more."

She heard the unspoken promise. "I'll think of you every time I do laundry."

"Only then?" A glimmer of his humor peeked from his shadowed eyes. "Always."

He kissed her good-bye, an intense, lingering kiss despite David and Maisie sitting at the table. Lifting his hat in salute, he disappeared down the street. She stood at the window, watching until she couldn't see him anymore.

Jerusha turned away from the window to find David and Maisie watching her. David wiggled his eyebrows dramatically. "I'm glad you two have finally made it past the Corporal and Miss Porter stage. When's he coming back?"

"He doesn't know." Her world suddenly felt empty except for cold crystals of fear. She sank into a chair beside Maisie.

"Does he know where he's going?" her friend asked quietly.

"No."

David nodded with sudden understanding and reached for her hand. " 'He shall give his angels charge over thee, to keep thee in all thy ways,' " he quoted softly. " 'A thousand shall fall at thy side, and ten thousand at thy right hand; but it shall not come nigh thee.' "

She recognized the words as Scripture and felt like he'd offered her a place beside a warm fire on a cold day. "Where are those verses from?"

"Psalm 91. The whole thing is good for times like this."

As Peace River Country winter slowly gave way to spring, Jerusha read the psalm every morning and every evening. For the first few weeks, it seemed like a thousand times a day she had to choose to trust instead of worry. Gradually, fear retreated, replaced by confidence in God's love.

Warm weather finally arrived, bringing with it a new water and sewer system for Dawson Creek. One Saturday, three weeks before David and Maisie's wedding, a delegation of men arrived at the parsonage. Jerusha invited them in for coffee and fresh bread.

"Thanks, Miss Porter, but we just have to speak briefly with the reverend." Big, gray-haired Timothy McEvan seemed to be acting as the group's spokesman.

David shook hands all around. "Do we need to go somewhere private?"

"No, no. It's this way, Rev. With you and Miss Clarke gettin' married, we figgered you might need more room in this here cabin. We hope you don't mind, but we've got a bit of a plan to show you. Greg, show Preacher what you've got."

The younger man spread a piece of paper on the table. "I heard Ma and Ruth and Mrs. Barry talkin' one night, and this idea came to mind. We can add another couple of rooms along the back wall, to give Miss Porter a new bedroom and her own sittin' room area, kinda. What is now Miss Porter's room could be expanded to be big enough for two by moving the wall into what is now the porch. We can also expand your present sitting room into the porch so you have more room for youth meetin's and such, and then build a new porch big enough for clotheslines for Miss Porter in the winter."

"That's a lot of work and lumber, Greg." David stated the fact without condemnation for the young man's idea.

"Which is why we're here, Rev." Mr. McEvan took over again. "There's another five or six men plannin' to get here soon, and with all of us workin', we can have everything done before nightfall." He held up a hand to stop David's objection. "We figure all of us together can carry the cost of the lumber. That and the day's work will be the church's wedding gift to you and Miss Clarke, though I know the womenfolk will add their own gifts later on."

David looked as overwhelmed as Jerusha felt. "How does it sound to you, Jerusha?"

She could only nod, amazed so many people wanted to put out the effort to make them more comfortable. "I'll go get my things out of the way."

True to their word, the men finished in a single day. They declined Jerusha's offer of supper, hurrying home to their families. David went to get Maisie so the three could explore their new home together. The new enclosed porch area ran the length of the parsonage now, with shelves on the north side and a trap door to a shallow area insulated with sawdust, which would keep vegetables cool in the summer and meat frozen in the winter.

Clotheslines had been strung across that end of the porch, as well. Shelves at the opposite end could hold boots and other items for storage. Pegs for coats extended from the doorway to the clotheslines. Only a small entry area was left from the old porch. A doorway to the right led to Jerusha's new quarters, which included both a bedroom and a small sitting room as promised. To the left of the entry, a doorway led directly into the enlarged main sitting room. The men had even created an alcove at one end for David's study area, complete with shelves. Jerusha's old room had also been enlarged to give David and Maisie plenty of bedroom space. Sturdy stairs beside the bedroom now replaced the old ladder up to the loft.

"They did this all today?" Maisie asked in amazement.

"Close to two dozen men worked on it," David explained.

"Still, it's incredible. They did it for free?"

"Welcome to a pastor's family, sweetheart." David put his arms around her. "Just when you begin to think no one notices you're living on a shoestring, the congregation will do something like this. They don't have much money, but they do have lots of heart."

Jerusha stuffed more wood into the cookstove. The changes in her house made the changes in her family more real. Though she and Maisie were close friends, what would it be like sharing cooking responsibilities and cleaning duties? How would Maisie want to decorate what would become her home?

∞

Maisie became Mrs. David Porter on one of the sunniest days Dawson Creek had seen yet that spring. Granted, it was also one of the muddiest, but no one noticed. Army Chaplain Tom Silverman had agreed to perform the ceremony. Mrs. Barry took charge of preparing refreshments for afterward, and it seemed every lady in the congregation had joined in the effort. Gifts poured in, even from people not connected with the church. Canned goods, linens, and dishes quickly filled the remaining shelf space in the parsonage. Uncle Cam and Aunt Vivienne sent two train tickets for a wedding trip back to Winnipeg, along with the promise of a similar holiday for Jerusha later in the year.

But as the summer unfolded, Jerusha found herself not inclined to leave town. Dawson Creek had become home. Maisie did make changes in the parsonage, but Jerusha felt they made the expanded cabin friendlier and brighter. Since Maisie loved to cook, something Jerusha had only done of necessity, Jerusha rarely had to prepare a meal. This left her with more free time than she could ever remember having, even after her laundry duties were done. She visited more often with the Murrays and became better acquainted with Mrs. Barry and Mrs. Pierce. And she wrote letters.

A brief note had arrived from Keith just before the wedding. She sent her reply to the address he'd indicated, but had heard nothing since. She kept writing, hoping her letters would catch up with him someday.

Her first letter from Mrs. Sutherland arrived while David and Maisie were on their wedding trip. When she'd first glimpsed the Colorado postmark, she'd been sure the letter contained the news she feared. It turned out to be just a letter of introduction. "Keith has written so much about you," it read, "that I almost feel like I know you. I think we could be great friends if we knew one another better. Since travel is out of the question, would you mind writing to me? I hear so rarely from Keith. It would be like a faint contact with him if I could hear from you." Jerusha wrote back immediately, apprehensive about writing to someone she didn't know, but eager to learn about Keith's family. From there the correspondence flourished.

Autumn replaced summer sooner than Jerusha thought it should. Winter came on even more quickly. Christmas held more excitement for her than ever before. Its story now told of Someone she was learning to know personally, rather than just being a religious story. Miraculously, a small package arrived from Keith—a lovely green, soft woolen scarf with matching gloves. Mrs. Sutherland sent several yards of royal blue silky fabric with a note. *I've had this piece for several years, but my husband isn't fond of the color. I would be delighted if it suits you.*

Sheila squealed with glee when she saw it. "This will look stunning. May I make it up for you? I know exactly what to do with it."

Jerusha described the new dress in as much detail as she could for Keith. *It has long sleeves, with cuffs that reach almost to my elbows. It also has a high collar with lace on it and on the cuffs. The skirt is long and full. It's absolutely luxurious to wear.* She went on to tell him as much Dawson Creek news as she could remember, including descriptions of new buildings that had been built. *You're not going to recognize this place when you get back. It's ever so slowly turning from a grubby army village into an honest-to-goodness town. Some areas are particularly pretty during the summer. They'd be ideal for long evening walks.*

"The scarf and gloves you sent me are just as beautiful as my new dress, only better. When I wrap the scarf around my neck, I feel almost like you've just hugged me. I can hardly wait for the real thing. Please keep yourself safe for me. With love, Jerusha."

In the spring of 1944, Sheila successfully birthed twin girls. Jerusha assisted with the delivery, a joyous experience so different from the previous year. She stayed for a couple of weeks afterward, helping Sheila adjust to two babies instead of the one she'd expected. Annie and Kerry, as the girls had been named, were happy, contented babies who seemed to flourish under the doting attention they received from their brothers.

"Our babies are the prettiest in Dawson Creek, aren't they?" Colin asked, his little chest thrust out proudly. "Did you know they're our babies, mine and Colin's, too?"

"Yes, Colin. They are pretty babies, and that's because you love them so much."

"Why does love make babies pretty, Auntie 'Rusha?" Bradley asked.

"I don't know, but it's worked with Annie and Kerry, hasn't it?"

Jerusha's second summer in Dawson Creek passed with little word from Keith and less hope of an end to the war. Christmas came again, this time without the letter she so anxiously awaited. Mrs. Sutherland's letter conveyed similar concern. *"It's been months since I've heard from our Keith. He's told me often not to worry, but in these days of unending war, I can't help myself. I try to be cheerful for the rest of my family, but I know you share my concern. Yet in spite of the worry, I feel if something had happened to him, I as his mother would know it. What a confusing mess emotions can be! I'm praying daily for his safe return and for continuing courage for you, as I trust you pray for me."*

The second anniversary of the explosion brought happy news to the Porter household. "I'm going to be a daddy!" David announced ecstatically one morning, after pounding on Jerusha's door. "My wife just told me, and I'm so thrilled I have to tell someone else. Sorry to wake you."

Jerusha laughed and hugged him, already looking forward to having a little one in the house. Maisie looked even more radiant as an expectant mother than she had as a bride. She didn't even feel nauseated in the morning, which brought out Irish indignation in Sheila.

"Sure, and it's not even fair!" she declared, her black eyes snapping. "You'll just have to pay for it with a fussy one instead of angels like my two."

Maisie just laughed and rubbed her tummy. "No, I think he'll have his daddy's happy personality."

Her only problem throughout her pregnancy was summer's heat. The least exertion caused her face to redden and her clothes to become soaked. Her feet and hands swelled. Dr. Pierce prescribed lots of rest, much to Maisie's dismay. David and Jerusha did what they could, taking her to the boardinghouse on laundry and bread-baking days to get her away from the additional heat, and preparing as many meals without cooking as possible.

Steven David Porter arrived early in the morning on September 2, causing only a little pain for his mother and an immense amount of pride for his father. Mrs. Barry came to visit the new baby, bringing with her a newspaper.

"I know those two won't be interested just yet," she whispered to Jerusha, "but I saw this headline and knew you'd want to read it." She thrust the paper at Jerusha and hurried to the bedroom.

Jerusha could barely believe her eyes. **WAR IS OVER**, the headline announced boldly. Details in the article proved it to be more than just a rumor. A tingly sense of anticipation went through her. She hadn't heard from Keith in almost a year, but neither she nor his mother had heard any bad news, either. She left the paper where David could read it if he ever took time away from his tiny son.

Steven fascinated Colin and Bradley as much as their sisters had. "He's pretty, too," Bradley observed, "but he shouldn't be 'cuz he's a boy."

"All babies are pretty, silly," Colin informed him with the immense knowledge of a youngster in his first year of school. "You'll know that when you learn to read."

Maisie regained her strength quickly. Within a couple of weeks, she was cooking again and taking the baby on daily trips to the boardinghouse. Often Jerusha spent those hours of quiet with her Bible. She'd read Psalm 91 so often she could quote it from memory, but she kept going back to read it again. *"He that dwelleth in the secret place of the most High. . . ."* The back door opened, but Jerusha ignored it. David had gone to the store for supplies and would holler for help if need be. She leaned her elbows on the table and continued reading. *"I will say of the Lord, he is my refuge and my fortress: my God; in him will I trust."* Strong khaki arms engulfed her in a hug from behind.

"I told you I'd come looking for you!" Keith's delighted voice growled in her ear.

She turned in his arms to look at the face she'd dreamed of countless times. He hadn't taken time to shave and looked like he hadn't slept in a week, but she thought he looked more marvelous than she'd remembered. "And I told you I'd make it easy for you to find me!" She hugged him back, hardly daring to believe she wasn't dreaming.

He kissed her with the intensity of two-and-a-half years' separation. "It took me long enough to get here. Let's not postpone our wedding any longer than we have to."

She laughed with the joy of the moment, his impatience making her feel supremely beloved. "Whatever you say, Corporal."

Hidden
Trails

To Kate and Norah
This book is a reality because of the support of four special people:
My editor, Rebecca Germany, whose patience has been admirable.
My critique partners, Kate and Norah,
whose encouragement made me feel like a genius.
My husband, Mark, who refused to let me give up.
To the four of you, I say "Thank you."
I couldn't have done it without you.

Prologue

England
September 1942

Phillip McEvan stood at attention before the commanding officer's desk, apprehension swirling in his gut. What had he done to earn the man's disapproval?

The sparse, bristle-haired man wasted no time in chitchat. "The Dutch underground is in trouble." His words came out in bursts of precisely articulated syllables. "The Nazi Secret Service has identified far too many of them and is watching many others. They've tapped most of our wireless network, so we can't be sure which messages are real and which are false intelligence. I'm looking for a wireless operator to find out as much as possible about the situation and get the information back to us."

Relief washed over Phillip, followed by tingling anticipation. Rather than delivering a rebuke, the CO was offering an opportunity for which Phillip had waited ever since his arrival in England.

The CO's words imprinted themselves in his brain. "I also need someone who is willing to work as a courier for information that is too sensitive to risk radio transmission. Since our supply of operatives is abysmal, I'm hoping for one man to volunteer for both duties." He paused. His steely gaze made Phillip feel as though his innermost thoughts were laid open for evaluation.

When the CO spoke again, his voice was quieter but more intense. "If you volunteer, don't expect to see the end of the war. You couldn't be more at risk if we sent you directly to Hitler's headquarters. Just the same, every little bit you can do before being captured will help us beat that German horror. Any questions?"

Phillip would never forget the utter clarity of that moment. It felt as if this was what he'd been born to do. Each of his senses recorded an impression of the moment—the lemony smell of furniture polish, the stiffness of his muscles as he held himself erect, the sound of rain pounding the window, the taste of fear, the look on his superior's face as Phillip said, "Only one question, sir. I don't speak any Dutch. How do I find out what you need to know if I can't speak the language?"

A glimmer of something that might have been approval showed for a second in the officer's eyes. "Most of the people with whom you'll be working speak English and Dutch. You'll be surprised at what you can understand when your life depends on it."

A period of intense training followed. The strength and endurance developed through years of physical labor on the farm became his greatest assets. Though shorter than most of his companions, he found himself able to move more quickly. His broad shoulders soon became accustomed to the weight of heavy rucksacks.

Reluctantly, he learned to use a variety of weapons and how to kill quickly and quietly. As soon as he learned, he wished he could forget. Yet he knew someday someone else's life might depend on his ability to do what he loathed. Other physical skills became second nature—survival in open territory, equipment usage, mapping and charting, surveillance.

Nothing prepared him for his first jump into Holland. Parachute training had been fun. The actual leap into occupied territory made him feel as if he'd come alive for the first time since birth. The suck of gravity and the wind shearing past his entire body overloaded his senses immediately. Then came the painstaking count of seconds, the jerk on his rip cord, the jolt of his chute snatching his body from free fall. The instant after his parachute opened, Phillip felt the texture of the night. As the smell and sound of the aircraft that had dropped him faded, he discovered the darkness had a personality. It hovered around him with reassuring whispers and fresh, clean smells. Every sense tingled with alertness as he landed expertly with the relaxed roll and tumble that prevented injury. Adrenaline sped his concealment of his chute while keeping all senses on the razor edge of alertness for signs of other humans.

His body turned into a finely tuned antenna, poised to gather the details that would not only keep him alive, but provide Allied intelligence with the details it needed to plan the liberation of this Nazi-oppressed segment of Europe.

In the next few days, he became an expert people-watcher, always searching eyes for signs of potential help or harm. He met members of the Dutch Resistance, surreptitiously gathered information on the strength of Germans and their sympathizers in an area, scouted roads and bridges for possible access routes by Allied forces. Never had he felt more alive.

And never had his emotions been stretched so close to a breaking point.

His personal exhilaration in following his orders contrasted starkly with the bleak conditions around him. Dutch faces rarely smiled. Clothes hung on gaunt frames stooped from the effort of survival. Fear, often mingled with indescribable sadness, flickered in every gaze. Yet indestructible courage also showed. In the eyes of the few who knew his identity or origin, he saw gratitude of such depth he wanted to weep.

Everywhere, stern German eyes kept watch. Cold expressions, harsh tones, and the haughty carriage of conquerors reinforced the fear that hung in the air. One glance into a pair of those eyes never failed to remind Phillip of the terrible consequences should his purpose be detected.

He couldn't feel afraid for himself. The nightmares that woke him in cold sweats showed the faces of those he might betray under the pressure of Nazi interrogation. Within days of his arrival, he saw what such interrogation could do to bodies. Some of his most reliable contacts had suffered more than one attempt to make them turn informer. He heard about the horrifying speed with which information obtained through torture resulted in further suffering.

He returned to England from his first mission grateful to be alive and determined to go back as soon as possible. By the end of his second mission, he knew he'd never again be happy at a desk job.

In May 1943, he made his third jump into the tiny country. His first two visits had each been only a few days in duration—parachute into an area near an ocean port, deliver the badly needed wireless set, gather the information for which he'd been sent, and meet up with the merchant marine vessel that smuggled him back to Britain.

On this trip, he had no scheduled return. His only link with the home office would be a biweekly wireless transmission sent in code just moments before he left a particular hiding place. He stepped out of the plane knowing it would be a miracle if he ever saw Allied soil again.

His parachute opened with a reassuring snap and the starless night enveloped him in a dank chill. Cloud cover almost obscured his target. He felt no welcome in the darkness, only a deep need below him; a sense of lurking danger strained every sense to the maximum. *I don't care if they get me,* he told himself as his parachute gently lowered him into the unknown. *I'm alive at this moment and that's what counts.* He suddenly understood the fear that shrouded this country and felt the silent resolve that propelled the resistance movement.

He hit the ground with a thump and stumbled across uneven ground. He turned quickly and rolled his chute into a bundle that he fastened to the pack on his back. He couldn't leave any evidence of his arrival. His hands worked quickly while he strained to catch the slightest signal of another human presence. He'd just secured the last knot when he felt, rather than saw or heard, someone approach. Holding himself motionless, he waited. The figure passed silently. Phillip followed through the blackness.

The man's silence reinforced Phillip's sense that he was a friend. The Germans usually appeared in groups with shouts and floodlights. This man moved stealthily, making his way across fields and along back roads with the confidence of a man in his own territory. At last he paused at a farmhouse door and rapped once. When the door opened, Phillip found himself alone, facing an older woman encased in a massive housecoat and a ruffled night-cap.

"My sister gave birth to a boy," he whispered, as he'd been instructed.

She beckoned him inside. Only after the door had been shut and bolted did she light a candle. The tiny light guided them down a steep set of stairs into a cellar barely high enough for Phillip to stand upright. A cot draped with a well-worn blanket sat in one corner. *"Danke,"* she whispered.

Even if Phillip had not understood the Dutch word for thanks, the gratitude in her eyes would have eliminated the need for translation. She turned quickly and vanished back upstairs.

He stretched out on the cot fully clothed. Early in his training, he'd learned how to drop from full alertness into sleep in moments. Rest must be claimed when available. Only a few hours later, the feeling of an approaching presence awoke him. He lay motionless, letting his eyes adjust to the darkness. He sensed motion on the stairs; his eyes detected a thickening of the shadows. Still he did not move. If a friend approached, he would reveal himself in his own time. If an enemy were attempting to ambush him, he would gain nothing from disclosing his wakefulness.

The stranger made his way to the side of Phillip's bed. Suddenly a match flared, and the steady glow of a candle lent a gentle light to the room. The dark eyes peering down at him softened with approval. "You are not a man to be surprised," a deep voice said quietly, with only a hint of a Dutch accent.

Phillip swung himself upright without comment, studying his companion. Average height, light-colored hair, slender build. Nothing remarkable in his appearance. Yet Phillip felt an inexplicable kinship with him, a trust that went beyond the need to elude a common enemy.

The man spoke again. "The Germans went looking for you last night."

Phillip raised his eyebrows in unspoken question.

His expression grave, the man answered. "We don't know how they knew. We saw them in the field where you landed, combing every inch for your parachute." His gaze rested briefly on Phillip's pack with the silken bundle still attached. "If they'd found it, they would have raided every house in the area. My contact says they think you aborted and will be watching again tonight."

Thus the pattern for the next several months established itself. Always, Phillip managed to stay barely ahead of the Gestapo. He slept every night in a different cellar or barn to minimize his chances of being caught. He talked with Resistance members in attics, fields, barns, cellars, even in the occasional automobile. He scouted bridges, roads, towns, and dikes, feeling always the German threat behind him like hot breath on the back of his neck. He went nowhere without a cap covering his distinctive red hair. Nothing he learned made its way into writing because any notes might fall into the wrong hands. He forced himself to remember the tiniest details. He even became proficient in the Dutch language.

But his friendship with the man he met in the cellar was sealed long before he learned the language. With the ever-present fear of capture and interrogation, Phillip deliberately learned little of Jan's background and nothing of his family. He didn't even know if Jan was the man's real name. Nevertheless, necessity made them partners. Somehow, Jan always had the information Phillip needed. He proved invaluable in helping him learn his way around the country. The Dutchman also taught Phillip to recognize the faces of men he must avoid. As they worked together, mutual respect made them friends.

Then came the morning of May 15, 1944. Phillip felt the train's approach long before he saw or heard it. Vibrations rumbled from the ground up through the wheels of the chair that was the cornerstone of his latest disguise. He hated the feeling of dependency upon the companion behind him, yet his life depended on his ability to portray helplessness. Still, he couldn't force his eyes to cease their constant searching of the faces around him. He felt the threat in the air.

His sensitivity to his surroundings had been what made him so successful in this world of espionage. He'd learned how to spot danger and how to respond appropriately. Now, no matter what he saw, he must not respond. No doubt, SS men were watching for him, expecting to see him board the train that couldn't arrive quickly enough for his tautly stretched nerves. If they caught him, he would have no choice but to swallow the contents of the tiny packet issued to him on his first mission.

He forced himself not to look at the man who had become his best friend. The courageous young Dutchman stood off to one side, as though casually waiting for an arrival. If anything, including a glance from a man in a wheelchair, singled Jan out from the crowd, his arrest would be certain. The SS had long suspected him of being part of the Resistance and were continually watching for him. He'd been detained, questioned, and even beaten more than once, but always managed to walk free. Phillip suspected Jan's youthful appearance convinced the authorities the Dutchman was far less influential than he actually was. If they'd known the extent of his contacts, the legendary reputation of his exploits, and his invincible reputation, they'd never have let him go.

With a head-splitting blast of the whistle, the overdue train rumbled to a stop. It seemed like an eternity before Phillip's attendant pushed the wheelchair forward. On the periphery of the crowd, Phillip saw the dreaded green uniforms with their red swastika patches. His pulse accelerated. He pushed on his knees to force himself to stay seated. Then, in the instant before he was pushed onto the train, he let himself glance toward Jan.

The man talking with him wore no uniform, but Phillip recognized the face. A band of dread tightened around his chest. He knew the man's mission—delay Jan's boarding of the train until it was too late. Then the uniformed men would move in and make a quiet arrest.

He wanted desperately to call out to his friend, to create some kind of diversion that would foil the plan unfolding before him. Yet he knew he'd put countless more lives in jeopardy if he did so. He forced himself to look away as the uniforms approached the man now isolated on the station platform. Phillip swallowed back the nausea created by his own helplessness. He knew Jan hadn't expected him to do anything differently, had in fact drilled him on his response should these events occur. But that knowledge would never be enough to take the taste of failure from his mouth.

Chapter 1

Dawson Creek, British Columbia
June 1951

Twenty-seven-year-old Phillip McEvan shifted his weight from his right foot to his left, jammed his hands into his pants pockets, and then pulled them out again. His sister, Ruth Pierce, placed a gentling hand on his arm. His fidgeting paused as he looked down into her face. Red-rimmed hazel eyes held as much concern for him as grief for her own loss of the adopted grandmother they both adored. Her empathy intensified the feelings he didn't want to acknowledge. *Men don't cry,* he reminded himself fiercely, though a quick look at his father's face revealed the lie for what it was. Timothy McEvan stood behind the chair where his wife sat, one hand on her shoulder and the other thumbing away moisture from brown eyes so similar to Phillip's own. The rust-colored hair covering his bowed head also proclaimed their family resemblance. Phillip allowed himself the nervous gesture of passing a hand through his own red, close-cropped hair.

Phillip moved his gaze to the tall, skinny man leaning against the kitchen cabinet reading Grandma Lucy's will aloud. Though Lionel Spencer's eyes also showed he'd been crying, he read in a firm voice, as if his mother's death were not a catastrophe. Suddenly, the boardinghouse kitchen in which Phillip had spent many happy hours felt entirely too small. He was preparing himself to make a bolt for the back door when the sound of his name from Mr. Spencer's lips riveted his attention.

"To Phillip McEvan, who has been as much my grandson as if he were born to one of my children, and to my granddaughter, Tabitha Spencer, I leave the care of my boardinghouse."

Phillip felt as if all air had been forced from his lungs. Grandma Lucy's death had left him without the anchor on which he'd come to rely in the past two years. The responsibility her will had just bestowed on him made him feel as if he hadn't lost her entirely. He felt her love just as surely as if she had placed a plate of his favorite raisin cookies in front of him. He shook his head as if to dislodge the tears pushing at the back of his eyes. He had to get out of this crowded room or he would break down for sure.

As unobtrusively as possible, he ducked out of the kitchen into the hallway. Three quick strides took him out the back door where late spring sunshine struggled around thickening clouds. A weathered wooden bench with a low back sat to the left against the back of the house. At the sight of the place where he and Grandma had often spent a summer evening, his feeling of loss overwhelmed him. He slumped onto the bench, put his face in his hands, and let his feelings surface.

Deep down, he'd known his living arrangement with Grandma Lucy couldn't last, but he'd never thought it would end like this. He'd fully expected his inner emptiness to propel him out of town in search of meaningful employment. Instead, Grandma Lucy died.

The memory of that awful morning just a week ago pushed itself to the front of his mind. He still didn't know what had awakened him. Usually, Grandma Lucy tapped on his door and started his day with a cheery, "Breakfast is almost ready, Phillip." That morning he awoke to silence. Early morning sunlight glowed behind the curtains at his window.

More curious than alarmed, he dressed quickly and left his room to go down to the kitchen where Grandma had always been busy by daybreak. He glanced at the tall grandfather clock in the upstairs hallway, which indicated the morning time was 6:45. Since Grandma served breakfast promptly at 7:00 every morning, he knew with a stab of alarm that something was wrong.

When no answer greeted his gentle rap followed by firmer knocking, he cautiously opened the door to her bedroom. She lay curled on her side under the covers. Only the awkward dangling of her arm off the edge of the bed looked amiss. He touched the callused hand only to find it cold. Though he knew immediately that she couldn't be helped, he still sprinted across the street to his sister's house to summon her husband, Dr. Theo Pierce. Ruth accompanied them to the boardinghouse to scramble some eggs and toast some bread for the boarders before her own three boys awakened. Dr. Pierce confirmed that Grandma had indeed passed away during the night.

The three men living at the boardinghouse looked as stunned by the news as Phillip felt. They promptly offered to move to the hotel for a few days, though they asked to move back if the boardinghouse remained in business.

Phillip straightened himself on the bench and forced his thoughts back to the present. He and his new business partner would need to contact the absent boarders as soon as possible. Two of the three men had been long-term residents at the boardinghouse. Their room and board would provide a steady income over the next three or four months, while still leaving four other rooms open for short-term guests.

His stomach knotted at the thought of running the place without Grandma. Still, he felt a sense of challenge that had been missing since he'd left Holland, which was exactly what Grandma Lucy had hoped for, he realized. An image of her twinkling blue eyes danced through his mind as he pictured her carefully writing her will to include him.

The partnership was a puzzle to him, though. Five years older than Tabby, his path had rarely crossed with hers. She seemed to him to be an intense woman who took life very seriously. Phillip remembered the last year he'd spent in a one-room schoolhouse. Tabby had been in grade one that year and even then seemed to feel she had something to prove. Had she proved herself yet? Phillip couldn't guess. He only hoped her intensity wouldn't make their partnership impossible. He frowned, considering the potential for conflict.

"I brought you some lunch."

He lifted his head at the sound of his sister's voice. She stood on the step, a full plate in her outstretched hand. He stood to take it from her. "Thanks, Sis."

"Are you going to eat it or just use it to help you hold down the bench?" Her expression reminded him of her teasing efforts to lure him out of a pout when they were children.

He pulled on one of the short, auburn curls framing her face. "I'll eat."

"We're all going to miss Grandma Lucy a lot. I'm glad she left the boardinghouse to you and Tabby rather than having it sold." She eased herself onto the bench. "It's going to be strange seeing this place running as usual, but without her."

Phillip hunched his shoulders against the fresh stab of loneliness. How could he explain, even to his beloved older sister, what the older woman had meant to him? He'd returned from the war broken by failure and longing for the impossible. Grandma Lucy's own experiences in World War I had given them a shared point of reference. She understood his nightmares and his memories that wouldn't go away. With the patience and gentleness uniquely hers, she'd helped him find himself again. In recent months, he'd begun to feel whole again. But her death had reactivated certain hurts, wounds he knew no one else would understand.

Ruth didn't push his confidence. Instead, she simply sat beside him until he finished the food she'd brought. That was one of many things he appreciated about his older sister. She didn't feel compelled to fill silence with words as did many women he knew, nor did she get offended when he didn't feel like talking. Wordlessly, he handed the empty plate back to her.

"It would be nice if you'd come back inside." Though her eyes pleaded with him, her tone stayed neutral.

"Why?"

"Because the rest of the family is together in there, and we would like to have you with us. Besides, Tabby might want to talk business with you."

Tabby. As uncomfortable as he felt with the partnership, his love for Grandma motivated him to try to make it work.

He dutifully followed Ruth into the kitchen, where more than twenty people circulated around a heavily laden table and chatted in subdued voices. Out of the corner of his eye, he noticed Tabby watching him. Her expression indicated she felt no more pleased about their partnership than he did. He decided to pretend he hadn't noticed her just yet.

He looked around the room awkwardly, not sure what to do with himself next. He felt as if he ought to take charge somehow, but what was there to take charge of?

Involuntarily, he glanced Tabby's way again. At least he had the advantage of having lived here. He knew the current boarders, as well as the daily routine. Tabby wouldn't know that much. He realized with a jolt that the bulk of the work would fall to her. Grandma Lucy had made this a home for her guests. He knew nothing about running a home. At least Tabby would have learned a little from her own mother. Then another thought struck him. Tabby would have to move into the boardinghouse. That meant he'd have to move out. It wouldn't look right if the two of them lived under the same roof. But where would he go?

It seemed the only sensible course of action was to chat with his new business partner. He looked in her direction and found her still watching him. He tilted his head in the direction of the parlor. She nodded.

Away from the crowd of their families, he felt more awkward than ever, but he forced himself to lift his gaze from the floor.

Her smile came and went quickly, as though she felt as awkward as he. But when she spoke, her tone reminded him of his instructors at boot camp. "What did you want?"

His brain responded automatically to the reminder of those days of discipline and order. He'd excelled in circumstances far more hostile than anything this slender young woman could produce. He hoped his voice sounded casual, yet businesslike. "It looks like we're business partners now."

"Um-hmm." Her voice lost none of its crispness. "How much do you know about the business?"

It felt as if she were evaluating whether he would be an asset or a liability. *A valid concern*, he conceded mentally. Since she would be burdened with the bulk of the day-to-day responsibilities, it only seemed natural that she investigate how much assistance he could give. "A bit. I know where Grandma Lucy kept things and the kind of routine she had. She also had me help her once or twice with her bookkeeping, but I don't know much about that."

"We can figure that out later. At least you're familiar with enough to get us started." She sounded almost relieved, which surprised Phillip. Her bearing and expression betrayed no glimmer of uncertainty. "The first step will be finding you a different place to live. It wouldn't look right if we lived here together, and it's too far for me to drive in from the farm every day."

He hoped his smile reassured her. "I'd already thought of that, and I think Ruth and Theo would be willing to let me stay with them for a while."

"That would be perfect, with them being just across the street. If you would stay here one more night, then I'll go home with my folks and get settled in here tomorrow. Give me a couple of days to get used to things, and we should be ready for business by the end of the week."

He opened his mouth to agree, but a pounding at the front door stopped his reply. They moved toward the kitchen together, only to find that everyone in the room was waiting for them to answer the summons. He and Tabby looked at each other simultaneously, and then she took a step backward. "Go ahead. You're the man of the house."

Feeling awkward with all the attention focused on him, Phillip moved into the mudroom. The sense of responsibility settled even more heavily on him. He opened the outside door.

Four strangers looked at him questioningly. A middle-aged man with graying dark hair sat in a wheelchair. Two empty pant legs had been folded up over stumps that ended at midthigh. His blue eyes held both sorrow and kindness. Behind him, hands resting on the handles of the wheelchair, stood a younger man in neat, but casual clothing. A gracious-looking middle-aged woman stood beside the younger man, her light brown hair pulled back in a manner that enhanced her refined features. Her gray eyes communicated the same gentleness he'd so often seen in his mother's face.

But it was the wheelchair occupant in front of her that held Phillip's attention. She looked pale, with smoky blue eyes strikingly similar to the older gentleman's. Her black hair showed the dishevelment of travel, wisps of it dangling on either side of her face. Small and fine-boned, she looked fragile and worn.

The woman behind her spoke. "The gentleman at the train station said you might have a place for us?"

Chapter 2

Adrianna wished she could turn away from the red-haired stranger's forbidding face and run in the opposite direction. Not a shred of welcome brightened the eyes under thick red eyebrows drawn together in a frown. No friendly response to her aunt's question lightened the moment. Unfortunately, polio at age eleven had robbed her of independent movement. Now, she could only hold herself as erect as possible in her wheelchair and wish she were somewhere else.

Then, she noticed the grim expression on his face shift, like the breeze stirring a drapery, just for an instant revealing deep shadows in his brown eyes. He spoke with a husky tone. "This isn't the best time for guests—" he began before being interrupted by a brisk voice behind him.

"Of course they're welcome."

He stepped to one side, revealing a young woman with short blond hair and intense green eyes. Adrianna noticed those eyes held the same kind of sadness that hid in the man's. She also had the feeling neither would welcome her perception. The young woman smiled tightly. "Please excuse our disorganization. We've just inherited this boardinghouse from my grandmother and we're trying to sort ourselves out."

Adrianna became aware of a babble of conversation building behind the two in the doorway. From her all-too-familiar perspective below the waists of the two in the doorway, she couldn't see the gathering. She just hoped there were fewer people than the noise seemed to indicate. As if he could read Adrianna's thoughts, the host's face softened a little. "We've just finished reading the will, so the family is still all gathered here. They'll be able to help us get your rooms ready shortly."

"This is a bad time for you," Aunt Caroline said softly. "We're sorry to impose. It's just that we'd rather stay in a place where we don't have to deal with a lot of stairs."

"That's perfectly understandable," the man replied, giving each of the wheelchairs a passing glance. "We're glad you've come here, provided you don't mind a little confusion just at first."

Adrianna searched his face for the slightest sign of acknowledgment and saw none. She caught his glance at Uncle James and then the quickly averted gaze as if he couldn't bear to see evidence of a handicap. So far, he hadn't acknowledged her presence by even a look. It was as if her chair made her invisible to him. The fourteen years since her illness had given her plenty of experience with that reaction. It was the one that infuriated her the most.

The object of her growing ire apparently found his voice and gestured toward the back of the house. "How about if we get you settled in the parlor until your rooms are ready?"

"Thanks, Son," Uncle James responded, causing his niece to look at him questioningly. The tone of his voice told her he liked this man. Adrianna couldn't fathom why. The man grasped the front of her chair while Uncle James's nurse, Neil Harris, lifted the back. Easily and smoothly, they carried her up the two stairs into the mudroom. Though Adrianna couldn't see any overt staring, she felt on display as Aunt Caroline pushed her through a kitchen teeming with people and down a short hallway. Their hostess led them through a doorway into a smaller side room.

The young woman moved a footstool out of the way to make room for both wheelchairs. Once Aunt Caroline had settled herself onto a needle-point-covered chair, the girl extended her hand first to Adrianna, then to Aunt Caroline. "I'm Tabby Spencer. Phillip McEvan is my business partner only." She smiled again as though it were an effort. "We've had a rough day so far, but we're glad to be of service. If you'll excuse me, I'll go prepare some tea for you."

"That would be lovely," Aunt Caroline responded.

Rather than taking the one response as answer for both women, Tabby turned to Adrianna with meticulous politeness. "Is tea okay for you, or would you prefer something else?"

Adrianna tried to put her at ease with a smile. "Tea would be fine." Miss Spencer's strained good manners gave Adrianna the same feeling as the man's obvious discomfort. No matter what, her handicap would always give her a disadvantage. People just didn't know how to respond to someone obviously different from themselves. She wished she could hide her handicap as easily as her long skirt hid her legs.

Tabby paused in her exit to allow Neil and Uncle James through the doorway. After confirming that tea would be acceptable to them, as well, she left the four alone.

Uncle James took a careful look around the room, then peered out the window behind Adrianna. "So far this looks like a comfortable, friendly place. I think I could stay here awhile."

"How long is awhile?" Adrianna couldn't resist asking. They had embarked on this trip to satisfy her uncle's desire to see the end of the Canadian Pacific rail line. Now that they were here, she knew he wouldn't return immediately, but hoped he didn't plan to take up residence for the entire summer.

"Oh, I don't know," he responded with a casual, yet teasing smile. "Are you in a hurry to get back to Toronto?"

"No," Adrianna admitted. "But you know how Mother and Father worry." The thought of her parents brought both loving warmth and a faint chill of dread. Since her illness, her parents had made sure she had no reason to leave their house. Every provision had been made for her comfort and entertainment, to the point that she felt stifled.

At first, she had been determined to prove to them that she could be independent and useful. But her parents' conviction that the outside world would be too difficult for her had slowly woven itself into her perspective. She hated feeling helpless and useless. They assured her they didn't see her as useless, that her presence in their lives brought them joy. For a long time, the assurance had worked. But since her twenty-fifth birthday seven months ago, she'd found herself longing for more. Though she dared not put words to the feeling, she knew she wanted to experience life rather than just observe it. She fingered the gold cross necklace that had been a birthday gift from her aunt and uncle. Their offer to bring her with them on this adventure had seemed like the perfect opportunity. Her parents could hardly object to Aunt Caroline's promise to look after her, especially since a registered nurse would be along to see to Uncle James's needs. Adrianna knew her father would have preferred a female nurse, but he'd chosen to leave his objection unspoken.

"They worry too much," Uncle James pronounced with a snort. "It's time they learned you'll do just fine without them."

The arrival of the tea tray took away the need for Adrianna to reply. She let the other three discuss the flavor of the tea and the red jelly provided for the generous slices of bread. Her own thoughts couldn't be voiced at the moment. Had she made a mistake venturing this far from the comfortable home she'd always known? *It's not like I've moved here permanently,* she assured herself. Uncle James would certainly want to return to the city before the chill of winter arrived. But that thought only increased her unease. She hated the feeling of vulnerability creeping up on her ever since the young man at the door had refused to look at her. His response, coupled with that of his partner, only made her more conscious of the fact she could never forget—she was crippled, forever destined to be only half of a person. Why, then, did her heart insist she could, and should, reach for more?

∞

Phillip hated himself for the relief he felt when both wheelchairs disappeared into the parlor. He knew he'd been impolite, even rude, but he'd felt helpless to stop himself. Those chairs had brought back memories he thought he'd successfully buried forever. Thankfully, Tabby had stepped in before he'd driven away their guests, and his usual ability to mask his feelings had reasserted itself. He promised himself never to let a slip like that happen again. He hadn't missed the look of hurt in the young woman's blue eyes and knew himself to be a cad. The combination of dignity and vulnerability in her expression made him want to show his best self rather than his worst.

He stood to one side, watching the bustle in the kitchen as the extended families prepared to leave. Tabby was in the thick of it, directing the distribution of leftover food as if she'd been doing it for years. How easily she'd moved into her new role! He should be the one with the confidence.

Instead, the memory of the months he'd spent assisting Grandma Lucy just made him feel more awkward than ever. If she were here, she would have given him a list of things to do. He could have simply followed orders, leaving the responsibility to her. Now, as partner in the venture, he felt as though he should take some initiative, but he hadn't a clue where to start. Grief mingled with a desire to reclaim the past ten minutes and change his reaction to one that would create happiness rather than pain. The futile wish held him detached, as if he had no role in the activity about him.

"Is that okay with you?"

Tabby's words barely penetrated his fog. He stared at her in a daze. "Sorry? I didn't hear what you said."

"I've asked Mom and Dad to bring some of my stuff from home tonight. With our new guests, I figured I should probably move in sooner rather than later. Do you mind?"

At this point, he didn't care. He was just grateful someone was making the decisions. "Sounds good to me."

She turned back to her parents, listing the items she'd need. Soon they left, followed by Tabby's brothers and sisters and their spouses. Then his own parents moved toward the door.

Mother stopped in front of him and placed a gentle hand along the side of his face. "I love you, Son. You're going to do just fine." Her eyes shimmered with restrained tears.

He pulled her into his arms, intending to comfort her, but found himself being comforted instead. It had always been this way with her. Even while grieving herself, she managed to impart some of her own strength to him. He realized afresh just how much like Grandma she was, despite the fact there was no blood relationship between them. The thought made him hug her all the tighter, then let go before he gave in to the tears pushing for release. His dad laid a hand on his shoulder but said nothing. Dad never used words when actions would do.

Finally, only Ruth and her husband, Theo, were left. Phillip could tell Ruth wanted to hug him again, but wasn't sure how he'd take it. He gave her a playful half hug to release some of the emotion between them. "Hey, Sis, do you think your love nest has room for your little brother?"

Ruth and Theo exchanged a look similar to the ones Phillip had often seen between his parents. The result was also the same. A mutual decision was reached without a word being said. He envied that kind of understanding.

Ruth's eyes twinkled as she answered. "Sure, we have room for you, provided you don't mind being awakened some morning by one of your nephews bouncing on your chest."

Phillip felt a grin tug at his mouth, the first time he'd felt like smiling since he'd found Grandma. Ruth's three boys could be noisy and mischievous, but he enjoyed their enthusiasm for life. "Can't be worse than sharing a room with three brothers." Another squeeze of her shoulders communicated his thanks. "I'll be over when we get our new guests settled."

Ruth turned to Tabby. "Do you need any help?"

Tabby turned to Phillip. "I'm not sure what all needs to be done, but Phillip and I can probably handle it."

Phillip could see Ruth forming an insistent response, but her husband steered her toward the door. "If we don't linger here, we can get our boys settled for the night and still have time for a walk before Phillip moves in."

Ruth's eyes sparkled in the way only Theo could make happen, and she followed him willingly across the street.

Left alone now with Tabby in the kitchen, Phillip found himself looking anywhere but at her. He knew they needed to get busy, but he couldn't figure out where to start. He felt as if his roiling emotions had disconnected his brain.

Once again, Tabby came to the rescue. "I guess we need to figure out where we're going to put our guests. The downstairs rooms are all in use, aren't they?"

Phillip thought for a moment. "Grandma usually put her long-term guests in these rooms because they're bigger, but I'm sure the men who have been staying there won't mind moving. We probably need to let them know we're open for business again."

"Are you sure they're coming back?"

Phillip thought he heard an uncharacteristic quiver in Tabby's voice. It prompted him to face her directly so she could see the confidence he felt. "Those three guys have been living at this boardinghouse for three years now. The day Grandma—" His voice broke, and he had to swallow hard, twice, in order to continue. "They told me they were only moving to the hotel to make things easier on the family, but that they wanted to know as soon as the future of the boardinghouse had been settled. It seems pretty settled to me." He forced a small grin to soften his face.

She studied him for a long time, though her eyes betrayed that her thoughts were anything but personal. Finally, she gave voice to her thoughts. "I just hope I can do as good a job as Grandma did. You lived with her, so you know the basics. I've never done anything like this before. What if I make us lose the business?"

He honestly hadn't thought that far ahead. Thinking about the future was, in fact, something he'd avoided doing since elementary school. Back then, he'd discovered that the moment held far more appeal than a misty future that couldn't be predicted. Recent years had shown him that the moment was also his only refuge from the past. Any plans for the future inevitably circled around to shadows he had to leave behind.

Tabby's words made him realize how fundamentally Grandma's bequest had changed his world. As a partner in a business, he would have to learn to think ahead. It wasn't just about honoring Grandma's memory; another person would now be affected by his choices. He took a deep breath, then rolled his shoulders as if to dislodge the invisible weight that seemed to be growing there. "We both have a lot of learning to do, but Grandma wouldn't have given this to us if she hadn't thought we could handle it. You've done a great job so far, which is more than I can say for myself."

"Your manners could use some polishing." Her teasing tone took any sting out of her words. "If I can learn to cook for a dozen, I'm sure you can learn to be polite."

He fervently wished his reaction at the door had simply been bad manners. His stomach tightened as he remembered the feelings that had crashed over him as soon as he saw their new guests. Obviously, his heart remembered things he'd tried to make his brain forget.

Chapter 3

The rest of the evening passed in a flurry of activity. Tabby prepared and served the Trentons a simple meal while Phillip did his best to prepare rooms for them. He felt uneasy about relocating the long-time occupants of these rooms, but he hoped they'd understand. Digging through their belongings in their absence increased his discomfort, as did his repeated trips past the dinner in progress. If he accidentally made eye contact with anyone, including Tabby, he stretched his lips into what he hoped was a friendly smile.

Mr. Johnson's room looked deceptively easy. As a schoolteacher, he kept all of his belongings orderly. Phillip emptied the bureau and carefully put its contents in a matching bureau upstairs. He stripped the bed and replaced the sheets with fresh ones from the linen closet. Then he began moving the books.

Countless trips later, he realized that Mr. Johnson's orderliness had concealed the true size of his collection. Since Phillip had no way of remembering how the books had fit on the shelves previously, he stacked them as neatly as possible on the floor. He then carried the bricks and boards that comprised the shelves up to the new room and set up the shelves for their owner to fill on his own.

Mr. Watters's room presented its own challenge. Though it was clean, there seemed to be no logic to the way the belongings were arranged. Phillip simply carried them to their new location, put them away as if he were organizing his own things, and hoped Mr. Watters wouldn't be offended.

The third room, which opened off the kitchen, had just recently been claimed by a young fellow, Adam Dodd. Phillip vaguely remembered him telling Grandma he'd come from up north to look for work. A single bureau drawer held what appeared to be the extent of his possessions. Phillip wondered if his finances might be similarly sparse. Should he have a chat with the young man before inviting him back?

As quickly as the question raised itself in his mind, he answered it. Grandma would never have asked anyone to leave because of lack of money.

He probably should raise the issue later with Tabby, though.

It took some effort to get the Trentons settled. Mr. Trenton requested rearrangement of the furniture in his room, then wheeled himself across the kitchen to look at the room opposite. "This is where my niece will be sleeping?" At Tabby's nod, he wheeled himself inside, then backed out. "I'd prefer she be in the room beside ours. I think it will be quieter for her."

Phillip agreed with the man's logic, though a part of him wanted to take offense. Yet, as Grandma had told him often, the guest was always right. He smiled in what he hoped was a hospitable fashion. "Would you like anything in her room moved around?"

"Perhaps you should ask her." Mr. Trenton's eyes held a shadow of rebuke.

Phillip forced himself to look at the young woman's face. If he concentrated hard enough, he could pretend the wheelchair didn't exist. But then he became uncomfortably aware of the clear blue eyes, thick dark hair, and delicate features. "May I move anything for you, Miss Trenton?"

She pushed at the wheels of her chair, but it was obvious she didn't have her uncle's expertise. Phillip felt a flutter of interest. Had she only recently acquired the chair? What had taken away her independence so early in her life? A strange urge to protect almost made him reach for the offensive chair, but Tabby moved first. Mr. Trenton stopped them both with a restraining gesture.

Phillip's curiosity increased, but he squelched it. Though a story hovered in the background, he didn't want to interest himself in any part of any of their lives. He'd once made the mistake of overinvolvement. The consequences still haunted him.

∞

Adrianna felt the dampness of sweat on the back of her blouse as she did her best to propel her chair toward the door Uncle James had indicated. In the months immediately following her illness, she'd tried to learn to move herself around. It soon became a futile effort. One of her parents or a servant always hovered near, ready to help anytime she so much as gestured toward her wheels. She remonstrated with them again and again, but the answer remained the same: "At least we can do this much for you." It seemed as though her parents carried guilt that she'd become ill in the first place. They tried to compensate through an abundance of material comforts, but Adrianna was just beginning to realize how they'd leached away her independence.

She sensed their hostess moving up behind her to help, then on the edge of her line of sight, saw Uncle James's restraining gesture. She supposed she should be thankful to him for encouraging her independence, but how she hated to struggle, especially under the grim appraisal of their red-haired host. Her arms quivered with exhaustion by the time she reached the bedroom door. She peered through the doorway, prepared to accept whatever she saw.

But Uncle James had a different idea. "Go on in, girl. Make sure you can get around in there without any furniture getting in the way."

Adrianna propelled herself into the space that would have easily fit inside her dressing room back home. The bedroom she'd lived in all her life was the size of the kitchen she'd just left. A window directly opposite the door framed a view of a tree that filtered light into the room. A bed just wide enough for one person sat in the corner to the left of the window, and a plain, but clean washstand to the right. A bureau occupied the wall opposite the bed. She didn't see how rearranging furniture would make any difference. The room looked pleasant and comfortable enough for the few days they'd be here. Since she'd never learned to turn her chair around on her own, she simply called out, "It looks very nice."

Wrapping her arms around herself, she stared out the window. She told herself she was just giving her arms a break. Something inside told her the reason had more to do with the grim-faced young man she didn't want to see again.

A knock at the front door made her exhale deeply in relief. At least now someone else would be the center of attention. Rustling skirts behind her indicated Aunt Caroline's presence, confirmed by the light, flowery scent uniquely hers.

"Are you all right?" Aunt Caroline asked in a gentle tone, settling herself on the edge of the bed. Even there, she looked ladylike and refined, back straight, clothing smooth and unwrinkled, the unfashionable length of her skirts only making her look more genteel.

Adrianna nodded. "Just tired from getting myself in here."

"Did you mind your uncle insisting you do it alone?"

She looked into her aunt's concern-filled eyes. "I came on this trip because I wanted to be more independent. It's his way of encouraging me."

"But. . ." A smile accompanied the gentle prodding.

"But I wish that man would go away."

"Our host?" Aunt Caroline guessed.

Adrianna nodded again. "Every time he looks at me, I feel smaller than this chair, as if this chair is all he can see. I hate that feeling!"

"I'm sure I don't have to tell you that some people feel uncomfortable around anyone who is obviously different from them. With both you and your uncle here, he should get used to your chairs in a couple of days."

Adrianna didn't feel so certain. Something she'd glimpsed in his averted gaze told her he wasn't merely uncomfortable. He was afraid.

∞

Phillip helped Tabby and her father carry her things upstairs. Instead of taking the big room in the south corner, which had been Grandma's, she started into his smaller one across the hall, then backed out abruptly with a flushed face. "Oops. I'm sorry. I didn't know that was yours."

"I'll be moving out tonight, so you can have it if you want." He tilted his head toward the closed door of the bigger room. "But there's no reason you couldn't move into there. It even has its own bathroom."

Her eyes shimmered with moisture for a moment, then hardened. "I'd rather take the smaller one."

Feeling rebuked, Phillip looked at Tabby's dad, who shrugged, then moved closer to her. "Are you sure, honey? Grandma's room would probably be more comfortable for you."

"I am not taking Grandma Lucy's room." With set lips, Tabby stood away from the door in a pointed gesture for Phillip to clear out his belongings.

He set down the crate he'd been carrying and slid past her into what had been his room. His feelings of loss stirred to life again. He wondered how long Tabby planned to keep Grandma Lucy's suite closed. He knew from experience that ignoring a loss didn't make it less of a fact.

It took only a few minutes to move his belongings out of Tabby's way and set them in the common area from which the six upstairs rooms opened. One look at her set face told him she wanted to be left alone.

It was close to midnight by the time he left the boardinghouse. He hadn't felt right leaving Tabby until her dad was gone, the kitchen cleaned up, and their guests settled for the night. Force of habit led him out the back door to bring in enough wood to fill the wood box beside the stove, then two trips to the hand pump on the back porch filled the water reservoir in the kitchen stove. Though the house had been modernized by running water two years ago, Grandma had liked to have that reservoir kept full. Until Tabby told him differently, he'd do the same for her.

Carrying his few personal belongings in two wooden crates, he crossed the street, then turned to his left and walked past three other buildings before reaching a two-story, frame building. Theo, a medical doctor, served the town out of three rooms on the ground floor. The back half of the same floor contained a large kitchen and a formal parlor area. Phillip eased the back door open, tiptoed inside, then shut it quietly behind him. Footsteps on the stairs told him Ruth had waited up for him. The loving warmth of that thought put a genuine smile on his face when he saw her. "I didn't wake you, did I?"

She grinned. "You know better than that. I was enjoying a good book while I waited. Do you need a cup of tea or anything?"

He became aware of a hollow feeling, reminding him he'd worked while the others ate. Emotional overload had stolen his appetite later in the evening. "Any leftovers from supper?"

With a quiet snicker, she turned toward the icebox Theo had had installed a year ago for her for Christmas. "How about a meat loaf sandwich?"

His stomach rumbled in response. "You're a great sister. Should I take my stuff up to the guest room?"

She nodded, already busy with a bread knife. He moved as quietly as possible up the stairs, avoiding the creaky stair second from the top.

The room he'd always used on his many visits to his sister's home faced the street and gave him an unobstructed view of the boardinghouse. No light showed in the window of his old room. He moved to the bureau and quickly put his clothing away, then laid his Bible on his nightstand. Though he didn't read it often, somehow the sight of it beside his bed always brought a sense of rightness. He placed his shaving items in the center of the bureau just as Ruth came into the room with his sandwich and a glass of milk.

"It's good to have you here, little brother."

"Thanks." He bit into the sandwich, reveling in the flavor familiar from their childhood. "Tastes just like the ones Mom makes."

She accepted the compliment with a smile. "That's high praise indeed. I'd recommend sleeping with your door closed so your nephews don't disturb you. They tend to get up with the birds."

He shrugged. "I should get up early anyway. Tabby could probably use the help, at least until we get a routine figured out."

With a light touch on his arm, Ruth left him alone. Three mouthfuls finished the sandwich, and two long gulps drained the glass of milk. It took only a moment for him to undress and settle into his bed. Though his body ached with weariness, sleep hovered just beyond his reach. Inactivity left his mind and emotions defenseless against the enormity of his loss. Worse, memories he'd held at bay for two years clamored for attention, stirred to life by the wheelchairs. Now, more than ever, he couldn't afford to let them in. Skills developed from long practice helped him force his body to relax and his restless thoughts to still. He needed rest in order to cope with the challenges daylight would certainly bring.

Chapter 4

Early morning light released Phillip from the grip of terror. He sat bolt upright in his bed, his breath coming in uneven pants. His heart thundered in his chest. Heaviness held his legs immovable. He blinked against the light, and reality slowly seeped into his consciousness. He forced cool, calming air into his lungs, then untangled the quilts that had his legs prisoner.

When he'd first returned from Holland, the nightmares had been a nightly occurrence. Lately, there'd been spaces as long as a week between the haunting dreams. The all-too-familiar cloak of helplessness and failure wrapped itself around him. How many more times would he be jerked from sleep by the memories he had no power to change?

He forced aside the painful thoughts, only to have them replaced by others just as miserable. This morning he wouldn't have Grandma Lucy's gentle wisdom to help dispel the effects of his memories. He'd never had to tell her when night had held more terror than rest for him. Somehow she'd always seen it in his eyes and always known what to say to ground him in the present once again.

Still lying beneath the tangled bedding, he forced himself to focus on the details of the familiar room—the Lord's Prayer sampler Ruth had stitched and hung on the wall facing the bed, the rag rug she'd braided to lay beside the bed, his personal belongings on top of the bureau where he'd put them last night.

The clock showed 5:00 A.M. Time to put his multiple griefs behind him, where they belonged, and focus on being a proper business partner and host. He shaved, then quietly pulled on denim pants and a dark green cotton shirt. A cloudless sky indicated another warm day as he crossed the street to the boardinghouse. He slipped into the boardinghouse kitchen and silently lifted one of the lids on the cookstove. Not even coals were left from yesterday's fire.

The routine of building a fire, as he'd done so often for Grandma, helped ease the heartache that clung to him. Opening a trapdoor at the front of the stove near the floor, he scraped the collection of ashes into a bucket. If the ash box became too full, he knew the fire wouldn't be able to draw as much air and thus wouldn't burn as well. He set the bucket aside to empty later. Closing the trapdoor, he opened the two draft levers. The draft on the stovepipe sucked smoke up the pipe and out of the house. The second draft at the back of the stovetop allowed extra air into the firebox to encourage the fire to start.

Next, he lifted a rectangular section of stovetop out of the way to give him unhindered access to the firebox. A crumpled piece of newspaper between pieces of kindling caught quickly when he held a match to it. When the kindling began to burn, he added a couple larger pieces of wood. He replaced the lid over the hole. He carried the bucket of ashes out the back door and dumped the ashes into a large wooden box near the seldom-used outhouse. When he returned to the kitchen, a faint crackling from the stove assured him the fire had caught. He closed the stovetop draft to encourage heat to circulate around the oven just in case Tabby needed it for breakfast preparations.

Still alone in the kitchen, he felt the shadows of the night begin to approach again. Looking for an activity to keep his mind occupied, he filled the coffeepot with water and put in the coffee grounds as Grandma had shown him. Though he knew their guests wouldn't be awake yet, perhaps Tabby would appreciate an early morning hot drink.

∽

The rattle of cookstove lids and a faint smell of wood smoke awoke Adrianna. Her bedroom at home was in its own quiet suite of rooms, so the normal noise of a functioning household never reached her. It felt good hearing the sounds of another person starting the day. Though she knew her mother would have been offended by the smoky odor, Adrianna found comfort in it. To her, it symbolized freedom. Far from the restrictions of her pampered upbringing, she now had the opportunity to explore independence, find out how far she could go, and what she might want to achieve with her discovery.

A soft tap on her door let her know her aunt was also awake. Adrianna called out a welcome. In the early days of the trip, their party of four had naturally fallen into a routine that worked well for them all. Part of Mr. Harris's job as Uncle James's companion was to assist him in getting out of bed and dressed each morning since that part of his care was simply too strenuous for Aunt Caroline. Thus, while the two men worked together, she slipped over to Adrianna's room to assist her.

Again this morning, as she had done often since the beginning of this trip, Adrianna couldn't help but compare her aunt's assistance with what she received at home. The servants at home, while affectionate and caring, viewed Adrianna as her parents did—helpless and in need of constant care. She felt like an overgrown baby while her maid dressed her, arranged her hair, and pushed her chair to the breakfast room. Aunt Caroline, on the other hand, allowed Adrianna to discover the limits of what she could do for herself. They discovered it worked best if Adrianna dressed before getting out of bed. She needed her aunt's help with her undergarments, but could manage her blouse and skirt by herself. With her aunt's daily encouragement, she even practiced moving herself from bed to chair. She hadn't yet made the transition independently, but she no longer felt like a puppet held by silken strings. As her physical strength increased, so did her confidence. She hadn't yet given much thought to what lay beyond being able to care for herself and move herself around, but she felt as though exciting options lay just around the corner.

Aunt Caroline helped her tuck her feet into hand-crocheted slippers, and the two made their way to the breakfast table. Uncle James and Neil sat conversing with their host while Tabby bustled around the cookstove preparing something that smelled delicious. Adrianna noticed dark rings under Phillip's eyes, betraying a less-than-restful night. He poured himself a cup of coffee, then moved to the table with the ease of one who had lived in this house for awhile. Just as he started to settle onto the bench, he seemed to recall his role as host. "I'm sorry. Could I get coffee for anyone else?"

Both Uncle James and Neil accepted the offer. Phillip barely glanced at Adrianna when she said, "No, thank you." He made her feel invisible, which reminded her of the way her father sometimes treated her—as though her handicap made her incapable of thinking for herself. After two weeks of being treated like a fully functional adult by her aunt and uncle, she wasn't going to let this stranger return her to her old status. A glimmer of self-assertiveness stirred in her. The least he could do would be to acknowledge her existence. "I would appreciate some tea, though."

The way his gaze snapped to her face, she knew he hadn't expected to hear anything further from her. She decided to rub it in some more. "With cream and sugar, please." She wanted to chuckle at the stunned look in his eyes, which slowly gave way to embarrassment as a flush crept up his neck.

Phillip felt rebuked. Once again, he'd allowed his emotional reaction to the wheelchairs to block out his awareness of the people in them. With her simple request, his guest had reminded him that she had feelings every bit as real as his. He wished he knew how to apologize without drawing even more attention to his problem. Instead, he turned his attention to warming Grandma's flowered teapot. When the pot of water on the stove came to a boil, he poured it into the warmed pot, then added tea leaves to steep.

Mr. Trenton filled the silence, which had begun to thicken. "If you're in any need of bookkeeping help, Neil is pretty good with numbers."

Surprise and relief forced Phillip's head up to meet the man's friendly gaze. To be honest, he hadn't given a thought to finding out the financial details of this business they'd acquired. He looked over at Tabby, whose face registered strong disapproval.

While it might be unconventional to allow a stranger access to such personal records, he knew they needed the assistance. "We'd appreciate the help, sir. I only helped Grandma Lucy—" he had to swallow hard around the sudden lump in his throat "—with day-to-day details. Her finances were a private matter."

Tabby nodded sharply as though she felt that was the way things should stay.

The nurse spoke his first words of the morning. "Just let me know when you need my help. I don't want to interfere if you want to handle it on your own."

Phillip appreciated the respectful reserve he saw in the man's brown eyes.

Phillip glanced Tabby's way again. She still looked prepared to do battle. "Good thinking, Mr.—?"

"Just call me Neil," the young man said with an almost bashful smile. He extended his hand to Phillip, though his gaze slid toward Tabby before meeting Phillip's. Phillip returned the handshake. "I'm Phillip."

"As long as we're making friends, I'd like you to call me James." The older man maneuvered his chair so he could also shake Phillip's hand. "My wife's name is Caroline, and you and my niece can sort out how formal you'd like to be with each other." His eyes twinkled as if he were enjoying a private joke.

Though Phillip had avoided looking directly at the dark-haired young woman all morning, he now felt compelled to meet her gaze. While her cheeks took on a touch of color, her voice held a refined challenge. "My name is Adrianna." She extended a small hand in greeting.

With a silent promise to himself never to overlook her as a person again, he grasped her hand lightly. "Please call me Phillip." The hand felt slim and fragile in his. Awareness of her femininity jolted through him. His gaze met hers, and for an instant he felt as if she understood and forgave his clumsiness. He withdrew his hand, hoping no one else had noticed the spark between them.

He moved back to the counter to give himself something to do. The tea looked ready, so he poured some into Grandma's best china cup, accompanied by a saucer and a small silver spoon. He found the matching sugar bowl and cream pitcher, which he filled, then placed within Adrianna's easy reach. He wanted nothing more than to escape to the back step, but with a heightened awareness of his manners and responsibilities along with an unfamiliar inner tremble, he resumed his seat. To his relief, Tabby handed out plates of steaming pancakes and sizzling sausages, which occupied everyone around the table.

His thoughts swirled around the attraction he felt for the young woman he'd met only yesterday. During his school years, he'd had plenty of friendly companions, both male and female, but no romantic interests. It had surprised him to discover upon his return from Europe that his service in the war had turned him into a hero. He found himself the subject of intense speculation by females in his age bracket and the recipient of dinner invitations from their mothers. The heartache he brought back with him left no room for romance, however. Though many of his admirers expressed interest in his war experiences, he always turned the questions aside with a joke. The memories were too dark to share with someone who had already placed him on a pedestal. Thus, he became the town's local man of mystery. Eventually, the girls found other companions, and he remained alone with his shadows.

But this polished woman touched something hidden within him. She obviously held no delusions about him; she'd seen him at his worst. Her eyes played none of the flirtatious games he'd seen before; rather, they demanded that he see her as a person—nothing more and nothing less. As he responded to that demand, he found himself responding to much more. He couldn't see her as a person without being drawn to her as an attractive woman.

∽

Adrianna's right hand still felt warm where Phillip had grasped it. She tucked it into her lap, hidden under her left as though some visible evidence existed of the impact of their touch. Granted, he'd dismissed her rudely, but for a moment, he'd acknowledged her, been aware of her as a person. That awareness had triggered a responding awareness in her. For the first time, she knew how it felt to be aware of a man, to be drawn to him because of his masculinity. She felt jarred by the experience, almost wounded, for now that her perception of him had changed, she wanted him to experience the attraction, too. It could never be, she knew that. This chair would always be a barrier between her and the rest of the world.

Still she could cherish the memory of that one moment, the instant in which she felt as though they might be kindred spirits.

Chapter 5

I n the days that followed, Tabby kept Phillip too busy to think or feel anything but tired. Room by room, she went through the upstairs with a broom and scrub brush. At her request, he moved beds, bureaus, and shelves so she could clean every cranny. The only area she left untouched was Grandma Lucy's room. He wished her cleaning frenzy would carry her beyond the closed door. If they sorted through Grandma's belongings together, perhaps they'd both find the solace they needed to carry on without her. But Tabby refused all such suggestions. She offered no explanation or confidences.

However, her frantic housecleaning halted for an hour before each meal so she could cook. Phillip used those breaks to become better acquainted with their guests. To his surprise, they seemed to have no agenda other than enjoying each other's company. James and Neil often matched wits over checkers or chess, while the ladies read, stitched, or wrote what Phillip assumed to be letters home. The first day, James challenged Phillip to beat him at checkers, and from then on, Phillip joined the games whenever he had an opportunity.

Conversation flowed easily among the five of them, even during the most intense chess match. Phillip learned that Adrianna was the only child of James's brother, Gilbert, and his wife, Lucille. James was the elder of the two brothers, and it seemed a close relationship existed between them. Neil wasn't related, but Phillip thought he might as well have been from the easy familiarity that existed between him and the Trentons. The obvious respect with which James treated the quiet nurse told Phillip this was a man who could be trusted.

On the afternoon of the third day, Tabby declared the upstairs fit for their previous guests to return. Her attention turned toward the pantry and kitchen. Since she seemed to need no assistance from Phillip, he decided to risk showing the financial records to Neil. Tabby would probably have a fit, but he'd deal with it when the time came. For now, they needed to know how to project their income and expenses.

Entering Grandma Lucy's room gave Phillip no difficult emotional reaction. Having only entered the room for the first time the morning she died, he discovered it was the one place in the house that held no memories for him. Yet in some intangible way, it felt as if her presence had just left, like the lingering fragrance of a savory meal.

To the right just beyond the door, a large, rolltop desk sat against the wall.

"What a beautiful desk," Neil whispered, his fingers caressing the edge.

Phillip looked at the old piece of furniture. He knew nothing of its history, and to him it was too scarred and beat-up-looking to be beautiful. He glanced doubtfully at his guest.

Neil's smile showed understanding. "Old furniture is a hobby of mine. This looks like it's seen better days, but a bit of refinishing could make it glow in no time. The wood grain is what appeals to me. It looks like it's made out of some fine wood like cherry or mahogany."

Phillip shrugged. "If you say so." He hoped his smile took any unintended sting out of his words.

"It's just the kind of project I love doing in my spare time back home." Neil reached for the slim book Phillip had retrieved from the center drawer of the desk. "This would be your grandmother's record of business?"

Phillip nodded. He'd often seen Grandma Lucy writing in the large red hardbound book at the kitchen table after their guests had gone to bed.

"Shall I look through it here, or take it downstairs?"

"Let's take it into the parlor, so Tabby doesn't suspect. No need for her to catch us in the act." Phillip grinned, feeling as he had during his school days just after he'd pinned a girl's braid to his desktop. Neil's normally pleasant expression looked troubled, as if he felt uncomfortable. But, in his typical fashion, he said nothing.

Phillip led the way back downstairs. In the parlor, Aunt Caroline and Adrianna sat discussing a needlework pattern, while Uncle James read a novel. Neil lowered himself into a chair, the ledger already open in his hands. He turned pages in silence.

Phillip experienced a moment of panic when Tabby arrived with a tray of cookies and a teapot.

"Oh, you're down here," she said to him. "I thought I heard you doing something upstairs."

"I just went to make sure the taps in Grandma's bathroom weren't leaking," he improvised quickly. That would justify his entrance into the room, if she wondered.

She seemed to accept the explanation. "I'll bring you a cup for tea, unless you'd prefer coffee."

"Tea is fine," he replied, not wanting her to linger. When she'd delivered the cup and left again, he gave a mental sigh of relief, then looked at Neil. "What's the verdict?"

Neil turned a few more pages until he reached Grandma's last entries. "Your grandmother was a careful businesswoman." He flipped through the blank pages until he encountered more writing and nodded. "I wondered about this." He studied the numbers for a few moments, then asked, "Have you made plans to go to the bank?"

Phillip shook his head. "I hadn't thought about it. Should I?"

"You might want to talk to your grandmother's banker today, then," Neil suggested. "The records show that the boardinghouse has been turning a small profit. According to your grandmother's tally, there's a good sum of money in the account." He turned to the beginning of the book and turned it so Phillip could read the tidy columns of numbers. "This column is the date of each transaction. She also set up columns to record where the money was spent, the person from whom income was received, and the amount. It looks like she also made up a separate page for each guest. Most of your guests look up-to-date, except for this one."

Phillip studied the page with Adam's name at the top. It had been close to a month since he'd paid. "That's strange. Grandma Lucy usually collected each Friday. I probably should talk to him about that before I invite him to return."

"You have returning guests?" Adrianna asked.

Phillip thought he saw a hint of worry in her eyes. He framed his answer with care, to calm whatever concern she had. "There were three men staying here the morning Grandma Lucy died. They moved to a hotel until we got things settled and asked us to let them know if and when the boardinghouse opened for business again."

Her nod of polite interest gave no clue of her feelings. He wished he knew her better so he could more easily guess her thoughts. It would be even easier if he had the right to ask her about them. But such familiarity would mean sharing his thoughts with her, and thus, his past as well. Those issues were better left untouched. Friendly distance was the only kind of relationship available to him.

Other concerns pushed Adrianna out of his mind as soon as he left the boardinghouse after lunch. Looking at Grandma's tidy ledger had made him realize how little he knew about managing finances. His rule had always been to spend the money when it was available and bide his time when it wasn't. This philosophy had served him well until now. Now that he was jointly responsible for a business, he'd have to learn about budgeting and record keeping.

Arriving at the bank, he realized with a shiver of apprehension that he had no idea who to talk to. His casual attitude toward money had made a bank unnecessary. He looked around the small room, his ingrained habits of observation causing him to register as many details about the place as possible. Four people waited in single file for one of the two tellers to become available. The tellers stood behind a counter topped with metal grating. Off to the right, four steps led up to a second level, half of which had been closed in by walls. A secretary's desk sat in the open area, and a door led to the room behind the walls. A wooden sign on the door read "Mr. Wilke, Bank Manager." A high window looked down over the tellers and customers.

"May I help you?"

The polite question from the teller to his right interrupted Phillip's observations. He hadn't realized the line would move so quickly. He stepped up to the counter. "I need to speak with someone about the accounts for Barry's Boardinghouse."

"Certainly, Mr. McEvan. I'll see if Mr. Wilke is available."

He felt uneasy at having been identified so quickly. Though he'd grown up in this town, he couldn't recall having seen either of the tellers before. Yet they recognized him. It brought back memories of the days when anonymity meant the difference between life and death. He looked nervously around the room again, then noted with relief that the teller had returned to her place. His memories receded as a balding, paunchy man wearing a wide smile moved around in front of the counter. "I'm Ben Wilke," he said, extending his hand toward Phillip.

Phillip shook the man's hand. "Phillip McEvan."

"We've been expecting you," Mr. Wilke assured him. "Would you like to have a seat in my office?" He gestured ahead of him toward the stairs and the room beyond. Once inside, he shut the door firmly and indicated a chair close to the large wooden desk. "Condolences on Mrs. Barry's death." He seated himself behind the desk. "She was one of our community's finest ladies. I assume you're here to discuss the financial arrangements she made for you and Miss Spencer."

The banker's knowledge brought Phillip an instinctive feeling of distrust. He had to forcibly remind himself that no one here meant him ill will. Both his family and Tabby's were well known in the community and respected. "You seem familiar with our situation," he managed to say.

Mr. Wilke smiled reassuringly. "Mrs. Barry discussed her wishes with me in detail many months ago, and yesterday Mr. Spencer brought me a copy of the will. He told me to expect you or his daughter to come in here and asked me to help you in whatever way I can."

Phillip hoped his internal relief at the perfectly rational explanation didn't show. "I'd like to know how much money is in the account, please."

"Certainly." Mr. Wilke opened a desk drawer and removed a folder, which he opened onto his desk. "Mrs. Barry opened three accounts with us. One is the fund she used for the daily operations of the boardinghouse. She brought deposits from her boarders' rent at the end of each week and made withdrawals at the end of each month to pay her various accounts with local merchants. About six months ago, she opened two other accounts. One is in your name and the other is in Miss Spencer's name. According to the will and what Mrs. Barry explained to me at the time she opened them, you and Miss Spencer are free to use what is in each of your accounts as you see fit. Withdrawals from the boardinghouse account require a signature from each of you. Your personal account is a private matter between you and the bank, and Miss Spencer's account is similarly private." He wrote on a piece of paper and handed it to Phillip. "That is the balance of the boardinghouse account, and this," he handed over another paper, "is the balance of your account. Do you need to make a withdrawal today?"

Phillip studied the two sets of numbers. Never had he had access to money like this. Though the amount in his personal account was quite a bit less than the boardinghouse account, there was still more there than he'd ever seen at one time. Grandma Lucy's generosity brought a lump to his throat. He felt as he had the many times in his boyhood when she'd quietly tucked a penny or a nickel into his pants pocket and told him to "buy yourself a treat from me." He couldn't let himself think right now about how much he missed her. He cleared his throat. "I'll take five dollars out of my personal account, please."

"I'll take care of it right away," Mr. Wilke assured him and hurried downstairs. By the time he returned with the cash, Phillip's sadness had passed, replaced with an eagerness to share the news with Tabby. He forced himself to shake Mr. Wilke's hand with dignity and leave the bank in the manner he thought an experienced businessman would. Once out onto the street, however, he broke into a run.

As soon as he entered the kitchen, he knew he'd have to wait. Tabby stood at the counter pummeling a lump of dough as he'd often seen Grandma Lucy do while making bread. Where Grandma's movements had always been smooth and rhythmic, Tabby's were sharp and forceful. The tension in her back told him her mind was occupied with more than the bread. She glanced over her shoulder at him, her hands not pausing in their work. "You look like you have good news."

He nodded, unsure of how much to tell her. The last thing he wanted to do was stir up a fight. "I've been to the bank. Grandma left each of us a bit of money in private accounts."

Surprise flashed in her eyes, then faded. "I hope there's enough in the business account to replenish the pantry. I'm almost out of flour."

"There's a good sum there. Perhaps after dinner tonight we can go over the numbers together?"

She nodded. "We definitely need a budget. If you stay for supper, we can talk after I get the dishes done."

"What can I do for you in the meantime?"

"Just keep the woodbox full." Though the words were abrupt, her tone sounded less sharp.

He shrugged to himself as he headed toward the back door. Tabby never had been one to gentle her words. She always said what she thought and kept her emotions on a tight rein. He did wish she'd let him do more than fill the woodbox. Grandma had always had a variety of tasks for him to do—lifting a pot of soup, filling the dishpan for washing dishes, removing cookies from the baking pan. Even when she didn't have a task for him, she encouraged his company while she worked. But he had a feeling Tabby wouldn't welcome his lingering. Until she made room for him in the world she was making her own, he'd have to step carefully. Three armloads of wood topped off the woodbox. He would check again in an hour. In the meantime, he felt as if he should be busy.

Perhaps he should chop more wood. Though the pile was still sizable, there could be no such thing as too much wood for the stove. Especially if Tabby intended to work out her frustrations in the kitchen.

∞

From the parlor, Adrianna watched Phillip's repeated trips between the back door and the kitchen. For the first time in years, she felt the stab of envy. He moved without conscious effort, carrying each armful of wood as if it had no weight. The feeling surprised her. Long ago, she'd resigned herself to living the rest of her life as a spectator, unable to join in the everyday activities other people took for granted. At home it was easy to be content in her chair. A bevy of people surrounded her constantly, eager to accommodate her every need and desire. She'd wanted to experience life beyond her luxurious home. She hadn't expected to be seized by a desire for independence, a longing to participate in this less-sheltering world.

Uncle James laughed in triumph as he beat Neil yet again in one of their endless games of chess. The sound ignited a flicker of hope in her. Though he was far more physically handicapped than she, he never seemed limited. He'd already encouraged her to expand her own limits by teaching her to propel her own chair, then insisting she practice at every opportunity. Perhaps she could learn more from him.

The subject of her thoughts startled her with a loudly voiced question. "Phillip, could I speak with you when you have a moment?"

To her surprise, the red-haired young man responded right away. "Yes, sir?" He came to the doorway and looked in eagerly. He had become so at ease with them, Adrianna felt as though she'd known him since childhood. Her thoughts darkened. Her childhood included the days when she could walk and she felt certain that in his mind, she and the chair were inseparable. How could she fault him for that? She'd taught herself to think the same way. Long ago she'd learned not to torture herself with thoughts of how life had been before her illness. She turned her attention back to the conversation.

". . .explore your town a bit," Uncle James was saying. "Would you be willing to escort me?"

Adrianna saw alarm flash in Phillip's eyes before he quickly neutralized his expression. "Actually, sir, Tabby's brother, Tom, who manages the train station, would be a far better guide than I. He knows the history and sights of this town well."

Uncle James studied the young man for a moment. Adrianna recognized his intent. She knew from experience how perceptive he could be, often recognizing hidden feelings in a person before that person was aware of them. She could tell he saw something in Phillip he wanted to explore.

She felt an unfamiliar though pleasant sense of anticipation. She'd seen Uncle James take people under his wing before, and the results were always positive. It would be fun to watch what his influence could do for this intriguing man.

Chapter 6

Apprehension skittered up Phillip's spine. An instinctive understanding of people had saved his life more than once. Now that instinct told him this man's request was anything but casual. He made a final attempt to dissuade him. "I'm sure Tom could answer your questions far better than I could—"

The man interrupted firmly. "But yours is the company I want." The statement held a strange gentleness. "If you're concerned about Tabby needing help, Neil would probably be willing to assist her." He glanced at his nurse and received a nod for confirmation.

Phillip wondered why his presence was so important to the older man. To inquire would seem rude, so he simply said, "When would you like to leave?"

"Immediately." He pushed at the wheels of his chair with the ease of much practice, propelling himself toward the doorway. "I'll grab a jacket from my room just in case the day turns cool."

In less time than seemed possible, James paused in the doorway of the mudroom. "You don't need to keep lunch for us, Tabby. If I have my way, Phillip and I won't be back for a while." He grinned at Phillip with the cheekiness of a ten year old.

Phillip grasped the handles of the wheelchair to maneuver it down the stairs. The cold metal brought back Phillip's worst memories. He could feel the chill of the metal frame around him, the feeling of frozen helplessness as cold-faced men stopped his friend. If he'd known it would be the last time he saw Jan—

"Seems too beautiful a day for such a rush."

Phillip returned to the present with a welcome jolt. They were now a full block away from the boardinghouse, and he was pushing the wheelchair as if they were being pursued. He slowed to a more sedate pace. "Sorry about that," he mumbled, hoping James wouldn't ask questions.

The older man just reached for the wheels of his chair. "How about if I push myself for a while? That way you can walk beside me. It will make conversation easier."

Gratefully, Phillip matched his stride to his companion's progress along the board sidewalk. He mentally sorted through what he knew of the town's history so that he could begin a commentary. "I'm not sure where to start in telling you about our town. I've lived in the area most of my life, but I'm afraid I haven't learned much about what makes it unique from other places."

"It's definitely unique," James assured him. "Being here feels like stepping back in time about ten years. Did the town feel different to you after you returned from the war?"

Phillip felt as if a cold wind had stolen his breath and his ability to speak. He concentrated on helping the wheelchair off the boardwalk, across the street, and up onto the next boardwalk before replying. "It's a completely different world," he finally stated. "How did you know I'd been a soldier?"

Knowing blue eyes looked up at him with compassion. "I was there, too, young man. I recognize the look in your eyes even when you think you're revealing nothing. I suspect those of us who fought the horror will always recognize each other." He gestured toward the train station at the end of the street. "How long has the railway been here?"

Grateful for the change of subject, Phillip let the happier memories wash over him. "It arrived in 1932." He felt the smile move his lips. "I was just a youngster at the time, but I still remember the excitement. You see, the entire town moved two and a half miles east to meet the railway. School let out for the day so we could watch the co-op store being moved. It was one of the few days my dad did anything but work on the farm. I still remember the thrill when our schoolteacher actually stopped to talk with my sister and me. I was utterly in love with her."

"Where is she now?"

Phillip chuckled. "She married my dad. My mother and three brothers had drowned two years before when we were moving to the Peace Country. Ida was the best thing that could have happened to our family. It seems strange to remember that she hasn't always been my mother."

"Was your grandma Lucy Ida's mother?"

"No. She's actually not related to us at all." Too late, he realized he'd spoken of her in the present tense. "I mean, she wasn't related to us." He had to swallow hard to get around the lump that had suddenly filled his throat. "Ida lived in the boardinghouse with her before marrying my dad. Both Ida's parents had died before she moved here, so Grandma Lucy became the only family she had. When she joined our family, Grandma Lucy just became our grandma, too."

"How did you and Tabby end up in partnership?"

Phillip shook his head. "I'm not sure." Usually, he avoided answering personal questions. It had been a necessity during his years overseas and had since become a habit. But for reasons he couldn't define, talking with this man felt comfortable, even comforting. "My best guess is that she saw the business as a way of helping us both. It's too big a responsibility for one person. Her eldest son lives in England, and her only other son is Tabby's dad, who has a successful farm. All of Tabby's brothers and sisters have families and careers of their own. Tabby is the only one with the time and interest to invest in the business. Since I've been living with Grandma for the past two years, I guess she figured I was the one best able to help Tabby."

"Tabby isn't an easy person to help." A small smile deprived the statement of any rancor.

"She's always been independent to an extreme." He realized they'd reached the main intersection of town. Pointing toward the co-op store on the other side of the street and the large hotel diagonally across from them, he mentioned another historical event. "This area of town was almost flattened in 1943. An explosion in a building nearby just about destroyed everything in this area and blew the glass out of most of the windows in the downtown area."

"What happened?" James's face lit with interest.

"I wasn't here at the time." Phillip shared a small smile of understanding with his companion. "But what I've been told is that the U.S. Army had stored some dynamite and percussion caps in a livery. Somehow, the building caught fire, and the dynamite and percussion caps did what they were invented to do."

"What a mess! Were many people killed?"

"Reports vary. The military put the town under martial law until the worst of the mess was cleaned up, then brought in town planners to redesign the downtown area. Also, by way of apology, they gave the town a much-needed new water and sewer system."

"What was the American military doing in Canada?"

"They built the highway that provides a land route from here to Alaska. They were concerned about the possibility of Japanese invasion from the north."

"That must have brought quite a few changes to your hometown." James put his chair in motion again.

Phillip nodded, remembering his return from the war. It had been more difficult than his most harrowing escape from the Gestapo. War had dramatically changed both him and his hometown. Reminding himself that James still waited for a reply, he tried to give an objective answer. "When I left, Dawson Creek had a population of around five hundred. Grandma Lucy told me about the army's arrival. Overnight, the railroad brought five thousand soldiers." He pointed toward the gentle ridge to the east of the town. "That hillside was covered with tents. There wasn't a reliable sewer system here yet, so most families still used outhouses. She said within forty-eight hours of the soldiers' arrival, every outhouse in town had a padlock on it."

He joined in James's laughter, then continued. "With this being the southern staging point for the construction, the town's economy got a real boost. Once the highway was finished, the economic benefit continued. We have a steady stream of people passing through on their way north, as well as plenty of opportunities for newcomers to find their niche."

He heard the faint note of longing in his voice and hoped the older man hadn't noticed. The bustling activity of his hometown had seemed the perfect place to establish a new life for himself, far removed from the horrors of war-torn Holland. Many other young men of his acquaintance had happily established themselves in business or on a farm and found wives. He had stumbled from job to job trying to lose his memories. But his experiences had turned him into a man who would never again fit easily into the predictable world of crops and animals, local commerce, or carefree community events. Moving in with Grandma Lucy had helped him find a certain measure of peace, but he still longed for a solid sense of direction for his future.

James said nothing for the next couple of blocks. When he spoke again, it was a question about the farms that surrounded the town and provided the basis for its existence. Phillip answered easily, relieved to be able to discuss something that didn't stir unwanted emotions.

They wandered past a variety of businesses as they talked. James didn't appear to have a particular objective in mind, seeming to prefer viewing whatever there was to be seen and asking questions about whatever caught his fancy. Phillip wondered at his stamina. Sunshine made the day a warm one, but the older man didn't seem to be breaking a sweat. For the first time since the Trentons' arrival, Phillip saw James as a complete person. The wheelchair became a mere appendage. While the man needed assistance in certain things, he in no way could be described as helpless.

With that realization came a startling thought: Perhaps James could help Phillip find a way to conquer his nightmares. Phillip couldn't believe his own line of thinking. The only person to whom he'd entrusted even a few of his memories had been Grandma Lucy. Others had asked about his war experiences, but he always sidestepped with a joke. Laughter invariably distracted people from their investigation into the mixed darkness and Technicolor of his memories. His listeners wouldn't understand the combined stimulation and heartbreak of surviving on the precipice between death and life. They would hear only the details he wanted to forget. He knew his silence stimulated their curiosity, but he refused to expose the part of himself that might never heal.

James pointed toward a sign ahead of them. "Jean's Cafe. Makes me think of lunch. What would you say to a couple of sandwiches to go, my treat. I'd rather not be cooped up indoors while we eat, if you can suggest an alternative."

"You don't have to buy my lunch," Phillip protested.

James waved the objection away. "It's something I'd like to do. You just think of a place where we can eat without a crowd surrounding us."

"There's a shady spot just a couple of blocks up, in front of the train station. It's off to the side, away from where most folks are coming and going."

"Sounds just right." He purchased the sandwiches, then accepted Phillip's offer to push the chair to their picnic spot. Phillip wasn't sure why he'd asked for the job he'd been afraid of just over two hours earlier. Somehow, it felt different now.

The sandwiches were almost eaten by the time he'd figured out how to lead into the questions he wanted to ask. "How long were you in the war?"

"Which one?" James grinned, then continued. "I served in the First War and came through without a scratch. So, when World War II started, I volunteered almost right away. I did fine until Dieppe. I only lost my legs. Too many of our men lost their lives."

While in England before his return to Canada, Phillip had met a few soldiers who had lived through Dieppe. Not a one of them would talk about it. Their eyes held the look of men who had seen things no sane person wanted to remember, much less discuss. But James's eyes were different. He had the look of a man who had not only lived through the worst but conquered its effect on his soul. "How do you live with it?" He knew the question came out badly, but he couldn't think of any other words.

James's face softened with understanding. "It's not been easy. Sometimes I still wake up in a sweat. I'll never forget lying on that beach, unable to move while my blood drained out onto the sand, hearing shells raining all around me." Memories whitened his face. "I'll also never forget the two men who risked their lives to carry me off that beach or the nurses who stayed by my bedside until the infection cleared up. Most importantly I'll never forget how my wife flew over to England as soon as she heard I'd been wounded; she refused to let me give up. Once my body began to heal, she made me talk about the memories that haunted me. Even now, she can tell when I get a flashback. She won't let me forget that God brought me through two wars for a reason. He kept me alive, and on a daily basis He provides what I need to cope with what I can't forget."

Phillip wished he could say the same. He, too, had a collection of good memories. They were what had pulled him back to Holland on assignment after assignment. But for him, all the good memories were overwhelmed by the worst one of all, the one that haunted his dreams and the one he'd never be able to tell another soul. "What about the nightmares?"

"Caroline and I have spent many nights talking through those, too. A lot of guys I know have retreated into themselves and won't tell anyone what they've been through. I wouldn't have made it if Caroline hadn't been willing to share my burden."

Phillip knew what he meant. Grandma had been his refuge. Though there were many things he hadn't told her, she knew enough of his experiences that he hadn't felt completely alone. "Grandma Lucy listened to me. She was a nurse in World War I so she knew what I was talking about."

"Now you have no one," James commented softly. "You don't have any friends among the other young men from here who served?"

"I don't want to talk with them." Phillip shook his head. "I did some unusual things, the kinds of things that people find thrilling to hear about. They don't understand what was at stake."

"France or Holland?"

The quiet question focused Phillip's attention on James's face. The compassion written in his eyes assured Phillip his companion respected both the adventure and the heartbreak. "Holland."

"Whew! No wonder you have nightmares."

For the first time since Grandma's death, Phillip felt the crushing weight of loneliness ease. "It was the most fulfilling work I've ever done, but it haunts me, too."

"How did you get into espionage work?"

He felt himself smile at the memory. "I kind of stumbled into it. When the war began, I signed up to get out of Dawson Creek. I'm not a farmer, which has made me a round peg in a square hole as long as I can remember."

James chuckled with appreciation. "I'm not sure I'd have made a good farmer, either. I can see how that could create an identity crisis around here. Was the army any better?"

"It was a brand-new world. I found something I was good at. Being a farmer's son, I was in pretty good condition, which put me ahead of a lot of guys. Before I knew it, I was offered a chance for extra training. The rest of my troop went to Italy or North Africa. I was told to report to the Special Operations Executive in England."

He let the memories take over, needing to be reminded of what had started him on the path that ended in his nightmares. "That's where I learned of the Resistance movement. It awed me. I couldn't imagine the courage it took for people in the Nazi-occupied countries to work under the occupation for its overthrow. I was assigned to the radio room, where I heard communications from field operatives throughout Europe. When a courier returned safely from a mission, we all felt relief so intense it seemed tangible. When news came of an operative captured or killed, I felt more determined than ever to do whatever necessary to help end Hitler's rampage."

Phillip paused. He couldn't find the words to describe the deep changes that occurred inside him during that time. Having been open and friendly since childhood with everyone he met, he had learned how to temper his friendliness with caution. A sixth sense awakened in him as he evaluated each new acquaintance. A few he trusted immediately, but most he kept at arm's length. His natural affability soon became an impenetrable guard around the secrets he had to hoard.

Then came the thrill of his first jump and the heartbreak of seeing what Nazi occupation had done to the once-beautiful country of Holland. Over and over, he returned to that little country, responding again and again to the courage of its people.

Only when his voice broke did he realize tears had filled his eyes. He looked into his listener's face, not sure what he'd see there.

Matching tears and deep empathy filled the eyes gazing back at him. After several quiet moments, James said softly, "You lost a friend."

Coming so closely on the heels of his vivid memories, the man's uncanny perception roused all the instincts that had kept Phillip alive under impossible circumstances. Without any forethought, he responded, "Spies have no friends."

Chapter 7

The rain started that evening. Once in bed, Adrianna kept herself awake to enjoy the rhythmic patter. Her parents' stone mansion didn't permit such sounds to be heard indoors. She felt a new wave of gratitude toward her aunt and uncle for making this trip possible. Her thoughts drifted toward Uncle James's lengthy absence today. She'd been surprised when he arranged for Neil to stay behind, though not too surprised to notice how pleased Neil was with the arrangement. A smile curved her lips in the dusky dimness. It had been funny to watch Neil's attempts to assist a ferociously independent Tabby. She'd had no choice but to let him keep the woodbox filled. At one point she'd gone so far as to request his help lifting a large pot off the stove. Beyond that, she gave every indication of wanting to be left strictly alone.

Adrianna couldn't help but feel sorry for Neil. He'd been Uncle James's nurse ever since the older man's return from England and, as such, had spent a great deal of time with the Trenton family. Gilbert and James shared a close bond that only became tighter after James's injury. In fact, Adrianna remembered, Father had tried to convince Uncle James and Aunt Caroline to move into his stone mansion in a prominent area of Toronto. Uncle James preferred their more modest, though certainly not shabby, home in a close-by neighborhood. Because of the affection between the brothers, the two families spent countless hours together. As a result, Adrianna had come to know Neil quite well, even looked on him as the brother or cousin she'd never had. The thought that he might have a crush on their prickly hostess made her want to giggle.

No two people could be more dissimilar. Neil had a quiet competence about him. While capable enough, Tabby bristled with pent-up frustration. She moved around the boardinghouse as if she had more tasks to do than her lifetime would allow. Adrianna just tried to keep out of the woman's way. Had her parents been here, she knew they wouldn't have stayed more than a night. They expected, and usually received, deferent courtesy. But Uncle James and Aunt Caroline seemed to have settled in here. Aunt Caroline appeared to have formed an affection for the brusque young woman. If anyone could find gentleness under that gruff exterior, Aunt Caroline could.

She and Uncle James had never had any children. Uncle James often teased that because she had no brood of her own to cluck over, she tried to mother the whole world. Innumerable young men and women had found emotional sustenance in the Trentons' home. In fact, Adrianna realized Aunt Caroline had filled a void in her life that her own affectionate but society-oriented parents hadn't been able to recognize.

Aunt Caroline wasn't the only giver in the family, either. Uncle James selected fewer protégés, but he invested himself in younger people just the same. In fact, Adrianna could tell when he left the boardinghouse this morning that the trip was less to satisfy his curiosity than it was to get to know their host.

As nearly as Adrianna could perceive, the plan had worked. There seemed to be an easy camaraderie between the two men that hadn't existed this morning. All through supper and during their after-dinner conversation in the parlor, she sensed Uncle James trying to make the young man feel part of their family. From the way in which they reached out to the younger pair, her aunt and uncle might have been the hosts. The role reversal didn't seem at all odd to Adrianna. Of all the places in town they might have chosen, how typical that they'd instinctively found the one place they were needed.

She refused to let her thoughts linger on Phillip. Anytime she happened to be in his presence, her emotions became violently contradictory. Part of her feared he would single her out for attention born of misguided pity. Another part tingled with awareness of him and longed for him to feel the same toward her. Since their memorable handshake, he'd treated her with considerate detachment. She wondered if it was her handicap that held him off or if he simply didn't feel any interest in her.

At least he seemed more comfortable around her uncle. He'd gone so far as to push Uncle James to the parlor after supper, which caused her to exchange a grin with Aunt Caroline. Usually, Uncle James became downright cranky if someone tried to do anything for him he felt he could do for himself. When Phillip grasped the handles of his chair, Uncle James had settled back as if he'd hired the man to be his personal servant.

Though she hated to admit it, something about Phillip made her want to find out what lay behind his troubled brown eyes. But even if she were able to learn what haunted him so, it would only make her care more about him. She'd kept tight rein on her heart up until now. No matter how much she cared about anyone, she couldn't expect a healthy, active man to want to spend the rest of his life with a cripple. She'd come to terms with that in her early teens. An emotional partnership such as Uncle James and Aunt Caroline shared just wasn't possible for her. But it seemed the older she got, the more she struggled against being as limited emotionally as she was physically.

She closed her eyes as if to shut the door on any more such thoughts and focused her attention on the drumming rain. Was it her imagination, or had it become heavier since she'd come to bed? No matter. If the sound was louder than before, it only proved more helpful in escaping into sleep. She drifted into slumber with the mental image of sorrow-darkened brown eyes not entirely banished. Each time she woke from a troubling dream in which she fell out of her wheelchair trying to reach something invisible, the continuing rain lulled her back to sleep.

∞

Phillip also listened to the rain throughout the night. His discussion with James in front of the train station wouldn't let his mind rest. Though James hadn't shown any offense at Phillip's abrupt termination of their conversation, his eyes told Phillip he understood what Phillip couldn't say. The friendship James had asked about, and Phillip had denied, sat at the center of Phillip's inner turmoil. His sense of failure had never faded, and tonight it kept Phillip awake. He knew if he shut his eyes, the nightmares would intrude. While conscious memory brought him pain, at least he could control it. The horrors of the night made their own agenda. At their core lay the unanswerable question: Could he have done more?

Logic told him he'd done everything possible. Had he blown his cover by leaping from the wheelchair to help Jan escape, he knew, without a trace of arrogance, he could have jeopardized the liberation of Holland. The SS would certainly have freed Jan if they'd been able to capture Phillip. Phillip's years of espionage work gave him knowledge and experience that made him highly valuable to both sides. The Germans needed him out of their way as desperately as the Allies needed him to continue his work. So, in that moment of horror, he'd chosen to let his friend be captured. Only weeks later, Holland regained its freedom.

Phillip managed to stay in Holland for the next three and a half years, officially to help with reconstruction. Unofficially, he searched for his friend, using every means at his disposal. At long last, he had to admit to himself that Jan was one of the many who had disappeared into the abyss of Nazi terror.

Even now, battling nothing more than memories, physically safe in a warm bed, Phillip found a small amount of solace in his lack of knowledge about Jan's family. Becoming friends as they had was more of a risk than espionage work allowed. Knowledge of Jan's loved ones was out of the question. Even as he'd left Holland for the last time, Phillip had known intense relief that he'd never had to answer to his friend's family for his loss. His mind told him Jan had known the risks and accepted his fate. His heart told him he had failed.

Finally, dawn slipped over the horizon, the daylight lightening the gloom around him. His clock showed 5:00 A.M. when a squeak just outside his room caught his attention. His pulse quickened in the aftermath of his memories, then slowed as he felt an indulgent smile widen his mouth. He waited silently for the door to move ever so slightly, confirming his suspicions. "Come in," he invited in a loud whisper.

As he expected, two small bodies scurried into the room. Four-year-old Danny wasted no time clambering up onto the bed to sit on his uncle's chest, while seven-year-old Teddy eyed Phillip with disappointment. "How did you know we were there?"

Phillip reached out to give the boy's arm a manly squeeze. "It's not you, Ted. The floor squeaked."

"I tried to keep Danny off that board, but he doesn't know about spying yet." Teddy gave his younger brother a disdainful look.

Phillip could see the beginnings of an all-out argument. "How about the three of us sneak downstairs together? Maybe if I carry Danny, we can miss the squeaky stairs."

Teddy's glowing eyes conveyed his excitement. Danny bounced with the delight of being included, his enthusiasm inflicting serious discomfort on Phillip's rib cage. Phillip grunted and lifted his nephew down to stand on his own feet. "If you'll get off of me, young man, I can pull on some pants."

"I already have on pants," the four year old informed him, forgetting to whisper. " 'Cept they're jammy pants, not real pants. Mommy says I always have to wear jammies to bed or I'll get cold."

"Your mommy is a smart lady," Phillip whispered, "but if we don't be quiet, she's not going to be happy with us."

Danny clapped his hand across his mouth, while Teddy proceeded toward the door with exaggerated care. Phillip lifted Danny to his shoulders, then showed Teddy how to step on the outside edge of each stair to avoid the creaks. The boys' enthusiasm pulled Phillip into their childish adventure, slowly freeing him from the tentacles of his memories. At the bottom of the stairs, he made a big deal about peering around the corner "to check for an ambush." They tiptoed to the kitchen, where he let the boys perch on the table with their feet resting on the bench.

He knew his sister wouldn't approve of the arrangement, but the boys seemed to think it great fun. He cut three slices of bread and spread each with a generous portion of Ruth's homemade raspberry jam. She appeared just as he was pouring a round of milk.

"We didn't wake Uncle Phillip up," Danny assured his mother, as though in answer to an unspoken reprimand. Ruth gave him a hug of reassurance, then lifted him onto the extra block of wood in the middle of the bench that helped him sit high enough to reach the table. Teddy quickly slid onto the bench while informing her, "He helped us sneak down here so we wouldn't wake you up."

The twinkle in Ruth's eyes both reproved Phillip for letting them sit on the table and let him know she hadn't missed a thing. She assured Teddy he'd been "wonderfully quiet." Phillip admired her ability to boost her son's confidence without resorting to untruth. He wished he were still young enough to be encouraged so easily.

"Do you want breakfast here or were you planning to eat at the boardinghouse?" Ruth's gentle inquiry reminded him of his responsibilities. He hurried upstairs for a quick shave, then across the street, where he found the kitchen empty. A full hour later than usual, he'd expected Tabby to be miffed that he hadn't arrived sooner. He went about his customary duties, starting the fire, setting the coffee on, heating a pot of water for Adrianna's tea.

He sat at the table waiting for the coffee, trying to stifle a sense of alarm. Should he go check on Tabby? He resisted the memories of another morning not so long ago.

The hiss of coffee boiling over pulled him back to the present. Phillip poured himself a cup of the black liquid, then moved the pot to the back of the stove. A rustling sound behind him attracted his attention. A weary-eyed Tabby stumbled into the room, bringing a smile of relief to his face. "Good morning," he greeted her, offering the steaming cup, which she accepted without comment. He poured another for himself. "Rough night?"

She wrapped her hands around the mug as if she were cold, then took two sips of the hot liquid. "You might say that. There was a leak right over my bed. I woke up a couple of hours ago to a soaked bed and spent the rest of the night on the floor."

"Let's move you into Grandma's room today, then," he suggested.

The look on her face conveyed anything but enthusiasm. "I'd like to check out the other rooms first."

The now-familiar question about her motives troubled him, but he didn't know how to encourage her confidence. "I'll go with you to see if there are any other drips."

"After breakfast?"

It took him a moment to realize she was requesting his input. "Sure." To extend the friendliness of the moment, he asked, "Is the coffee okay?"

She nodded. "It's good. Your mother taught you well."

"It was Grandma Lucy, actually." The moment the words left his mouth, he knew he'd said something wrong. Tabby's face hardened and she turned toward the counter. Not sure how to mend his error, he changed the subject. "We didn't get a chance last night to discuss my visit to the bank. Do you have a moment now?"

She studied the wall clock for several moments, her stance suggesting a decision of massive importance. "I should get potatoes boiling for hash browns, but if you can talk while I work, I'd like to know what you found out."

He tried not to notice the difference between her harried motions and what had been Grandma Lucy's comfortable way of moving about the kitchen. Tabby had always had her own way of doing things. "It's not complicated. She set up an account for each of us, in addition to the main business account." He named the amount in his own account and in the main one. "Mr. Wilke said he'd talk to you personally about your account."

"I'm going to put the money back." Her voice held a strangled tone.

Phillip sat speechless. After mentally searching for a neutral reply, he put his only thought into words. "Why, don't you want Grandma's gift?"

She shot him a look filled with exasperation. "It's not going to be easy to make this business work as well as Grandma made it work. It was fine for Dad to bring her produce and meat all the time, but we can't let him do that for us. We not only have to make the business self-supporting, but make it support us, too."

"But Grandma's gift will support us until the business turns a profit for us."

"I don't care if you take yours. The boardinghouse is all we have left of Grandma—" Here her voice broke for a moment, but she swallowed and continued. "And I'm going to do everything I can to make sure it succeeds."

Her determination gave him the perfect opening to confess what he'd done with Neil. "I feel the same way, Tabby. That's why I went ahead and showed Neil Grandma's record book." He waited for the storm to break over him.

Her glare could have withered a forest. "I can't change what you've already done, but I wish you hadn't."

"I know." He made his tone as conciliatory as possible. "But it seemed to me we'd be better off getting advice now from someone we trust, rather than muddling through on our own and possibly making serious mistakes later. Besides, if Neil hadn't have looked at the records, we wouldn't know about the money in the bank."

She shrugged as if it made no difference, and he didn't pursue the conversation. With the matter of their finances now an open subject between them, later would be soon enough to discuss future plans.

Chapter 8

With his new awareness of their financial situation, Phillip watched Tabby prepare breakfast. He noticed for the first time what went into the hearty meals he took for granted. The coffee and tea he'd already prepared had to be purchased from the local co-op. The potatoes for the hash browns, eggs, smoked meat, milk, cream, and butter all came from Tabby's father's farm. Though he didn't know what ingredients went into the bread, he had a feeling most of them had to be purchased from the co-op as well.

While Tabby's father had refused to allow his mother to pay for items he regularly brought to the boardinghouse, Phillip knew that arrangement would have to change.

With a quiet but cheerful "good morning," Neil crossed the kitchen from his room to James and Caroline's. Phillip responded with a smile and a nod, though Tabby didn't seem to have heard their guest. Again, Phillip wondered what troubled Tabby so deeply. Though she'd always been a bit withdrawn around strangers, he'd never seen her so sullen and moody. Neil could be of immense assistance to them in understanding Grandma Lucy's ledger and setting up a projection of income and expenses. That is, if Tabby would accept his help.

The door to James and Caroline's room opened again, and Caroline gave them a pleasant greeting on her way to her niece's room. Phillip's thoughts turned toward the younger woman. After spending yesterday with James, he'd made a kind of peace with the two wheelchairs. Somehow, getting to know a person in a wheelchair as a human being made the dark memory lose part of its power, perhaps because now it wasn't his only real experience with someone in a chair. With that barrier in his perception crumbled, he wanted to find out more about the young woman who had sparked his interest.

A door creaked open, and he watched Adrianna push herself into the kitchen. Her black hair was coiled around her head in some kind of braid that accented her pale, delicate features and her blue eyes. Her gaze met his, then dropped as a flush crept into her cheeks. In that moment of eye contact, Phillip saw an emotion in her eyes that struck an answering chord in him. He preferred not to analyze the feeling, though he couldn't escape the sense that they carried similar burdens. Logic told him that couldn't be possible. She'd been nowhere near the war. *If so,* an inner voice argued, *what has she experienced to put such shadows in her?*

He banished the uncomfortable questions under a layer of courtesy. "Good morning, Caroline, Adrianna. Coffee or tea?"

They each requested tea, so he busied himself filling their cups and providing honey and milk. "How was your rest?"

A soft smile brought life to Adrianna's eyes. "I've never been lulled to sleep by rain before. It's a lovely sound."

Phillip considered for a moment, then nodded in agreement. "When you're warm and snug inside, it is a wonderful sound. It's not so nice when you have to sleep in it, though." He made sure a smile let her know he meant no criticism.

"Why did you have to sleep in the rain?" Aunt Caroline wanted to know.

"During the war." It was more of an explanation than he'd offered to anyone other than Grandma Lucy.

"You look far too young to have been a soldier," Aunt Caroline commented with a smile. "Where did you serve?"

"Mostly in England as a wireless operator." This was the cover story that had served him well since his return. No one expected someone who hadn't left England to have any stories to tell, so the questions usually stopped. Just then he noticed that James had joined the table. He wondered what the older man would think of his evasion. But James's eyes showed only understanding and support.

"Mmmm. The smell of fresh coffee starts any day out right," he commented to the room in general.

Phillip answered the broad hint with a smile, hoping his face also communicated his gratitude for diverting the conversation. He served coffee to both James and Neil, then helped Tabby carry heaping platters from the stove to the table. He noticed she still remained behind a wall of silence.

But when he approached her after the meal about asking for Neil's help, she responded with less rancor than before. "He's already seen the records, so we might as well benefit. If we can set up a budget of what we think we'll need, then we'll know how long the money in the bank can carry us."

He noticed she avoided a direct reference to Grandma. Maybe it was just a woman's way of dealing with grief. Whatever the cause of her moodiness, she seemed quite at ease when the three of them settled around the end of the table for another look at Grandma's tidy records.

"Income appears in this column," Neil explained, using a pencil to point to the figures, "and expenses are here. These are bills she paid right away, and these are her charge accounts at the co-op and the lumber mill. It looks like she hasn't used her account at the mill in some time."

Phillip nodded. "Any repairs I've done in the past two years have been minor enough that she paid cash for supplies."

Little lines of tension showed around Tabby's mouth. "Hopefully, it won't cost much to fix the leak in my room. It doesn't look like income has been that great over the winter."

Neil pointed to the income column. "With only three guests at one dollar a night, she was just making ends meet. As we noticed yesterday, one of the guests hasn't paid at all this month. She must have been living on savings."

"Which we can't afford to do," Tabby declared. "From what I see here, it looks like there's enough in the bank to keep us going for six months. Summer is usually a busier time than winter, so maybe we can keep all the rooms filled from now until the end of September. If we do that—" she paused and reached for Neil's pencil and the ledger. Making some small, tidy ciphers on a blank page, she turned the book so Phillip could see the results. "Eight rooms at one dollar a night for the next three and a half months will give us $856. The ledger shows expenses of about $50 a month. Since we'll have to spend more than she did on groceries, we can say $75 a month. That's $262, which will give us almost $600 at the end of the summer. It will get us through the winter, but it won't give us much for spending money."

Phillip wanted to point out that they each had more than enough spending money in the bank, but didn't want to resurrect Tabby's temper. If she wanted to live on a shoestring, that was her choice. As far as he could tell, the boardinghouse could support itself for the next year without him giving up what Grandma had wanted him to have.

Tabby wasn't finished planning. "Next time Dad stops by, I'll have a chat with him about paying for the food items he brings in."

Phillip felt a stab of resentment that she didn't feel a need to include him in the discussion. He hoped her urge for independence or whatever it was that motivated her wouldn't destroy the possibilities that lay before them both. He listened to her next thoughts.

"In the meantime, let's take a look at the rooms upstairs. I'd like to get my stuff moved and then contact the other guests to return. We need their income as soon as possible."

He paused long enough to thank Neil for his help, then followed Tabby up the stairs, where the drumming of the rain was even more pronounced. At the doorway of the room she had chosen, she stood back to let him enter. He saw immediately where a leak had formed in the corner above her bed. He stood for several moments, contemplating the steady drip. He knew little about carpentry, but this didn't look like a minor problem. "Let's check the other side of this wall." He tapped the wall that separated Tabby's room from the one in which he'd put Mr. Johnson's things. "Hopefully this is our only leak."

Tabby peered into the next room first. Her look of horror prepared him only slightly for the disaster before them. The area that dripped onto Tabby's bed gave a steady stream directly over Mr. Johnson's collection of books. Shelving had protected some of them, but a couple of books were drenched. A stain of wetness spread across the entire ceiling. His feeling of uneasiness intensified. He peered into the next room, which showed signs of dampness but no visible leak yet. The two rooms on the south end of the house seemed to have escaped damage so far.

He rejoined Tabby in Mr. Johnson's room, where she pulled books from the shelves as quickly as her hands could move. "One thing I know for sure," he offered, taking a stack from her, "we can't do any kind of repairs until the rain quits. Let's just pray things don't get any worse."

"What are we going to tell Mr. Johnson?" Her eyes darkened with dread.

He shrugged. "What else is there to tell him except that we needed his room downstairs and didn't know that this one leaked. Let's hope he understands our dilemma." After a moment of thought, he added, "He'll be in school until 3:00. I could walk over to the school around that time and see if I can speak to him before he goes back to the hotel. Mr. Watters probably isn't working today because of the rain, so perhaps we could get him to come take a look at this mess. Being a carpenter, he'll be able to tell us what needs to be done."

They moved Mr. Johnson's belongings into one of the smaller, but dry, rooms and stacked his undamaged books on the bed. Tabby carried the wet ones down to the kitchen to dry. As soon as Caroline saw the problem, she offered assistance. "Let me take those into the parlor. I can put them in front of the fireplace and keep an eye on them while I work on my needlepoint. Adrianna and I will keep the pages turned so that they'll dry more quickly."

To Phillip's amazement, Tabby only said, "Thank you."

He built a small fire in the parlor fireplace, then helped Caroline lay out the damp books. He noticed Adrianna wore a thick shawl over her shoulders as she worked on some kind of lacy stitchery. The sight made him realize how cool the room must be for someone who couldn't walk around. He wished he'd thought about the fireplace earlier. He built a fire, then tended it carefully throughout the morning.

It felt so natural to share a meal with these five, he noticed. In less than a week, Neil and the Trentons had become much more to him than guests. Though Tabby remained an enigma, she felt like less of a stranger than she had in the moments they'd first learned of their inheritance.

After the meal, he carried dishes to the sink as he had often done for Grandma, then reached for a dishtowel. Tabby snatched the cloth out of his hand. "I can manage!"

Instinct told him the attack had little to do with him. He moved away from the counter to sit beside the table. "We didn't get your things moved to a different room," he pointed out. "Your only option is Grandma Lucy's room."

"I'm not moving." Her tone was quiet but implacable.

"Tabby, you can't sleep in a wet bed or on the floor. You know your dad gave Grandma's room every luxury he could think of. Why won't you use it?"

"Because it's hers."

"But she's not here anymore."

"The room is still hers. I'm not taking it away from her."

He couldn't resist the comment he knew wouldn't make things any easier. "You're not being reasonable."

The look she turned on him bristled with temper. "Just what do you mean by that?"

He'd already stuck his foot in a mess. He might as well say his piece and take the consequences. "You know as well as I do Grandma is dead. She won't ever need her room again. You might as well—" The shaking of her shoulders stopped his flow of words. He couldn't think of anything to say or do. As he watched sobs shake her whole body, he wished he'd just kept his mouth shut.

Then Aunt Caroline moved into his line of vision and wrapped her arms around the weeping woman. "It's okay to grieve, honey. Just let the hurt all out," she murmured soothingly as one hand held Tabby's head against her and the other stroked the blond hair.

Phillip felt guilty for causing the storm and even more guilty for watching so helplessly. Without conscious thought, his steps took him to the parlor. James and Neil sat hunched over the chessboard as usual. Adrianna looked up at him with concern in her eyes. "Is Tabby okay?"

Phillip shrugged. "I said something stupid and got her upset."

James's chuckle attracted Phillip's attention. "I wish I had a penny for every stupid comment I've made to get Caroline upset. If anyone can help Tabby come to terms with her loss, it's Caroline."

Phillip still felt baffled. "What do you mean? Tabby seems to think Grandma is going to need her room sometime soon."

James contemplated the chessboard. "Some folks deal with grief that way. By not facing the empty room, she doesn't have to admit to herself that she's lost someone she loves very much."

"So can you explain to me why she's been so crabby?"

Neil's eyes reproached him, but James only gave another small, knowing smile. "It's the difference between men and women, son. We men like to vent our emotions in physical activity. Women tend to carry the hurt inside until someone loves them enough to give them permission to let it out. She needs lots of love right now and Caroline has lots to give."

Not many minutes passed before Phillip heard the companionable sound of the two women working together. He couldn't make out the details of the quiet conversation, but it sounded as though the crisis had passed. He suddenly itched to get out of the boardinghouse. Maybe now would be a good time to visit the hotel and talk with Mr. Watters. He'd also see if he could track down Adam Dodd. Even if the young man didn't want to return to the boardinghouse, there was still the matter of his unpaid bill.

Chapter 9

Phillip spent the afternoon slogging through the rain and mud from one place of lodging to another. At the first hotel he visited, the desk clerk confirmed that Mr. Watters was a guest, but had stepped out for awhile. No record of an Adam Dodd existed. Phillip stopped by the second hotel and checked with Mrs. Sealy, who occasionally rented out a couple of rooms in her two-story house. No one had seen a person matching Phillip's description of Dodd. He mulled over the mystery on his way to the school. He didn't even want to think about what Tabby would say about the lost income.

To make matters worse, Mr. Johnson didn't take the news about the leaky roof as calmly as Phillip hoped he would. He accompanied Phillip through the still-falling rain to the boardinghouse in silence, surveyed the water-damaged books in the parlor, and then turned his most forbidding schoolmaster look back to Phillip. "Young man, I do not appreciate your mishandling of my belongings."

Conscious of Adrianna and Caroline seated nearby, Phillip tried to gesture the irate man to the kitchen. He didn't want them to have to hear the reason Mr. Johnson's books had been moved, nor did he want to subject them to what was building into a nasty scene.

"Nor do I appreciate being interrupted," the short, gray-haired man continued as if they stood alone. "I have inconvenienced myself by living in the hotel to give you time to adjust to your grandmother's loss, and you repay me by this invasion of my privacy, not to mention the destruction of my property. This confirms my suspicion that the excellent, respectful lodging I've enjoyed for the past five years is no longer available to me. School lets out at the end of next week, and I shall find alternate accommodation thereafter. In the meantime, please have my belongings delivered to the hotel." He strode toward the front door, then turned at the last moment. "I shall also expect financial compensation for my damaged books. You may do whatever you like with them as they are no longer useful to me."

Phillip shut the door behind the departing man and turned to see Tabby staring at him. He thought he detected panic in her eyes.

"Phillip, you didn't even try to get him to stay! We can't afford to lose customers. Besides, you can be sure he'll tell everyone he knows about what happened."

He resented her inference that he could have done something to avert Mr. Johnson's departure. "You want to have him stay here to find fault with everything we do?"

"I can live with it," she asserted. "We need the money."

He couldn't share her desperation. Grandma Lucy had never worried about her clientele. She gave them her best service, and if they didn't like it, she bid them a cheerful farewell. For the first time since the will had been read, he wondered if there was a way out of this awkward partnership. He had no alternative employment, but returning to the family farm might be preferable to Tabby's uptight approach to business. Before he could say anything he might regret, however, a knock on the door diverted his attention.

Cecil Watters stood on the doorstep, water running down his uncovered balding head. A tall, bulky man, his face wore a perpetually pleasant expression. "The hotel gave me the message you needed to see me?" He tipped his hat in Tabby's direction. "I can't tell you how glad I am you two young folks are keeping Miz Barry's business going. It's a fine tribute to her memory."

"Thank you," Tabby responded from her place in front of the stove, her voice sounding choked. "We're looking forward to having you back with us."

Mr. Watters looked back to Phillip. "Is there a problem?"

"Actually, we need your help to determine that," Phillip said quickly before Tabby could reply. "We have a very wet ceiling upstairs. I know little about carpentry, so we were wondering if you'd look at the problem and assess the damage for us."

He nodded and slipped off his wet boots. "I'd be glad to help. Let's go take a look."

Once upstairs, Phillip pointed out the three rooms that gave evidence of the problem. Mr. Watters peered at the ceiling in each room. He spent the longest amount of time in the center room. After several minutes of silent study, he pulled a folding measure out of his back pocket and extended it to poke at the boards above them. The ruler made an indentation. "Just as I thought," he muttered. He moved out to the upstairs common area, where he focused his attention on the area where the stovepipe extended through the roof. Finally, he looked at Phillip.

"Would you mind if I looked in there?" He gestured toward what had been Grandma Lucy's room.

"No problem." Phillip opened the door. "Come on in." He and Mr. Watters moved toward the right side of the room together. But while the carpenter's attention centered on the damp ceiling, Phillip examined the desk below it. Water had dripped onto the rolltop cover, puddling in the grooves. Even Phillip's untrained eyes could detect staining. The piece of furniture, which had seemed unimportant just yesterday, now touched a tender spot in him. He could easily envision Grandma Lucy hunched over this desk, penning the letters that had meant so much to him during the war. Maybe he should talk with Neil about refinishing it. At the moment, however, it needed to be protected from further damage. He pulled one end away from the wall.

"Let me help." Mr. Watters grasped the other end, and together they moved it to stand beside the bed. "Do you want to call Miss Spencer up here so I can give you the news together?" His tone indicated it wouldn't be happy news.

Phillip knew better than to holler at his partner. Quickly, he descended the stairs. In the kitchen, she stood at the counter stirring something in a huge bowl. "Mr. Watters wants to talk with us upstairs," he told her. "Can you spare a couple of moments?"

She quickly wiped her hands on a towel and hurried upstairs, not even waiting for him to follow.

Mr. Watters waited for them in Mr. Johnson's room, the room with the most visible damage. "It looks to me like your roof needs to be replaced." He poked at the wet ceiling with his wooden measuring stick. "You can see here where water has run into the attic and rotted out the ceiling boards." The stick made more little indentations in what Phillip had thought was solid wood. "Damage this severe doesn't occur overnight. It means water has been getting into the attic for quite some time, gradually rotting out the structure. I have no way of knowing how severe the problem is until I get inside the attic, but I'd say you're looking at some major rebuilding. The leak in your grandmother's room comes from the ventilation pipe from the plumbing. It looks like the seal around it has come loose, which has let water seep into the attic and now through the ceiling."

From the edge of his vision, Phillip saw Tabby whirl from the room. Her footsteps echoed into the room she'd refused to enter until now. He wished he knew whether or not to follow. He decided it was more important to continue their business with Mr. Watters. "Can you give us an estimate for materials and labor?"

The carpenter pondered the ceiling in silence. At last he replied in the slow, thoughtful way typical of him. "I'd guess materials will cost close to four hundred dollars. Labor would be about half that."

Phillip knew he'd have to tell Tabby the news. Materials alone would consume most of the money in their business account. She would be even more adamant about putting Grandma Lucy's gift money into the business. He wondered if he should feel guilty for not doing the same, but he didn't. He didn't want to relinquish the last tangible reminder of the special relationship he'd shared with Grandma.

A question from Mr. Watters pulled him out of his thoughts. "Which room did you put my things in?"

"The next one over." Phillip moved to the less-damaged room beside the one that had housed the schoolteacher's belongings. If he'd chosen rooms differently, perhaps the more easygoing guest would have suffered the damage. On the other hand, he doubted Mr. Johnson would have been happy in any case.

The carpenter looked over the bed, washstand, and bureau. "I could be quite comfortable here." He gave Phillip a direct look. "Frank Johnson told me what happened to his books. I wanted to tell you I think you did the right thing, the only thing you could have done under the circumstances. Those people downstairs need the bigger rooms." He paused, looked out the window for a moment, and cleared his throat. "I have a proposal for you. If you and Miss Spencer would be willing to let me continue living here, I'd oversee the repairs free of charge. I figure six months' free room and board would be quite adequate compensation. Talk it over with Miss Spencer tonight, and get word to me in the morning. Regardless of your decision, I'd like to move back here as soon as you're ready for me." He gave Phillip a firm handshake to seal the deal.

Phillip wondered if he knew anything about the third former guest. "Do you know where Adam Dodd might be staying? I tried to get word to him, but he seems to have vanished."

Mr. Watters nodded with a wry expression. "I'm not surprised. The morning we left here, he mentioned taking the train to the city. Did he leave anything behind?"

"Not much." Phillip chose not to mention the unpaid bill. If Dodd really had left town, there wasn't much they could do to collect. The less said, the better.

Mr. Watters made his departure, and Phillip made one more tour of the upstairs rooms, except for the one from which Tabby had not yet returned. He didn't feel ready to deal with one of her emotional storms. To be honest, he didn't feel ready to face his own feelings. All he knew for sure was that this business of Grandma's was threatening to ask more of him than he wanted to give. If he and Tabby decided to get the repairs done, they'd be committing themselves to working together for a long time. First, there would be the months of structural work, then months of rebuilding the business. Would it ever earn enough to support the two of them? He couldn't imagine himself working as an innkeeper for the rest of his life. Not even for the foreseeable future, if he were honest.

The stray thought that had been teasing the edges of his brain for days tantalized him again. Why not just take the money Grandma Lucy had left him and disappear from town? He had no obligation to anyone here. If he'd learned anything in the past two years, it was that he and this town just didn't fit each other. Would he head north into even more remote locations or south or east to the city?

The restlessness in his soul moved his feet down the stairs. He noticed Adrianna sitting alone by the fireplace in the parlor. The quietness in her face, so at odds with the turmoil he felt, drew him in. "May I join you?"

She looked up from her book with a smile that shortened his breath. "I'd be happy for the company." A furrow appeared between her brows. "You look troubled. I'm a good listener if you need one."

Though airing his feelings had been the last thing on his mind as he came down the stairs, he found himself describing the problem with the roof. "According to Mr. Watters's estimate, we do have just enough money to make the repairs. But I keep asking myself if I really want to do it. I've never thought of myself as a business owner. I don't think I like the responsibility." He hoped his wry grin told her he knew how selfish he sounded.

But her thoughts seemed to have gone in a different direction. "Do you know why your grandmother left the business to the two of you? I mean, it sounds like your families are large enough that any number of people could have taken over."

Were he and Tabby so obviously mismatched? Uncle James had asked a similar question just days ago. "I don't know for sure," he admitted. "I assumed that since Tabby and I are the only ones not married and involved in other things, we got it by default."

When Adrianna didn't respond, Phillip lifted his gaze from the floor to meet the blue eyes regarding him soberly. "You don't agree?"

Color flooded her face. "It's not my place to comment."

Again, he found himself wondering what thoughts tumbled behind her gaze. "Perhaps your perspective would help me figure things out. I'd like to know what you think, if you don't mind telling me."

Her words came out slowly and carefully. "It seems to me that since your grandmother took the time to put her wishes into writing, she made a conscious choice about whom she wanted to give her business to."

Phillip hadn't thought of it that way. For the first time since the will had been read, he felt a sense of curiosity. Grandma Lucy knew him well enough to be aware that he'd find the responsibility she gave him burdensome. She wasn't the kind of person to inflict burdens on other people. Rather, in all the years he'd known her, he'd watched her time and again try to relieve others' burdens. So what had been her intention for him? He wondered if he'd ever be able to find out.

Chapter 10

P hillip!" Tabby's voice from the top of the stairs shattered the moment in the parlor.

Phillip stood. "It sounds like I'm needed. Thanks for listening. You gave me something to think about."

Though Adrianna made no move to touch him, the look in her eyes made him feel as if she had. "I'd like to know what you discover." Her tone suggested a faith in him he was sure he couldn't live up to.

Yet, he realized as he took the stairs two at a time, he wanted to be worthy of that faith. Whatever she saw in him, he wanted to prove that it wasn't an illusion. However, at the moment, more practical matters beckoned. As soon as he reached the top of the stairs, Tabby hurried ahead of him into Grandma's room. He followed with a sense of caution.

Inside the room, Tabby turned to face him. He saw the evidence of heavy crying, but her eyes looked brighter than they had since the funeral. She stood with one hand on the desk, in much the same gentle gesture Neil had used. "I'm ready to move in here," she announced in her typically abrupt way. "I've come to terms with reality. Now I'm ready to work with you to make this boardinghouse a tribute to her memory."

"That might not be possible." He hadn't intended to say it so bluntly, but the words just seemed to fall out of his mouth. "Mr. Watters says we're going to have to replace most of the ceiling, attic, and roof. The materials will take most of what we have in the bank, though he says he'll do the labor in exchange for six months' free room and board."

"So when does he start?"

It was, he thought, as if her acquaintance with reality hadn't gone nearly deep enough. "Tabby, we're talking about major reconstruction here. Months of upheaval during which the main floor will be the only one fit for guests. Even if we find a way to keep the place running during that time, what guarantee do we have we'll turn a profit after it's all done? With two hotels in town, why would people choose a boardinghouse?"

Her lips thinned. "We'll just have to make sure we're the best."

He decided to let her have the undiluted truth. "And what about people like Adam Dodd? Do you realize he left town without paying for over a month's worth of room and board? It would take only one guest like that to put us in a real bind."

"I'll collect rent every night if that's what it takes."

The intensity of her determination frightened him. Did she not even see the potential problems? Should he just tell her now that he wanted out? Her touch on his arm caught his attention.

Her eyes were wide in her face, full of conflicting emotions. Her voice came out softer than he'd ever heard it. "I know there's every chance in the world I won't succeed. But this is all I have left of Grandma Lucy. I have to give it everything I've got so that if I do lose it, I'll know I did all I could."

He noticed she didn't include him in either the effort or the results.

With an abrupt change of subject, she caught him off guard again. "I want to find someone to restore this desk. It's a beautiful piece of furniture."

"Neil said the same thing." Again, his response came without forethought. "He said something about working with furniture in his spare time."

"Really?" Her eyes lit with anticipation. "I'll talk to him at supper. Maybe he'll work on this for me while he's here."

Neil's eyes sparkled similarly when she made her request. "Provided James doesn't mind sharing me, I would be delighted to help you out. I don't know how long we'll be here, but I'll do as much as I can in the meantime."

James's smile hinted at inner secrets. "I'm in no hurry to be anywhere else. Let's just say we'll be here at least until the desk is completed."

"That's settled then," Tabby declared, "and I'm most grateful. I should tell you, though, that the house will be under construction for the rest of the summer, most likely. We'll take pains to keep the noise and mess to a minimum. I'd be willing to offer you a reduced rate for your inconvenience."

"Nonsense." James could be as dogmatic as Tabby, Phillip noted. "We're far more comfortable here than we would be in any hotel."

Phillip caught the triumphant look Tabby shot in his direction before she replied with a gracious nod. "I appreciate your confidence."

Once again he felt as if she saw herself as sole owner of the business. *Not that I care,* he hastily assured himself. If it weren't for the mystery of Grandma's intentions, he'd sign the whole mess over to Tabby and be gone. He had no clue how he would solve the mystery, but until he'd given it his best effort, he couldn't bring himself to abandon Grandma Lucy's gift.

After supper, Tabby surprised him by accepting Aunt Caroline's help with the dishes. He wished he had Aunt Caroline's ability to slip past Tabby's stubbornness. Yet, if he could do so, would he really insist they abandon their inheritance?

He turned his mind away from the unanswerable questions as he and Neil eased the large desk down the narrow stairway. They agreed the kitchen would be the best place for the refinishing work, though Neil warned the smells might be objectionable at mealtime.

"We'll cope," Tabby replied. "If keeping the front door open doesn't help, then we'll just have to eat out in the summer kitchen."

"That sounds intriguing," James replied. "My mother had a summer kitchen while we were growing up, but city homes don't have such things. I'd like a look at yours, just for memory's sake."

"Sure." Phillip didn't have to be hit over the head to know when it was his turn to play the gracious host. Tabby was elbow deep in hot sudsy water. He led the way down the hall, knowing James would follow as effortlessly as if he still walked on his own feet. When they reached the back door, Phillip opened it. Glancing down as he stepped over the threshold, he realized the wheelchair would have trouble getting over the uneven boards. He stepped aside until James stopped at the doorway, then Phillip, with an ease which amazed himself, reached for the handles of the chair to tilt it over the awkward place. From there, an open porch led to a screened-in area to the left, which housed the outdoor work area. Three walls about four feet high partially enclosed a rectangle of space that was completed by the back wall of the house. Posts extended upward from the half-walls to support a roof that protected the room from rain and winter snow. A large barrel stove sat in the middle of the room, and cupboards lined the perimeter. Canning pots and jars filled some of the shelves, while buckets sat on others. Huge metal laundry tubs hung from nails driven into some of the posts that supported the roof.

This was one area of the house Phillip hadn't visited since before Grandma Lucy's death. He easily envisioned her at work out here, washing clothes or putting endless piles of vegetables into canning jars. The memory jolted through him, accompanied by a longing to have just one more chat with her, ask her just one more question. . . .

∞

Wiping the last pot carefully with the damp tea towel, Adrianna felt the exhilaration of accomplishment. It had been a whim tonight, to ask Aunt

Caroline for the towel. The counter was low enough that she could reach the wet dishes Tabby placed on there for drying. It felt good to participate in routine work rather than just watching. With that thought in mind, she turned her chair toward where Neil still sat looking over the old desk as if it were treasure. It still took strenuous effort to propel herself across a room, but the effort seemed to grow less each day. The feeling of independence more than compensated for the sore muscles.

"Tell me what you see," she invited.

With the teasing grin of an older brother, he obliged. "I see a lovely young woman whose newfound independence suits her better than cosmetics."

She felt the blush brighten her cheeks, even as her heart warmed under the lighthearted praise. Neil's opinion meant almost as much to her as her aunt's and uncle's. "Thanks for the flattery, but I meant what do you see in that desk."

"Oh." He nodded as if he'd just now caught her meaning. Gazing again at the interlocking pieces of wood that formed the rolltop cover, he ran his fingers lightly over the grooves. "I see hands. First the hands that made this, roughened by hours of work, possibly scarred by a slipped tool. Then the hands that bought it. I'm thinking probably a man's hands, buying this as a gift for his fiancée or his new wife. Then the lady's hands that used it. I can't envision anyone other than their grandma Lucy." He tilted his head in Tabby's direction. "Though they say she wasn't that old when she passed away, her hands probably looked much older than her age. They take it all in stride, but it's still a hard life out here."

Adrianna had to agree. While electricity lit Dawson Creek's homes and telephones connected the residents to each other, the town as a whole still felt remote from the rest of the world. The variety of services and entertainment she took for granted simply didn't exist in this place. These people worked, and worked hard, for everything they had. "I wonder what it was like here before the railroad came. I can't imagine living without electricity or telephones or running water."

"You should talk with my mother," Phillip offered from where he'd entered silently behind her.

She turned toward him, glad to have an excuse to find out more about him. "What does she remember about those days?"

He grinned and shrugged as if he were a small boy caught sneaking cookies before dinnertime. "To be honest, I don't remember. I didn't listen very carefully to what I thought were her boring stories. All I know for sure is that she came before the railway and watched this town grow. I'll bring her in for a visit one of these days and you can ask her questions to your heart's content. She'll be glad for an interested audience." He turned his attention to Neil. "So what's the first step?"

Neil traced the edge of the top drawer as if he could hardly wait to get started. "We should pull out all the drawers and make sure there's nothing left inside." At Phillip's nod, he suited action to words. Three drawers on the left side yielded a variety of writing materials and several bundles of letters.

Overcome by curiosity, Adrianna reached for the top of two large drawers on the right side. Puzzled, she pushed the drawer back in to look at its front again. "Neil, look at this. The front looks like it should be a deep drawer, but when I open it, it's just a shallow one."

A gleam lit her friend's eyes. "The drawer has a false bottom." He glanced at Phillip. "Do you mind if we snoop to see what's under it?"

"Not at all." Phillip shook his head. "I doubt Grandma Lucy had any terrible secrets."

Neil poked at the drawer's false bottom until a loose panel revealed itself. With a little more pressure, it flipped up, revealing a compartment underneath. Adrianna leaned over the drawer to get a better look. A well-worn notebook lay inside. "Do you think that would be her journal, Phillip?"

The red-haired young man peered over her shoulder, then drew back. "Possibly. Go ahead and lift it out."

She glanced toward the stove to see if Tabby would offer any objection. The young woman paused in scrubbing the floor. Adrianna raised her eyebrows in question, and Tabby responded with a silent nod. Only then did Adrianna reach for the notebook.

It turned out to be a stack of notebooks, each filled with small, careful script. Dates on the outside indicated the order in which the books had been filled. Adrianna opened the top one, which still contained several blank pages. "It is her journal," she whispered. "I've never looked at someone else's private papers before." She looked up at Neil and Phillip, only to find them watching her intently. "Should we be reading these?"

Phillip looked over at Tabby, who only shrugged as if it made no difference to her. The look he directed back at Adrianna showed both curiosity and sadness. "She's not here anymore to say yes or no. I'd like to learn more about who she was. She told me she'd been a nurse in the First World War, which is where she met Mr. Barry."

"Your father is her son?" Neil asked Tabby, who nodded.

"She was born and raised in England. She was married with two children when the war broke out. She lost her husband in the war and joined up as a way of supporting her family. When she came to Canada with Mr. Barry, only my father wanted to come with her. My uncle was already married at the time, so he and his family stayed there."

Adrianna hadn't heard their hostess say so much at a time since their arrival. The unusually gentle look on her face betrayed how much family meant to her. Adrianna gained a new appreciation for how much the young woman still must hurt over her grandmother's unexpected death. She risked another glance at Phillip, whose eyes also showed his inner hurt. An idea slowly took shape. "I'd like to learn more about her also. Could we read these together in the evenings while Neil works on the desk? I'm pretty good at reading aloud."

Tabby's face still held its softened look. "I'd like that."

"I would, also," Phillip agreed. "If Neil will show me what to do, I'll even help with the desk."

Adrianna looked back down into her lap where the journals rested. "Shall we start now?" When no one voiced dissent, she pulled the notebook that rested on the bottom of the stack. After scanning the first few sentences of the first entry, she grinned at Neil. "It looks like your imagination was right. Listen to this:

May 3, 1910
    I've never kept a journal before, but the hidden compartment in my new desk begs for written confidences. My dear husband, Kelvin, presented me with a lovely rolltop desk for our anniversary this year. I've been thinking for some time of writing down some of my thoughts, and this is as good a time as any to begin.
    My life is so blessed. My loving husband grows more dear to me with each day as do our two sons, Kelvin Jr. and Lionel. Sometimes I feel I ought to credit God more for these blessings and in some way show my gratitude, but my days are too full of happiness. I hope He knows how my heart feels and doesn't hold my silence toward Him against me.

She read aloud through page after page. The young Lucy's life seemed a lot like her own, comfortable in material things and happy except for a vague longing that surfaced again and again in her entries.

The pile of dismantled desk pieces grew as she read, and eventually Tabby's busy hands found nothing else to occupy them. Still, the young woman lingered, with what Adrianna knew to be uncharacteristic inactivity. Though Adrianna had never met the woman whom Tabby and Phillip loved so dearly, she felt just as absorbed in these thoughts as they seemed to be. Only when her voice began to grow hoarse did she close the book, and each of them roused slowly as if emerging from a joint dream.

Later that night, Adrianna dreamed of herself as Lucy, free to walk on her own, assume responsibility for a family, and live the life of privilege to which she'd been born. She woke in the dark with tears on her cheeks. Did she weep for herself or for the woman in the journal? She had no idea. All she felt for sure was the certainty that the pages she would read aloud in coming days would change her life.

Chapter 11

After another two days of intermittent rain, sunshine broke through. Cecil Watters moved back in and began work on the roof in the evenings. Despite his misgivings over the decision to rebuild, Phillip accompanied the carpenter up the ladder. Even if he eventually decided to leave town, at least this way he could say he'd done his part to help secure the future of the business for Tabby.

The only regret he felt as he ripped one rotten shingle after another off the roof was that he had to miss out on listening to Adrianna read from Grandma Lucy's journal. He had a hard time imagining the young woman who had penned the words, but they still made him feel closer to the grandmother he'd known and loved.

He and Cecil put in three hours of hard work before Cecil declared a halt. "Ten o'clock is late enough for any project," he announced with a grin.

Phillip followed him down the ladder, back already aching from his labor. Just inside the back door, Cecil bid him good night and headed up the stairs to his right. Phillip moved toward the kitchen as quietly as his work boots would permit. To his surprise, a light still shone in the parlor. Adrianna sat beside the dying fire, Grandma Lucy's journals in her lap.

"Hello," she called softly as he passed.

He stopped and took a step backward so that he stood beside the doorway. "Hello yourself. I thought everyone would be in bed by now."

Was it the firelight, or did a blush color her cheeks? "I thought you might like to hear what we read in the journals tonight."

Pleasure warmed him through. He couldn't believe this gentle woman had altered her schedule for him. "I'd like that very much, though I should probably take a quick shower first."

"I'll be waiting," she promised.

He stepped into the bathroom beside the stairs and stripped off his dusty clothing. Tomorrow he'd be prepared with a clean change. But for tonight, just rinsing the dirt and sweat off his body would have to do. Before returning to the parlor, he sneaked into the kitchen for two glasses of milk and some of the cookies he knew Tabby had baked that day.

That evening set the routine for the ones to follow. Phillip soon looked forward to the quiet time beside the fireplace as his favorite part of the day. He found Adrianna's voice delightful to listen to, and it felt good to share Grandma's thoughts with her.

Saturday morning, Cecil announced he'd spend the day at the boardinghouse. "The framing job I've been working on this week finished up yesterday, and the next house I'm supposed to start doesn't have the foundation finished yet." He gave Tabby a deferential smile. "That means, Miss Spencer, your house is one day closer to being finished."

She just nodded in response, but Phillip saw the anticipation in her eyes. He wished more than ever that he could share her dream. Later, on the roof, he used his unusual vantage point to try to gain a different perspective on his hometown. He only saw the same weathered buildings, wood sidewalks, and dirt streets. Cars and trucks had replaced the horses and wagons of his childhood, but the town still felt the same.

That night, dreams haunted him again. These weren't the clear flashbacks of his nightmares. Rather, he felt himself tumbling through the air in a free fall. He felt helpless to stop the pull of gravity or change his direction. He rose early Sunday morning to warm the cookstove in the boardinghouse and start coffee for Tabby, then returned to his room at his sister's home.

His thoughts had grown only more tangled during the night. He didn't feel able to cope with either food or conversation until his mind cleared.

He waited until the sounds of Ruth's family had faded, indicating they'd already left for church. Then, he made his way alone to the familiar setting. As he expected, a sizable crowd had already gathered by the time he arrived. The building was nothing fancy, but a comfortable hush permeated it. Families sat together on benches, quietly awaiting the start of the service. The little bit of visiting that took place happened outside by the steps.

He could see his parents and younger siblings seated near the front. To his surprise, the boardinghouse guests had also come. James and Adrianna's wheelchairs fit neatly at the end of two benches nearest the wall to his left. Phillip slipped into a place near the back, still preferring to be alone. He felt himself relax, as though an invisible hand wiped his mind clear of its frustrating thoughts. He remembered moments like this during the war when this same peace had invaded his spirit and provided guidance that went beyond experience or instinct. Eager to recapture the fulfillment of those days, he let himself absorb the quietness. An inexplicable sense of expectancy crept over him.

He stood with the rest of the worshippers and listened to the hymns they sang. He'd never been able to figure out how to make his voice produce melodious sounds. Though he could whistle any tune he wanted, singing was beyond him. He'd whistled the hymns as a boy, but couldn't bring himself to do so as an adult.

By the time the singing portion of the service was over, the room had become stuffy in the summer warmth. The men nearest the windows opened them to admit fresh air. Without being aware of his choice, Phillip found himself at the window beside Adrianna. He raised it a couple of inches, then looked at her to be sure the draft wouldn't chill her. She nodded at him with the soft smile that made him feel singled out for a special privilege. He moved back to his seat before he made a spectacle of himself. A few outside sounds drifted in through the open windows, but no one seemed to have a problem staying focused on what the pastor had to say.

A tall, thin man with a receding hairline and a permanent smile, Pastor David Porter had lost none of the enthusiasm that had brought him to Dawson Creek to lead this congregation and help them build the building in which they now sat.

"My text this morning comes from three verses, Proverbs 16, verse 9, Proverbs chapter 19, verse 21, and Philippians 2, verse 13." Pastor David moved out from behind the rustic pulpit, his Bible held in one hand while two fingers of the other marked his places. Phillip could hardly ever remember seeing the man preach any other way. The rustling of pages gradually stilled as the members of the congregation located the references. "Proverbs 16:9 says, 'A man's heart deviseth his way: but the LORD directeth his steps.' Then chapter 19, verse 21 reads, 'There are many devices in a man's heart; nevertheless the counsel of the Lord, that shall stand. Finally, in the New Testament, Philippians 2:13 says, 'For it is God which worketh in you both to will and to do of his good pleasure.' Has anyone caught the common theme here yet?"

Laughter rippled through the crowd. Phillip had always enjoyed listening to the pastor mingle humor and scriptural teaching.

"The first verse we read talks about how we set up a general direction we'd like to take. For instance, Dr. Pierce," the pastor smiled in Theo's direction, "knew when he was still in grade school that he wanted to be a doctor. I've heard he also knew he wanted to marry Ruth McEvan." Again, laughter met his comments. "However, I've heard Dr. Pierce tell about the ways

God guided him through his training and back to our community. By way of personal illustration, I was a teenager when I knew God had called me to preach. That was my general direction. God's specific steps for me led me to Dawson Creek and to the beautiful lady who is now my wife." His glance settled briefly on Maisie and their four children in the front row.

"Then if we look again at our verse in Philippians, we see that God not only shows us His direction for us, but He also gives us the will to do it. Many people have a hard time with this concept, because they see God's will as being primarily something that demands we do something different from what we want to do."

Phillip felt as though God had betrayed his personal struggle to the pastor, yet the man's gaze neither studied Phillip nor avoided him. Phillip leaned forward, his chin resting in his hand and his elbow propped on his knee, focusing intently on what Pastor David would say next.

"There are times when what God asks of us is not comfortable or easy. However, this verse doesn't have a qualifier in it or around it. It doesn't say sometimes He works in us or He may work in us. It says definitively He does work in us both to will and to do."

Pastor David closed his Bible, holding it now with one hand. "No matter how big the challenge, if we quiet our objections long enough to listen to Him, God will give us the 'want to' for whatever He's asking of us. The second verse we read in Proverbs tells us that God's plans prevail no matter what we decide to do. I think each of us here would agree that we want to see His will done through us, not in spite of us."

A quiet "Amen" came from several of the listeners.

"God's will is sometimes an easy thing and sometimes a heartbreaking thing. Sometimes submission to Him means embracing greater joy than we've ever known. Sometimes it means acknowledging that even the painful experiences in our lives are still within His control and wrapped in His love. We can't always explain Him, but we can choose daily to trust Him.

"In closing, I'd like to leave you with a quote I read recently. 'God is too loving to be unkind and too wise to make a mistake.' Let's ask Him together for the grace to trust His leading in each of our lives." He finished with a short prayer.

Quiet conversation followed the close of the service, gradually building in volume as people greeted each other and children scrambled outside to run off the energy that had accumulated during their enforced stillness. Phillip sat alone at the end of the bench, trying to absorb everything he'd heard. Grandma Lucy had lived by the principles the pastor had talked about this morning. Though the motives behind her will remained a mystery, Phillip had to consider the possibility that that very will had become God's direction for him. Responsibility still loomed over him and questions lingered, but a grain of peace made the burdens easier to bear.

∞

Adrianna had never before been part of a simple church service like this one. She let her eyes roam around the emptying room. Pine board walls and floor, clear glass windows, basic low-backed benches. Amid the simplicity, she felt something no stained glass edifice had ever given her. There was peace here; not so much in the building, but in the people who used it. The pastor used no fancy words or complicated phrases, yet his sermon provoked more thought in her than any other. He spoke of God as if He were as close to her as her wheelchair, and even as necessary. One sentence echoed in her mind. "God works in you both to will and to do." Did God concern Himself so much with her that He would give her desires and then fulfill them? Dared she consider for even a moment that He might grant her deepest desire? The thought thrilled, then devastated her. If she were meant to find love, surely he wouldn't have allowed the handicap that stood between her and a normal relationship with a man. Yet if that desire couldn't be met, perhaps He would still help her find a means of usefulness. She'd come on this trip to learn a bit of independence. Now she longed for more.

Tabby had lunch on the table soon after everyone returned to the boardinghouse. Adrianna picked at her food, her mind still occupied by what she'd heard. As soon as could be considered polite, she excused herself to the privacy of her room. The journals on top of her bureau caught her attention. She enjoyed reading aloud while Tabby went about her unending duties and Neil sanded down each piece of the desk. However, her greatest joy came during the late reading with Phillip. Though the words were the same, she felt them differently when he listened.

Last night they'd read of Lucy's impatience with her country's "obsession" with the war that had broken out as the result of the murder of a prince. Her entries became more consistent and laced with worry as her husband contemplated his part if England should join the conflict. Then came the heartbroken words about his departure for the front and her decision to send her two sons to live with their grandparents in the northern part of England.

On this quiet Sunday afternoon, Adrianna couldn't resist the urge to continue reading on her own. It wouldn't bother her to reread pages this evening by the cookstove and again by the fireplace. She felt as if these pages might contain the answer to her puzzling thoughts. She opened the notebook and found the place where she'd left off. The next entry made her catch her breath in sympathy for the young woman she had come to know and love.

September 15, 1914

My heart is shattered. Yesterday, I awoke in such anticipation of our fifteenth wedding anniversary, which would have been today. Though Kelvin could not be with me, I knew his thoughts would be here, and I planned a special dinner of celebration even though I would be the only one eating it. Just after noon, my doorbell rang and there stood two men in military uniforms holding a black-edged piece of paper. I knew without reading it what the message would be.

Apparently, I fainted, because the next thing I remember was waking up this morning in my bed with my neighbor Chelsea keeping watch. It took but a moment for me to recall what had so overwhelmed me. As graciously as I could, I sent Chelsea away so I could be alone with my grief.

Alone. Never has the word carried such devastation for me. Oh, this horrible, horrible war! If it weren't for some foreigners who can't settle their disputes in a civilized fashion, I wouldn't be a widow today.

Adrianna pulled a handkerchief from her bureau drawer and continued reading. Page after page revealed the outpourings of Lucy's heartache. Adrianna wept along with Lucy. The young widow's feelings were so similar to Adrianna's own when she discovered she would never walk again. Though the losses were very different, each of them had lost something precious. From what she'd heard about Phillip and Tabby's grandmother, she'd obviously found a way to fill her life with happiness in later years. Adrianna wanted to know how. When she reached the last entry in the notebook, she reached eagerly for the second book.

This one was tattered and stained. The cover hung loosely. Adrianna opened it and returned to war-torn England. The entries became shorter, more sporadic, and increasingly bitter. Just four sentences revealed Lucy's decision to change the course of her life.

November 3, 1914

I've signed up as a WAC. I hope to be sent overseas soon, hopefully to serve as close to the front as possible. If God has any compassion, a bullet will allow me to rejoin my husband. I can do this with a clear conscience, knowing my sons will be raised well by their grandparents.

More entries recorded Lucy's arrival at the front where she wanted to be, then her still-increasing bitterness over the devastation she witnessed. Adrianna realized the stains on the cover came from blood, and she felt closer than ever to the woman whose thoughts she read. Then, after a paragraph dated March 23, 1916, the writing stopped. When it resumed on the next page, the date was June 1, 1916, and the script looked shaky and weak. The first few sentences told briefly of being shot at while on the way to an aid station. Lucy wrote how she couldn't remember anything after the first shot, but how she'd been told that the vehicle in which she'd been riding had been blown up. She'd been thrown clear, but her two companions had died. Again, the young woman railed at God for His lack of care in the world He'd created.

But as Adrianna read, she began to notice a gradual change in tone. What had been rantings at God became questions rather than accusations. Bits of Scripture verses began to show up, apparently found in a Bible borrowed from one of the nurses.

June 13, 1916

They tell me I'm healthy enough to return to the front and that I'm desperately needed. Because of my injury, I could refuse to go, and no one would fault me. But I sense my Heavenly Father leading me back into service. I went the first time in rebellion against Him, daring Him to take my life, wanting to punish Him for altering my world so irrevocably. He chose not to take my life, but as the psalmist says, "He weakened my strength in the way." He put me in a place where I could do nothing but lay still and listen to Him speak.

Now I want to go back to the war, this time to help others find the peace I've discovered. I wish I could understand why He allows the things He does.

But since I can't, I will trust what I've learned about Him these weeks. His Word echoes with the message of His love for mankind, in spite of man's continual rejection of that love. I cannot help but respond to His love. Even though my heart still aches with loss, I know now that He has been good to me. He has brought me to the end of myself so I can see Him. That is enough.

Adrianna lifted her gaze from the page. That was the key to what she'd heard this morning. She realized that the preacher hadn't spoken of a God who planned humans' lives the way Uncle James and Neil planned their chess moves. Rather, God cared personally for each individual, at least according to what Lucy had written.

Never had she thought of God as being interested in her, Adrianna Jean Trenton. If He were, then He could help her find a fulfilling life in spite of her useless legs. More than that, she felt a longing to know Him the way Lucy had come to know Him. Her notations talked about a God who could be approached informally, just as a child would approach her parent.

Hesitantly, Adrianna put her longing into whispered words. "God, I don't know You, though I've heard Uncle James and Aunt Caroline talk about You. They say You're the reason Uncle James is still alive and such a wonderful man to be around. Will You become part of my life and help me come to know You? And if it's possible, would You help me find a way to become useful?" Though her prayer contained no formal conclusion, she had a strong feeling of being heard. A gentle feeling of love enveloped her. For the first time since her illness, she felt totally accepted, both in her inner being and in her physical condition. She also felt, for the first time, a sense that her life had purpose. Time would show her what it would be.

Chapter 12

The next day, Phillip began a series of excursions with Neil and the Trentons, who requested his escort around Dawson Creek and its outlying areas. He felt no guilt for spending so much time away from the boardinghouse. Tabby seemed happiest when left alone to do what she felt necessary. He couldn't work on the construction without Cecil, who was working at a paying job that kept him busy during the day.

Wednesday morning, Phillip borrowed Tabby's brother's car for a trip to the old town site, then to his parents' farm. There was barely enough room in the car for all five people, so the wheelchairs had to stay behind.

It had been months since Phillip had visited the family farm. He'd never before noticed how picturesque the two-story house looked, tucked at the end of a tree-lined lane. Until now, it had symbolized the way of life he wanted to get away from. Today it just looked like home.

"The original house was a single-story, two-room cabin," he explained, bringing the car to a stop. "From what Dad and Ruth have told me, there was nothing on this land when we arrived. Neighbors helped put up the cabin and a barn, and Dad gradually improved it to what you see now." With fresh appreciation, he looked around at the corrals, two barns, storage sheds, and greenhouse positioned around the neat yard.

"Your parents have done well," James observed.

Phillip felt an unfamiliar glow of pride. "I didn't appreciate it as I should have while I was growing up, but I see it now."

Mom hurried from the house with a wide smile of welcome. "Phillip, what a pleasant surprise! Hello again, Mr. and Mrs. Trenton." She looked back at Phillip. "We met on Sunday. Can you stay for lunch?"

Phillip pondered for a moment. While it would take a bit of effort to get James and Adrianna into the house, he knew his parents would make them feel at home. "If you have enough for five extra, sure."

"Of course we do." Mom looked toward one of the barns for a moment. "Greg and Tim are out seeding, but Dad's in the barn. Here he comes now." The soft smile she saved only for her husband lit her face.

Phillip swallowed a sudden lump. Wouldn't it be wonderful to have someone smile at him like that? Involuntarily, his eyes turned toward Adrianna, and their gazes collided. For an instant, he saw in her the same longing he felt. He scrambled out of the car before the momentary connection could blossom into something more intense.

Dad greeted him with a rough hug. "Good to have you drop by, Son. Shall we help your guests come inside?" In the matter-of-fact manner so typical of him, he positioned himself beside Neil to assist James into the house. Mom and Caroline followed, already chatting as if they were long-time friends.

Phillip again looked at Adrianna, this time with a feeling of apprehension. Should he wait for Neil? The thought seemed ridiculous. The dainty young woman couldn't weigh any more than the bundles of shingles he'd stacked beside the house last night. He couldn't leave her in the car alone, yet something in him resisted the idea of having her in his arms.

⟳

Through the front window of the car, Adrianna tried to guess Phillip's feelings. The fact he made no move toward her indicated he felt reluctance to help her into the house. Often in recent weeks, she'd resented her chair and the restrictions it represented. Now she realized just how much freedom it gave her. Had her chair been available, she could have made her own way into the house.

At the moment, though, she had no choice but to wait until either Phillip decided to assist her or Neil returned. Phillip moved slowly toward her side of the car. Was her handicap so repulsive he didn't even want to touch her? She felt the shame of it begin to creep up her spine. If ever she wished to be a whole woman, this was the moment. What she wouldn't give to be able to meet this man on equal ground rather than to be dependent on him! The intensity of the longing blocked out her awareness of anything else until a pair of strong arms lifted her from the seat. Just a moment before impact, she realized he had misjudged. Her head crashed against the door frame. A heavy thud echoed through her skull, causing her to cry out in pain. Involuntarily, she tightened her grip around the one who held her. The pain slowly subsided, but not before it had left tears in her eyes. She tried to blink them away before he saw. With his right arm under her legs, his left around her waist, and her arms around his neck, there was no way either could avoid eye contact. The self-loathing she'd felt moments before now showed in his gaze.

"Honey, I'm so sorry." His voice hitched on the last word.

The endearment and the gentle tone shook her more than the bump on the head. Could he really care so much? By the time she'd gained the courage to look into his eyes for confirmation, they'd reached the house. Neil swung the door open for them, and Phillip carried her into a roomful of people. He set her down as if she would shatter if jarred too suddenly. She found herself in a high-backed wooden chair with arms worn smooth from use. Phillip pushed her chair close to the large table that took up most of the kitchen area. Conversation flowed around her. She felt as if everyone could read in her face the emotions swirling inside her. Aunt Caroline gave her a glance as if to confirm her presence, but it didn't linger. Grateful that her aunt had noticed nothing amiss, Adrianna was still amazed that her feelings couldn't be read by all.

Phillip's mom knelt beside her, concern evident on her face. "Phillip told me what happened. Are you okay?" she asked softly. "If it still hurts, I can get you a cold cloth."

Adrianna shook her head. "I'm fine, thanks. Tell him not to worry so." Her smile began as friendly reassurance to the woman beside her, but she found herself wanting another look into Phillip's face. He stood off to one side with one shoulder propped against the wall, his gaze moving from person to person as though checking for an intruder. Only after watching for several minutes did she realize his eyes always returned to her. The warm wonder of it shook her again. With effort, she refocused on the room as a whole.

Uncle James sat at the other end of the long table with Aunt Caroline beside him. Two girls who looked to be teenagers moved from stove to counter to table, filling dishes with food and placing them on the table. Two younger girls moved around the table laying out place settings. Adrianna figured the younger two must be twins as their hair color was the only distinguishing characteristic between them. One had the blond hair of their mother, while the other had the tousled red locks of their father and their older brother. The door behind her opened again, and she heard two more male voices. With a joyful look in his eyes, Phillip moved to greet them. The three met in a tangle of mock punches right beside her chair.

"Phillip! I didn't see you on Sunday. How's the businessman?" The youngest of the three still had the lean, rangy look of a teenager. The family resemblance was obvious, though he topped Phillip by several inches. He caught his brother in a headlock, which Phillip broke with a punch to the stomach. The third man avoided most of the fray. He looked enough like Phillip to be his twin, though Adrianna noticed his eyes looked a lifetime younger.

"Let's eat."

Adrianna barely heard Mrs. McEvan's quiet statement above the chatter, but her family responded with the swift attention of years' practice. A bit of jostling took place as the brothers teased each other and the girls tried to claim seats closest to Phillip. He ended up along the side of the table, immediately to Adrianna's right. With a few quiet words, Mrs. McEvan directed Neil to Phillip's right, and the rest of the family found places along the benches. In a moment, everyone stilled. Mr. McEvan said a short blessing, then the chatter of a large family resumed.

It was all so different from the rarefied atmosphere in which Adrianna had been raised. She felt Aunt Caroline's attention on her again, and the two exchanged understanding smiles. Though it never would have fit in her mother's dining room, she found the noisy interaction fun. Even the twins' squabble over the butter felt like love in action.

⌒⌒

It feels good to be home, Phillip mused, spreading a slice of bread with a thick layer of apple butter. Though one of his sisters might have made the bread, it still tasted like Mom's. He couldn't resist a glance at Adrianna to see how she was taking all the commotion. To his surprise, she looked as if she were having the time of her life. Her usually pale cheeks glowed, and a sparkle of fun in her eyes made him want her attention all for himself. She certainly didn't look like a woman who'd been given a crack on the head. He couldn't shake the feeling of failure. Her handicap meant she needed exceptional care and gentleness, not a concussion. He wasn't sure whether he should spend the rest of her visit trying to make it up to her or just avoid her altogether. Before he could make up his mind, his mother's question gave him something else to occupy his mind.

"After church, I heard Tabby telling her mother about the repairs at the boardinghouse. What are you doing?"

Phillip gathered his thoughts as best he could. "The ceiling upstairs started leaking. It turns out a lot of the roof is rotten."

"That sounds expensive." Concern darkened her eyes.

He shrugged. "It is, but there's no way around it. Cecil Watters has offered to donate his labor in exchange for six months' free room and board. That helps quite a bit. I'm working with him so we don't have to pay another

439

laborer. It just means the job will take longer."

"When you're ready for a work crew, let us know," Dad offered. "Greg, Tim, and I can probably spare a Saturday or two from the farm."

"I'll talk to Mr. Watters about it. You know how little I know about construction." He chuckled at his own expense, then felt amazed at the affection he heard in the laughter among his family. That started a string of stories about his woodworking mishaps.

"As you can tell," Dad began, addressing his comments to James and Caroline, "this house has had its share of expansions. The first time, we added two rooms to the original two-room cabin. Phillip was only seven at the time, but he managed to nail his jacket to the floor. The next time we expanded, we built a second story. That was the time he fell off the roof. The third time we added on, we sent Phillip over to a neighbor's farm to keep him safe."

Laughter rippled around the table, making Phillip feel embraced by affection. Not so long ago, he would have felt like a misfit, like the butt of a bad joke. When had he changed? Where would he go from here? The mention of Ruth's name brought him back to the conversation.

"Ruth and Theo and the boys came out for Sunday lunch," Mom was saying. "Theo was talking about hiring Cecil Watters to do some construction work on their house. They're thinking about expanding."

"The family or the house?" Tim asked, with an impish grin.

"Both." The look Mom and Dad exchanged was pure joy. Phillip shared their excitement over another baby in the family, even while he felt as if he'd missed something important. How could he be living under the same roof as his sister and not know what was happening?

"Theo is thinking of moving his practice out of the house." Dad added to Mom's comments in the way they had of finishing each other's thoughts. "He wants to find someone part-time to help with the record keeping so Ruth doesn't have to do it anymore."

"She's indignant that he'd even think such a thing," Mom added, "but Theo says with four children, she'll have enough to keep her busy."

Phillip laughed. "As if there's ever enough to keep Ruthie busy."

Dad sent Mom another intimate look. "She's a lot like her mom that way."

The rest of the family added their chuckles. It was a long-standing family joke that Ruth and Ida couldn't have been more alike in personality if they had been biologically related.

The meal soon finished. Tim and Greg returned to the field, while the older girls cleaned up the kitchen. Mom sent the twins out to weed a couple rows of carrots. "Might as well have them squabbling outdoors as in here where we have to listen to them," she explained while refilling coffee cups.

They lingered into midafternoon. Phillip enjoyed watching the interaction between his parents and the Trentons. He noticed his mom even managed to draw Adrianna into a quiet conversation.

When it came time to go, he promised himself he'd let someone else look after Adrianna. He would not risk hurting her again. But as had happened earlier, it seemed everyone assumed he'd help her. He'd only look boorish if he refused. When he picked her up, she felt even more delicate than before. Yet the twinkle in her eye was anything but fragile. "You don't have to be scared of me," she said softly as he carried her out into the sunlight. "I promise I won't bite or break."

He smiled, but said nothing as he carried her to the car. How could he tell her that what he feared most lay within himself?

Chapter 13

Later that evening, Cecil and Phillip finished removing the last of the shingles. It was easy to see where the roof of the expanded building had simply been patched over the roof of the original. "There's the problem." Cecil pointed to the small peak running perpendicular to the long peak of the newer roof. "That roof was already worn when the new one was put on. Water seeped through the old shingles and through the seams between the old and the new. Now even some of the trusses are rotten."

Phillip stood carefully straddling a truss, his feet braced on wood he'd already tested. So much of the structure was rotten, it would be easy to fall through. He looked between the open roof structure into the attic area. Originally filled with wood chips for insulation, the area now harbored piles of rotting wood.

Cecil gingerly lowered himself into the attic. "We're going to have to pull all these chips out." He kicked at the top layer, then used his hammer to scrape down to the wood that formed the ceiling for the upper story. "There's no telling how much of this ceiling is rotten, so watch your step." He continued poking through the mess. "I think the easiest way of doing this is to use shovels. We'll move all the wood chips to the back side, where it will be easier to dump them over into as neat a pile as possible. We'll make quite a mess of the area behind the house, but it can't be helped."

With no shovels on hand, the men quit early. Phillip felt only relief. He still felt guilty for the accident with Adrianna earlier in the day, even while he didn't want to acknowledge stronger feelings that had stirred in him. After cleaning the work dirt off his face and hands, he ventured into the kitchen, where he found the scene he'd hoped for: Tabby stood hunched in front of the oven, checking the progress of a pan of muffins. Neil carefully rubbed sandpaper over pieces of the dismantled desk. And off to one side, her gentle voice putting expression into every word, sat Adrianna reading from Grandma Lucy's journals. Phillip tried to slip unnoticed into a seat at the table, but she stopped.

"You're off early." Her smile scrambled his thoughts.

His mouth suddenly dry, he had to try twice to force the words out. "I got impatient for my story. Please continue."

He couldn't have told anyone what she read in the next hour. He studied the tabletop so as to not be caught staring, but her face remained imprinted in his mind. Her delicate weight as he'd carried her this afternoon remained imprinted on his arms. Was it possible he'd actually fallen in love?

When he dismissed that thought, another just as disturbing took its place. He really should go have a chat with Ruth and Theo. Despite living in their home, he'd seen little of them in the past week. He left each morning before they awoke. The work on the roof kept him up until well past their retiring time. Since they were expecting another baby and planning to renovate their home, he should find another place to stay. He knew Ruth would object to his reasoning, but he also knew they'd need his room for other things.

Which then brought him to the question of his own future. On Sunday, he'd come to terms with making no immediate plans. Yet the more he worked on the roof project, the more he committed himself to seeing it through. Once he finished the repairs, he wouldn't be able to leave until the boardinghouse was on secure financial footing. No contract could bind him to it more securely than his own feelings of what Grandma Lucy would have wanted him to do. But something else warred with that loyalty. He just couldn't see himself spending the rest of his life in the boardinghouse. He wanted more. But what?

The question continued to plague him long after he'd gone to bed, once again, well after Ruth and Theo had done the same. It woke him early in the morning and hovered over him as he prepared the cookstove for Tabby.

He watched eagerly for Adrianna's appearance at the breakfast table. When she wheeled herself out from her room, he hurried to her with a cup of tea. "How is your head?"

Her smile had lost none of its effect on him. "There's a sore bump there, but I'll be fine." Her eyes told him she didn't want him to fret over it.

Then the kitchen filled with the other guests and he busied himself offering tea and coffee. Tabby put steaming platters of blueberry muffins and scrambled eggs on the table. He made sure everyone, including Tabby, was served before helping himself. It wasn't until he reached for seconds that he remembered Dad's offer the day before. "Cecil, I forgot to mention to you that my dad and two brothers offered to come help us some Saturday. I told him I'd talk to you about the best timing."

Cecil nodded, then swallowed. "Miss Spencer, your cooking is every bit as marvelous as your grandmother's." Transferring his attention to Phillip, he continued. "Extra hands would be useful after we get the ceiling replaced. I'd rather not have too many people up there until we get something solid under our feet. We should be ready this Saturday to put the new ceiling in, if you can check with the lumberyard for materials. I'll give you a list before I leave this morning."

James speared the last muffin off the platter in front of him. "From what Phillip was telling his parents yesterday, that's quite a project going on up there."

Cecil nodded again. "This building has been around for awhile, so it's due." Tossing back the last of his coffee, he pushed his chair back from the table. "Thanks for breakfast, Miss Spencer." His work boots thumped on the wooden floor as he made his way up to his room.

"Tabby. Phillip." James seemed oddly ill at ease. "When you have a few moments this morning, Caroline and I would like to talk with you."

Phillip noticed Adrianna look at her uncle as if she, too, were puzzled by his demeanor. Tabby seemed alarmed. "Is there something amiss with our service? I'd be happy to change anything to make you more comfortable."

James held up a hand to stop her flow of words. "It's not a matter for you to worry over, Tabby. It's because we're so comfortable here that we've come up with an idea we'd like to present to you."

"I can listen, then, while I clean up." She began gathering sticky plates and empty cups with nervous movements.

James seemed to gauge her mood correctly and didn't insist that she finish her unending chores first. "Very well. Please stay, Neil." He stopped Neil's attempted departure and kept a hand on Adrianna's arm to keep her in place, also. "We'd like you and Adrianna to hear our thoughts as well. Our plans could involve you if you so choose."

Phillip wordlessly refilled coffee and teacups to cover his own sense of tingling anticipation. Still, he felt totally unprepared for what came next.

"Caroline and I would like to invest in your business if you're willing to consider a suggestion we have." He paused as if to give Tabby and Phillip time to object. Tabby remained with her back to the table, though Phillip detected a stiffening in her shoulders. In himself, he only felt the anticipation increase, as if James were about to present him with the fulfillment of a dream.

James reached for his wife's hand. "You have a lovely home here, in a beautiful setting. You probably don't realize how peaceful your community is. The close proximity to a rural lifestyle only adds to the appeal. We'd like you to think about turning your boardinghouse into a recovery home for veterans. There are many men out there who need the tranquillity here, men who are still struggling to find themselves after experiencing the worst war can offer. I have the contacts back in Toronto to keep your home filled year round."

Phillip's spine tingled. Could this be the answer to all the searching he'd done in the past three years? The idea appealed to him as no opportunity had since Holland. Even the possibility of a house full of wheelchairs didn't bother him. His friendship with James and Adrianna had helped him come to terms with the physical objects, though the associated memories still lingered. He'd done all he could for Jan. Perhaps through helping others, he could make peace with what he could never forget. He didn't know what he could offer the men James described, but if there were a chance—

"No." The single, forceful syllable turned everyone's attention toward the sink, where Tabby continued washing dishes with the rhythm of long practice. She turned around just enough to look James in the eyes. "We're not turning Grandma's boardinghouse into a hospital." She turned back to her dishes as though the discussion were concluded.

Phillip wanted to snatch the words out of the air and return them to her unspoken. He wanted to hear more details of the plan. But with her feelings made so plain, it felt pointless to resurrect the topic. The sound of Cecil's returning footsteps broke the silence. Cecil handed Phillip a piece of paper with a tidy list written on it. "See if they can have these supplies to us by Thursday afternoon," he said. Then with a nod to the others around the table, he picked up the bag lunch Tabby had prepared for him and disappeared out the front door.

Silence reigned behind him. Phillip didn't know what to say next. Adrianna wheeled quietly over to the counter where Tabby worked, picked up a dishtowel, and began drying the dishes Tabby had washed. Neil studied the back of Tabby's head as if he could read her thoughts. To Phillip's surprise, James and Caroline didn't look at all put out. They smiled at each other as if the discussion had gone the way they wanted it to.

Aunt Caroline moved calmly to the counter and laid a hand on Tabby's stiff shoulder. "Just think about it," she encouraged softly.

James turned to Phillip with an inquiring look. "After you get finished at the lumberyard, I'd like your escort to the grain elevators. I've never seen anything like that up close."

Phillip immediately thought of a friend of his dad's who would be able to satisfy James's curiosity. "Sure. My dad is friends with the manager; he would probably give you a detailed tour of the operation."

But Phillip's mind was far from grain processing as he walked the twenty minutes to the lumberyard. He could envision all kinds of possibilities for the idea James had introduced. For one thing, with other residents around all the time, he could easily live at the boardinghouse without raising any improper speculation about him and Tabby. Frustration coursed through him. If people could read his thoughts about his business partner at the moment, there wouldn't ever be any lewd suggestions. He wanted to jar her stubbornness loose with a good shake.

Alternatively, he could just disappear from town, leaving her with the headaches of rebuilding. But he knew that was nothing more than a passing thought. Yesterday, he'd rediscovered his inner connection to his family. For the first time since Grandma's death, he felt less than totally alone. For the first time in as long as he could remember, his hometown offered him a reason to stay.

He talked to the manager at the lumberyard, obtained an estimate for the boards Cecil needed, and arranged for delivery on Thursday. With the written estimate in hand, he retraced his steps to the boardinghouse. Perhaps the numbers on this paper would change her mind. The replacement shingles alone would eat up most of what was in their bank account. He didn't see how they could afford to keep the business running as it was.

On impulse, he detoured to his sister's home before returning to the boardinghouse. He found Ruth in the kitchen looking wan while her three boys each clamored at Ida, who seemed to have just arrived. Phillip watched the commotion in silence, struck by an unexpected sense of belonging. This was family, his family. Even if he were to leave town again, whenever he chose to return, they'd welcome him. When the excitement settled a bit, Ruth handed each of the boys a piece of bread and shooed them out the back door. "Whew!" She sank down wearily at the table. "I'd love to have their energy."

"It will get easier in another month or so," Mom said soothingly.

They appeared to notice Phillip at the same time. "Hi, Phillip." Ruth greeted him with an effort at a smile. "What brings you here at this time of day?" She started to get up from her seat, but he pushed her gently back down.

"Just sit. You look exhausted. Are you okay?" Ruth's energy never flagged unless she were really sick.

This time her grin brightened her face. "Just pregnant. I'm always washed out for the first few months."

Though she looked considerably worse than "washed out," he couldn't help but respond to the glow of joy in her shadow-rimmed eyes. "I'm happy for you, Sis, though why you'd want to feel this way is beyond me," he teased. "Would a cup of tea help?" He relished the look of surprise that passed across both faces.

Ruth nodded. "That would be nice."

"Didn't know I could make tea, did you?" When she grinned as he'd hoped, he shrugged as if it meant nothing. "I've had to learn to make myself useful now that Tabby's in charge."

"How is it going over there?" Ruth asked. "I haven't had either the time or the energy to stop in, and you're always up and gone before I can even say good morning." From anyone else, it might have sounded like a complaint, but that wasn't Ruth's way. One of the things Phillip loved most about her was her directness. If she were unhappy about something, she said so.

"We have the four new guests who arrived last week. The schoolteacher has moved out, Mr. Watters is staying to help us repair the roof, and we haven't heard a word from Adam Dodd."

As usual, Mom's question took a more personal approach. "What about you and Tabby? Are you working together all right?"

It surprised Phillip that he didn't feel bothered by the question. From anyone else it would have been annoying. He shrugged again. "As good as can be expected, I guess." The kettle whistled, so he got up to fill the teapot. It gave him opportunity to find words for what he really wanted to discuss. He brought the teapot and three mugs to the table, then found the honey he knew Ruth liked to put in hers. "I have something I want to ask you both about." He was suddenly glad Mom was here, too.

She winked. "Romantic troubles?"

Instantly, he recalled the feeling of Adrianna in his arms. He wasn't ready to discuss that with anyone, not even himself. "Nope. This is business." He looked at both of them. "What do you think Grandma Lucy would think if we did something else with the boardinghouse?"

Ruth answered first. "Depends on what that something else is."

After a moment of silence, Mom responded, "I'm not sure that matters. Grandma Lucy gave the business to you and Tabby. What you choose to do with the gift is totally up to you."

Phillip shook his head. "It still feels to me like her business, like something she trusted us to take good care of."

Mom laid her hand on his. "Phillip, Grandma Lucy is with the Lord now. As much as you love her, you can't make your decisions based on what you think she would have done. The boardinghouse doesn't matter to her anymore."

The feel of her work-roughened hand on his brought back memories of Grandma so intense his eyes stung. He looked into her eyes and saw the depth of caring he'd often seen in Grandma Lucy's eyes. Then understanding dawned. He'd clung to the maternal love Grandma offered him without ever seeing that the woman he'd called "Mom" most of his life offered the same. Another wave of intense emotion clogged his throat. It felt as if a long-sealed door in his heart were slowly creaking open. He forced his thoughts back to the topic of discussion. "I doubt Tabby would agree with you."

Mom returned her hand to her mug. "So you have an idea you've discussed with Tabby?"

"Sort of." He quickly told them about James Trenton's offer. "The more I think about it, the more it sounds like something I want to do. But Tabby is determined not to change anything. I don't think the business can survive that way." He took a drink of the tea, which had cooled. "I guess that's something I'll have to sort out with her. I didn't realize she could be so unreasonable."

Both Mom and Ruth laughed. "I'm sure Theo thinks the same about me sometimes," Ruth offered, "though I do remember Tabby being quite certain of her own opinions even as a child."

"Be patient with her," Mom advised. "People are often the most stubborn about things they don't understand. Running the boardinghouse is her first taste of being independent from her family. Perhaps she's afraid of losing that. Or maybe she's afraid she'll lose her memories of Grandma if she changes Grandma's business. We'll pray with you, Son, that the two of you will be able to come to a decision that works for both of you. God cares about you both even more than we do."

Her parting hug lingered with Phillip even during lunch and the game of chess with James that followed. His chat with Mom and Ruth hadn't solved any of his problems, but it had shown him he wasn't, and never had been, as alone as he'd felt. No matter what happened with the boarding-house, he still had family. The feeling of belonging began to ease the heartache he'd carried for so long.

Chapter 14

For days, Adrianna basked in the peace that followed her Sunday afternoon prayer. She found her thoughts shifting from her own limitations and struggles to the matters that interested the people with whom she spent time.

The tension between Tabby and Phillip bothered her. She didn't know why Phillip wanted so much to accept Uncle James's offer, nor why Tabby remained so opposed to it. Still, she longed to help the two find a common ground.

She also discovered an insatiable desire to learn all she could from the Bible Aunt Caroline had loaned her. Though her parents were faithful churchgoers, the services had never been more than formal rituals for her, the Bible only a collection of unfamiliar phrases. Now, it seemed to glow with personal meaning. She loved to sit by the big window in the parlor, reading bits of Scripture, then staring out the window while she thought about what she'd read.

Aunt Caroline had recommended she start with John's gospel. She'd read the first fourteen chapters in two days. But chapter fifteen slowed her down. Not that she couldn't understand what she read. Rather, she found it almost too incredible to believe.

Thursday morning after breakfast, she joined Neil and her aunt and uncle in the parlor, as had become their routine. Each day a different one took a turn reading aloud a portion of Scripture, then they all discussed it. Their informal devotional time finished with each of them praying aloud about any concerns they had. Today was her turn to read. She opened to John 15 and read the first seventeen verses. "This feels like an incredible treasure I can't quite reach," she confided to the other three. "Jesus says we're supposed to abide in Him. What does that mean?"

After a few moments of thoughtful silence, Uncle James responded. "It's like us and these wheelchairs," he said with a grin that seemed to say only the two of them would really understand his point. "We don't wake up each morning wondering if our chairs are going to work that day. We don't spend the day trying to keep our weight off the chairs so they don't break down. We just relax into the chairs and appreciate the mobility they give us. God wants us to trust Him in the same way and make Him a part of our everyday lives just like our chairs are part of our lives. Just like you and I can't go anywhere without these chairs so Jesus says we can't live the joyful lives He intended for us without Him."

"I never thought about it that way before," Neil offered. "I seem to think more in terms of what I can do to please Him, rather than simply appreciating belonging to Him."

Aunt Caroline looked up from where she'd been studying the open Bible she shared with Uncle James. "The only things in this passage He says to do are to abide in Him, bear fruit, obey His commands, and love each other. Abiding in Him and loving others are attitudes. When you think about a tree bearing fruit, it doesn't have to work at it. It just absorbs sunlight, water, and air and the fruit appears. So, the only 'doing' is obeying His commands. In another part of the Gospels, He says that His commandments can be wrapped up in two statements: Love God and love each other. It sounds like if we focus on loving Him and loving each other, we're doing what's most important to Him."

Adrianna was still puzzled. "But what does bearing fruit mean?"

Aunt Caroline held a finger in the place where she'd been reading and turned some pages. "The book of Galatians gives a list of what is called the fruit of the Spirit—love, joy, peace, long-suffering, gentleness, goodness, faith, meekness, and temperance. Again, they're more attitudes than actions, but attitudes are what govern our actions. Jesus says in John 15 that the fruit we produce, or perhaps the attitudes we display, are what will identify us as people who love Him."

Adrianna felt a growing sense of excitement. If what they were saying was true, then she could be as pleasing to God as people who had full use of their legs. Though she didn't voice it during their prayer time, her heart sent a request to the One she was learning to love. *Heavenly Father, please show me how to abide in You, love You, and show love to others. Please show me how to produce Your kind of fruit.*

The prayer stayed with her throughout the day as she busied herself with crocheting, more reading, and a game of chess with Uncle James. If he and Aunt Caroline were aware of the conflict between Tabby and Phillip, they made no mention of it. She wished she knew either of her hosts well enough to try to mediate. At lunch, Tabby served in silence. Though Phillip carried his part of conversation well enough and ate as well as he usually did, Adrianna sensed his distress. She helped with dishes, as usual, and that was when the idea blossomed. If she couldn't solve the problem, perhaps she could help Phillip in a different way. She'd never done anything so forward, but it felt like the right thing to do. As soon as she'd dried the last pot and hung her towel over the rack on the wall, she went in search of Phillip before she lost her nerve.

The back door slightly ajar gave her a clue as to his whereabouts. She'd never tried to manage a door by herself but decided this was as good a time as any to try. She wheeled her chair almost to within arm's reach of the door, then leaned forward to pull it open. With one hand bracing the door and the other pushing the wheel of her chair, she managed to make lopsided progress until she was beside the open door and her chair could serve as a doorstop. From there, she managed to maneuver herself over the threshold onto the small back porch.

It took only a minute for her to spot him in the porchlike area off to the left. He stood with his back against the half-height wall, facing the yard area behind the house. He appeared absorbed in thoughts far from where he stood. Though the flooring was rough, she successfully wheeled herself close enough to him to make herself heard without announcing her business to the world in general. "Phillip?"

He gave a small start, but his expression became welcoming as soon as he saw her. "Hi, Adrianna."

Before her resolve withered, she put her thoughts into words. "I was wondering if you have time to do a favor for me."

"I'd be glad to. What do you need?"

She swallowed the huge lump in her throat. This was the hardest part. "I'd—I'd—would you mind taking me for a walk?" She couldn't read the expression in his eyes, so she hurried on with the explanation she'd concocted. "Aunt Caroline is busy with her needlework, and I heard Neil and Uncle James discussing another chess game. I'd just like to get out of the house for awhile."

"You don't need to explain yourself." Gentleness warmed his tone. "If you're willing to spend time with me, it would be my honor to accompany you."

A new emotion, far beyond nerves, gripped her. Never had a young man made her feel as if her company were a privilege. She'd made her request from a simple desire to give Phillip something to think about other than the tension between him and Tabby. Immediately, the proposed excursion had taken on an entirely different tone. She hoped she wasn't misinterpreting his sentiments. She dared to lift her gaze to his face and saw in his eyes the same warmth she'd heard in his voice. In fact, there hovered in his expression something that made her heart beat faster. It was almost as if he'd wanted her to seek him out, as if her request were something he'd hoped for.

Before she lost herself in an emotional haze and did or said something embarrassing, she turned her attention back to her chair. As she'd carefully watched Uncle James do, she put most of her effort into pushing the wheel on her left while allowing the wheel on the right only a small amount of movement. To her relief, the chair turned as she'd hoped. A sense of pride welled through the other emotions churning inside. She really was becoming a little more independent all the time. She wondered if Phillip understood what her achievement meant to her. Whether he did or not, she appreciated the fact he didn't rush to push her chair. The area around the house looked far too rough for her to pass over, so she wheeled herself toward the back door and Phillip followed.

Aunt Caroline accepted her quick explanation without comment, though a twinkle accompanied her smile. Phillip offered no comment as they passed through the kitchen. He seemed to sense the precise moment when she needed help at the front steps. At the boardwalk, he paused. "Which direction would you like to go?"

She couldn't brave another glance at him, so she looked first right, then left. "I'd like to see whatever you want to show me."

"Then let's go this way. Would you like me to push?"

This time her gaze snapped to his face without effort, her sense of gratitude so intense she had to give it words. "Thank you for giving me the choice, and, yes, I would appreciate your help."

"You mean people don't ask your permission before pushing you around?"

She smiled, though he couldn't see it. "You'd be surprised. Because I can't walk, some people assume I can't think, either."

"What about your parents?"

"They can be the worst of all." She had never spoken her feelings aloud, but she wanted to let this man see her inner self. "I know they love me. But sometimes I wonder if they see me as a whole person in spite of my useless legs."

Phillip said nothing in response, which Adrianna appreciated. A glib reply would have hurt. If he'd tried to explain her parents, that would have made an even deeper wound. The silence made her feel as if she'd really been heard.

At the end of the block on which the boardinghouse stood, he turned left and took her several blocks until the town thinned. The street turned into a well-trodden road that tracked through a field before dropping off a shallow bank into a flow of water. Adrianna stared at the water, unable to decide if it were a very large stream or a very small river. The dilemma amused her until a giggle forced its way into the stillness. "What do you call it?"

"Dawson Creek," he answered with an accompanying chuckle. He dropped down onto the grass beside her.

She looked around at the small trees clinging to the edge of the creek, then back toward the open area between them and the town. If anyone happened to see them out here, there could be no improper accusations.

He again seemed to read her thoughts. "This is a popular courting spot. It's a bit private, but still very visible. I hope you don't mind my bringing you here."

Courting. The word stuck in her brain. Never in her wildest imaginings had she thought she might ever be courted. *Then again, maybe that's not what he means at all,* she reminded herself. He might be exceptionally thoughtful of her, and there might be moments of intense awareness between them, but rash assumptions on her part could easily destroy the friendship they'd formed. "If this is where you wanted to come, I'm glad you were willing to bring me with you."

He turned a questioning look toward her, but neither of them prolonged the eye contact. Easy silence enveloped them again. Then, with his gaze focused somewhere on the other side of the creek, he inquired, "Do you mind if I ask why you wanted to get out of the house? I can't imagine you were getting cabin fever."

The droll comment injected just enough humor to keep her thoughts from becoming hopelessly jumbled. "I thought you might enjoy a break."

Another space of silence and then, "A break from what?"

She tried to word her answer carefully. "I know you and Tabby are at odds over Uncle James's offer. I just wanted to help you find something pleasant to think about instead."

To her amazement, he reached for her hand. "Thank you."

Every nerve in her body seemed to focus on the warmth of his touch.

Although his hands were roughened by the calluses of hard work, his touch was surprisingly tender. Unsure as to how she should respond, she laid her free hand over his, then let her gaze meet his. Had she misinterpreted his gesture?

The warmth in his eyes stole her ability to breathe as he hitched himself closer to her chair. "You don't mind if I hold your hand?" His voice held as much uncertainty as she felt.

His vulnerability gave her courage. "No. I like it." This time their gazes didn't skitter away from each other.

"Adrianna, may I court you?"

The question stunned her. "Why?"

Hurt flashed in his eyes before he looked away. "I guess I shouldn't have asked that. I'm sorry."

She tightened her grip on his hand so he couldn't pull it away. "Phillip." She waited until he looked at her again. "I think I'd like you to court me. I just never expected anyone to want to be around me in that way."

He didn't pretend to miss her meaning. "There are some people who can't see anything other than your wheelchair. I know, because I felt that way when you first arrived. Your chair stirred up too many memories I've been trying to outrun. Then I began to see the person in the chair. First, your courage as you've struggled to learn to do things for yourself. Then, your caring as you've figured out ways to help Tabby even though she doesn't seem to want help. The other day when I bashed your head," he interrupted himself with a shamefaced grimace, "I could hardly stand myself for inflicting pain on you. That's when I realized you've come to mean more to me than I thought possible. Since I left Europe, I've thought I wouldn't be able to fall in love. But," his voice dropped to a husky whisper, "I think I'm falling anyway."

Adrianna felt as if her heart were being squeezed by the unbearable sweetness of the moment. "Phillip, you've made me feel as if I were a whole person rather than a cripple. I think I started falling for you the night we arrived and you stood in the doorway glaring at us like a bear awakened from hibernation. It seems too incredible that you might actually care for me."

"Oh, I do." His hand tightened its grip. "But the feeling still scares me. I have nothing to offer you except my heart. I can't even predict how I'll earn a living next week. I'm not ready to promise anything because I have no idea how I'll be able to follow through. All I know is that I do care about you very much. You've given me a special gift by returning my regard. Do you mind if we explore our feelings slowly and take time to see where they lead us?"

Time. The thought didn't bother her at all. "I never dreamed I'd ever be courted. I'd like nothing better than to take it slowly enough to savor every moment. We have all the time in the world."

Chapter 15

Once again, Phillip had a hard time falling asleep. Though his body ached for rest after four hours of hard work on the roof, his mind wanted to replay those unbelievable moments on the creek bank. How far he'd come from the moment not so long ago when he just wished the wheelchairs and their occupants would disappear. He felt a grin tug at his mouth and knew it was probably one of those silly ones that told the whole world its wearer had fallen in love. Thankfully, he was alone and in the dark. He didn't feel ready to share his secret yet. For now, it was enough that Adrianna knew and shared his feelings. Time would let them both know whether what they felt would last.

Friday morning, he awoke earlier than usual and rushed to the boardinghouse kitchen, impatient to see Adrianna. What would their fledgling connection look like in the light of a new day?

But before he had a chance to find out, Tabby delivered a startling announcement over breakfast preparations. "I'd like to accept Mr. Trenton's offer."

Phillip had never felt more foolish, staring at her as though he hadn't a working brain cell in his head. How did one respond to such an abrupt change? "Are you sure?" He knew the question sounded inane, but he couldn't think of anything else to say.

With a brisk nod, she turned back to the potatoes she'd been chopping for hash browns. "Neil talked with me yesterday afternoon while you and Miss Trenton were out. He helped me understand the business value of what Mr. Trenton is offering us. I thought about it overnight and realized it would be the ultimate betrayal of Grandma's trust if I were to refuse to change just because I'm afraid of losing control."

Her abrupt silence told him not to expect any further confidences. That part didn't matter. The only important thing to him was that Tabby was willing to share the dream being offered to them. He resisted the urge to grab her in an enthusiastic hug. "Let's talk with James right after breakfast, then." He paused, then added, "Thanks for reconsidering. It means a lot to me."

She favored him with a small, quick smile before turning to the pan sizzling on the stove.

As soon as Cecil left and the dishes had been cleared away, everyone but Tabby reassembled at the table. She remained busy with bread dough, but her face showed a sparkle of interest that Phillip hadn't seen before. He knew there had to be more to it than a simple business decision. But rather than puzzling over something he couldn't solve, he made sure coffee cups and teacups were full and fresh pots set on the stove to brew. Adrianna sat at one end of the table, Uncle James to her right, and Aunt Caroline beside him. Phillip slipped easily into place at Adrianna's left. Her quick, pleased smile made him feel like he'd done something extraordinary.

Before he became too distracted by his feelings, he turned his attention to James and Caroline, only to find their attention fixed on him and Adrianna. A glance at her showed her cheeks turning pink, which matched the warmth in his own face. He cleared his throat. "James, Tabby and I talked this morning, and we'd like to accept your offer of financial partnership, if it's still open." He didn't miss the glances exchanged by Neil and Tabby.

James and Caroline looked at each other with obvious delight. "That's great news!" James responded. "Do you have any terms for us?" His question seemed directed more at Tabby than Phillip.

Phillip hadn't given any thought to putting terms on the partnership, but he waited to see what Tabby would say. Apprehension showed in her eyes, but she said briskly, "I assume Phillip and I will still have some say in how the new business is run?"

James didn't wave her concern away with an easy answer. "Caroline and I may be putting money into this venture, but you and Phillip are contributing the land, the building, and the basic structure of the business. To my way of thinking, you two have the most to lose if things go wrong. I'd like to think of us as equal partners, but we'll vote on major decisions. Caroline and I will share a vote, and you and Phillip will each have a vote. How does that sound?"

To Phillip it sounded more than generous, and he held his breath until Tabby slowly nodded. He still couldn't figure out what had her so worried, but James seemed to be doing a good job of allaying her fears.

"Phillip, if you'll provide Adrianna with pencil and paper, I'd like her to take notes of our discussion. This afternoon I'll draft a letter to my lawyer in Toronto directing him to draw up a formal business agreement among us."

Phillip opened his mouth to protest that such a thing wasn't necessary, but Tabby had a different opinion. "I'd appreciate that," she said, for once turning her back on her work at the counter. "It's not that I don't trust you, because I do." She swallowed hard. When she spoke again, her voice wasn't as steady as it had been. "It's just that this boardinghouse is all I have left of my grandmother. This is my only chance at building a future for myself other than becoming an old maid on my parents' farm." She abruptly turned back to the counter.

James didn't linger on her admission but directed the discussion into concrete planning. "Since our focus is going to be veterans, we're probably going to need more rooms that are accessible by wheelchair. Any ideas?"

"I'd have to talk with Cecil, but I don't think it would be hard to build a ramp to the upstairs," Phillip offered. "The two center rooms up there are about the same size as the ones down here, so they'd work well for wheelchairs."

Neil put in his first comment of the morning. "I would suggest enlarging the bathroom up there to make room for a patient and a caregiver."

"Which brings to mind another thought," Uncle James added. "We should have easily accessible medical staff. Neil will certainly be an asset while we're here, but Caroline and I won't be able to live here year round, which means he goes, too. I'll let Adrianna make up her own mind, though." Grins rippled around the table.

An idea began to grow in Phillip's mind. "Tabby, I think Theo has been thinking about moving his office out of their house. What do you think about offering him space here? We'd have to add on to make room, but it would help him and us."

When she did respond, it was with a nod of approval. "If we build an addition for his office, then he can have his own entrance and his patients won't have to track through my kitchen."

"We have a lot of construction to be done," he warned. "It might take Cecil and me awhile to finish it."

"I've been thinking about that," James put in. "Caroline and I would be happy to pay his wages if he's free to come work on our project full-time. We could probably also afford extra help for him when he needs it. There's no need for work to drag on for months." He directed a questioning glance at his wife, and when she nodded, he continued.

"Here's another thought for you. We were wondering if you'd be willing to let us build our own suite at the back of the house. We'd like to be connected to the main building, but since we plan to live here at least part of the year, we don't want to be underfoot all the time."

Phillip liked the idea immensely, but again waited for Tabby's opinion. She looked at the older couple with the softest smile he'd ever seen on her face. "It would be nice to have you around as often as you'd like to be here."

Planning continued throughout the morning. Caroline and Adrianna contributed ideas about the layout of the renovated building. When Tabby wondered how they would attract residents, James assured her his contacts in Toronto could send them all the business they had room for. That brought up the subject of fees. Uncle James named a weekly charge that staggered Phillip. One look at Tabby's face told him she felt just as amazed.

But Neil confirmed James's suggestion. "You're offering a rehabilitation center, not just room and board. It's a specialized service, so you have to charge enough to make it worth the effort and expense."

"We can also reevaluate as we go along," Phillip pointed out. "What if we hear of someone who needs to come but can't afford our fee?"

Tabby set a plate of sandwiches in the middle of the table. "I have a thought. Could we set aside one room for which we don't charge? That way anyone who needs us can come." When her idea received enthusiastic acceptance, she added, "I'd like to do it as a tribute to Grandma and name the room in her memory."

To Phillip's surprise, tears stung his eyes. It was just the kind of idea Grandma Lucy would have loved. For the first time since the war, he felt as if he were making a difference in lives other than his own. But one question diluted his joy. When would Adrianna choose to return home? The rehab center offered her far less than her own family's home in Toronto. He wished he could provide a compelling reason for her to stay. But even that lay beyond his abilities. He could only enjoy having her near enough to greet each morning she chose to remain.

∞

Adrianna had never been so close to so much excited activity. Within a week of the conference around the table, Cecil had finished his other work and began renovating the boardinghouse. He and Phillip spent long hours rebuilding the roof and ceiling on the upper story. As much as she would have liked the opportunity for more time alone with Phillip, she loved the look of fulfillment in his eyes even more. For the first time since she'd met him, he looked happy.

Uncle James seemed to be in his glory. He mailed bundles of letters to friends who could recommend potential clients. Anytime he, Phillip, and Tabby were in the same room, he had ideas, questions, and encouragement for them. He and Aunt Caroline spent hours drawing and redrawing their ideas for the design of their suite. Aunt Caroline simply glowed with the delight of seeing her husband so happy.

Though he had less of a direct contribution to the activity, Neil looked no less affected by it. He spent every free moment working on the desk, though Adrianna privately wondered whether it was the desk or Tabby's company that drew him. She didn't overhear much conversation between them, but they seemed to smile more when the other was near.

The most remarkable change was in Tabby. For all of her earlier opposition to changing the way the boardinghouse would be run, she now thrived under the influence of the changes. The moody woman of earlier days had been replaced by a gentler, more companionable one. She'd mellowed so much that Adrianna even found the courage to ask for cooking lessons.

"I've never been this close to a kitchen before," she confided. "I'd like to learn what I can."

"There's no reason you can't do everything I do except the actual stove work," Tabby declared in her determined way. "Let's start with a batch of cookies for lunch tomorrow." Within a matter of days, the two women found an easy rhythm together. To Adrianna's amazement, Tabby even chatted with her as though they might be friends and sometimes even stopped her endless work for a cup of tea. It didn't surprise Adrianna to find Neil also in the kitchen during those times.

"They're fun to watch," she told Phillip one evening when they managed to steal a few moments alone together on the back porch. "They don't flirt or even talk much with each other, but it's obvious they love to be together. How do you think she'll handle it when Neil has to go back to Toronto with Uncle James?"

Phillip shrugged and reached for her hand. "I wouldn't even try to predict Tabby. I know how I'll feel when you go back, though." His eyes grew shadowed and his grip tightened. She wished she could assure him she wouldn't leave. The more she came to know of this man, the more she loved him. When the time was right, she would have no regrets exchanging the comfort of her parents' lifestyle for the much rougher one here. She even hoped to learn enough from Tabby to become a genuine asset to the rehab center. But until he asked her to stay, she had to plan on returning when her aunt and uncle chose to do so. She formed her reply carefully. "I haven't heard Uncle James talking about going back just yet."

The silence that fell between them grew heavy with unspoken thoughts neither of them felt ready to discuss. His reticence only increased her respect for him. Though conversation flowed easily between them on most occasions, she knew he'd never give her empty promises. When he eventually put his feelings into words, she'd know he meant every syllable. Cecil's voice from the rooftop called Phillip back to work, leaving her without any discontent over what hadn't been said.

The next afternoon as she wrote her weekly letter to her parents, she spent more time than usual pondering what to tell them. This marked the fifth week of what had begun as a six-week absence. She knew she should let them know not to expect her as soon as she'd originally planned. Father would have a fit. When he found out about Uncle James's investment and that their return would be delayed because of the project, she knew the reaction wouldn't be pretty.

But what else could she tell him? She made the bulk of her letter as chatty as she could, telling them about her cooking and Neil's progress on the desk. The last paragraph consisted of just three careful sentences. "We won't be home as soon as we'd planned. Uncle James and Aunt Caroline are enjoying Dawson Creek so much they're talking of spending a few more weeks. I'll let you know when we plan to arrive."

Chapter 16

Within a month, all the interior renovations had been completed, and work had begun on the office area for Theo, who had enthusiastically accepted the offer to become part of the new project. Two reservations had already come in, with the new guests due to arrive in ten days' time. To Adrianna's delight, Uncle James had asked her to write the notes of confirmation. When a request for information arrived in the next day's mail, he asked her to respond to that, as well. It wasn't long before all mail relating to the rehab center became her unofficial responsibility. Neil finished the desk, and it stood polished and shining in the far corner of the kitchen.

The next afternoon, as Adrianna prepared to work on correspondence at the end of the table, Tabby suggested, "Why don't you use the desk? Since you're doing all the secretarial work, you should have your own work space."

Adrianna couldn't believe her ears. This was the woman who had been fiercely protective of anything connected with her grandmother. "Are you sure you don't want this up in your room?"

With a gentle expression, Tabby nodded. "It's too beautiful to hide away upstairs. Besides, the work you're doing is just as much a part of our tribute to Grandma as the meals I cook. I'd like you to use the desk as your own."

Adrianna's other delight was the newly installed ramps. No longer was she confined to the main floor. It took days of consistent practice, but eventually her arms gained enough strength to propel her upstairs. This meant she could assist Tabby in routine housekeeping chores, yet another learning experience. She felt giddy with accomplishment. At long last, she'd found a setting that allowed her to be useful.

But best of all were the hours she spent with Phillip. Construction ceased on Sundays, and those afternoons became their special times together. She'd been out to visit his parents three times and felt more comfortable with his family each time she saw them. She'd even tried out her biscuit-making skills in his mother's kitchen. The men of the family praised her efforts, but the most meaningful compliment was his mother's. "You can come share my kitchen anytime." Adrianna sensed Ida's welcome applied to more than just the room that housed the cookstove.

No matter what other activities occupied a Sunday afternoon, Phillip always found a way for them to have some time alone. She came to trust him with thoughts she'd never put into words before as she told him about her illness and the lonely years that had followed. He in turn told her of his years in Europe. Her heart ached with his as he told of his friend, Jan, and the futile search long after the war ended. After hearing what a wheelchair had cost him, she felt new amazement that he'd ever seen past hers. The fact that the mutual attraction seemed to be growing at the same pace left her breathless with wonder.

It was after one of their private chats by the creek bank that her idyllic world exploded. She was still laughing at one of Phillip's stories about his childhood as he helped her up the steps into the boardinghouse. She propelled herself out of the mudroom, only to have the laughter die in her throat. Her father sat at the opposite end of the kitchen table, looking ready to boil over. Her mother sat to his left, a profound distaste in her eyes. They appeared utterly out of place in the rustic environment.

Adrianna tried her best to start the conversation casually. "Hello, Father, Mother. It's good to see you." She pushed herself toward their end of the table to greet them with hugs. Father declined her gesture, and Mother barely touched her shoulders.

"What have they done to you?" Mother whispered. "You poor child, having to push yourself around." The cloying concern in her voice wrapped itself around Adrianna's heart as if strangling her hard-won independence. She forced a laugh, hoping to show them she didn't need to be pitied or rescued. "I taught myself to do this, Mother. I've also learned to cook, clean, and make beds." Her announcement sounded less triumphant than she intended.

"James." Father's voice came out in an ominous rumble. For the first time, Adrianna noticed her aunt and uncle seated nearby. "I trusted you to take care of my daughter, not turn her into a housemaid. You of all people should know how delicate she is. And who is this ruffian who has followed her here?"

Adrianna looked at Phillip in horror. After an insult like that, she wouldn't blame him if he walked away from her permanently. With a tone of much patient experience, James replied, "Gilbert, meet our host, Phillip McEvan. He and our hostess, Tabby Spencer, have not only made us very comfortable here, but agreed to become business partners with Caroline and me."

"Knowing you," Father replied with grudging respect, "it's a splendid idea that will provide you even more money to give away to people who don't appreciate it. My concern is with my daughter. How could you treat her so carelessly?"

Adrianna despised being discussed as though she couldn't speak for herself, but her newfound confidence had withered under her parents' all-too-familiar patronizing. When her mother suggested in another whispered comment that she "retire for a rest," Adrianna simply did so. She knew she'd be on the next train east, her parents hovering on either side, and there was nothing she could do to prevent it.

∽

Phillip watched Adrianna wheel herself to her room. He recalled the first night he'd seen her attempt this feat. How far she'd come in just six weeks! He looked over at the large man still glowering at him from the other end of the table. Once again, his people-reading skills asserted themselves. His own experience with unrelenting guilt enabled him to see it in the other man's eyes. Gilbert Trenton hid an aching heart behind his bluster.

James spoke softly. "Gilbert, your daughter hasn't come to any harm. Can't you see how well independence suits her?"

Gilbert studied his brother for a moment, then turned toward Phillip. Phillip returned the steady gaze. Finally, it was Mrs. Trenton's voice that caused her husband to break the eye contact. "Gilbert, do you think she's really happy here?"

It was Aunt Caroline who replied, "Why don't you ask her?"

∽

Adrianna rolled her chair over to the window. Bracing her chin on her hands, she looked out as though seeing the view for the last time. Another house sat not far away, but beyond that she could see the rolling fields that surrounded this little town. When would she see these fields again or fall asleep hearing rain patter against the windowpanes? Then, like a lance slicing into her heart, came the awareness that she'd lose Phillip. Even if her parents could bring themselves to accept him, he could no more live in the city than she could parachute from a plane.

She let her gaze travel around the room, taking in the details that had seemed so rough when she first arrived and now just felt like home. Lucy Barry's journals on her nightstand caught her attention. She reached for them and put the stack of notebooks in her lap. She and Phillip had almost finished reading through them. Just a few pages in the last notebook remained. She riffled idly toward the end, then stopped as Phillip's name caught her eye.

May 21, 1951

  I've been so tired lately; I wonder how much longer I can maintain the boardinghouse. God has used it to provide well for me throughout the years, blessing me with much more than material goods. If it hadn't been for my business venture, I might never have met Ida Thomas and become honorary grandmother to the McEvan brood. Though each of my grandchildren has a special place in my heart, young Phillip is most on my mind these days. I'm glad to have been able to offer him shelter and kindness this past year as he's struggled so hard to adjust to a world without war and intrigue. You know how tender his heart is, Father, and only You can give him the healing he needs.

  I also carry a burden for my granddaughter, Tabby. With all of her brothers and sisters gone from the family farm, she needs a place to call her own. Father, if You haven't prepared a special husband for her, I know You'll provide a place uniquely her own.

  The others have found their trails to Your will so much more easily than these two. It's as though Tabby and Phillip, each for different reasons and in different circumstances, are having to search harder for the path You wish them to take.

A few other entries followed this one, each containing a mention of either Phillip or Tabby or both. Finally, Adrianna came upon the last entry.

June 4, 1951

  Today I talked to a lawyer about revising my will. God has impressed upon me that He's not finished with the house after He calls me home. For no reason other than that I feel His leading, I've decided to bequeath my business to the two grandchildren who've been on my heart so much of late. What they do with it after I'm gone doesn't matter. I just ask, Father God, that it be used for healing, first for them and then through them for others.

Adrianna's breath caught. Tears stung her eyes. Such love radiated through these words. "A place of healing." Wasn't that what the rehabilitation center would be? Following in the mood of what she'd just read, she turned her thoughts into a prayer. "God, I'm just learning to call You Father, and what I've read of You in this journal and in the Bible is so different from my natural father. I want to find the trail of Your will for me. Would You really lead me away from this place of healing, as Lucy called it, and away from the finest man I've ever known? Would You ask me to give up without a fight the usefulness I've struggled to acquire and the love I never hoped to find?"

She sat for long moments with her head bowed. Tears spilled down her cheeks. She felt as if she'd come so far only to have to give it all up. Then, like the gentle warmth of morning sunshine, hope began to warm her heart. Since she wasn't physically capable of complete independence, she couldn't insist on remaining here indefinitely. However, she knew without asking that Aunt Caroline and Uncle James would welcome her with them as long as they remained. Perhaps if her departure weren't so abrupt, she could bear to leave when the time came.

With courage born only of hope, she dared to return to the kitchen before her mother came to get her. She could see as they turned to face her that even this small bit of independence startled both parents. Deciding to press her advantage, she launched her announcement immediately.

"Father, I appreciate your concern for me, but I won't be going back to Toronto tomorrow." The shock on his face gave her the courage to continue. "I know you and Mother won't be able to understand this, but I've found something here I'm not ready to give up."

"You can't possibly have fallen in love—" Father started to interrupt, but for the first time she could remember, she didn't let him silence her.

"Please let me finish. You might as well know that I do care very much for Phillip, but he's not the only reason I want to stay. I have to stay because I am useful here. I like being able to make a difference in someone's life besides my own. Our first guests are due in just a few days. I would like to be able to help get them settled. If you'll let me stay until Uncle James and Aunt Caroline come home, I promise I'll come with them without complaint. I just want to enjoy a little more usefulness."

Father's gaze didn't waver from her face until he reached for her with a strangely unsteady hand. "Don't you know how much a difference you make to my life and to your mother's? You're useful in our lives just by being yourself." His tone carried an odd note of pleading.

She met his hand with her own. "I know you love me, Father, but I'm not truly useful in our home. We have servants who provide everything I need almost before I know I need it. I like being independent for a change."

Both her parents looked as if she'd struck them. Then Mother stood to enfold her in a hug that was genuine this time. "I couldn't bear to live in this primitive place, but it can't be all bad if you're happy here."

Father cleared his throat loudly. "I never could refuse you anything." He scowled at James. "It appears I have to trust you with my daughter for a few more weeks. Don't let me down this time."

Before James could reply, Phillip spoke up. "Mr. Trenton, sir, may I have your permission to try to win your daughter's heart before she has to return to you? I don't have much to offer her, but I'd like her to share my life once we get the rehab center operational."

Joy made Adrianna's heart feel as if it skipped a beat or two. This wasn't the way she'd envisioned hearing Phillip declare himself, but the setting didn't matter nearly as much as the look of hopeful devotion he sent her. She let her eyes show all the love she felt. She wanted him to know her heart already belonged to him. For the second time in less than ten minutes, she saw her father struggling for words. He looked from Phillip to her and back again, then to his wife as if she could tell him what to say.

Finally, he let out a heavy sigh. "Son, if you're good enough for my brother to choose as a business partner, I can't very well say you're not good enough to court my daughter. Just treat her carefully, you hear?" Rare sentiment roughened his voice as he turned toward Adrianna once again.

But Adrianna wanted only Phillip's arms around her. How quickly God had answered her prayer! From within Phillip's gentle embrace, she knew no matter how hidden His trail for them might be from this point on, they would seek Him together.

Epilogue

A drianna pulled aside the heavy silk draperies in front of her bedroom window. Welcome sunshine warmed her face. Never had she greeted spring so eagerly.

"Anything else to go in this trunk, miss?" her maid, Jeanette, asked.

Adrianna turned back to the packing in progress. "I'm expecting another delivery of bedding from Eaton's sometime this afternoon. We should be able to fit some of it into that trunk and then the rest in the bottom of the trunk with the wedding presents." Her thoughts drifted to her fiancé, whom she hadn't seen since Christmas.

She'd left Dawson Creek last September when Uncle James and Aunt Caroline returned to Toronto. The love between her and Phillip only grew stronger during the separation. She wrote him daily, and he responded weekly in letters that told of a full rehab center and a growing waiting list.

In early December, he had arrived for a surprise visit. Her Christmas present from him was a dainty engagement ring, three small diamonds set on a plain gold band. She could tell her mother would have preferred something flashier, but Adrianna loved the ring's simplicity. Then Phillip had announced that the rehab center had brought in enough profit that he would be able to build a suite for him and Adrianna adjacent to Uncle James and Aunt Caroline's suite.

So Adrianna had waited through the long days of winter. Her mother wanted to plan a huge society wedding in the city. Adrianna wanted to say her vows in front of her loved ones and Phillip's in the church where she'd first begun to know the God she now called Friend. She and Phillip set a wedding date of June 5, the anniversary of Grandma Lucy's death. To some it might be a morbid thought, but they did it as a tribute to the woman from whom they'd learned so much.

Since Mother couldn't have the gala she wanted, she compensated by posting a huge notice in the paper. Mother and Father's many friends and acquaintances throughout the city sent gifts of congratulation that now filled the parlor. Mother had wanted Adrianna to open the gifts right away and put them on display, but Adrianna refused. She wanted Phillip to enjoy with her the fun of discovering what each package contained.

Father's gift to them was a bank account in Adrianna's name with an initial deposit of one thousand dollars. "Your wedding here in the city would cost twice that, so I'd like you to have the money to spend however you wish," he'd explained. "I'll add to it each Christmas so you'll have your own source of income."

She felt immense relief when Phillip didn't take offense at the gift. He seemed to understand her father's need to continue caring for her in some way. When she told him she wanted to invest some of the money in the rehab center, they discussed many options by mail. Eventually, after a suggestion from Tabby, they'd decided quality bedding for every room in the center would be a good start. Her purchases used only a fraction of the bank balance. The rest she left untouched for now. It could be used later to furnish their home or perhaps meet other needs in their business.

Now only days remained until she could board the train that would take her to her new home. The sheets, blankets, and coverlets arrived, along with twelve dozen plush towels of varying sizes and colors. She supervised their placement around the edges of the two trunks that would be filled with wedding presents tomorrow. The following day she would pack her clothing, and on the third day, she would depart Toronto with Mother and Father.

∞

Phillip gulped the last of his lunchtime sandwich when he heard the whistle of the incoming train. He felt the grin that started deep within. In just a few minutes he would see, and hold, the woman who'd become part of his heart. One week from today, he'd pledge in front of a church full of witnesses to cherish her for the rest of his life.

He hurried out the front door of what had become a busy rehabilitation center for veterans. The dream sparked by the Trentons had become a fulfilling reality. The building stood proudly refurbished with a new roof, new siding, and additions extending from either side and off the back. He could hardly wait to show Adrianna what they'd accomplished in the months since she'd left.

He arrived at the train station just as passengers began to disembark.

Several people he knew greeted him as they passed, but his attention remained focused on the steps. Then she appeared, her father carrying her down the stairs while an attendant waited at the bottom with her chair. He moved quickly to her before her father could put her down. "May I?" he asked them both.

With a smile, Mr. Trenton relinquished his daughter into Phillip's arms.

She touched his face with gentle fingers as though to assure herself they were really together again. "Hello, my love," she whispered.

Phillip bent his head to touch her lips with his in the lightest of kisses, then replied, "Welcome home, darling."

A Letter to Our Readers

Dear Readers:

In order that we might better contribute to your reading enjoyment, we would appreciate you taking a few minutes to respond to the following questions. When completed, please return to the following: Fiction Editor, Barbour Publishing, Inc., P.O. Box 719, Uhrichsville, OH 44683.

1. Did you enjoy reading *British Columbia?*
   - ❏ Very much. I would like to see more books like this.
   - ❏ Moderately—I would have enjoyed it more if _____
   _____
   _____

2. What influenced your decision to purchase this book?
   (Check those that apply.)
   - ❏ Cover   ❏ Back cover copy   ❏ Title   ❏ Price
   - ❏ Friends   ❏ Publicity   ❏ Other

3. Which story was your favorite?
   - ❏ *River of Peace*   ❏ *Winding Highway*
   - ❏ *Beckoning Streams*   ❏ *Hidden Trails*

4. Please check your age range:
   - ❏ Under 18   ❏ 18–24   ❏ 25–34
   - ❏ 35–45   ❏ 46–55   ❏ Over 55

5. How many hours per week do you read? _____

Name _____

Occupation _____

Address _____

City _____ State _____ Zip _____